The Roman Empire was famous for its network of roads. By following the path of these thoroughfares, Shelley Lindgren, wine director and co-owner of the acclaimed San Francisco restaurants A16 and SPQR, and executive chef of SPQR, Matthew Accarrino, explore Central and Northern Italy's local cuisines and artisanal wines.

Throughout each of the eight featured regions, Accarrino offers not only a modern version of Italian cooking, but also his own take on these constantly evolving regional specialties. Recipes like Fried Rabbit Livers with Pickled Vegetables and Spicy Mayonnaise and Fontina and Mushroom Tortelli with Black Truffle Fonduta are elevated and thoughtful, reflecting Accarrino's extensive knowledge of traditional Italian food, but also his focus on precision and technique. In addition to recipes, Accarrino elucidates basic kitchen skills like small animal butchery and pasta making, as well as newer techniques like sous vide—all of which are prodigiously illustrated with step-by-step photos.

Shelley Lindgren's uniquely informed essays on the wines and winemakers of each region reveal the most interesting Italian wines, highlighting overlooked and little-known grapes and producers—and explaining how each reflects the region's unique history, cultural influences, climate, and terrain. Lindgren, one of the foremost authorities on Italian wine, shares her deep and unparalleled knowledge of Italian wine and winemakers through producer profiles, wine recommendations, and personal observations, making this a necessary addition to any wine-lover's library.

Brimming with both discovery and tradition, *SPQR* delivers the best of modern Italian food rooted in the regions, flavors, and history of Italy.

SPQR

MODERN ITALIAN FOOD AND WINE

SPQR

MODERN ITALIAN FOOD AND WINE

SHELLEY LINDGREN and MATTHEW ACCARRINO with KATE LEAHY

Photography by Sara Remington

TEN SPEED PRESS
Berkeley

CONTENTS

Recipes

INTRODUCTION

Ancient Information Highways

Americans have learned a lot from Italians. We embrace Old World traditions, such as buying cheese from a cheese maker we know by name or building relationships with farmers that grow our tomatoes. Now, as in Italy, we appreciate how wine can season a meal as well as any ingredient. These are just a few of the reasons why we celebrate Italy's culinary contributions at SPQR, a small restaurant on the west side of Fillmore Street in San Francisco. The name, an acronym for the Latin translation of The Senate and the People of Rome, is a proclamation of Roman democracy. The restaurant itself is modest—wooden tables in the dining room surround a marble bar containing the small open kitchen—but the experiences offered nightly are nowhere near plebian. Our guests may sample spring lamb wrapped in chard leaves on one night and pillows of agnolotti filled with fava beans and black truffle the next, swirling glasses of wine that hail from the coast of Liguria to the Adriatic Sea. In this setting, Shelley Lindgren champions little-known Italian wines while Matthew Accarrino composes menus with ideas gleaned from Italy and California.

This book, however, is not intended to be a restaurant cookbook. Rather, it is a slow-paced *passeggiata*, an Italian stroll, taken along the ancient Roman roads of central and northern Italy. Each chapter begins with Shelley's description of regional wines, focusing on the people and grapes that distinguish the area. The second half offers Matthew's recipes inspired by memories, traditions, and travel.

Rome's ancient roads were once information conduits of Western culture. The networks of cobblestone roads—the first structurally sound pathways in Europe—linked the hinterlands to Rome. These roads also opened up markets, supplying goods and information to all corners of the peninsula long after Rome fell in AD 476. Even though Italy was not unified until 1861 (and even then, borders remained in flux well into the twentieth century), the foundation of a collective Italian consciousness was set early on by these networks, and these roads remain woven into the country's cultural fabric.

Contemporary information highways aren't as tangible as the ancient Roman roads. Yet the Internet and international travel have hastened the spread of Italian culture throughout the world, including in our corner of California. In between visits to Italy, we stay in touch with Italian winemakers, chefs, and restaurateurs through phone calls and email. We also encourage our Italian friends to visit SPQR, pour their wines, and share their stories. This book is inspired by these friendships.

A Roman Road Guide

The chapters of this book are divided along Roman roads, with each road marking one or two Italian regions. Here is a sketch of their geography and history.

VIA APPIA. When the Romans broke ground in 312 BC on the Appian Way, they wanted a faster route between Rome and Campania. It became the prototypical Roman road.

VIA SALARIA. The ancient Salt Route, which facilitated the trade of salt along the Tiber River, predates Rome—in fact, it is often credited for the inception of Rome. Via Salaria was later extended to Le Marche.

VIA FLAMINIA. This road cut through Umbrian territory to the coast, making the heart of the peninsula accessible to Roman rule.

VIA POSTUMIA. Linking Genoa with Aquileia, this road facilitated trade across Northern Italy.

VIA CLAUDIA AUGUSTA. This was the first major path through the Alps connecting the Italian peninsula and northern Europe.

VIA AEMILIA. The Emilian Way allowed the Romans to control the Po Valley. The major cities of Emilia-Romagna, including Bologna, formed along its path.

VIA FRANCIGENA. Comprising several ancient roads, the Via Francigena emerged during the Middle Ages as the path for pilgrims en route to Rome.

VIA AURELIA. This coastal road once ran from Rome to France. Today the road is Strada Statale 1.

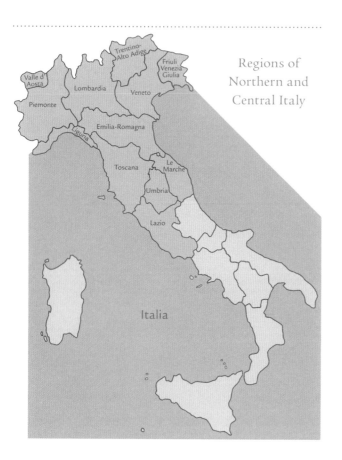

Regions of Northern and Central Italy

La Strada del Vino

My immersion into the world of Italian wine began in the Mezzogiorno, the southern portion of the country. In 2004 while we were opening our first restaurant, A16, the wine emerging from Campania, Puglia, and Sicilia was just starting to show its potential. These wines were incredible values and worked like magic in food pairing, which made it easy for me to focus my wine list on southern Italy. But just as I became hooked on the wines of Mount Etna, I'd hear the buzz about enticing discoveries beyond the Mezzogiorno, like Timorasso, an uncharacteristically rich white wine from Piemonte. Gradually, my tastings crept north. One day I'd sample a zesty Frascati from Lazio, the region around Rome. The next I'd sip a mineral-tinged Verdicchio from Le Marche. Before long, fragrant Nebbiolo wines from Roero in Piemonte and Donnas in Valle d'Aosta were on the table. How could I possibly pass up a chance to share these finds with customers at my restaurant?

That opportunity came with a second restaurant, SPQR. Although our list needed to be small (the restaurant has nearly no storage space), I wanted it to offer a range of wine styles from all over Italy. With my oldest son, Phineas, then only a baby, tucked under one arm, I tasted and spat my way through central and northern Italy, making many discoveries along the way. As I sampled and researched the wines, I came to realize that central and northern Italy had just as many unheralded wines as the South, like Sagrantino from Umbria and Ribolla Gialla from Friuli-Venezia Giulia. With some trepidation, I also dipped into giant wine producing areas, like Soave and Chianti, and found plenty of artisan wines to pour. Perhaps our guests were primed from experiences with new wines at A16, but I was amazed at how willing they were to take a chance on unfamiliar bottles. When Matthew joined the team, the discoveries continued. His knack for balancing dishes with acidity gave me more options for wine pairings, and soon I was pouring a Gewürztraminer from the Alto Adige, a region that borders Austria, with everything from fried rabbit livers to farro-stuffed quail.

Part of the appeal of these wines is their diversity. Italy has a deeper pool of native grapes than any other wine-producing country. The peninsula's natural

advantages—its mountains, temperate weather, tufa and limestone soils, and sea breezes—encouraged *Vitis vinifera* to spread throughout the country and adapt to its microclimates. Grapes literally grow everywhere, and they come in every color and shape imaginable, from the speckled golden Pigato to inky Ancellotta. They cling to slopes facing the Adriatic and trellises at the base of Mont Blanc. The vines struggle to survive in the poor rocky soil of the Carso or they unfurl in the rich farmland of the Po River valley.

Yet even though Italian viticulture is as diverse as it is ancient, the dynamism seen within the Italian wine community is relatively recent. While European nobles enjoyed aged wines from their cellar, the majority of Italians historically consumed simple table wines. Farmers picked their grapes and then crushed and fermented the field blends for table wine. These light, fresh farmhouse wines had more in common with fizzy Lambrusco than brooding Barolo. As post-war Italy prospered in the 1960s and 1970s, however, winemaking became a serious endeavor. Looking to France's Appellation d'Origine Contrôlée (AOC) system for inspiration, the Italian government launched the DOC (Denominazione di Origine Controllata) system (on page 5). Many saw it as a way to affirm the quality of the country's most historic wines. More important than a wine classification system were advancements in cellar technology. The crisp white wines that put Friuli on the wine map would have been impossible without temperature-controlled stainless steel tanks, which only began to be used in the 1960s. Italians also expanded their horizons beyond their local wines by tasting wines of other regions and countries.

Growing fascination with French grapes spurred the development in the 1970s of Super Tuscans, high-end wines made in a style akin to Bordeaux, and Cabernet Sauvignon and Merlot plantings spread across the country. In Piemonte's Barolo and Barbaresco zones, some winemakers abandoned *botti*, the old Slavonian oak casks that held anywhere from 2,000 to 6,000 liters of wine, in exchange for the 220-liter *barrique*, the French oak barrels used in Bordeaux. Those who stuck with *botti* argued for more subtle wines focused on terroir, while those who switched to *barrique* focused on cellar innovations. The tension between the so-called modernists and traditionalists became one of the most well-documented style debates in recent Italian wine history.

Today the debate has moved beyond modern versus traditional to focus instead on winemakers' personal style. Many have taken to calling themselves farmers, and while some of these changes are more talk than action, the best producers are keenly in sync with the health of their land. At one extreme of this trend are natural wines, which are made without commercial yeasts or other additives. These unusual, captivating wines offer a glimpse at how wines made in preindustrial times may have tasted—and perhaps how the wines of tomorrow will evolve.

Now the pendulum has swung away from international grapes—Cabernet, Merlot, Chardonnay—and toward native varieties. In nearly every corner of Italy, vintners are focusing their attention on these once-forgotten varieties, like Lacrima di Morro d'Alba in Le Marche and Pignolo in Friuli. The investment in regional grape varieties is one of the reasons that Italy is such a beguiling country for a wine professional. No matter how much I study, I continue to come across Italian wines that make me want to reexamine everything I think I know about viticulture and enology. This happened the first time I tried Josko Gravner's Ribolla Gialla wine, aged underground in amphorae, terra-cotta vessels used thousands of years ago for wine transport. Although it was a white wine, it behaved like a red, slowly opening up in the glass and lingering on the palate for a long finish.

Beyond its wine diversity, Italy enchants me for the simple reason that, there, wine is an intrinsic part of a meal. Because wine is an everyday event, winemakers respond by making two styles of wines. The same producer in Montalcino that makes ageworthy Brunello also produces a Rosso di Montalcino to drink while the Brunello ages. The same is true in Barolo, and I have yet to meet a Barolo producer who drinks the rich, noble wine every day (they more often turn to Barbera or Dolcetto). Italians have mastered the art of living a balanced life between work and play, food and wine. My life may not always be as optimally balanced, but I try to infuse that same philosophy into my restaurants in San Francisco. While some might say that Italian wine is having a moment, I say that its moment is here to stay.
—SHELLEY LINDGREN

DOC and DOCG Designations

Italians have documented regional wine quality since Roman times, but it wasn't until relatively recently—1963—that they rolled out a modern wine classification system that emulated France's Appellation d'Origine Contrôlée (AOC) system. In an attempt to ensure the quality and elevate the stature of the country's viticulture industry, the Italian Ministry of Agriculture and Forestry put together a list of rules that classified the grapes, growing locations, and aging requirements of established wines. The broadest category in the classification system, with the fewest regulations, is Vino da Tavola (table wine). It is followed by Indicazione Geografica Tipica, which indicates wines "typical of the geographic growing area." But the wines most mentioned, commented on, and debated are those carrying the DOC and DOCG designations. I use the two terms frequently in this book.

DOC stands for *Denominazione di Origine Controllata* (controlled and guaranteed place of named origin). DOCG tacks on *garantita* (guaranteed), implying a more prestigious level of quality control and craftsmanship. Both categories include wines that are sparkling or still, white or red, young or aged, and dry or sweet. As with most endeavors within the Italian legal system, however, there are some true head scratchers within the DOC system. While some deserving regions have yet to garner the prestige of a DOCG wine, other regions with strong *consorzios* racked up the distiction. Consequently, while DOC and DOCG wines are a good place to start when learning about the wines of a region, it isn't necessary to stick within the DOC or DOCG boundaries to find a great bottle of Italian wine.

La Strada della Cucina

EVERY CHEF has a point of view that fuels creativity. Mine stems from two places: Italy and America. My extended family lives in Puglia, the southern region that stretches down the heel of the boot. Visits to Puglia inevitably included walks in the hills outside of Manfredonia to forage for wild greens. It was on these walks that I first learned that some wild plants were not only edible but also delicious.

Years later, I traveled to Labico, a small town outside of Rome, to work for Antonello Colonna at his namesake Michelin-starred restaurant. I continued this journey of discovery, encountering the best places around the town to forage for porcini mushrooms, but I also saw Italian food from a new perspective. Instead of the rustic family meals I enjoyed in Manfredonia, here each plate was polished and modern, a style of food that was more closely aligned with the aesthetics I saw in New York City, where

I had cooked for much of my career. Yet even though this modern restaurant served some of Rome's wealthiest residents, a soulful sense of place remained. The restaurant was right along one of the main roads of Labico, and its office and wine cellar (an ancient cave) were across the street. Every time someone ordered a bottle of wine, the sommelier dodged traffic to fetch it.

But while I feel very much at home in Italy, I am American. I was born in the Midwest, I trained as a chef in New York City, and I have run restaurant kitchens in California. In San Francisco, my pantry is stocked with local Meyer lemons and cans of chipotle peppers as well as *aceto balsamico* and extra virgin olive oil. I forage here too, but what I find is different than what I encountered in Labico and Manfredonia. Here I pick dried wild fennel, harvest nettles and lamb's quarters, and garnish delicate dishes with edible flowers. I cook from experience, but I also cook what inspires me based on where I live and work.

In America, our understanding of Italian cooking has transformed over time. We now know that Italy offers not one cuisine but instead a patchwork of regional specialties. Yet sometimes we get hung up on this idea of authenticity, which can hamstring opportunities for creativity. For me, Italian food is not an artifact to be replicated; it is an inspiration. Like the country's wine, Italian food is dynamic. It changes with shifts in technology, family life, politics, and climate. (If nothing ever changed in Italy, we'd never know the joys of pasta with tomatoes or polenta made of cornmeal, both of which rely on ingredients indigenous to the Americas.) Great chefs throughout Italy have elevated classic Italian flavors and textures and created nuanced menus that push our levels of understanding of one of the world's most beloved cuisines.

The recipes in this book are inspired by my travels in and memories of Italy. Some of them evoke familiar Italian dishes, liked beef braised in Barolo, while others are more whimsical and interpretive, like scallops with hibiscus *agrodolce*. When I compose a dish, sourcing seasonal ingredients is merely a starting point. From there, I look for the best ways to handle ingredients to achieve optimal flavor. It is not just about making something taste like what it is—a carrot tastes like carrot already—but making that carrot taste better by deepening its flavor or accentuating it in a different way.

Often, this approach uses cooking techniques that may be somewhat unfamiliar to home cooks, like *sous vide* (see page 271). But only by challenging yourself to learn new techniques and methods do you become a better cook. Once a farmer brought me a whole crop of green rhubarb—some of the sourest stuff I'd ever tasted. It had been grown with care, but it was not in the form I was used to. I wanted to use it, but how? Then it occurred to me that instead of making a pickle by adding vinegar to something neutral or sweet tasting, I could add simple syrup to something tart. Essentially, I was pickling in reverse.

Cooking from this book requires the same sort of instinct. Technical skills are crucial, since technique enables you to execute a new idea. But cooking from your gut is just as important. Instinct can steer you away from bad ideas and toward good ones. When both sides—the technical execution and the personal perspective—fuse together, great ideas can happen.

While all of these recipes were tested in a home kitchen, every kitchen performs a little differently. Given differences in air circulation, burner strength, and the ingredients themselves, forty minutes for a simmering sauce might not be long enough, or it might be too long. Taste, observe, and adjust as needed. Cooking is as much about following instinct as following recipes.

It's also okay to acknowledge the limitations of your schedule. Many of the recipes in this book are recipes-within-recipes, and a number of the components are outstanding on their own. The semolina gnocchi (page 34) are not hard to make and pair well with a simple tomato sauce. Free-form *blècs* (page 98) are an easy pasta to master, and they taste delicious even if you don't serve it with a ragù of suckling pig.

No matter what I cook, I always take with me the core lessons that traveling and cooking in Italy have taught me: a respect for flavor and quality, the habit of supporting communities of artisan food producers, and the craft of cooking, from making pasta to curing meat. Yet the most important lesson is appreciating the value of spending an entire day (or three) cooking one meal, and then slowing down to savor every bite.

—MATTHEW ACCARRINO

VIA APPIA—
LAZIO

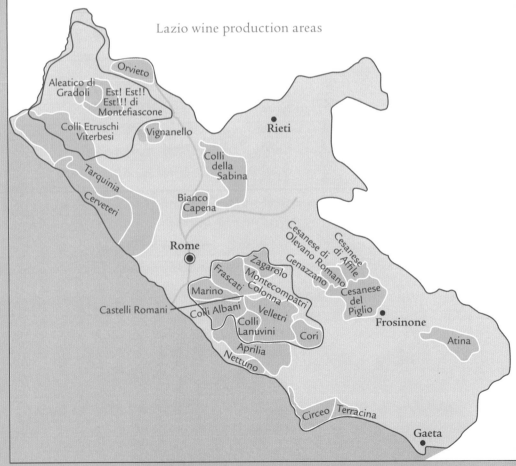

Lazio wine production areas

Orvieto

Aleatico di Gradoli

Est! Est!! Est!!! di Montefiascone

Colli Etruschi Viterbesi

Vignanello

Rieti

Colli della Sabina

Tarquinia

Cerveteri

Bianco Capena

Rome

Cesanese di Olevano Romano

Cesanese di Affile

Zagarolo

Genazzano

Frascati

Montecompatri Colonna

Cesanese del Piglio

Marino

Castelli Romani

Colli Albani

Velletri

Frosinone

Colli Lanuvini

Cori

Atina

Aprilia

Nettuno

Circeo   Terracina

Gaeta

VIA APPIA—LAZIO

Rome is a city of contrasts. Its ancient walls and streets either gleam or have been marred with graffiti. It is expensive but can feel cheap, especially when one pays dearly to sit at an uncomfortable table in a jammed restaurant. And its pedestrian-friendly cobblestone streets run alongside the constant rumble of traffic from main arteries, a problem that has plagued the city since the time of Julius Caesar. And still, I can't seem to get enough of Rome, its history, its people, and its wine culture.

Here, the past coexists comfortably with contemporary times, a point of which I'm reminded every time I walk by a manhole inscribed S.P.Q.R., a tribute to Rome's ancient government. Rome also is a cultural crucible in which the relaxed sensibilities of the Mezzogiorno collide with those from the progressive, industrialized north. Is Rome a northern city in the south or a southern city in the north? The answer is neither: Rome is Rome.

I first visited the city with my husband, Greg, on our honeymoon. We drove our rented Renault from Sardegna off the ferry at Civitavecchia, leaving the sleepy, isolated island in exchange for the urban adventure of Rome. After a few white-knuckle moments and several trips around congested traffic circles, we found ourselves facing the beautiful Hotel Eden. Sitting in a car covered in Sardinian dust, Greg and I contemplated whether this five-star property was within our budget. The answer was no. But after that harried drive, we surrendered, splurging for a single night of luxury and relaxation. Since that visit, I visit the Hotel Eden every time I am in Rome. Instead of staying the night, I enjoy a glass of the best bubbles *del giorno* at the terrace bar and watch the sunset over St. Peter's Cathedral, reveling in the glory and beauty of this great city.

For centuries, Rome has supplied travelers with lasting memories. Yet it is the Eternal City's magnetism that makes it easy to overlook the fast-evolving wine industry in Lazio, the central Italian region that surrounds the city. One can visit Rome's vibrant wine bars, like Cul de Sac in Piazza Pasquino, and sample wines from all over Italy without noticing the red Giacchè grape from Cerveteri or the white Bellone grape, which the ancients called *uva fantastica* for its abundant, sweet juice. It's not that wine from Lazio was ever scarce. Even though wineries here sold a high volume of wine, they could hardly keep up with the demand of Rome alone, and quantity trumped quality.

But times are changing. While working in Rome's substantial shadow, Lazio winemakers have quietly refined their techniques and improved their wines. In 2003, for instance, the region did not have a single DOCG wine. Today it has three: the white wines Frascati Superiore and Canellino Frascati in the Colli Romani hills south of Rome, and red Cesanese del Piglio in Frosinone, a province southwest of Rome. The confluence of lower yields in the vineyards, more nuanced cellar management, and a resurgence of regional pride in indigenous grapes, has made the wines of Lazio ripe for rediscovery.

Spring is when the region feels most alive. Every field appears to be full of artichokes and every table offers them fried, braised, or roasted. While many wine connoisseurs hold up a white flag when asked to pair wine with artichokes, I never encounter trouble in Lazio. Here, a red wine like Cesanese handles the task admirably, offering another example of the truism that what grows together, goes together. When spring comes to San Francisco, I also turn often to Frascati because the wine's ripe stone

fruit and orange blossom nuances never overwhelm the nuances of fresh fava beans, peas, and tender greens.

Lazio has natural advantages for viticulture, from grape diversity to hilly terrain, much of it volcanic, which imparts acidity to the grapes. Meanwhile, the region's warm climate is tempered by breezes from the Tyrrhenian Sea on the coast and Lake Bolsena inland near the Umbrian border. The most productive growing areas are the Castelli Romani and Colli Albani hills south of Rome, where Frascati and Marino wines come from, yet wines are also made in northern Lazio near Umbria as well as by the coast around Cerveteri. The majority of wines produced here are white, and most are made with the same grapes, mainly Malvasia and Trebbiano and an assortment of other varieties, like Bombino Bianco and Passerina. Pockets of the region also make red wines with grapes rarely grown elsewhere.

Lazio's south also is evolving quickly. Southeast of Rome near the coast, the Casale del Giglio estate grows French grapes in Agro Pontino, marshland that Mussolini had drained in the 1930s. And in the ancient hill town of Cori, Marco Carpineti biodynamically farms rare grapes like Arciprete, Nero Buona di Cori, and Greco Moro. In Olevano, Damiano Ciolli replanted his family's Cesanese vines, replacing the traditional pergola trellis system with the lower-yielding French *guyot* system instead. When he started green-harvesting grapes—cutting away unripe grapes to concentrate flavors of the remaining grapes—his father tried to hide the grapes so neighbors wouldn't mutter about waste. Damiano's perseverance paid off, however, and wines like Silene have garnered great attention for Cesanese.

Lazio's history in wine production goes back centuries. In the summer, popes, aristocrats, and artists would escape the heat of Rome by heading to the Castelli Romani hills, where they would drink the local Malvasia wine. *Sagras*, festivals stemming from pagan Roman rituals, are still common throughout the Italy, but the area around Frascati claims some of the more elaborate. During the annual fall Sagra dell'uva di Marino, for instance, the public fountains fill with wine. (One year, after a municipal water snafu, residents also had wine running from their faucets.) Frascati bakeries also offer an icon for wine: *la pupazza di Frascati*, a doll cookie with three breasts, two for milk and one for wine.

In northern Lazio, there is the famous story about how the DOC Est! Est!! Est!!! de Montefiascone earned its name. The legend goes that a bishop traveling to Rome sent his servant ahead to find the inns with the best wine. He wrote *est*, Latin for "it is," on the doors of inns that met the bishop's standards. By the time the servant arrived in Montefiascone, however, he found the wine so good that he scribbled *est! est!! est!!!*

Even today, Lazio's past is never far from reach. In the 1980s, when Fabrizio Santarelli was building his winery, Castel de Paolis, workers discovered ancient cisterns under the topsoil. I was also reminded about the region's bottomless well of history in Cerveteri. Right outside the town walls lies a large Etruscan necropolis, which contains the family of the first king of Rome. Its existence is one of the reasons that Fiorenzo Collacciani, the patriarch of nearby winery Casale Cento Corvi, insists that the origin of his prized red grape, Giacchè, predates Rome.

Yet the best contemporary producers rely on hard work, not ancient history, for success. The Montefiascone area is better known today for Falesco, a winery on the Lazio-Umbrian border, than for a breathless messenger. Here, the Cotarella brothers have shown the potential for Merlot in the area, especially in their revered wine, Montiano. Falesco also makes a lauded medium- to full-bodied white wine from the local grape Roscetto. And then there's Sergio Mottura, whose work with Grechetto has turned the overlooked grape into one of central Italy's premier white varieties.

Lazio wine advocates like Paolo Latini have helped to get the word out about these and countless other notable producers. I met Paolo at the end of a research trip. With a free day in Rome, I wandered from the Spanish Steps into Rome's designer shopping district until I stumbled upon an unassuming wine bar. Seeking refuge from window shopping, I stepped inside to order a glass of wine. At the time, apart from a handful of Frascati producers, it was difficult to find wines from Lazio in San Francisco. But here was a wine list entirely focused on Lazio, and many bottles were new to me. With my curiosity piqued, I struck up a conversation with Paolo, the bar's gentle sommelier. After discovering that we both made a living out of curating wine lists of quality-focused winemakers, we clicked. When I meet up with Paolo today, the conversation inevitably turns to how much has changed for the better in Italian wine. With each region offering wines worth championing, both of us feel as if we are working during a wine renaissance, a recapturing of past glory. There may be no better place to celebrate this than with a glass of wine in hand in the center of Rome. —SL

White Grapes

BELLONE

This *uva fantastica* is a wonderful eating grape. Because it was easy to cultivate and resistant to disease, it was used often in the region's numerous white-wine blends. In recent years, better pruning techniques have brought out the grape's stone fruit and apple characteristics. Bellone, which is sometimes called Bello, may be a clone of Arciprete and Cacchione, two equally juicy local grapes.

RECOMMENDED PRODUCERS: Castel de Paolis, Marco Carpineti, Cincinnato

ROMANESCO

This greenish grape is the same color as Romanesco broccoli. Known in Rome since ancient times, it makes a light, everyday wine seemingly designed for hot Lazio afternoons. It is more often found in a blend of Malvasia and Trebbiano, but varietal bottlings of Romanesco are on the horizon.

RECOMMENDED PRODUCER: Castel del Paolis
SEE ALSO: Grechetto (page 70), Moscato (page 201), Trebbiano (page 71)

MALVASIA

Brought to Italy from Crete during the time of Magna Graecia, Malvasia is one of Italy's most widely planted—and diverse—grape varieties. It has more than twenty subvarieties, which vary from savory to flowery to aromatic. Some vines even produce red grapes. Yet not all Malvasia is created equal. In Lazio, where Malvasia has long been used for blending, winemakers are shifting away from Malvasia di Candia, a resilient, reliable strain that produced large bunches, to Malvasia del Lazio (also called Puntinata), a strain that yields smaller bunches with more intense berries. Malvasia del Lazio is harder to grow, yet its complexity shows through in the wines. Through efforts from producers like Fontana Candida, whose Luna Mater bottling is made solely with Malvasia del Lazio, the grape is regaining its prestige in Lazio.

Malvasia is also important in other regions. In the Colli Piacentini, a hilly wine region on the border shared by Emilia-Romagna and Lombardia, the crisp, dry, and floral Malvasia di Candia aromatica strain is used by both *frizzante* wines and natural wines, made with extended skin contact by estates like La Stoppa. In Friuli, Malvasia Istriana offers notes of green almond and acacia honey. It is especially good with the seafood from the Adriatic (try Vie di Romans).

RECOMMENDED PRODUCERS

- **Lazio:** Conte Zandotti, Casal Pilozzo, Fontana Candida, Ludovisi
- **Emilia Romagna:** La Stoppa, Medici Ermete, Castello di Luzzano, Camillo Donati
- **Toscana:** Massa Vecchia, Querciabella, Ricasoli, San Giusto a Rentennano
- **Fruili-Venezia Giulia:** Vie di Romans, Kante, Zidarich, Zuliani
- **Umbria:** Paolo Bea, Carlo Massimiliano Gritti
- **Piedmonte:** Cantina Sociale di Casorzo, Fracchia Voulet, La Sera

Red Grapes

ALEATICO

Historically made into an excellent sweet wine in both dried-grape (*passito*) and fortified (*liquoroso*) styles, Aleatico was once an important grape variety on the shores of Lake Bolsena and in the southern region of Puglia. These days, it's not grown nearly as much, though that might change as producers like the Tuscan Falvo family have started making outstanding *passito* Aleatico on the island of Elba. Sweeter styles of this grape are giving way to dry versions that express notes of spice and strawberry, which I find pair unexpectedly well with seafood and pasta.

RECOMMENDED PRODUCERS: Sociale di Gradoli, Falesco, Valdana (Lazio), Fubbiano (Toscana)

CESANESE

The main red grape of Lazio's southern Frosinone province, Cesanese has shot up from obscure local variety to regional hero in only a handful of years. For most of the twentieth century, it was sold as a blending grape for bulk red wines (it still is), but Cesanese producers started to believe the grape was capable of much more. These possibilities came to fruition when Cesanese di Affile attained DOCG status in 2008. The grape produces medium-bodied wines with alluring notes of cloves, black pepper, and black cherry.

RECOMMENDED PRODUCERS: Damiano Ciolli, Casale della Ioria, Terenzi, Cantine Volpetti, Corte dei Papi, Coletti Conti

GIACCHÈ

Indigenous to the area around Cerveteri since the times of the Etruscans, this grape was on the verge of extinction until the Collacciani family of Casale Cento Corvi took an interest in it. Even though there were only two vines remaining in the vineyard, the family decided to propagate the variety to produce a unique Lazio wine. It's a small grape with thick skin and a lot of seeds. When vinified, Giacchè tastes like a blend of blueberries and blackberries spiced with black pepper and star anise.

RECOMMENDED PRODUCER: Casale Cento Corvi

Going Wild

THERE IS something magical about walking into the woods empty-handed and coming out with a bag full of raw ingredients. I first learned how to forage with my extended family in Manfredonia, Puglia. But I never thought of doing it in a restaurant setting until 2000 when I arrived in Labico, a town southeast of Rome, to work for Antonello Colonna. Apart from one weekly delivery from Rome with more worldly supplies, everything the Michelin-starred chef used in the kitchen, from local cheeses to the olive oil, came from around the town, and wild edibles from the Lazio countryside were a natural fit.

One day I hitched a ride to the restaurant with Alessandro Pipero, the sommelier. Alessandro pulled over, hopped off the Vespa, and started walking toward the woods as I trailed behind. About a hundred feet in from the pavement, we came across a patch of porcini. It was the first time I had seen porcini growing in the wild, and the idea that such prized ingredients grew so readily in the Lazio countryside took me by surprise. Soon I was going out with Alessandro, Antonello, and other staff members and finding miner's lettuce, chamomile, and fiddlehead ferns. But local porcini were the true prize, and when they could be found they were always on the menu. On these fortunate days, we would sit down for staff meal to a pot of risotto speckled with the mushrooms' trimmings.

In Rome, it is easy to dine anonymously. But in the towns outside of the city, like Labico, restaurants are as much about community as business. Through expeditions into the countryside and our meals together, I felt as if I had connected to the local fabric—a feeling that I try bringing to my cooking today.

—MA

SPICED RICOTTA FRITTERS *with* Smoked Maple Syrup

During the Middle Ages, street vendors sold *frittelle di ricotta*, treats made with cheese, egg whites, and nuts. I've borrowed the idea for a contemporary antipasto, in which I drizzle fritters with smoked maple syrup. Countering the sweetness of the syrup are curry powder, cayenne, and fennel pollen. Fennel pollen might sound exotic, but wild fennel grows all over northern California. I pick it after the blossoms have dried and then shake out the pollen.

Maple syrup can be smoked on the stove using a stove-top smoker or a disposable aluminum pan (see page 274). Bits of ash remain in the syrup after it is strained, but that's on purpose: I like how the ash visually reinforces the smoke.

MAKES 30 TO 36 FRITTERS; SERVES 6 TO 8

Ricotta Fritters

350 grams • 1¹/₂ cups drained ricotta (see page 281)

45 grams • 1¹/₂ tablespoons crème fraîche

100 grams • 2 eggs

20 grams • 1 egg yolk

13 grams • 2 teaspoons honey

3 grams • ³/₄ teaspoon kosher salt

85 grams • ¹/₂ cup plus 1 tablespoon all-purpose flour

2 grams • ¹/₂ teaspoon baking powder

1 gram • ¹/₄ teaspoon baking soda

1 gram • ¹/₄ teaspoon curry powder

a pinch of cayenne

blended oil for frying (see page 278)

280 grams • 1 cup pure maple syrup

30 grams • ¹/₈ cup sugar

1 gram • ¹/₄ teaspoon curry powder

1 gram • ¹/₄ teaspoon fennel pollen

1 gram • ¹/₄ teaspoon ground cardamom

smoked salt (optional)

To make the fritters: In a bowl, whisk together the ricotta, crème fraîche, eggs, yolk, honey, and salt. Sift together the flour, baking powder, baking soda, curry powder, and cayenne then gradually fold this into the ricotta batter.

In a large, wide pot, heat about 3 inches of oil to 355° to 360°F. Cook one fritter first as a test: carefully drop 1 tablespoon of batter into the oil and fry until golden on both sides, about 1 minute per side. When it's cool enough to handle, tear the fritter open to ensure it's cooked in the center. If it's still raw, either take more time frying the rest of the fritters or make them smaller. Fry the remaining batter in uncrowded batches, returning the oil to temperature between batches. Using a skimmer or slotted spoon, remove the fritters and drain on paper towels.

Soak and drain about ¹/₂ cup of apple- or cherry-wood chips suitable for stove-top smokers. Smoke the maple syrup in a stove-top smoker according to the instructions for smoking liquids on page 274. Using tongs or a metal spoon, scoop some of the ash into the syrup and soak for 20 minutes. Strain the syrup through a fine-mesh strainer.

To serve: In a large bowl, mix together the sugar, curry powder, fennel pollen, and cardamom. Toss the hot fritters in the bowl to coat lightly with the sugar mixture. Sprinkle with smoked salt and serve with a side of maple syrup for dipping.

FRIED RABBIT LIVERS
with Pickled Vegetables *and* Spicy Mayonnaise

In an average, no-frills grocery store outside of Rome, not only will you find whole rabbits cut up for sale, you will also find a wide selection of livers, tendons, tongues, and tripe. I share the same sentiment in my cooking, often focusing on "extras" like livers, and building dishes around them. Dipped in batter, deep-fried, and served with quickly pickled vegetables, rabbit livers make a simple antipasto to pass around the table. I add a dab of chipotle in the mayonnaise for a smoky, savory accent. If rabbit livers are hard to find, chicken livers are a good substitute.

SERVES 4 TO 6

420 grams • 6 to 8 rabbit livers (14 ounces), halved or quartered (yielding about 20 pieces)

Spicy Mayonnaise

60 grams • 1/4 cup white wine vinegar

30 grams • 1 heaping teaspoon chopped chipotle peppers in adobo

30 grams • 1 heaping teaspoon Dijon mustard

20 grams • 1 egg yolk

10 grams • 1 1/2 teaspoons honey

3 grams • 3/4 teaspoon kosher salt

250 grams • 1 1/4 cups grapeseed or canola oil

50 grams • 1/4 cup extra virgin olive oil

blended oil for frying (see page 278)

100 grams • 2/3 cup Wondra flour (see page 283)

50 grams • 1/3 cup semolina flour

1 gram • 1/4 teaspoon cumin seeds, toasted in a dry pan and ground

1 gram • 1/4 teaspoon smoked paprika

1 gram • 1/4 teaspoon cayenne

kosher salt and black pepper

110 grams • 1/2 cup buttermilk

1 cup pickled vegetables (page 281)

about 5 baby radishes (such as French breakfast or icicle), stemmed and sliced thinly

extra virgin olive oil

about 1/4 cup buckwheat or radish sprouts (optional)

1 lemon, cut into wedges and seeded, for serving

Trim off the visible vein that connects the liver lobes. Soak the livers in ice water for 3 hours or overnight. Drain, pat dry, and refrigerate until ready to fry.

To make the spicy mayonnaise: In a food processor, blend the vinegar, chipotle, mustard, yolk, honey, and salt into a paste. While the processor is running, gradually drizzle in the oils to form a creamy emulsion. Taste and season with more salt if needed. You should have just over 1 cup of mayonnaise.

To prepare the livers: In a large, wide pot, heat about 2 inches of oil to 360°F. Place a cooling rack over a baking sheet and line with paper towels. Set aside. In a small bowl, mix together the Wondra and semolina flours with the cumin, paprika, cayenne, and a pinch of salt.

Pat the livers dry with paper towels and season them with salt and pepper. Dip the livers in the buttermilk and dredge through the flour until evenly coated. Pat off any excess flour, then gingerly drop the livers, one by one, into the oil (the livers may splatter and pop when they hit the oil). Fry in uncrowded batches until crisp, 2 to 3 minutes. With a skimmer or a slotted spoon, lift the pieces out of the oil and drain on the paper towel–lined rack. Season with salt and pepper. Return the oil to temperature between batches.

Drain the pickled vegetables and toss in a small bowl with the radishes, a drizzle of olive oil, and pinch of salt.

Spread a dab of mayonnaise on the bottom of each plate. Scatter equal amounts of livers, pickled vegetables, radishes, and sprouts on top. Serve more mayonnaise and the lemon wedges on the side.

CRISPY PIG EARS *with* Pickled Green Tomatoes, Jalapeño, *and* Radish

Rome is known for fried foods and dishes derived from the *quinto quarto*, the so-called fifth quarter of the animal: the variety meats. Fried pig ears combine the city's two specialties. I season them with chile oil, pickles, and lemon juice for dimension, then serve a cooling radish salad alongside to counter the heat. The result is an unexpectedly refreshing fried antipasto. The pickled vegetables also benefit from time spent in the brine. I pickle jalapeños separately from the other vegetables to avoid making all the vegetables spicy. The elements of this antipasto need to be made at least a day in advance, but they come together quickly before serving.

SERVES 4 TO 6

650 grams • 4 (6-ounce) pig ears
35 grams • 4 tablespoons basic meat cure (page 276)
150 grams • 1/2 white onion, chopped
160 grams • 1 carrot, chopped
50 grams • 1 stalk celery, chopped
5 parsley stems
907 grams • 4 cups water
340 grams • 1 cup white wine
3 grams • 3/4 teaspoon kosher salt

Pickles

20 grams • 1 jalapeño
190 grams • 1 cup green cherry tomatoes or small tomatillos
150 grams • 1/2 yellow onion, sliced thinly
8 grams • 2 garlic cloves, sliced thinly
1 gram • 1/2 teaspoon mustard seeds
a pinch of turmeric
397 grams • 1 3/4 cups pickling liquid (page 281)

1 watermelon radish
about 6 assorted small radishes (such as Easter egg, French breakfast, icicle), stemmed

blended oil for frying (see page 278)
a few drops of Calabrian chile oil (page 278)
1 lemon, cut into wedges and seeded
kosher salt and black pepper
1/2 cup baby dandelion greens
1 or 2 sprigs parsley, stemmed
a pinch of coarse salt

Singe any hairs off the pig ears, then rinse, pat dry, and place in a storage container. Season evenly with the curing salt, cover, and refrigerate at least 6 hours or overnight.

Preheat the oven to 325°F. Rinse the pig ears, pat dry, and place in a heavy-bottomed pot over medium heat. Add the onion, carrot, celery, and parsley stems, then pour in the water and wine. Season with the salt and bring to a simmer. Cover with a tight-fitting lid and transfer the pot to the oven. Cook the ears until they are completely tender (when the tip of a paring knife can pierce the ear without any resistance), about 2 1/2 hours.

Let the pig ears cool in the braising liquid at room temperature for at least 1 hour. Remove the ears and place on a parchment paper–lined baking sheet. Place a piece of parchment paper on top, then place another baking sheet on top and put a few cans or other heavy items to weigh down the sheet (this will force the pig ears to flatten as they cool). Refrigerate until the ears are chilled and firm, at least 3 hours or overnight. If desired, refrigerate the braising liquid for another use (before refrigerating, strain and discard the vegetables).

To make the pickles: Slice the jalapeño into thin disks and soak in ice water (this helps tame the heat). In a large Mason jar or nonreactive heatproof container, pack in the tomatoes, onion, garlic, mustard seeds, and turmeric. In a small pot over medium-high heat, bring 1 1/2 cups of the pickling liquid to a simmer. Pour into the jar and cool completely. Cover, and refrigerate at least overnight or up to 3 weeks.

Drain the jalapeño and place in a small Mason jar or a heatproof bowl. In a small pot over medium-high heat, bring the remaining 1/4 cup of pickling liquid to a simmer

{continued}

and pour over the jalapeño. Cool completely, cover, and refrigerate at least overnight or up to 1 week.

To serve: Peel the watermelon radish and dice finely. Slice the remaining radishes into thin disks. Drain the pickled vegetables (if using tomatillos, halve or quarter them) and place in a bowl with the radishes.

In a large, wide pot, heat about 2 inches of oil to 375°F. Blot the pig ears dry and slice into 2-inch triangles or ¹/₂-inch strips. Using a skimmer, lower the ears into the oil and fry in uncrowded batches until crisp, about 3 minutes. (The ears will bubble and pop quite a bit; hold a mesh splatter guard over the pan to lessen the mess.) Drain the ears on paper towels, then place in a mixing bowl and toss with a few drops of chile oil, a squeeze of juice from a lemon wedge, and a few pinches of salt and pepper.

Mix the dandelion greens and parsley into the radishes and tomatoes. Spoon the vegetables onto a platter or individual plates. Place the pig ears on top. Drain a spoonful of pickled jalapeño slices, then scatter them on top of the pig ears. Serve with lemon wedges and coarse salt for seasoning at the table.

SPRING VEGETABLE VIGNAROLA SALAD

Vignarola celebrates the first tender vegetables of the season. I approach it like a curator, compiling the best of what grows nearby, from fava beans and sugar snap peas to foraged greens like chickweed, miner's lettuce, and watercress. The success of this salad lies in the fundamentals. Take time to properly blanch the vegetables. I tell my cooks that blanching a vegetable is cooking it until the vegetable has texture but no raw bite. Use a large pot of salted water for blanching, and add salt to the ice bath. This reinforces the vegetables' seasoning rather than washing it away. The tough light-green shell of fava beans is easier to remove after blanching, but I do it beforehand to preserve the beans' texture.

SERVES 4 TO 6

Dressing

120 grams • ¹/₂ cup buttermilk

50 grams • ¹/₄ cup crumbled fresh goat cheese

55 grams • ¹/₄ cup extra virgin olive oil

30 grams • 2 tablespoons red wine vinegar

kosher salt and black pepper

227 grams • 8 ounces whole fresh fava beans (¹/₃ cup shelled but unpeeled)

32 grams • ¹/₄ cup shelled peas

40 grams • ¹/₄ cup trimmed wax beans

45 grams • ¹/₄ cup raw asparagus sliced thinly on a bias

35 grams • ¹/₄ cup raw sugar snap peas sliced thinly on a bias

extra virgin olive oil

about 1¹/₂ cups country bread cut into ¹/₂-inch cubes

kosher salt and black pepper

about 2 cups washed and trimmed baby lettuces

¹/₄ cup spring onions sliced thinly on a bias

¹/₄ cup pea shoots

¹/₄ cup packed picked fresh herbs, such as mint, tarragon, parsley, and chervil

a handful of local wild greens, such as watercress, chickweed, and miner's lettuce

about ¹/₂ cup crumbled goat cheese

12 slices lemon confitura (page 279)

To make the dressing: In a food processor, combine the buttermilk and goat cheese. With the machine running, drizzle in the olive oil and vinegar. Season with salt and pepper. If the dressing needs more acid, add another teaspoon of vinegar. You will have about 1 cup of dressing.

To prepare the vegetables: Bring a large pot of water to a boil and season with salt. Shuck the fava beans and discard the pods. Shell each fava bean and remove its germ. Blanch until al dente, about 3 minutes. Shock in ice water seasoned with salt. Blanch (2 to 3 minutes) and shock the peas, followed by the wax beans (3 to 4 minutes). Drain the vegetables and combine with the asparagus, and snap peas.

Heat about a half-inch of olive oil in a straight-sided sauté pan over medium-high heat. Add the bread cubes in a single layer and fry until golden, about 3 minutes. Drain the bread cubes on paper towels and season with salt and pepper.

Pour off excess oil, stir in the vegetables and cook until warmed through. Season with salt and pepper.

In a large bowl, gently mix together all of the lettuces, spring onions, pea shoots, herbs, and wild greens. Scatter the goat cheese, lemon *confitura*, and fried bread over the greens, then add the warmed vegetables. Drizzle the dressing into the bowl (you may only need to use half of it) and mix well but gently. Season with additional salt and pepper if needed and serve immediately—the delicate greens wilt quickly.

BUCATINI *with* Nettles, Pancetta, *and* Black Pepper

When I worked in Italy, one of the first things I learned to make was *cacio e pepe*, Roman *bucatini* with cheese and pepper. A springtime variation on the classic incorporated foraged nettles. Nettles are collected in early spring when the shoots are young (the mature leaves sting). Here, puréed leaves lightly blanket the hollow spaghetti-like strands.

The nettle purée may make more than you need for this pasta, but making less of it won't purée as well in the blender. Extra purée can be mixed into eggs in a frittata or frozen in ice cube trays for future use.

SERVES 4 TO 6

Bucatini

150 grams • 1 cup 00 flour

100 grams • ³/4 cup farro flour or whole wheat flour

1 gram • ¹/4 teaspoon kosher salt

100 grams • 2 eggs

25 grams • 2 tablespoons water

4 cups nettle leaves, packed, plus ¹/2 cup for garnish

2 cups spinach leaves, packed

kosher salt

115 grams • 4 ounces pancetta, diced into small cubes

1 to 2 tablespoons unsalted butter

black pepper

a block of Parmigiano-Reggiano for grating

a handful of herb flowers, such as garlic, sorrel, onion, or chive blossoms

To make the *bucatini*: In a stand mixer with the paddle attachment, mix together the flours and salt. In a bowl, whisk together the eggs. With the mixer running on low speed, drizzle in the eggs and water. Mix the dough for 2 to 3 minutes until the dough just comes together. Turn the dough onto a floured counter and knead for several minutes by hand; it will feel dry and slightly crumbly. Flatten the dough into a rectangle, wrap in plastic wrap, and leave on the counter for 30 minutes to soften and

hydrate. Follow the instructions for extruding pasta on page 274.

Prepare an ice bath lined with a mesh strainer. Bring a large pot of water to a boil and season with salt. Blanch the 4 cups of nettles and the spinach until soft, 1 to 2 minutes. Using a skimmer or slotted spoon, remove the greens and plunge into the ice bath. When the greens are cold, remove them from the ice bath and squeeze out some of the excess water with your hands until it is still wet but no longer dripping. In a blender, purée the blanched greens until smooth. If the purée seems dry, add a couple of tablespoons of water. Season with salt. You should have about ³/4 cup of sauce, more than you need for the pasta.

Heat a large sauté pan over medium-low heat. Scatter the pancetta in one layer in the pan and gently render until crisp, about 3 minutes. Drain the pancetta on paper towels and save the rendered fat for another use. Return the pancetta to the pan.

Bring a large pot of water to a boil and season with salt. Stir in the *bucatini* and cook until al dente, 4 to 5 minutes. Drain, reserving about 1 cup of pasta cooking water, and add the *bucatini* to the pan with the pancetta. Over medium-high heat, swirl in a tablespoon of butter and fold in the nettle leaves, then simmer the *bucatini* gently for a minute or two, thinning with the saved pasta water if necessary. Stir in about ¹/3 cup of nettle purée, just enough to lightly coat the *bucatini*. Cook until heated through. Season to taste with salt and pepper, adding more nettle purée, butter, or reserved cooking water if the pasta looks dry.

Serve on warmed plates and grate Parmigiano-Reggiano over each portion. Sprinkle herb flowers on top to finish.

WHOLE WHEAT FETTUCCINE *with* Funghi Trifolati *and* Spring Garlic

A good rule of thumb is to pair pasta with a sauce or condiment of similar texture and size. A velvety ragù melds well with a ribbon of noodles while a sauce of chunky vegetables is more suited for short pasta shapes. To complement the flat, long fettuccine noodles, I sauté wispy mushrooms, such as black trumpet, yellowfoot, and chanterelle, in olive oil. For contrast in textures, I garnish the pasta with garlic chips, which echo the fresh spring garlic mixed into the mushrooms. To ensure the garlic fries evenly, first blanch it in milk and water. This removes some of the sugars and mellows the garlic's pungency. Fry it in enough oil to keep the slices from sticking to the pan.

SERVES 6

Fettuccine

125 grams • 3/4 cup plus 3/4 teaspoon whole wheat flour

125 grams • 3/4 cup plus 1 1/2 tablespoons 00 flour

1 gram • 1/4 teaspoon kosher salt

100 grams • 2 eggs

15 grams • 1 tablespoon warm water

semolina or 00 flour for dusting

extra virgin olive oil

228 grams • 8 ounces mixed mushrooms, such as chanterelle, black trumpet, oyster, and hen of the woods, cleaned, dry, and sliced lengthwise into 4 to 6 pieces (about 3 cups)

kosher salt and black pepper

30 grams • about 2 tablespoons unsalted butter

28 grams • 1/4 cup minced spring garlic, mostly white parts

8 grams • 2 garlic cloves, minced

18 grams • 1 shallot, minced

40 grams • 1/4 cup vermouth

115 grams • 1/2 cup heavy cream

30 grams • 6 garlic cloves, sliced thinly

240 grams • 1 cup whole milk

205 grams • 1 cup water

23 grams • 1 1/2 tablespoons crème fraîche

2 grams • 2 tablespoons minced chives

a block of Parmigiano-Reggiano for grating

To make the fettuccine: In a stand mixer with the paddle attachment, mix together the flours and salt. In a bowl, whisk together the eggs and water. With the mixer running on low speed, drizzle in the egg mixture. Mix the dough for 2 to 3 minutes, turn onto a floured counter and knead for several minutes by hand; it will feel dry and firm. Flatten the dough into a rectangle, wrap in plastic wrap, and leave on the counter for 30 minutes to soften and hydrate.

Roll out the dough according to the instructions for laminated pasta on page 273. Cut the pasta into 12-inch sheets and dust with flour. Remove the pasta machine rollers and replace with the fettuccine cutters. One at a time, feed the sheets through the cutters. As the noodles emerge from the cutter, catch them with your other hand. Shake the noodles loose, then curl them around your hand to form 3 to 4-ounce nests. You will have about 4 nests. Place the nests on a lightly floured baking sheet and keep on the counter. (If you are cooking the pasta that day, you don't need to refrigerate it.)

To make the ragù: heat a thin film of olive oil in a large sauté pan over high heat until almost smoking. Scatter a quarter of the mushrooms in the pan in an even layer. Let the mushrooms sear without trying to move them until they begin to brown, about 1 minute. Give the mushrooms a stir and season with salt and pepper. When they're nearly cooked, about 4 minutes, swirl in a small dollop of butter and cook until the butter browns, about 30 seconds. Drain the mushrooms on a paper towel–lined platter and repeat with the remaining mushrooms.

Wipe the pan clean with a paper towel, then heat a thin film of olive oil over low heat. Stir in the spring garlic, minced garlic, and shallot and sweat until soft but not caramelized, about 2 minutes. Deglaze with the vermouth and simmer over medium heat until the pan is almost dry. Pour in the cream and simmer until the cream has reduced by about a third. Stir in the cooked mushrooms and simmer to warm through for 2 to

3 more minutes. Season to taste with salt and pepper and transfer the ragù to a bowl.

To make the garlic chips: in a small pot, bring the garlic slices to a simmer with 1/2 cup of the milk and 1/2 cup of the water. Drain and return the garlic to the pot. Pour in the remaining 1/2 cup of milk and 1/2 cup of water and bring to a simmer. Drain the garlic again, cool, and pat dry. Heat about 1/2 inch of olive oil in a small sauté pan over medium-high heat. Scatter the garlic pieces in one layer in the pan and gently fry until crisp, about 30 seconds. Transfer to a paper towel–lined plate and season lightly with salt.

Bring a large pot of water to a boil and season with salt. Stir in the pasta and cook until al dente, 3 to 4 minutes. Drain, reserving about 1/2 cup of pasta cooking water, and return the pasta to the same pot. Over medium-low heat, stir in the ragù, crème fraîche, and chives. Grate a handful of Parmigiano into the pot, then simmer the pasta gently for a minute or two, thinning with a tablespoon at a time of saved pasta water if necessary. Taste, adjusting the seasoning with salt if needed.

Serve the pasta on warmed plates and sprinkle with more Parmigiano. Finish each serving with a few garlic chips, a drizzle of olive oil, and a few grindings of pepper.

CLEANING MUSHROOMS

It's rare to find a wild mushroom that doesn't contain some grit, and biting into a speck of dirt is as appetizing as encountering eggshell in an omelet. To clean mushrooms thoroughly, I submerge them in water. Water won't destroy mushrooms or dilute their flavor if you handle them gently. The trick is to soak the mushrooms only briefly, just long enough to dislodge dirt and sand.

For mushrooms that hold a lot of dirt and leaves, like black trumpets, I split them open before rinsing. Less porous mushrooms, like porcini, can be left whole. I put the mushrooms in a large bowl filled with water for about 30 seconds, agitating the water to shake out any grit. I let the grit settle to the bottom of the bowl, then I lift the mushrooms out of the water. If the water is very dirty, I submerge the mushrooms in fresh water, repeating the same steps until the soaking water is relatively clean. Once the mushrooms have been washed, I gently spin them in a salad spinner. Before storing or cooking them, I set them out on towel-lined trays to dry.

BRAISED OXTAIL
in Cabbage Leaves *with* Cranberry Beans

Coda alla vaccinara—oxtail stew—is a classic Roman dish prepared by braising oxtails in tomatoes, broth, and wine until the meat starts to fall off the bone. I refine the presentation by shredding the braised oxtails, mixing the meat with breadcrumbs and seasoning, and tucking the mix into neat cabbage bundles. If you have leftover lamb ragù (page 34), you can use it instead of braised oxtail meat. The oxtail also makes a great filling for ravioli. I like to serve the stuffed cabbage leaves with simply seasoned cranberry beans, a side dish that comes together quickly when you have soffritto (page 282) and cooked beans (page 277) on hand.

SERVES 6

1180 grams • 2 pounds 10 ounces (4 or 5 pieces) oxtail

kosher salt and black pepper

extra virgin olive oil

200 grams • 1 1/2 carrots, diced

200 grams • 1 yellow onion, diced

200 grams • 3 stalks celery, diced

7 sprigs mint

4 sprigs rosemary

2 sprigs thyme

a sachet of 4 black peppercorns, 2 star anise, and 2 fennel seeds
   (see page 282)

490 grams • 2 1/4 cups red wine

260 grams • 1 cup brown stock (page 283)

Filling

200 grams • 1 yellow onion, sliced

8 grams • 2 cloves garlic, minced

5 grams • 1 teaspoon Calabrian chile oil (page 278)

a pinch of dried red pepper flakes

100 grams • 1/2 cup soffritto (page 282)

200 grams • 1 cup canned tomatoes, passed through a food mill

50 grams • 1/3 cup dried breadcrumbs

3 grams • 1 tablespoon chopped mint

50 grams • 3 tablespoons unsalted butter, softened

50 grams • 1/2 cup grated pecorino

kosher salt and black pepper

Cranberry Beans

extra virgin olive oil

200 grams • 1 cup soffritto (page 282)

35 grams • 4 cloves garlic confitura (page 279), mashed

6 grams • 2 teaspoons smoked paprika

200 grams • 1 cup canned tomatoes, passed through a food mill

720 grams • 3 cups cooked and drained cranberry beans
   (see page 277)

kosher salt and black pepper

extra virgin olive oil

1000 grams • 2 pounds, 2 ounces savoy cabbage (about 1 head)

113 grams • 4 ounces prosciutto (about 15 slices)

100 grams • 1/2 onion, sliced

100 grams • 1/2 carrot, sliced into 1/8-inch rounds

50 grams • 1 celery stalk, sliced into 1/8-inch pieces

5 to 8 mint leaves, coarsely chopped

a block of pecorino for grating

Pat the oxtail pieces dry, then season with salt and a few grindings of pepper. Heat a thin film of olive oil in a large straight-sided sauté pan over medium-high heat. Sear the oxtails until evenly browned on all sides, then transfer to a heatproof storage container. Cover the oxtail with the carrot, onion, celery, mint, rosemary, thyme, and sachet. Pour off any excess fat from the sauté pan and add the wine. Put the pan over medium-high heat and use a wooden spoon to dislodge any brown bits from the bottom. Once the wine reaches a simmer, pour it over the oxtail. Cool, cover, and store oxtail in the marinade in the refrigerator overnight or up to 3 days.

Preheat the oven to 300°F. Strain the marinade into a small, high-sided pot and set over low heat. Bring the marinade slowly to a simmer, using a ladle to skim away coagulated proteins that float to the surface. Put the oxtail, vegetables, and sachet in a Dutch oven or heavy-bottomed pot. Using a fine-mesh strainer, strain the marinade directly into the Dutch oven, then pour in the stock and 1 cup of water. Bring to a simmer, cover with a

{continued}

tight-fitting lid and transfer to the oven. Cook the oxtail for 3 to 3¹/₂ hours or until tender enough to shred with a fork. Let the meat cool in the braising liquid for 2 hours.

Remove the oxtail pieces from the braising liquid and pick the meat off the bones, discarding any connective tissue. You will have about 1¹/₂ cups of meat. Strain the braising liquid through a fine-mesh strainer into a clean pot and discard the vegetables and sachet. Simmer over low heat, skimming the fat from the surface, until the braising liquid has reduced to about 1 cup and tastes very flavorful.

To make the filling: Heat a thin film of oil in a large straight-sided sauté pan (or a wide pot) over medium heat. Sweat the onion until soft, about 2 minutes, and then stir in the garlic and sweat for 30 seconds more. Stir in the chile oil, red pepper flakes, and soffritto, then pour in the tomato. Cook, stirring occasionally, until the tomato begins to thicken, about 4 minutes. Add the oxtail meat and a few tablespoons of the braising liquid and cook gently for 5 minutes to meld the flavors. Cool the filling to a warm room temperature.

Transfer the filling to a large bowl. Using your hands, mix in the breadcrumbs, mint, butter, pecorino, and a couple of pinches of salt and pepper until the mixture is tacky, thick, and well seasoned. Cover, and refrigerate until needed.

To make the beans: Preheat the oven to 325°F. Heat a thin film of olive oil in a pot over medium heat. Sweat the soffritto for 1 minute or until warmed through. Add the garlic confitura and paprika, then stir in the tomato.

Bring to a simmer, mix in the beans, and cover with a parchment paper lid (see page 277). Bake the beans for 30 minutes. Remove the parchment and taste the beans, adjusting the seasoning with salt and pepper if needed. Drizzle in a few tablespoons of olive oil and keep warm.

Prepare an ice bath and line baking sheets with paper towels. Bring a large pot of salted water to a boil. Pull off the outer leaves of the cabbage head and discard, then cut out the core with the tip of your knife. Peel off the leaves, taking care to keep them in whole pieces. When you reach the heart, slice the small, tender leaves and set aside to use for garnish. Keeping the water at a constant boil, blanch the leaves in small batches until tender, about 1 minute. Shock the leaves in the ice bath. Once cold, drain the leaves on the prepared baking sheets.

To ensure that the cabbage leaves lies flat, remove part of the thick center vein: Lay a leaf on a cutting board. With your knife blade parallel to the board, shave away the center vein until it is nearly level with the rest of the leaf (leaving part of the vein keeps it in one piece).

To assemble each cabbage roll, place two leaves of cabbage face up on a work surface, slightly overlapping. Near the root end, place a generous spoonful (about ¹/₄ cup) of filling across the layers. Roll the root end up over the filling, then tuck in the sides and roll the cabbage up like a burrito. Wrap each bundle with a strip of prosciutto, then tie butcher's twine around the center to secure. You will have 12 to 15 bundles. Refrigerate in a single layer until ready to serve.

BRAISING AND COOKING MEAT

I braise boneless meat in *sous vide* (see page 271) but I cook bone-in meat, such as oxtail, the traditional way. I dredge the meat in Wondra flour (see page 283), sear it on all sides, and then braise it in the oven until tender but not quite falling apart. In some instances, I also marinate the meat overnight and then use the marinade as the braising liquid. Without exception, I always cool the meat in the braising liquid for at least one hour before I do anything else. If I were to pull the meat out of the braising liquid when still hot, it would toughen and become dry—it's like slicing into a roast without letting it rest. When it cools in its braising liquid, it relaxes, absorbing more liquid as it cools. For best results, I braise meat the day before I plan to serve it, refrigerating it overnight in the braising liquid.

Preheat the oven to 300°F. Place the rolls in a single layer in a 9 by 13-inch baking pan and pour enough braising liquid in to cover the bottom of the pan. Cover the pan with aluminum foil and bake until hot in the center, 15 to 20 minutes.

Meanwhile, heat a thin film of olive oil in a sauté pan over medium heat. Sweat the reserved center cabbage leaves as well as the onion, carrot, and celery, until tender, about 3 minutes. Season with salt to taste.

Snip the butcher's twine off of the cabbage rolls with scissors. Using a spatula, transfer the rolls onto plates or a serving platter and scatter the vegetable garnish and mint over the top. Grate pecorino over the cabbage, finish with a drizzle of olive oil, and serve with a side of cranberry beans.

....

GOAT CHEESE and Ricotta Crespelle with Orange–Caramel Sauce

Much like a local cheesemaker would do in Italy, Soyoung Scanlan personally delivers her Andante Dairy cheeses to our restaurant. Through this personal transaction, we can discuss with her the flavor differentiations that naturally occur in cheese throughout the year. The cheeses are bright, almost sweet, in the spring when the herds are eating new grass. As the season continues and the grass dries, the cheeses take on a straw-like character. This dessert is designed to emphasize the depth of flavor in Soyoung's cheeses. *Crespelle*, Italian for crepes, are neutral canvases, the ideal vehicle for tangy, rich goat cheese. For best results, make the batter the day before; letting it rest allows the flour to hydrate and the gluten to relax, yielding more delicate *crespelle*.

SERVES 6 TO 8

Batter

40 grams • 3 tablespoons unsalted butter

355 grams • 1¹/₂ cups whole milk

200 grams • 4 eggs

125 grams • ³/₄ cup all-purpose flour

40 grams • 3 tablespoons sugar

3 grams • ³/₄ teaspoon kosher salt

Filling

50 grams • ¹/₄ cup goat cheese

50 grams • ¹/₄ cup mascarpone

100 grams • ¹/₃ cup plus 1 tablespoon drained ricotta
(see page 281)

3 grams • ¹/₂ teaspoon vanilla paste

35 grams • ¹/₃ cup confectioner's sugar

1 teaspoon orange zest

a pinch of kosher salt

2 to 4 tablespoons unsalted butter

about 2 tablespoons granulated sugar

about 1 cup orange juice

1 orange for zesting

confectioner's sugar

To make the batter: Heat the butter in a small sauté pan over medium heat until it bubbles and browns. Cool to room temperature. In a small pot over medium heat, briefly scald the milk and cool slightly. In a blender, blend together the eggs and milk, then blend in the flour, sugar, and salt. With the blender running, drizzle in the butter. Strain the batter through a fine-mesh strainer and refrigerate for at least 30 minutes or overnight.

To make the filling: In a stand mixer fitted with the paddle attachment, mix together the goat cheese, mascarpone, and ricotta until smooth. Add the vanilla paste and mix on medium speed for 30 seconds. Add the confectioner's sugar, orange zest, and salt and mix on medium speed for another 30 seconds. Transfer to a pastry bag fitted with a large tip and refrigerate until needed.

To make the crespelle: Spread a couple of sheets of parchment paper on the counter. Heat an 8-inch nonstick sauté pan over medium heat. Spray with a little cooking

{continued}

spray, then wipe the pan clean. (A *crespella* won't stick if the pan is hot enough.) With a small ladle, spoon 1¹/₂ ounces of batter into the pan, then swirl to spread the batter evenly across the pan's surface. Cook for about 1 minute or until the top is almost dry. With a wrist-flick or a spatula, flip the *crespella* onto the other side and cook for 30 seconds more. Invert the *crespella* on the parchment paper. Repeat with the remaining batter, laying the *crespelle* in a single layer if space permits (If stacking *crespelle*, wait until they are cool, and separate the layers with parchment paper.) Add nonstick spray only if you need to—the less you add, the better the *crespelle* cook. You should have 16 to 18 *crespelle*.

To fill the crespelle: Once they're cooled to room temperature, pipe a few lines of filling (about 1 tablespoon) across the top third of each *crespella*. Fold the top end over the filling, tuck in the sides, and roll up like a burrito. Transfer to a parchment-lined baking sheet seam-side

down, cover with plastic wrap, and refrigerate for at least 2 hours or overnight.

Melt a pat of butter in two large sauté pans over medium-low heat (if you only have one such pan, keep the first batch of *crespelle* warm while you make the second batch). Place 8 or 9 *crespelle*, seam-side down, into each pan. Once the bottoms are lightly toasted, using a spoon, nudge the *crespelle* over so the seam sides are facing up. Sprinkle each batch of *crespelle* with about 1 tablespoon of sugar. Once the sugar starts to melt into the *crespelle*, pour in the orange juice, about ¹/₂ cup per batch. Simmer until the orange juice becomes syrupy, about 2 minutes. Swirl in another pat of butter and baste the *crespelle* with the juices until the sauce lightly glazes them. Place 2 to 3 *crespelle* on individual plates or a serving platter and spoon the sauce on top. Grate orange zest on top and dust with confectioner's sugar.

SPRING LAMB

Cooking a whole lamb is a rite of spring in central Italy. In San Francisco, building a menu around spring lamb not only gives me a reason to celebrate the season but also allows me to use a full array of cooking techniques, both classic and new. Starting in February, when spring lambs become available from Don Watson's Napa Valley Lamb Company, I buy two each week. Obtaining whole animals directly from the source guarantees quality while giving us the flexibility to butcher the meat in our own way. Yet the greatest value I find in preparing spring lamb is in how it reinforces the connection between respect for technique and respect for ingredient. Out of reverence for the animal, not one ounce goes to waste.

To best bring out the tender, delicate flavor of a young lamb, I use *sous vide* techniques extensively (see page 271 for detailed instructions). I wrap the belly in plastic wrap, then gently cook in a water bath heated with an immersion circulator, a process that renders the tough cuts tender. I bone out the leg, and from the leg trimmings make a mousse, which I wrap around the leg meat and encase in Swiss chard leaves. Since the lamb chops and loin are naturally tender, I prepare them simply, searing them and basting them in butter and herbs. Presented together with accompanying side dishes, spring lamb becomes the ultimate celebration of technique.

Any time I butcher a whole animal, I am left with trimmings and several bones. I grind the trimmings and use them in sausages and terrines, and I save the bones for stock or for fortifying braising liquid. Braised shoulders and shanks are transformed into lamb ragù served with semolina gnocchi. A spring lamb weighs 25 to 35 pounds; a more mature lamb can top 60 pounds. You can ask for a split carcass, which will give you enough to make most of these recipes. You can use older spring lamb to make the following recipes, but if you are using cuts from a more mature animal, use the estimated weights in the headnotes as a guide for how much meat you will need. Each lamb preparation will serve four to six people as part of a larger meal. All of the accompaniments included in this section—the steamed artichokes, the pickled Swiss chard stems, the sauce with Gaeta olives, or the semolina gnocchi—can be mixed and matched with any of the lamb preparations you choose.

LAMB RAGÙ *with* Semolina Gnocchi *and* Pecorino Pepato

These gnocchi are the perfect foil for velvety ragù made with braised lamb. Typically, *gnocchi alla Romana* are made from polenta spread onto a surface to cool. My semolina gnocchi has similar flavors as the traditional version, but I use a technique I learned while working for chef Thomas Keller. The base of the gnocchi is *pâte à choux*, the batter used for making éclair pastries. I pour the batter into a pastry bag, hold the bag over a pot of boiling water, and cut the gnocchi directly into a pot of simmering water using the side of an offset spatula. This recipe makes twice as much braising liquid than you will need for the ragù; save the remaining for other lamb recipes in this section.

SERVES 4 TO 6

Lamb Ragù

extra virgin olive oil

1000 grams • 2 pounds, 2 ounces lamb shoulders and shanks

kosher salt and black pepper

1 yellow onion, cut into large dice

1 carrot, cut into large dice

2 celery stalks, cut into large dice

1 garlic head, halved crosswise

a sachet with 10 black peppercorns, 1/2 teaspoon fennel seeds, 1/2 teaspoon coriander seeds, 1 star anise, 3 thyme sprigs, 1 bay leaf, and 1 rosemary sprig (see page 282)

1 cup white wine

4 cups water

1/3 yellow onion, cut into fine dice

2 pinches dried red pepper flakes

2 tablespoons tomato paste

1 cup diced bell peppers

1/4 cup soffritto (page 282)

1/2 cup white wine

1/2 cup crushed canned Italian cherry tomatoes

Semolina Gnocchi

205 grams • 3/4 cup plus 2 tablespoons water

115 grams • 8 tablespoons unsalted butter

5 grams • 1 teaspoon kosher salt

100 grams • 1/2 cup plus 1 tablespoon semolina flour

57 grams • scant 1/2 cup all-purpose flour

200 grams • 4 eggs

30 grams • 1/3 cup grated pecorino pepato

extra virgin olive oil

1/4 cup chopped parsley

2 tablespoons chopped rosemary

a block of pecorino pepato for grating

To make the ragù: Preheat the oven to 300°F. Heat a thin film of olive oil in a Dutch oven or large braising pan over high heat. Season the shoulders and shanks with salt and pepper. In batches, brown the shoulders and shanks on all sides until lightly browned, about 2 minutes per side. Set the shoulders and shanks aside. Tip out any excess fat from the pan, then add the large diced onion, carrot, celery, garlic, and sachet to the pan and cook for 2 to 3 minutes to soften the vegetables. Pour in the wine to deglaze the bottom of the pan. Nestle the shoulders and shanks into the pan and pour in the water. Bring to a simmer, cover, transfer the pan to the oven, and braise for 3 to 4 hours, until the meat has started falling away from the bone. Let the meat cool in its braising liquid for 2 hours.

Pick the braised meat from the bones and discard the bones, braising vegetables, and sachet. Remove the excess fat, connective tissue, and veins from the meat, but do not shred the meat too finely. Chop the meat into 3/4-inch pieces and set aside. Strain the braising liquid into a tall, narrow pot and let it settle so the fat rises to the surface. Skim off most of the fat, then place the pot over medium-low heat to reduce until the liquid is thick enough to lightly coat the back of a spoon, skimming the surface of fat as it simmers. Reduce the liquid to about 4 cups. Reserve 1 1/2 cups for the ragù; reserve the rest for other lamb recipes.

To finish the ragu: Heat a thin film of olive oil in a large Dutch oven or heavy-bottomed pot over medium-high heat. Sweat the finely chopped onion until soft, about 3 minutes, and season with red pepper flakes. Stir in the tomato paste and cook until it changes color from bright red to brick red, 2 to 3 minutes. Stir in the sweet peppers and cook until soft, about 10 minutes. Add the soffrito and cook until heated through. Pour in the wine and simmer until reduced by half. Add the tomatoes and cook until thickened, about 5 minutes. Pour in the reserved braising liquid and bring to a simmer. Cook for 10 to15 minutes to integrate the flavors. Season with salt and pepper, then stir in the shredded lamb. Remove from the heat and let sit, uncovered, for about 30 minutes to let the flavors come together.

To make the gnocchi: In a large pot, bring the water and butter to a boil. Add the salt and whisk in the flours, continuing to whisk until the batter starts to thicken, about 4 minutes. Cook over medium heat, stirring with a spoon, until the dough turns shiny and tightens up, about 2 minutes. Transfer the dough to a stand mixer fitted with the paddle attachment and mix on low speed for 1 minute so the dough cools slightly. Turn the mixer to medium speed and add the eggs one at a time, mixing well after each addition. On low speed, mix in the pecorino pepato just until incorporated. Transfer the batter to a pastry bag fitted with a medium round tip.

Bring a large pot of salted water to a boil. Oil a large baking sheet. Position the pastry bag over the water and, with one hand, in batches to avoid crowding the pot, pipe out the batter. Holding an offset spatula or paring knife in your other hand, cut the batter into 1-inch pieces. Poach the gnocchi for 2 to 3 minutes after they bob to the surface. Using a skimmer, lift the gnocchi out of the water and spread in a single layer on the baking sheet to cool. Repeat in batches until all the gnocchi batter is cooked.

Heat a thin film of olive oil in a large sauté pan over medium-high heat. Brown the gnocchi on all sides, swirling the pan occasionally, about 4 minutes, and season lightly with salt. Lower the heat to medium and add spoonfuls of ragù until it lightly coats the gnocchi (you will have some left over). Sprinkle with parsley and rosemary and toss to coat. Taste, seasoning with salt and pepper if needed. Serve the gnocchi in warmed bowls. Grate pecorino pepato over the top and finish with a drizzle of olive oil.

LAMB BELLY

Lamb belly is an undervalued cut with a lot of potential. It has a high ratio of fat to meat, which gives it a pleasant crispness, like bacon. Drawing these characteristics out requires time, however. Rolling the belly in plastic wrap and cooking it *sous vide* all day means the meat not only becomes tender but also forms into an easy-to-portion cylinder. I slice the belly into disks, which I sear in a pan to crisp the outsides and heat the centers. Lamb belly pairs especially well with steamed artichokes (page 41). For this recipe, use a lamb belly weighing around 800 grams.

SERVES 4 TO 6

1 garlic clove, coarsely chopped

1 sprig rosemary, stemmed

1 tablespoon lemon zest

kosher salt and black pepper

extra virgin olive oil

black pepper

800 grams • 1 (1pound, 12 ounces) lamb belly, boned and trimmed

sea salt

To make the belly: In a large water bath filled nearly to the top, set an immersion circulator to 155°F (see *Sous Vide*, page 271). In a mortar with a pestle, crush the garlic, rosemary, and lemon zest into a coarse paste. Season with a generous pinch of salt, then mix in 1 to 2 tablespoons of olive oil.

Season the lamb on both sides with salt and pepper. Rub the paste on the top side of the belly (the side that once held the bones and that has less fat). Roll the belly crosswise into a tight roll and wrap in plastic (see page 38). Place the lamb roll in the preheated water and cook for 18 to 20 hours.

Carefully pull the lamb roll from the water, place on a tray and let cool to room temperature, about 1 hour. Cut off the plastic ends, leaving the rest of the plastic in place. Drain out the juices that have accumulated, then wrap a few fresh layers of plastic over the roll and twist the ends as before. Cool the lamb completely in an ice bath and refrigerate.

{continued}

Cut the lamb through the plastic into 1/2-inch-thick slices, discarding the end pieces and the plastic wrap. Season the slices with salt and pepper. Heat a thin film of olive oil in a large sauté pan over medium-high heat. Sear the slices until caramelized on both sides and warm in the center, about 2 minutes per side. Season each slice with sea salt.

LAMB LOIN *and* RACK *with* Gaeta Olive Sauce

Spring lambs have smaller rack and loin chops, so I cut the meat into double chops (about 1 1/2 to 2 inches thick), allowing the lamb to caramelize on the outside while cooking to medium rare internally. If you have braising liquid from the lamb ragù with semolina gnocchi (page 34), use it instead. Otherwise, prepare a brown stock with lamb bones following the method on page 283.

SERVES 4 TO 6

kosher salt and black pepper
560 grams • 8 double lamb rib chops (2 1/2 ounces each)
900 grams • 8 to 10 lamb loin chops (4 ounces each)
extra virgin olive oil
2 to 3 tablespoons unsalted butter
2 sprigs fresh rosemary, stemmed

Gaeta Olive Sauce

1 1/2 cups brown stock (page 283)
10 dried black Gaeta olives (page 278), finely chopped
1 tablespoon small mint leaves

Preheat the oven to 350°F. Tie a piece of butcher's twine around the perimeter of each chop to ensure it keeps its shape while cooking. Season the chops with salt and pepper. Heat a thin film of olive oil in 2 large ovenproof sauté pans over medium-high heat. Sear the chops until they have caramelized on all sides, about 4 minutes per side. Transfer the sauté pans to the oven and roast until

the meat is medium rare with an internal temperature of about 125°F, 10 to 12 minutes. Remove the pans from the oven, place over medium heat, swirl in the butter and rosemary, and baste the meat with pan juices for 1 or 2 minutes. Transfer the chops to a rack to rest for about 10 minutes.

Bring the stock or braising liquid to a simmer and reduce until slightly thickened, about 5 minutes. Stir in the olives, mint leaves, season to taste, and keep warm. Cut off the butcher's twine and slice the lamb as desired. To serve, spoon the sauce over the meat.

LEG *of* LAMB Wrapped *in* Lamb Mousse *and* Swiss Chard

Leg of lamb tends to mean one large piece of meat slowly roasted and carved at the table. The trouble is, a whole leg of lamb can cook unevenly. By the time the thicker part is medium-rare, other parts are overcooked. To gain more control over the process, I bone the leg, trim the meat into even-sized pieces, and then cook them separately. I use the trimmings to make a mousse, which I wrap around the leg pieces, and then encase in Swiss chard leaves. To ensure the mousse and chard adhere to the lamb meat, I sprinkle the layers with Activa RM, transglutaminase enzymes that fuse proteins together (see page 275). The result is an elegant presentation that emphasizes the delicate flavor of lamb. When cooked *sous vide* (see page 271), it is a perfect pink all the way through. I like to serve lamb leg with Gaeta Olive Sauce (opposite) and a sprinkle of sea salt.

To make this recipe, you will need about 2 1/2 kilos (about 5 1/2 pounds) of lamb leg. If you're using a larger leg, save the trimmings for the mousse or grind it and add it to Bolognese (page 184). When making the lamb mousse, ensure the ingredients are very cold before you start. This will keep the mousse from breaking or weeping fat or liquid when it cooks.

Pictured on pages 38–39

SERVES 4 TO 6

2500 grams • 1 (5½-pound) lamb leg

1 teaspoon kosher salt, plus extra

2 egg yolks

⅓ cup crème fraîche

zest of ½ lemon

1 teaspoon chopped parsley

1 teaspoon chopped chervil

1 tablespoon finely chopped dried black Gaeta olives (page 278)

Activa RM (page 275)

3 bunches Swiss chard

sea salt and black pepper

Tracing the tip of a knife along the bone, with the blade facing the bone, cut out the femur and discard or save for making stock. With a knife, separate the muscles along the seams—where the muscles naturally separate. Trim the pieces into rectangles about 150 to 200 grams each. Refrigerate the trimmings to make the mousse (you will need 240 grams of trimmings).

To make the mousse, set up a mixing bowl over a bowl of ice. In a chilled food processor, blend the reserved lamb trimmings with 1 teaspoon kosher salt. Blend in one yolk at a time and pulse until well blended. Blend in the crème fraîche, then transfer the mousse to the bowl over the ice. Fold in the zest, herbs, and olives.

For each lamb piece, lay a large sheet of plastic wrap on a work surface. Using a palette knife, spread mousse in an even layer about ⅛ inch thick, as wide as one of the pieces, and long enough to be wrapped around the lamb. Lightly dust the mousse with Activa RM and season with salt. Place a lamb piece at one end of the mousse and roll the mousse around the lamb, using the plastic wrap to help guide the mousse around the lamb and peeling the plastic wrap back as you work. Repeat with remaining lamb pieces and place in the freezer until firm but not frozen, about 25 minutes.

Prepare an ice bath. Using a knife, cut out the stem of each chard leaf. (Save the stems for Pickled Swiss Chard Stems, page 41.) In a pot of boiling, salted water, blanch the chard leaves until wilted, 1 minute, and shock in the ice bath. Drain well.

For each lamb piece, lay a large sheet of plastic wrap on a work surface. Place the chard in overlapping layers in a rectangle about the same size as the mousse and trim the edges. Dust the chard with Activa RM. Remove the plastic wrap from a leg piece, place on the chard leaves, and roll, using the plastic wrap as an aid. Wrap several times in plastic wrap. Repeat with each lamb piece, and refrigerate for 6 hours so the layers bond together.

In a large water bath filled nearly to the top, set an immersion circulator to 139°F (see *Sous Vide*, page 271). Bring the leg pieces to room temperature. Cook in the water bath for 35 to 38 minutes. Pull the leg pieces from the water and let rest for 5 to 7 minutes.

To serve, slice off and discard the ends. Peel off the plastic and slice the meat into 1 inch pieces. Season lightly with sea salt, and serve.

STEAMED ARTICHOKES

To balance the richness of the lamb, I serve another classic spring ingredient: artichokes, which blanket the Lazio countryside in April. To infuse the artichokes with flavor while they cook, I steam them over an aromatic broth. They are especially delicious with the slow-cooked lamb belly (page 35). If you have leftover artichokes, add them to the Spring Vegetable Vignarola Salad (page 22).

SERVES 4 TO 6

2 lemons, halved

170 grams • ³/₄ cup water

1000 grams • 6 to 8 medium artichokes

240 grams • 1 cup white wine

120 grams • ¹/₂ cup verjus (see page 283)

1 tablespoon white wine vinegar

1 sprig rosemary

extra virgin olive oil

kosher salt and black pepper

1 or 2 sprigs parsley, stemmed and finely chopped

1 tablespoon chopped lemon confitura (page 279)

In a large bowl, mix the juice of half a lemon with cold water. Working with one artichoke at a time, snap off the tough outer leaves, stopping once you reach the softer inner leaves. Cut ¹/₂ to 1 inch off the top and trim the stem. Using a paring knife, strip away the skin of the stem, leaving as much of the stem intact as possible. With the blunt handle of a small spoon, scrape out the prickly, fibrous choke from the top of the artichoke. Submerge the artichoke in the acidulated water while you clean the remaining artichokes. Cut 6 to 7 of the cleaned artichokes lengthwise into ¹/₄ to ¹/₂ inch slices; leave 1 in the water to shave raw for garnish.

In a pot fitted with a steamer basket, pour in the wine, water, verjus, vinegar, and rosemary and bring to a simmer. In a bowl, mix the sliced artichokes with a few drops of olive oil and season with salt and pepper. Place the artichokes with the stem up in the steamer basket, cover, and steam the artichokes until tender when pierced with the tip of a knife, 4 to 7 minutes. Transfer the artichokes to a bowl and dress lightly with a splash of olive oil, a squeeze of lemon juice, parsley, and lemon confitura, and taste, adjusting seasoning if necessary. Using a mandoline or very sharp knife, shave the raw artichoke into paper-thin slices and toss with the cooked artichokes. Serve.

PICKLED SWISS CHARD STEMS

While often overlooked, chard stems have a texture that responds well to pickling. Sliced diagonally into diamonds, the stems are an elegant garnish for meat dishes, such as braised lamb and roasted chicken.

MAKES ABOUT 3 CUPS

1¹/₄ cups Swiss chard stems cut diagonally into diamonds

¹/₂ yellow onion, thinly sliced

3 garlic cloves, thinly sliced

2 cups white pickling liquid (page 281)

kosher salt

extra virgin olive oil

black pepper

In a pot of salted water, blanch the chard stems until just tender, about 2 minutes, and transfer to a heatproof container or pickling jar. Pack in the onion and garlic. Bring the pickling liquid to a boil and pour over the vegetables to cover them. Season with a generous pinch of salt. Cool and refrigerate at least overnight or up to a month. To serve, bring to room temperature. Drain and toss in a large bowl with enough olive oil to coat, then season with salt and pepper.

VIA SALARIA—
LE MARCHE

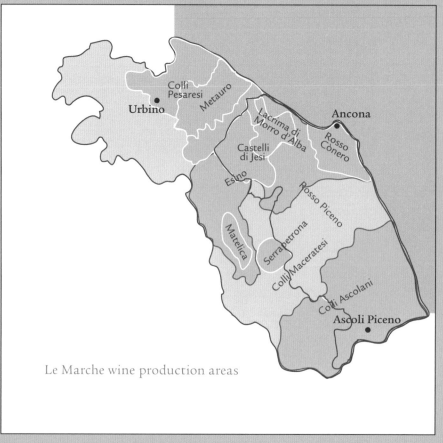

Le Marche wine production areas

VIA SALARIA—LE MARCHE

Ampelio Bucci collects old things. Screw presses once used to crush grapes, vintage typewriters, concave wooden butcher blocks, cast-iron cauldrons, antique irons, and stove-top coffee pots—all are displayed along the walls of the old farmhouse across the courtyard from the Villa Bucci offices. One breezy afternoon in April, I saw several metal molds with long, slender handles hung against a white-washed wall. Ampelio paused, removed one from its hook, and opened it up to reveal an intricate crucifix etched into the metal. He described how the molds were used to make communion wafers for Mass during in the Middle Ages: they would be filled with batter, clamped shut, and placed over the fire to crisp.

This is typical of the history lessons one gleans from spending a day with the estate owner of Villa Bucci, a premier producer of Le Marche's most recognizable white wine, Verdicchio dei Castelli di Jesi Classico. In moments like these, Ampelio—otherwise a forward-thinking wine producer—appears to be like a curator of the past, preserving as much as he can of Italy's craftsman history before it's gone. As a design and marketing professor and consultant based in Milan, Ampelio believes designers can learn a lot from the handmade products of the past. It's his attachment to quality and craft that has also driven him to produce wines that prove the worth of a native vine. "I always insist that you have to focus on the indigenous grape," he says. "It's the only way a small producer can be more of a craftsman."

Bucci is an old name in Le Marche. In the seaside city of Senigallia, about a half-hour's drive from the Villa Bucci winery, a Roman plaque in the center of town has "Bucci" chiseled into the stone. The family has owned a villa in Montecarotto, a Jesi hill town, since the eighteenth century. Ampelio's father bought the property in 1936, but the family's farming interests remained in commodity crops like wheat until the late 1970s. Ampelio, who took over managing the estate's agricultural interests, wanted to move away from crops whose prices were determined by the global commodity market. He decided to concentrate on vines and olive trees, crops that could be rendered into artisanal products not subject to commodity trading. In the early 1980s, however, this quality-over-quantity approach to winemaking was still rare in Le Marche. Ampelio found an ally in Giorgio Grai, an accomplished enologist from Alto Adige. Together, they gambled on the unproven native white grape, Verdicchio. Eventually, the push toward quality paid off. In 2005, the Villa Bucci Verdicchio dei Castelli di Jesi Riserva 2001 garnered the coveted *Gambero Rosso* white wine of the year award.

Improvement efforts focused on concentrating flavor, first by reducing the amount of fruit produced by each vine by better pruning methods, and second by aging the white wine in old Slavonian oak *botti*—large casks—in the winery, some of which dated back to when his father bought the estate. In the *botti*, the wines gently breathe as they age, allowing Verdicchio's trademark mineral quality to come through in the glass.

Although grapes have grown in Le Marche for centuries, the region historically was better known for its fields of wheat, sunflowers, sugar beets, and other common crops. Its propensity for agriculture comes from a forgiving landscape: all undulating hills with soft edges. The region's rich array of raw ingredients has long inspired creativity in the kitchen. In seaside cities like Senigallia and Pesaro, contemporary *crudo* dishes are served everywhere from simple tables to three-star Michelin restaurants. Saffron-infused *brodetto*, fish soup, is served in every town along the coast while inland, heartier food reigns, with dishes like braised rabbit, game birds, and roast pork. Le Marche also has its own version of Emilia-Romagna's lasagna, which is just as rich as the dish from its northern neighbor, and more so when studded with shavings of Urbino truffles. The diversity at table in Le Marche gives it the feeling of the entire Italian peninsula—northern sophistication, southern simplicity, mountain meals, seafood fare—on one plate.

Le Marche's enological reputation still hinges on white wine, in particular those made with the Verdicchio grape. Verdicchio dei Castelli di Jesi, a region surrounded by fourteen walled villages in the central province of Ancona, makes most of Le Marche's Verdicchio wines while the inland, higher-altitude Macerata province's Verdicchio di Matelica offers a more austere side of the grape. Both areas carry DOCG distinction for their *riserva* bottlings. While Verdicchio generally takes all the attention, other white wines are nibbling at its dominance. Just south of Urbino is the Bianchello del Metauro DOC, which produces round wines made with the local Bianchello grape that are best consumed when young. Offida, a southern Marche town, produces white wines made with light, floral Passerina and Pecorino, a once-forgotten grape that today is showing a lot of promise.

White wines are not the whole story here. Aromatic and lightly spicy red grapes, such as Vernaccia Nera, Vernaccia Rosso di Pergola, and Lacrima produce uniquely floral red wines, and widely planted grapes like Montepulciano have shown new life. In the Cupra Marittima hills near Offida, Marco Casolanetti and his dynamic partner, Eleanora Rossi, run an *osteria* and comfortable *agriturismo* at Oasi degli Angeli. But they are best known for their wines, especially cult favorite Kurni, made with 100 percent Montepulciano. With limited yields in the vineyard and use of *barrique* (French oak barrels), Montepulciano becomes a gripping, powerful, red wine redolent of star anise, bittersweet chocolate, leather, and tobacco. The wine was the first in the area to show the power of Montepulciano, and the couple's enthusiasm for caring for their land has encouraged others to improve how they farm their grapes.

North of Offida, the Rosso Cònero DOCG offers structured renditions of Montepulciano; these can be great deals considering the attention to quality they are made with. While the DOCG permits some Sangiovese in the blend, the best Cònero reds tend to be, like Kurni, Montepulciano only. While the grapes here benefit from a mix of volcanic and limestone soils, visitors benefit from the view: Monte Cònero juts out abruptly into the Adriatic, and is the highest point on the coast between Puglia and Friuli.

On the opposite end of the region, near the northern coastal city of Pesaro, red wines seem to come in a grab bag of styles, from wines made with French grapes to Sangiovese. Winemaking here seems to require an experimental temperament, and a lot of energy. Luigi Mancini, who volunteered to take me to his vineyard early one morning to see the sunrise over the Adriatic, has an abundant supply of both. Luigi's Pinot Noir vines grow on a vineyard so steep that it looks like it may slide into the sea. Pinot Noir might seem out of place with the rest of Le Marche, but the Mancini family has cultivated it since the mid-nineteenth century.

Alberto Taddei, a sommelier and good friend who also makes wine around Pesaro, looks beyond Le Marche for inspiration. Along with his brother, Alessandro, Alberto makes lush red wines under the family's Selvagrossa label, using Cabernet Franc and Merlot as well as Sangiovese and Ciliegiolo, two grapes common in Toscana and Umbria. In Le Marche, it seems, winemakers play fast and loose with the rules, and this can make it difficult to sum up the region's red-wine styles to others, and to tell its story abroad.

What is clear is that the wines keep getting better, which is one of the reasons that I find myself returning here on nearly every trip I take to Italy. It's also as close as I feel to home. Sitting outside around Alberto's table one warm afternoon while his mother, Anselma, made *passatelli*, we struggled to remember an Italian saying about drinking wine for your health. Alberto supplied it: "*L'acqua fa laruggine, il vino fa cantar,*" he said. Water makes you rust, wine makes you sing. —SL

White Grapes

BIANCHELLO

An ancient grape dating back to around 500 BC, Bianchello grows in the Metauro River valley near Fano, the town where the Via Flaminia meets the Adriatic. Bianchello del Metauro became a DOC in 1969. It is a rare wine that is both light and round at the same time, with floral notes that lift its flavor while it pleasantly fills your mouth. I drink Bianchello di Metauro when it is still young so I can enjoy the wine's fruit-forward flavors.

RECOMMENDED PRODUCERS: Claudio Morelli, Fiorini, Roberto Lucarelli, Terracruda

PASSERINA

Large-berried, late-ripening Passerina yields several styles around the La Marche's Offida growing area and in Lazio. Varietal Passerina wine is crisp and floral, bringing to mind apple blossoms, lemon-lime tartness, acacia honey, and flint. Like Bianchello, it is best when consumed young. Sparkling Passerina wines are refreshing *aperitivo*-like quaffs. The variety also is made into a honeyed *passito* (dried grape) wine.

RECOMMENDED PRODUCERS: Capestrano, Velenosi, Castello Fageto (Le Marche), Giovanni Terenzi, Luciano Pignataro (Lazio)

PECORINO

Pecorino is a a rising star grape in southern Marche and neighboring Abruzzo. I've heard several stories about how this delicate, light-golden grape earned its name. Here are a few: sheep used to spring up energetically after eating it; its ripe grape clusters looked like wooly sheep heads; the grapes grew best in the mountains where sheep graze. There may be little truth these stories, but they seem to indicate that early-ripening Pecorino grows well on the high-altitude hillsides. Today the chartreuse grape's small yields is one of the reasons it has endeared itself to contemporary winemakers. Pecorino is crisp, with notes of lemon verbena, white ginger, mandarin, and wet stone.

RECOMMENDED PRODUCERS: Ciù Ciù, Velenosi, De Angelis, Poderi San Lazzaro

VERDICCHIO

What Le Marche's signature white grape lacks in showy aromatics or voluptuous body, it makes up in refinement: layers of nuts and lemons tinged with citrus-pith bitterness. The best examples of Verdicchio come from two DOCG growing areas: Castelli di Jesi, which is a half-hour drive from the Adriatic; and Matelica, a valley within the Apennine foothills. Jesi is known for its pebbly, calcareous clay soil and mild, gentle weather, and its wines range from bone-dry to rich and full. A fraction of the size of Jesi, Matelica has hotter summers and colder winters and experiences greater variation between daytime and nighttime temperatures. Its wines exhibit chalky acidity and the aroma of fresh quince. If compared to the wines of the Loire Valley, Jesi Verdicchio is reminiscent of Vouvray while Matelica Verdicchio is higher in acidity, like Savenierres.

RECOMMENDED PRODUCERS: Villa Bucci, Garofoli, Bisci, La Monacesca, Conte Guido Baldeschi Balleani, San Lorenzo, Monte Schiavo, Montecappone, Sartarelli, Collestefano, Coroncino, Belisario

Red Grapes

LACRIMA DI MORRO D'ALBA

In the early 1980s, there were only seven hectares left of the unusual red grape in Lacrima di Morro d'Alba, a medieval town close to the coast. A few families also sought to keep the Lacrima tradition going. Stefano Mancinelli and his family began producing a Lacrima wine in 1979. Soon after, the Marotti Campi family became a major proponent of Lacrima di Morro d'Alba. Their stainless steel–aged Rubico wine was the first Lacrima di Morro d'Alba that I poured in San Francisco. This is not an easy grape to harvest. Its dark purple skins are fragile (it's called *lacrima*, tear, because broken skins would cause grapes to tear up). The grape yields a plum-hued, low-alcohol wine redolent of violets and dried roses, with subtle notes of ginger and cardamom on the nose.

RECOMMENDED PRODUCERS: Badiali, Luigi Giusti, Luciano Landi, Stefano Mancinelli, Marotti Campi

MONTEPULCIANO

As one of the most-planted grape varieties in Italy, Montepulciano used to be taken for granted: harvested too green or allowed to grow with unchecked vigor. Lately, though, its fortunes have changed. The success of Oasi degli Angeli's cult wine Kurni in southern Marche has shown the concentration that Montepulciano can reach in the area's clay soil. The volcanic and limestone soils of Rosso Cònero offer a different side of the grape. Here Montepulciano achieves tight tannins with bright acidity and a toned finish. Finally, there is Le Marche's largest red wine region, Rosso Piceno DOC. The best renditions have the richness of Montepulciano balanced by the tartness of Sangiovese. For a concentrated, *appassimento* style of Montepulciano, I often recommend Le Caniette's Nero di Vite Rosso Piceno, which appeals to Amarone aficionados.

RECOMMENDED PRODUCERS: Lanari, Le Terraze, Garofoli, Le Caniette, Moroder, Oasi Degli Angeli, Mattoni, Ciù Ciù

VERNACCIA NERA

While it holds the same name as the white grape Vernaccia used in historic Vernaccia di San Gimigniano (page 249), Vernaccia Nera isn't related. *Vernaccia* merely means vernacular, or indigenous. This grape was the local variety grown in Serrapetrona, a town in Le Marche's inland Macerata province. References to the grape go back at least to the Middle Ages, though the vine's lineage is probably much older. Today Serrapetrona is still the only place that cultivates the grape for the DOCG wine Vernaccia di Serrapetrona. But although the grape is made in lightly sparkling (*frizzante*), still, and sweet (*passito*) styles, production is tiny. It took me years to find someone who imported Vernaccia di Serrapetrona. As a *frizzante* wine, Vernaccia Nera is comparable to Lambrusco. When vinified dry, as in Ottavi's Pianetta di Cagnore, Vernacchia is imbued with tobacco and black pepper, similar to red wines from northern Rhône.

RECOMMENDED PRODUCERS: Colleluce, Ottavi, Quacquarini

VERNACCIA ROSSO DI PERGOLA

This grape goes by several names, of which Vernaccia Rosso, Pergola Rosso, and Vernaccia di Pergola are the most common. The grape's history in Le Marche dates back to the thirteenth century. Believed to be a clone of Aleatico, a grape that grows in Lazio, Toscana, and Puglia, the grape was traditionally made into a sweet, *passito*-style wine. More recently, vintners around the city of Fano renewed their interest in the grape by vinifying it dry. Without sweetness, Vernaccia Rosso tastes fresh and lively, though it maintains an illusion of sweetness with its fruit-forward flavor and velvety texture.

RECOMMENDED PRODUCERS: Claudio Morelli, Terracruda, Pandolfi Orsini

SEE ALSO: Sangiovese (page 248)

Instinctual Cooking

MOST CHEFS have a feeling for the distance between the burners and the counter, a layout in our unconscious mind that helps us to increase efficiency in every task we take on. When we step out of that environment to cook in someone's home, however, we are knocked squarely from our comfort zone, forced to rethink how we cook—and these are the moments when instinct and "cooking from your gut" matter most.

When I visited winemaker Ampelio Bucci's historic family villa in Montecarotto, a town in Le Marche's Jesi hills, I was faced with such a moment. That evening I had the opportunity to cook for Ampelio, his gracious wife, Vanda, Shelley, and some friends. Early that morning, Ampelio and I headed for the coast, to Senigallia. Within the city's nineteenth-century circular neoclassical arcade, Ampelio and I roamed among the stalls of the farmers' market, buying only what looked best—farm eggs, wild greens, lemons, oranges, bay leaves, thyme, dried cherries, rosemary, eggs, cheese, peas, asparagus, and cherry tomatoes. Before returning to Montecarotto, we stopped in Serra de' Conti, a town just as old as Montecarotto, if slightly more weathered. The local butcher shop had an excellent rabbit on display, and an employee graciously offered to slice pancetta paper-thin for me and to cut off a long piece of butcher's twine. Yet while I had purchased the best food I came across, I still didn't have a complete plan for the meal I was about to prepare.

Not only was the villa's kitchen unfamiliar territory, it was basic. With a small gas stove and a hearth, a sink and drying rack lining the back wall, and a kitchen table covered in a plastic tablecloth, it was the chef's equivalent of going unplugged. I quickly got to work, cleaning anchovies, picking herbs, washing greens, and peeling asparagus. One of my concerns was how to prepare the rabbit in a way that would be aesthetically pleasing and bring out the best it had to offer. In San Francisco, I might have turned to Activa RM, an enzyme that bonds proteins together. Instead, I wrapped the rabbit in plastic wrap and then poached it gently. Once it was poached, I unwrapped it, rewrapped it in pancetta secured with the butcher's twine, and tucked herbs under the string. It roasted in the hearth while I stewed the rabbit legs and shoulders. It was an enjoyable meal, one that came together without any modern kitchen gizmos. It was a Villa Bucci victory. —MA

FLUKE CRUDO, Sausage-Stuffed Olives, *and* Citrus

Senigallia, a cosmopolitan beach town on the coast of the Adriatic, has two of my favorite restaurants in Italy, La Madonnina del Pescatore and Uliassi. Both take advantage of the bountiful local catch, focusing heavily on seafood. It is a particular specialty of chef Moreno Cedroni, who in addition to running La Madonnina, operates a bar where he specializes in *crudo* and "salumi," made from fish. *Crudo* is seafood served in its freshest, purest form: raw. I find it pairs well with salty accents, like green olives stuffed with sausage and fried—a specialty of the southern Marche town of Ascoli Piceno. To match the briny flavors of the olives, I also garnish the *crudo* with sea beans, little vegetables that grow in the San Francisco Bay. Their salty crunch pairs particularly well with seafood. (Use capers if sea beans are unavailable.)

SERVES 6

Crudo

150 grams • 1 cup kosher salt

75 grams • 1/3 cup sugar

about 1/4 cup mixed citrus zest (orange, Meyer lemon, grapefruit)

5 to 10 mint leaves

227 to 340 grams • one 8- to 12-ounce fluke fillet, boned and skinned

57 grams • 2 ounces sweet Italian sausage meat

12 to 18 large green pitted olives, like Casteveltrano or Cerignola

32 grams • 1/4 cup Wondra flour (see page 283)

50 grams • 1 egg, lightly beaten

30 grams • 1/4 cup fine dried breadcrumbs

kosher salt

1 orange, segmented

1 Meyer lemon, segmented

1 grapefruit, segmented

1/2 cup sea beans

1/2 teaspoon coarse salt

1/2 teaspoon lime zest

extra virgin olive oil

6 to 12 small mint leaves

To make the *crudo*: Using your hands, rub the salt, sugar, zest, and mint leaves together to release the mint and citrus flavors. Lay out a long sheet of plastic wrap on a work surface. Scatter half of the cure on the plastic in an even layer about the length of the fish. Place the fish on top and cover with the remaining cure. Wrap the sides of the plastic wrap over the fish, forming a snug package and refrigerate for 2 to 2 1/2 hours.

To make the olives: Stuff the sausage meat into the hollows of the olives. Dredge the olives in Wondra, then egg, then breadcrumbs. Refrigerate until ready to fry.

Cut the citrus segments thinly crosswise and mix together in a small bowl. Bring a pot of unsalted water to a boil. Prepare the ice bath. Blanch the sea beans for about 1 minute, then drain and shock in the ice bath. Unwrap the fish, rinse it under cool water, and pat dry. Slice crosswise into 1/8-inch thick pieces. Lay the pieces on chilled plates.

In a small bowl, mix the salt and lime zest together. In a small pot, heat 1 inch of olive oil to 360°F and line a tray with paper towels. Fry the olives until the breading has turned golden, 1 to 2 minutes. With a spider skimmer or slotted spoon, lift the olives out of the oil and drain on the paper towels. Season with lime salt.

To serve: Spoon the citrus around and on top of the fish slices. Drizzle olive oil over the top and sprinkle with lime salt. Finish with the fried olives, sea beans, and mint leaves.

FRIED SURF CLAMS *with* Agrodolce *and* Onion, Fennel, *and* Cherry Pepper Salad

Unlike Manila clams, surf clams are too large to eat whole. I buy the clams already shelled, cleaned, and cut into strips, so all I need to do is bread and fry them. Lemon juice brightens fried seafood, and *agrodolce*, a sweet-sour condiment, takes on a similar role. The salad offers a refreshing finish. To complement the quickly pickled onions, I like to add a few pickled cherry peppers. Get a jar of nice Italian round peppers that aren't too hot.

SERVES 4 TO 6

Agrodolce

50 grams • 3^1/$_2$ tablespoons water

25 grams • 3 tablespoons sugar

25 grams • 2 tablespoons white wine vinegar

50 grams • 2 tablespoons liquid glucose (see page 280)

1 gram • ^{1}/$_2$ teaspoon cayenne

a pinch of espelette pepper

a pinch of kosher salt

Salad

150 grams • ^{1}/$_2$ yellow onion, thinly sliced

12 grams • 3 garlic cloves, thinly sliced

113 grams • ^{1}/$_2$ cup white pickling liquid (page 281)

50 grams • ^{1}/$_4$ fennel bulb, cored

6 to 8 pickled cherry peppers, halved, seeded, and sliced into ^{1}/$_8$-inch strips

about ^{1}/$_4$ cup parsley leaves

extra virgin olive oil

kosher salt

blended oil for frying (see page 278)

454 grams • 1 pound shucked surf clams, cut into strips

about 1 cup buttermilk

^{3}/$_4$ cup coarse semolina flour

^{1}/$_4$ cup Wondra flour (see page 283)

^{3}/$_4$ teaspoon smoked paprika, plus more for seasoning

^{1}/$_2$ teaspoon cayenne

1 tablespoon onion powder

^{1}/$_2$ teaspoon fennel pollen (see page 279)

kosher salt and black pepper

1 lemon, cut into wedges and seeded

To make the *agrodolce*: In a small pot over medium heat, simmer together the water, sugar and vinegar. Cook until lightly caramelized and syrupy, about 5 minutes. Stir in the glucose and bring to a boil. Swirl in the cayenne, espelette pepper, and salt and cool to room temperature.

To make the salad: Combine the onion and garlic in a nonreactive heatproof container. In a small pot, bring the pickling liquid to a boil. Pour over the onion and let cool to room temperature.

Using a mandoline, shave the fennel lengthwise. In a small bowl, soak the fennel in cold water. Right before frying the clams, drain the onion and the fennel. In a small bowl, toss together the onion and fennel with the cherry peppers, parsley, and a few drops of olive oil. Season with a pinch of salt.

To make the clams: In a large, wide pot, heat 2 inches of oil to 360°F. Place a cooling rack over a baking sheet and line with paper towels.

As the oil heats, in a bowl, soak the clams with just enough buttermilk to cover for a few minutes and drain. In a large bowl, mix together the semolina, Wondra flour, smoked paprika, cayenne, onion powder, and fennel pollen. Toss the clams in the flour mixture to coat, then lift out and shake off any excess.

Using a skimmer or slotted spoon, gently lower some clams into the oil. Fry the clams in uncrowded batches until crispy, 2 to 3 minutes. With the skimmer or spoon, lift the clams out of the oil and drain on the paper towels. Make sure the oil is at temperature before you fry the next batch. Season with salt, pepper, and a pinch of paprika. Squeeze a lemon wedge over the pieces.

To serve: Toss the clams in *agrodolce* and spoon onto a platter. Top with the cherry pepper salad and then drizzle more *agrodolce* on top. Serve with extra lemon wedges alongside.

BAKED ANCHOVIES

In nearly every region in Italy, anchovies find their way to the table. Piemontese cooks may infuse salted anchovies in butter for *bagna cauda*, while in Le Marche they serve them roasted. Baking is one of the best ways to prepare this small, immensely flavorful fish. If you are new to cleaning whole fish, this is a forgiving place to start. (The technique given here also works with sardines.) If you have a batch of garlic confitura (page 279), pour off some of the oil and use it instead of the olive oil called for in this recipe.

SERVES 4 TO 6

680 grams • 1 1/2 pounds whole fresh anchovies

extra virgin olive oil

kosher salt and black pepper

2 lemons

about 1/2 cup dry breadcrumbs

10 bay leaves

Clean each fish under cold running water: run a small spoon from the tail end toward the head to gently scrape away the scales. Rinse well. Using kitchen shears, make a cut behind the head and gills, stopping just short of cutting all the way through the belly. Let the head fall away and gently pull the innards out. Rinse the anchovy well and place on a bed of ice while you clean the remaining fish. Using kitchen shears, gently cut through the belly from the head toward the tail. With the shears, snip the spine just before the tail (leave the tail intact). With your fingers, open the anchovy up like a book. Gently pull out the backbone and pinbones.

Preheat the oven to 375°F. Oil a 9 by 13-inch casserole. Slice one of the lemons crosswise into rounds. Cut the other lemon into wedges for serving.

Spread the cleaned fish out on a baking sheet or platter and season with salt and pepper. Drizzle the fish with enough olive oil to coat, then sprinkle with about 1/4 cup of the breadcrumbs or enough to coat them lightly. Tuck

the anchovies crosswise into the casserole and sprinkle with more breadcrumbs to barely cover. Nestle the lemon rounds and bay leaves in among the fish. Drizzle with additional oil and bake for 8 to 12 minutes or until the breadcrumbs are golden brown and crisp and the fish is cooked through. Serve with lemon wedges on the side.

PASSATELLI EN BRODO

Made from a soft dough of breadcrumbs, egg, and cheese extruded through a potato ricer, thick *passatelli* noodles are commonly served in Le Marche and neighboring Emilia-Romagna. Anselma Taddei, a seasoned home cook from the coastal Le Marche city of Pesaro, makes *passatelli* by eye. She grates the lemon and nutmeg directly over untoasted breadcrumbs made from stale bread and then mixes the ingredients by hand, adding more breadcrumbs until the dough stops sticking to her hands. I think of *passatelli* as pasta, but some call it a soup since it's always served in a flavorful *brodo*, or broth. While I prefer using a parmesan-rind-infused chicken broth or consommé (page 182) for *brodo*, to make it Pesaro-style, use a light fish broth.

SERVES 4 TO 6

450 grams • 2¹/₂ cups breadcrumbs, plus more as needed

325 grams • 2¹/₂ cups grated Parmigiano-Reggiano, plus more
   to serve

50 grams • ¹/₄ cup 00 flour

2 grams • ¹/₂ teaspoon kosher salt

1 lemon for grating

10 gratings of nutmeg

300 grams • 6 eggs

1190 grams • 6 cups white stock (page 282)

Mix together the breadcrumbs, 2¹/₂ cups Parmigiano-Reggiano, flour, and salt. Pile the ingredients on a work surface and grate the lemon and nutmeg directly on top. Make a well and pour the eggs into the center. With a fork, break up the eggs, gradually pulling the dry ingredients into the eggs until a coarse dough forms. Fold in the sides and knead the dough for 3 to 5 minutes until completely smooth. If the dough is sticking to your hands, add more breadcrumbs.

Roll the dough into a log no wider than the well of your potato ricer. Cut off 2-inch pieces and push them through the ricer's largest plate. As the *passatelli* come out of the ricer, cut them into 4-inch strands with a paring knife.

Meanwhile, bring the stock to a simmer and taste, adding salt if needed. Keep warm.

Bring a pot of water to a boil and season with salt. Poach the *passatelli* in the water until the strands have been floating for a minute (about 2 minutes). Drain the *passatelli* and spoon into 4 to 6 bowls. Ladle in just enough stock to cover the strands. Sprinkle Parmigiano-Reggiano over the top to finish.

LASAGNA VINCISGRASSI

Vincisgrassi, a decadent baked pasta layered with *besciamella* (béchamel), veal ragù, and mushrooms, is Le Marche's answer to lasagna. I came across it early in my career while working for Todd English. The *vincisgrassi* that I make today is a special-occasion dish, more like a refined terrine than a lasagna. There is no single formula for making *vincisgrassi*. Some add truffles; others do not. The one factor that remains constant is the layers. Most Marchigiani use at least five layers; I prefer more.

SERVES 6 TO 8

Veal Ragù

75 grams • 5 tablespoons unsalted butter

395 grams • 14 ounces ground veal

kosher salt and black pepper

100 grams • 1/3 yellow onion, finely chopped

8 grams • 2 garlic cloves, minced

a pinch of ground cloves

110 grams • 1/2 cup soffritto (page 282)

15 grams • 2 tablespoons Wondra flour (see page 283)

120 grams • 1/2 cup white wine

200 grams • 1 scant cup brown stock (page 283)

1 bay leaf

Filling

100 grams • 3 1/2 ounces chicken livers

kosher salt and black pepper

125 grams • 4 1/2 ounces cooked veal sweetbreads (page 170), sliced into 1/2-inch pieces

113 grams • 8 tablespoons unsalted butter

75 grams • 1/4 yellow onion, finely chopped

150 grams • 5 1/4 ounces mixed mushrooms, such as chanterelles, black trumpets, oyster, and baby shiitake, cleaned and sliced lengthwise into 4 to 6 pieces (2 cups)

5 grams • 1/4 cup packed sage leaves

1 nutmeg for grating

15 grams • 2 tablespoons Wondra flour

100 grams • scant 1/2 cup Marsala wine

57 grams • 1 cup grated Parmigiano-Reggiano

40 grams • 1 1/2 ounces (5 slices) prosciutto, chopped

Pasta

500 grams • 4 cups 00 flour

2 grams • 1/2 teaspoon kosher salt

200 grams • 4 eggs

15 grams • 1 tablespoon extra virgin olive oil

Besciamella

100 grams • 7 tablespoons unsalted butter

115 grams • scant 1 cup all-purpose flour

660 grams • 2 3/4 cups whole milk

5 grams • 1 teaspoon kosher salt

freshly ground white pepper

1 nutmeg for grating

57 grams • 1 cup grated Parmigiano-Reggiano, plus extra to serve

To make the ragù: Melt the butter in a Dutch oven or heavy-bottomed pot over medium heat. Add the veal and season with salt and pepper, breaking the meat into smaller pieces with a wooden spoon as it browns. After the meat is mostly cooked, 5 minutes, stir in the onion, garlic, and clove. Continue to cook until the onion has softened, about 3 minutes. Stir in the soffritto, then sprinkle the Wondra over the pot and stir to combine. Pour in the wine and bring to a simmer, then add the stock. Drop in the bay leaf, cover, and turn the heat to a gentle simmer. Stew, stirring occasionally, for 30 minutes. Remove the lid and simmer for an additional 15 minutes or until the liquid has reduced enough to glaze the meat. Remove the bay leaf and season with more salt or pepper if needed. You will have just under 3 cups.

To make the filling: Trim away any discolored parts or visible veins from the livers. Soak in ice water for 3 hours to leach out any blood or impurities. Rinse, pat dry, and season evenly with salt and pepper. Season the sweetbreads with salt and pepper.

Melt 4 tablespoons of the butter in a large, straight-sided sauté pan over medium heat. When the butter starts to bubble, stir in the livers and sweetbreads and cook until lightly browned on all sides, about 2 minutes per side. Transfer the livers and sweetbreads to a plate.

Melt the remaining 4 tablespoons of butter in the pan over medium heat. Sweat the onion with a pinch of salt until softened, about 3 minutes. Increase the heat to medium-high and scatter the mushrooms into the pan. Season with salt and cook until the mushrooms begin to soften. Stir in the sage and 15 gratings of nutmeg. Sprinkle the Wondra over the mushrooms and mix well. Pour in the Marsala and simmer until the pan is nearly dry, about 4 minutes. Transfer the mushrooms and pan juices to a bowl.

Coarsely chop the sweetbreads and livers and mix into the mushrooms, then stir in the Parmigiano-Reggiano and prosciutto. You will have about 3 cups.

To make the pasta: In a stand mixer with the paddle attachment, mix together the flour and salt. In a bowl, whisk together the eggs and olive oil. With the mixer running on low speed, drizzle in the eggs. Mix the dough for 2 to 3 minutes, then turn the dough onto the counter and knead for several minutes by hand; it should feel firm and dry. With your hands or a rolling pin, flatten the dough into a rectangle. Wrap in plastic wrap and leave on the counter for 30 minutes to soften.

To make the besciamella: In a saucepan over medium heat, melt the butter. Stir in the flour and cook until it pulls away from the sides of the pan but hasn't started to brown, 2 to 3 minutes. Whisk in the milk until smooth. Cook, whisking constantly, for about 5 minutes or until the besciamella becomes thick enough to coat the back of a spoon and the flour taste has been cooked out of the milk. You will have about 3^1/$_2$ cups. Season with salt, several grindings of white pepper, and several gratings of nutmeg. Remove from the heat, sprinkle the Parmigiano-Reggiano on top, and gently stir into the besciamella until completely melted.

To assemble: Preheat the oven to 375°F. Butter an 8 by 12-inch baking pan. Clear a large workspace for making the pasta and set the rollers on your pasta maker to the widest setting. Roll out the dough according to the instructions for laminated pasta on page 273. Cut the sheets into 10-inch rectangles.

Spread a thick layer of besciamella on the bottom of the baking pan. Place an even layer of pasta over the besciamella, trimming the rectangles to fit as needed. Spoon a layer of veal ragù over the pasta, followed by a layer of pasta. Spoon a layer of chicken livers and mushrooms on top, followed by another layer of pasta. Repeat with layers of ragù and chicken livers. For the top layer, spoon ragù over the top, then dot with besciamella and sprinkle with Parmigiano-Reggiano.

Cover the pan with aluminum foil and tap lightly on the counter to expel any air bubbles. Bake for 15 to 20 minutes. Uncover and bake for an additional 15 to 20 minutes or until the top is lightly browned. Let the vincisgrassi rest for about 10 minutes before cutting into it. Serve with additional Parmigiano-Reggiano on the side.

RABBIT *a la* VILLA BUCCI

This rabbit is inspired by the meal I prepared at Villa Bucci: a poached and roasted rabbit roulade served with braised shoulders and drumsticks (see page 51). When wrapping the rabbit roulade, you can use prosciutto, pancetta, or speck, but be sure that the meat is sliced paper-thin.

SERVES 6

1360 grams • 1 (3-pound) rabbit, with heart and liver, legs and shoulders removed

kosher salt and black pepper

a pinch of dried red pepper flakes

1 orange for zesting

1/4 cup dried sour cherries

10 sage leaves, chopped

3 thyme sprigs, chopped

3 rosemary sprigs, chopped, plus more for roasting

2 dill sprigs, chopped

2 marjoram sprigs, chopped

2 wild fennel sprigs, chopped

2 parsley sprigs, chopped

extra virgin olive oil

2 cipollini onions, minced

1 garlic clove, minced into a paste

1/3 cup soffritto (page 282)

1/3 cup white wine

1 1/2 cups 1/2-inch cubes of country bread

1 egg, lightly beaten

113 grams • ounces (20 thin slices) pancetta

kosher salt and black pepper

Wondra flour (see page 283)

2 small carrots cut on a bias

2 cipollini onions, cut into sixths

1 small fennel bulb, cut into 8 to 10 wedges

2 tablespoons tomato purée

1 cup white wine

Cut the rabbit drumsticks (shanks) away from the thighs and set these aside with the shoulders. Turn the thighs so that the insides face up. Make an incision along the bone where it runs closest to the surface. Cut the meat away from the bone until you can remove the bone completely. Dice the thigh and reserve for stuffing the rabbit; set aside the bone with the shanks and shoulders. Open up the rabbit so it is lying flat and the belly meat is exposed.

Place the rabbit saddle on its back. Using a small knife, bone the saddle: start along the ribs working inward toward the spine. Once you reach the loin muscle, work from the head toward the tail with the knife until the loin releases from the vertebrae. Repeat along the other side of the rabbit. Remove the tenderloins from the saddle and set aside. Gently cut along the tops of the vertebrae to release the bones from the meat while ensuring that the rabbit saddle remains in one piece. Once boned, season the saddle with salt, pepper, and red pepper flakes. Grate orange zest directly over the meat, then cover the rabbit and refrigerate for 2 hours.

Soak the cherries in warm water until plump, at least 1 hour. Mix the chopped herbs in a bowl, and set aside. Heat a large, rectangular water bath fitted with an immersion circulator to 155°F (see *Sous Vide*, page 271).

Meanwhile, make the stuffing. Season the rabbit heart and liver with salt and pepper. Heat a film of olive oil in a sauté pan over medium-high heat and sear the heart and liver until golden brown on the outside but still rare in the center, about 1 minute. Let cool, then quarter.

Heat another film of oil in the sauté pan over medium heat. Sweat the minced onion with a pinch of salt until soft, about 3 minutes. Stir in the garlic and sweat briefly, about 1 minute. Add the soffritto and cook until warmed through. Pour in the 1/3 cup white wine and reduce until the pan is nearly dry, 3 minutes. Remove the pan from the heat and let cool to room temperature.

In a bowl, mix the rabbit thigh meat with the bread and egg. Mix in the onions and garlic. Drain the cherries and stir them in, then stir in half of the chopped herbs. To assemble the roulade, lay the pancetta slices in slightly overlapping layers crosswise across a large piece of plastic wrap so the slices form a large rectangle. Place the rabbit, skin-side down, across the center of the rectangle perpendicular to the pancetta strips. Spoon the stuffing

{continued}

in a 2-inch strip down the center of the rabbit. Dot the stuffing with the heart and liver pieces. Starting from the long end, roll up the rabbit, using the plastic wrap as a guide. Starting with the edge closest to the rabbit, roll the pancetta layer around the rabbit. Use additional plastic wrap to wrap the roulade into a tight roll as directed on page 272. Prepare the ice bath. Cook for 25 minutes in the water bath to set the shape, then plunge into the ice bath. Once the rabbit is completely cool (about 10 minutes), remove the plastic wrap. Tie butcher's twine around the rabbit 3 or 4 times crosswise. Tie one piece of twine lengthwise around the roulade. Tuck the remaining rosemary sprigs under the twine.

To braise the drumsticks and shoulders: Preheat the oven to 325°F. Season the drumsticks and shoulders with salt and pepper and dredge in Wondra, shaking off any excess. Repeat with the reserved bones. Heat a film of olive oil in a small Dutch oven over medium-high heat. Sear the drumsticks and shoulders on all sides and transfer to a plate. Stir in the carrots, onion pieces, and fennel and cook, stirring occasionally, until softened, about 3 minutes. Add the bones to the Dutch oven and gently brown, about 6 minutes. Stir in the tomato purée and cook for 1 to 2 minutes or until thickened. Deglaze with the 1 cup of wine and cook until the pan is nearly dry. Return the rabbit pieces to the pan and pour in just enough water to cover. Cover and braise for 1 hour.

Uncover, pick out the bones, cover and simmer over low heat, until tender, 35 to 45 minutes.

To roast the roulade, heat a large roasting pan on the stove top. Lightly coat the roulade in olive oil and lightly season with salt and pepper. Gently sear on all sides, then place the pan in the oven. Roast until the internal temperature reaches 150°F, about 35 minutes. Let the roulade rest 15 to 20 minutes before slicing.

Meanwhile, uncover the braised shoulders and drumsticks and simmer on the stove top for 10 more minutes, until the braising liquid thickens to a sauce consistency.

Slice the roulade into 3/4-inch rounds and put a round on each plate. Spoon the braised rabbit, braised vegetables, and sauce alongside. Sprinkle each plate with the remaining chopped herbs and finish with a drizzle of olive oil.

DRIED FRUIT and NUT BISCOTTI *with* Sweet Wine Granita

Biscotti are often baked too long and then forgotten about until they're brick-hard and dry as powder. There is no reason this delicious cookie needs to be treated this way. I lightly toast the outside, leaving the cookies almost—but not quite—soft in the center. Serving biscotti alongside sweet wine granita is a clean, refreshing way to end a meal. When making granita, use a shallow container (ideally stainless steel or plastic) with a lot of surface area—this makes it easier to scrape the granita as it freezes to form the icy crystals. For the wine, a sweet Moscato works well. You also can make the granita with dry wine by sweetening it with sugar to your liking.

MAKES 48 BISCOTTI

Granita

- 300 grams • 1 3/4 cups sweet wine
- 200 grams • 5 tablespoons water
- 30 grams • 3 tablespoons sugar
- 2 dried hibiscus flowers (optional)
- a pinch of kosher salt

Biscotti

- 150 grams • 10 1/2 tablespoons unsalted butter
- 365 grams • 2 1/3 cups sugar
- 250 grams • 5 eggs
- 9 grams • 1 1/2 teaspoons vanilla paste
- 400 grams • 3 1/8 cups all-purpose flour
- 12 grams • 1 tablespoon baking powder
- 6 grams • 1 3/4 teaspoons kosher salt
- 20 grams • 2 1/2 tablespoons almond meal
- 100 grams • 3/4 cup whole untoasted almonds
- 30 grams • 1/4 cup golden raisins
- 30 grams • 1/4 cup dried cherries
- 30 grams • 1/4 cup chopped dried apricots
- 2 grams • 1 teaspoon orange zest
- verbena hydrosol (optional; see opposite)

To make the granita: In a small saucepot over medium heat, simmer the wine, water, and sugar just until the sugar is dissolved. Pour into a freezer-safe container that is about 10 inches long and 3 to 4 inches deep and transfer to the freezer. Using a fork, stir or scrape the top of the granita every 30 minutes until it has frozen completely into icy crystals, 2 to 2 1/2 hours.

To make the biscotti: Preheat the oven to 325°F. Line two baking sheets with parchment paper. In the bowl of a stand mixer fitted with the paddle attachment, mix the butter until soft. Mix in the sugar and beat until fluffy, about 3 minutes. Crack four of the eggs into a bowl and mix in the vanilla paste. With the mixer running on low speed, gradually add the egg mixture to the batter and mix until well blended. In a separate bowl, combine the flour, baking powder, and salt. Lay a sheet of parchment paper on the counter and sift the dry ingredients into the center of the sheet. Mix the almond meal into the sifted dry ingredients. Pick up the long sides of the parchment paper to form a funnel. With the mixer running on low speed, tip the funnel into the mouth of the mixing bowl so as to gradually add the dry ingredients to the batter. Mix until the dough comes together, then stop the machine and fold in the almonds, raisins, cherries, apricots, and orange zest.

Scrape the dough onto a lightly floured work surface and divide into two even portions. Roll each portion into a long log about 2 inches in diameter. Transfer to the prepared baking sheets and flatten the logs slightly with the tips of your fingers. Blend together the remaining egg with a splash of water and brush the dough with this egg wash.

Bake for 30 minutes, then transfer to cooling racks. Once they are cool enough to handle (after about 10 minutes), cut the logs crosswise with a serrated knife into slices about 1/4 inch thick. Lay the slices on the baking sheets and bake until lightly toasted, 5 to 7 minutes. Cool completely before serving.

To serve, spoon the granita into small chilled glasses or bowls and serve the biscotti alongside. Before serving, spray a light mist of hydrosol over the granita.

HYDROSOLS

Making essential oils requires a distillation process. When the steam left behind from the distillation condenses, you have a hydrosol—water infused with the scent of the plant. A spritz of hydrosol over a dish right before it is served can accent its flavors like a sprinkling of sea salt, and can also evoke a sense of place. I like the selection of northern Californian hydrosols made by Marty Jacobson from Allstar Organics in Marin County: Douglas fir, laurel, coastal sage, verbena.

VIA FLAMINIA—
UMBRIA

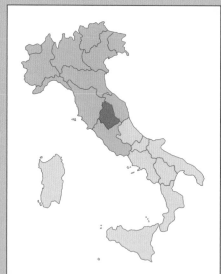

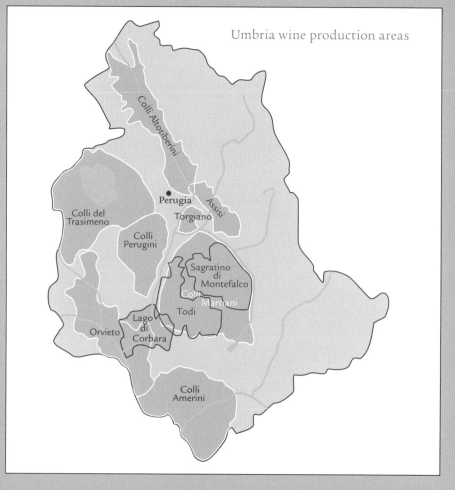

Umbria wine production areas

Colli Altotiberini

Perugia

Assisi

Colli del Trasimeno

Torgiano

Colli Perugini

Sagratino di Montefalco

Colli Martani

Colli Todi

Lago di Corbara

Orvieto

Colli Amerini

VIA FLAMINIA—UMBRIA

Looking at the patchwork fields of healthy olive groves and vineyards rolling down the gentle slopes of Montefalco, it's hard not to feel as if this storybook Italian countryside is an extension of Toscana. Medieval walled cities on hillsides hold court over valley floors. The region produces some of Italy's best extra virgin olive oil. And hearty pork preparations, from sausages made with *cinghiale* (wild boar) to *porchetta*, slow-cooked pork roast with addictively crispy skin, are menu staples. For all its similarities to its neighbor to the north, however, Umbria is much more than a Tuscan understudy.

"Umbria is the green heart of Italy," Marco Caprai asserts, quoting a line from a poem by Tuscan-born author Giosuè Carducci that has become a motto for the region. Slogan aside, Umbria is Italy's geographic heart. Walled off from Le Marche by the Apennines, it shares borders with Lazio to the south and Toscana to the west and north. As one of Italy's few land-locked regions, it is tied to the earth. The forests of Spoleto and Norcia harbor truffles and mushrooms. Many who live in Umbria cultivate vegetable gardens and raise chickens. Small green valleys support olive groves. And then there are all those vineyards.

Marco and his father, Arnaldo, deserve significant credit for bringing the world a taste of insular Umbria. Arnaldo Caprai bought vineyard land around Montefalco in 1971 with the intention of turning the little-known local Sagrantino grape into a serious red wine capable of aging like great Sangiovese or Nebbiolo bottlings. Gradually, through better clonal selection and winemaking techniques, the grape's reputation changed from regional curiosity (once used primarily for sweet *passito* wine) to rising-star red. While several producers make Sagrantino today, Marco initiated many of the early promotional efforts. Arnaldo Caprai's stern 25 Anni, a 100 percent Sagrantino wine released in 1993 to celebrate the winery's twenty-fifth anniversary, not only reflects Marco's direct personality but also is a testament to the Caprai family's vision, the grape with the spiky leaves, and the Montefalco growing area.

I first sampled 25 Anni in a restaurant in Orvieto, an ancient city perched on a cliff near the southwest border of the region. I asked the sommelier for a flagship Umbrian wine to pair with my dish, *umbricelli* pasta with black truffles. He poured Caprai's wine, which proved earthy enough to mirror the truffles without

overwhelming them, complementing the flavors with acidity, tar, leather, and dark berries. It was a classic pairing, a confirmation of the truism that what grows together, goes together (in this case, Sagrantino grapes and black truffles).

To think about choosing red wine in Orvieto over white used to be unheard of. The surrounding Orvieto DOC, which extends into Lazio, has been famous for white wine since the Middle Ages. Orvieto's volcanic tufa soil imparts acidic verve to white grapes while the city's ancient tunnels, bored into volcanic rock, kept white wines cool as they fermented and aged. In addition, Orvieto vintners always had a ready market for their wine. With its relative proximity to Rome, the city and nearby Lake Corbara became a destination for vacationing popes; its beauty also attracted artists, writers, and royals, all of whom spread the word about the honeyed white wine.

Like Frascati in Lazio, by the twentieth century Orvieto's wines started to become bland—light and refreshing but indistinguishable from one another. That is changing as winemakers adjust the blend of white grapes in the wine. Bright, acidic Grechetto, historically not the main white grape in the Orvieto DOC, is now the primary grape in the area; meanwhile, the use of Trebbiano Toscano, a less characterful grape, has declined. A few producers, such as Barberani, also still make classic Orvieto dessert wine with grapes that have attracted botrytis, the same grape bunch rot that creates the glycerine-rich grapes used in Sauternes.

Beyond Orvieto, more producers are turning out elegant wines with Grechetto. Sara Goretti, a fourth-generation winemaker at her family's winery in the rolling hills outside of Perugia, softly presses Grechetto grapes for her barrel-aged wine Il Moggio. Several producers of Sagrantino, including Caprai, also make varietal Grechetto. But despite the region's history of white-wine production, today more red wine is made here than white, and red wine claims Umbria's only two DOCG areas: Montefalco Sagrantino and Torgiano Rosso Riserva. In Torgiano, a northern Etruscan town with an ancient winemaking past, the late Giorgio Lungarotti caught attention for his red wine in the 1960s. Torgiano Rosso Riserva was the first DOC in Umbria, and was later upgraded to DOCG status. The designation was based on one wine: Lungarotti's Sangiovese-based Rubesco Riserva della Vigna Monticchio, a classic style of Italian red. Today the maker remains the primary producer of Torgiano Rosso Riserva. Elsewhere in Umbria, international plantings abound. Enologist Riccardo Cotarella makes modern, extracted reds with Bordeaux grapes at his winery, Falesco, which borders Lazio. And even in Montefalco, where Sagrantino is king, the less expensive, easy-drinking Montefalco Rosso often has a percentage of Merlot blended into its Sangiovese.

New oak and Merlot is a world apart from the goings on at Paolo Bea, a small, family-run winery that's walking distance from the ancient walls of Montefalco. Trim and smartly dressed, Giampiero Bea—an architect by training—manages the vineyards and wine production for the label. It's a family business with an admirable agenda: to maintain local traditions against a tide of international juice. Giampiero is a key player behind Gruppo Vini Veri (Real Wine Group), an organization of producers who make wines with natural processes but shun labels like organic or biodynamic. It's not that he's against modernity; his newly built winery with a plain,

modern façade is a testament to sustainable design. Rather, he seeks an equilibrium between the natural world and modern civilizations. That became evident as soon as I saw Giampiero's collection of Trebbiano Spoletino vines that climb up trees, some of which are more than 100 years old. Scattered among several small plots, the trees are remnants of a once-common practice in which a vine was married to a tree and both grew together. In 1995, when he saw residents cutting down these old vines and trees for firewood, Giampiero decided to rent plots containing the old vines, saving the tradition by paying the owners not to cut them down.

The Trebbiano "trees" stand about three meters high, with stark, wild vines that unfurl from the branches. By comparison, Bea's other vineyards look conventional. But they're not—exactly. There he employs more subtle touches, like planting artichokes in between Sagrantino vines to add iron to Montefalco's signature yellow clay and stone soil. His efforts in the vineyard alone make me feel honored to taste his small-production wines, from the rich, minerally Trebbiano Spoletino and the inky, natural Sagrantino. "In nature, it is necessary to observe, to listen, to understand, but never to dominate," Giampiero says. Perhaps such visionary efforts are the future for this region's green heart. —SL

White Grapes

GRECHETTO
Grechetto is a late-ripening, low-yielding grape with great acidity and thick, yellowish skins. While for years it was used as a blending grape, Grechetto is now singled out by Umbrian and Lazio winemakers as a grape with a bright future. Grechetto's name may have stemmed from Greco, an ancient Greek grape grown in southern Italy, though Grechetto doesn't share many characteristics with its southern counterpart. The grape has taken well to the mineral-rich soils of Umbria and northern Lazio, where producer Sergio Mottura was an early champion of the grape. His wine Poggio della Costa has long been one of the highest regarded Grechetto wines in Italy.

RECOMMENDED PRODUCERS: Fattoria Colleallodole, Goretti (Umbria); Castel de Paolis, Sergio Mottura, Monastero Suore Cistercensi, Lorenzo Costantini, Falesco (Lazio)

SEE ALSO: Malvasia (page 14), Sauvignon (page 117)

TREBBIANO

Nearly everyone who drinks Italian white wine comes across Trebbiano, one of the most planted white grapes in Italy. For all of its ubiquity, however, the most common subvariety, Trebbiano Toscano, tends to offer little beyond a neutral canvas, and other strains of Trebbiano (or other grapes entirely, as is the case in the Orvieto DOC) are being favored in its place. The subvarieties of Trebbiano are near endless. Procanico is another Umbrian variation on Trebbiano, used mainly as a blending grape. In Lazio, Trebbiano Romagnola is another workhorse variety that offers light notes of wildflowers and herbs. Alone, it is made in *spumante* or still styles. But the best rendition of Trebbiano might be Trebbiano di Lugana (also called Terbina). It grows primarily in the Lugana DOC, which stretches around the base of Lake Garda from Lombardia to Veneto. It also could be the same subvariety as Trebbiano Spoletino, a fantastic grape that Giampiero Bea grows up trees around Montefalco. When made with extended skin contact, as with Bea's Arboreus wine, Trebbiano Spoletino is capable of aging for several years.

RECOMMENDED PRODUCERS: Falesco (Lazio); Mancero (Le Marche); Ca'Lojera, Otella, Provenza (Lombardia); Suavia (Veneto); Camillo Donati, Tre Monti (Emilia Romagna); Capezzana (Toscana)

SEE ALSO: Malvasia (page 14), Sauvignon (page 117)

Red Grapes

CANAIOLO

Canaiolo plays a minor though historically important role in the red wines of Torgiano as well as in Toscana's Chianti and Vino Nobile de Montepulciano. The soft, juicy grape is native to central Italy, and some believe it descends from an Etruscan variety. Today the variety survives mainly as a blending grape to soften Sangiovese wines. The best-known example comes from Lungarotti. Torgiano Rosso and Torgiano Rosso Riserva wines comprise 70 percent Sangiovese and 30 percent Canaiolo.

RECOMMENDED PRODUCERS: Caprai, Lungarotti, Le Pogetta (Umbria); Castello della Paneretta, Bibi Graetz (Toscana)

SAGRANTINO

With unusual spiky leaves and dense purple fruit, Sagrantino is Umbria's most significant and strange native vine. No one knows for sure how it arrived in Montefalco. Some attribute its origins to Greece, others put faith on the followers of Saint Francis of Assisi, who may have brought the vines along on their journey to visit Umbria's famous saint. Sagrantino wines can be an inky wash of dark berry fruits. Some evoke iron, leather, and plums, and most pack a wallop of drying tannins. Until the 1970s, Sagrantino grapes were always dried first for making *passito* wines. (Some producers still make small amounts of this sweet dessert wine.) Its rise as a dry wine happened quickly. Between 2005 and 2007, production of Montefalco Sagrantino nearly doubled. When customers indicate that they like Bordeaux-varietal wines and want to try something new in a similar style, I frequently turn to Sagrantino. For elegant wines with floral aromatics, I recommend Paolo Bea and Perticaia. For special occasions, I go with Fattoria Colleallodole. Francesco Antano, the son of pioneering winemaker Milziade Antano, also makes decadent Sagrantino.

RECOMMENDED PRODUCERS: Antonelli, Caprai, Fattoria Colleallodole, Paolo Bea, Perticaia, Scacciadiavoli

SEE ALSO: Colorino (page 250), Sangiovese (page 248)

The Truffle Hunt

THE MOUNTAINS between Norcia and Spoleto in eastern Umbria are far removed from the crowded streets of Rome or the sunny coast of Le Marche. On my last visit, the only noise came from chainsaws (residents are permitted to cut down trees for firewood). While there were more than enough trees to go around, I had come in search of another natural resource entirely: Umbrian black truffles!

Piled in the back of an army-issue jeep, we headed partway up the mountain to an orchard maintained by Urbani, the region's largest truffle exporter. Truffles can't be farmed traditionally, but burying truffle spores around the right kind of trees can encourage their growth. From December through February, truffles emerge in the *pianello*, a two- to three-meter ring of acidic soil surrounding downy oak or maple trees. The roots and soil interact in a way that, with humidity and a little luck, results in truffles. Trained dogs sniff them out of the *pianello*, gently cradling them in their mouths before relinquishing them in exchange for a treat.

Alba in Piemonte gets plenty of attention for white truffles, but Umbria is Italy's largest source of black truffles. In America, truffles are a luxury. So I'm always happily surprised to see an *osteria* well off the main road shower a Sunday lunch tagliatelle with black truffle as if it were grated cheese. The result is an authentic taste of Umbrian terroir. —MA

SMOKED TROUT *with* Warm Potato Salad *and* Horseradish Gelatina

What Umbria lacks in coastline, it makes up for in lakes and rivers, and freshwater fish takes the place of seafood on the menu. In this recipe, smoke imparts a subtle earthiness to the trout, which is complemented by a warm potato salad. (This salad makes a small portion to accompany the smoked trout. Double the recipe if you would like to serve it as a larger side dish.) For a pop of acidity, I make a simple horseradish *gelatina*—essentially horseradish water set with agar-agar. I find hot-smoking trout can yield a dry, firm piece of fish, so I prefer to cold-smoke it just long enough to infuse it with smoke flavor (see page 275). Once the fish is smoked but still raw, I cook it *sous vide* for more control over the texture (see page 271).

SERVES 6

Smoked Trout

1500 grams • 7 cups water

120 grams • 3/4 cup plus 1 tablespoon kosher salt

75 grams • 1/4 cup sugar

5 parsley stems

2 thyme sprigs

1 bay leaf

2 grams • 1 tablespoon mixed whole spices, such as black peppercorns, star anise, coriander seeds, and fennel seeds

415 grams • 6 (4- to 6-ounce) boneless, skin-on trout fillets

extra virgin olive oil

Horseradish Gelatina

36 grams • 2 inches fresh horseradish, peeled

113 grams • 1/2 cup pickling liquid (page 281)

kosher salt

36 grams • 2 tablespoons simple syrup (page 281)

1 gram • 1 teaspoon powdered agar-agar (see page 276)

Potato Salad

335 grams • 2 cups small fingerling potatoes

kosher salt

5 parsley stems

2 thyme sprigs

1 bay leaf

1 tablespoon mixed whole spices, such as black peppercorns, star anise, coriander seeds, fennel seeds

2 tablespoons whole grain mustard

1 shallot, halved lengthwise and sliced

3 tablespoons extra virgin olive oil

1 tablespoon sherry vinegar

1 tablespoon chopped Italian parsley

black pepper

45 grams • 3 tablespoons crème fraîche

45 grams • 3 tablespoons heavy cream

extra virgin olive oil

black pepper

1/4 cup baby lettuces or foraged greens, such as chickweed, miner's lettuce, wild radish, or wild mustard

peeled fresh horseradish for grating

trout roe (optional)

To make the trout: Bring the water, salt, and sugar to a simmer to dissolve. Pour into a storage container, add the parsley, thyme, bay leaf, and whole spices, and steep for 2 hours. Submerge the trout in the brine, cover, and refrigerate for 1 to 2 hours. Remove the trout and pat dry. Place on a cooling rack and refrigerate, uncovered, for 2 to 3 hours. To create a tacky surface for smoke to adhere to.

Prepare a smoker according to the instructions for stovetop smoking on page 274. Place the trout on the perforated pan or rack as far away from the end with the wood chips as possible. Cover tightly with foil or a lid and smoke for 10 to 12 minutes. Take off the foil and remove the trout. It should still look raw.

Prepare a large ice bath. Heat a large, rectangular water bath fitted with an immersion circulator to 135°F (see *Sous Vide*, page 271). Pack the trout into 2 vacuum-seal pouches. Add a splash of olive oil to each pouch and

{continued}

vacuum seal. Cook the pouches in the water bath for 10 to 12 minutes. Remove and plunge gently into a large ice bath to chill completely.

To make the *gelatina*: Grate the horseradish with a microplane into a heatproof mixing bowl. In a small pot, bring the pickling liquid to a boil and pour it over the horseradish. Add a pinch of salt, cover, and refrigerate for at least 3 hours or overnight. Strain the liquid and discard the horseradish. Set aside 2 tablespoons of the liquid.

Spray a 4 by 6-inch glass baking pan or small flat dish with nonstick spray. Pour the remaining liquid into a bowl and mix in the simple syrup. (The weight of the liquid should be about 110 grams. You need 1 percent of the weight for the agar-agar measurement, which should be just over 1 gram.) Pour the liquid and agar-agar into a small pot and bring to a boil, whisking constantly. Boil vigorously, while whisking for 1 minute, then pour into the prepared pan. Refrigerate until set, 20 to 25 minutes. Once set, invert the *gelatina* onto a cutting board and cut it into small cubes. It will resemble a clear jelly.

To make the potato salad: Put the potatoes in a medium pot and cover with about an inch of water. Bring the pot to a simmer over medium heat, then season with a few pinches of salt. Mix in the parsley, thyme, bay leaf, and whole spices and cook until the potatoes are cooked through but not falling apart, about 15 minutes. To test the potatoes, lift one out of the pot and press it with the tip of a finger. It should yield to the pressure like a ripe avocado. Remove the pot from the heat and let the potatoes rest in the cooking water for 20 minutes; they will absorb more seasoning as they cool. Once the potatoes reach room temperature, drain and slice into 1/2-inch round pieces. In a medium bowl, whisk together the mustard, shallot, olive oil, vinegar, and parsley. Mix in the potatoes and season with salt and black pepper.

Whisk the remaining 2 tablespoons horseradish liquid with the crème fraîche until it forms stiff peaks. In a separate small bowl, season the cream with a pinch of salt and whisk the cream until it forms stiff peaks. Fold the crème fraîche into the cream and refrigerate until needed.

Preheat the broiler. Remove the trout fillets from the pouches and pat dry. Peel off the skins gently, then place the skins back on the fillets (they will protect the fish while it warms up, but they will not be served). Lay the fillets, skin side up, on a baking sheet and broil until warmed, about 1 minute. Take off the skins and discard.

To serve: Divide the trout among 6 plates, drizzle with olive oil, and season lightly with pepper. Spoon potato salad onto each plate, then add a few cubes of *gelatina* and a spoonful of the seasoned crème fraîche. Garnish with greens, freshly grated horseradish, and trout roe.

CHOPPED CHICKEN LIVERS *with* Wine Gelatina, Carrot Marmellata, *and* Grilled Bread

Taking humble ingredients—chicken livers and carrots—and transforming them into a sophisticated dish demonstrates the power of culinary technique. I pack the livers into glass jars and coat the top with Marsala *gelatina*, which sets into a glossy layer atop the liver. For a condiment, I make a carrot *marmellata*—marmalade—that echos the sweetness in the *gelatina*. If you have a vegetable juicer, juice your own carrots for the *marmellata*. Otherwise, high-quality store-bought carrot juice works just as well.

SERVES 6

250 grams • 1¹⁄₂ cups chicken livers

kosher salt and black pepper

3 grams • 1 sheet gelatin

extra virgin olive oil

150 grams • ¹⁄₂ yellow onion, diced

8 grams • 2 garlic cloves, minced

3 sage leaves

8 grams • 1 tablespoon Wondra flour (see page 283)

70 grams • ¹⁄₃ cup Marsala

50 grams • ¹⁄₄ cup reduced white stock (page 282) or water

2 grams • ¹⁄₄ teaspoon truffle oil (optional)

90 grams • scant ¹⁄₂ cup crème fraîche

Gelatina

3 grams • 1 sheet gelatin

80 grams • ¹⁄₃ cup simple syrup (page 281)

30 grams • 2 tablespoons Marsala

2 grams • ¹⁄₂ teaspoon kosher salt

Carrot Marmellata

5 grams • 1 tablespoon orange zest

38 grams • 2¹⁄₂ tablespoons orange juice

3 grams • 1¹⁄₂ tablespoons Meyer lemon zest

8 grams • 2 teaspoons Meyer lemon juice

100 grams • scant ¹⁄₂ cup carrot juice

90 grams • ¹⁄₃ cup plus 2 tablespoons sugar

185 grams • 1³⁄₄ cups finely grated carrot

7 grams • 1 teaspoon powdered pectin

2 grams • ¹⁄₂ teaspoon kosher salt

about 12 (¹⁄₂-inch-thick) slices country bread

extra virgin olive oil

1 garlic clove

coarse salt and black pepper

Trim away any discolored parts or visible veins from the livers. Soak in ice water for 3 hours to draw out blood and impurities. Rinse the livers, pat dry, and season evenly with salt and pepper. Set aside.

Soak the gelatin sheet in ice water to soften; set aside. Heat a thin film of olive oil in a large sauté pan over medium-high heat. Sear the livers on each side until lightly browned on the outside but still pink in the center, 1 to 2 minutes per side. Transfer the seared livers to a plate.

Wipe the pan clean and reduce the heat to medium-low. Coat the bottom of the pan with a film of olive oil. Add the onion, season with salt and pepper, and sweat, stirring occasionally, until caramelized and very soft, 8 to 12 minutes. Stir in the garlic and sage and sweat for 3 minutes or until aromatic. Dust the onion mixture with the Wondra flour and stir to dissolve. Pour in the Marsala and simmer until the pan is nearly dry, 1 to 2 minutes. Pour in the stock, bring to a boil, and cook for 1 to 2 minutes. Stir in the seared livers and cook until lightly glazed, 1 to 2 minutes. Squeeze out the excess water from the soaked gelatin sheet and dissolve in the liver mixture.

In a food processor in batches, pulse the liver mixture until the livers are nearly smooth but still retain some texture. Transfer the liver mixture to a large bowl over

{continued}

ice and fold in the truffle oil. In a separate bowl, whisk the crème fraîche into stiff peaks, then gently fold into the liver mixture. Taste and season with salt and pepper. Using about ¹/₂ cup per serving, portion the livers in 6 ramekins or glass jars. Cover with plastic wrap and refrigerate for at least 1 hour.

To make the *gelatina*: Soak the gelatin sheet in ice water until softened. In a small pot, bring the simple syrup and Marsala to a brief boil and then remove from heat. Squeeze out any excess water from the gelatin and dissolve it in the syrup mixture. Stir in the salt, then strain the syrup mixture. Cool to a warm room temperature. Spoon over the chilled livers and return to the refrigerator.

To make the *marmellata:* In a medium pot, combine the orange and lemon zests and juices. Stir in the carrot juice and all but 1 tablespoon of the sugar and bring to a simmer. Add the grated carrot and cook over medium-low heat for 10 minutes. In a small bowl, mix together the remaining tablespoon of sugar with the pectin and salt. Sprinkle over the carrots, stirring to prevent lumps. Simmer gently until the *marmellata* has thickened to the consistency of jam, 7 to 10 minutes. Cool completely. Once chilled, invert the *marmellata* onto a cutting board and mince it until it forms a thick paste. Refrigerate until ready to serve.

Preheat the broiler. Brush olive oil evenly on each slice of bread, then broil, turning the pieces over once, until toasted and lightly charred. Rub one side of each piece with garlic. Spoon *marmellata* into each ramekin. Sprinkle coarse salt and pepper on top. Serve with the grilled bread.

FAVA BEAN AGNOLOTTI
with Mashed Black Truffle

Thin pasta enveloping small pockets of savory filling—*agnolotti* look like delicate pillows. The pasta shape originated in Piedmont, where they are often dressed up with white truffles in the fall. Here I use the trimmings of black Umbrian truffles instead. This pasta shape can be used with several other smooth fillings: in winter, I use puréed white beans; in summer, sweet corn. To serve *agnolotti*, I glaze the delicate pasta with a light sauce of *burro fuso*, butter emulsified with water (see page 276).

Making *agnolotti* isn't necessarily difficult—in fact, this is one of the fastest filled pasta shapes to make once you get the hang of it—but the dough is thin and the filling needs to be piped in a straight line along its length. To get the scalloped edges, I use a fluted pasta cutter. *Agnolotti*, as with all fresh pasta, is best served soon after it's made. You can refrigerate the pasta pieces on a bed of coarse semolina overnight, but I don't recommend freezing them.

Pictured on pages 82–83

SERVES 4 TO 6

Filling

454 grams • 1 pound fava beans

60 grams • ¹/₃ cup drained ricotta (see page 281)

20 grams • ¹/₄ cup grated pecorino cheese

10 grams • 3 tablespoons chopped mint

5 grams • 2 tablespoons chopped parsley

kosher salt and black pepper

250 grams • scant 2 cups 00 flour

2 grams • ¹/₂ teaspoon kosher salt

100 grams • 2 eggs

10 grams • 1 tablespoon water

85 grams • ¹/₃ cup unsalted butter

about 1 tablespoon black truffle trimmings, mashed with a fork

about ¹/₈ cup small mint leaves

a block of pecorino cheese for grating

To make the filling: Prepare an ice bath. Shuck the fava beans and discard the pods. Peel each fava bean. You should have about 145 grams (1 cup) of peeled fava beans. In a pot of boiling, salted water, blanch the favas until very tender, about 4 minutes. Shock in salted ice bath. Set aside 1/4 cup of favas. In a food processor, blend the remaining 3/4 cup of favas with the ricotta, pecorino, mint, and parsley until very smooth. Season with salt and pepper to taste. You will have a little more than 1 cup of filling. Transfer to a pastry bag fitted with a small tip (no more than 1/2 inch) and refrigerate until needed.

In a stand mixer fitted with the paddle attachment, mix together the flour and salt on low speed. In a bowl, whisk together the eggs and water. With the mixer running on medium speed, drizzle in the egg mixture. Mix the dough for 2 to 3 minutes. Turn the dough onto the counter and knead for several minutes by hand; it will feel dry and firm. Flatten the dough into a rectangle, wrap in plastic wrap, and leave on the counter for 30 minutes to soften and hydrate.

Roll out the dough according to the instructions for laminated pasta on page 273. Place one sheet parallel to the edge of the work surface and keep those you are not using covered with a towel to prevent them from drying out. Starting about 1 inch in from the bottom edge of the sheet, pipe one long, thin line of filling along the length of the sheet. Lightly mist water over the pasta with a spray bottle. Fold the bottom edge over the filling, then tap a plastic bench scraper along the length of the filling, expelling any excess air. You will now have a long tube of pasta covering the filling. Using your index finger and thumb, pinch the tube into pieces no bigger than 3/4 inch long, pressing firmly to seal off each piece and leaving about 3/4 inch of space in between. The *agnolotti* will look like a row of pillows stuck together.

With a fluted pasta wheel, trim off the top edge of pasta dough in one long strip, leaving enough space that you won't cut into the filling or ruin the seal. With the same pasta wheel, cut between each piece. You should have about sixty 1-inch pieces. Place the filled pasta on a baking sheet lightly dusted with flour; refrigerate until ready to cook.

With the butter and 2 tablespoons of water, make the *burro fuso* according to the instructions on page 276; keep warm. Bring a large pot of salted water to a boil. Drop the *agnolotti* in the water and cook until al dente, about 4 minutes. Lift the *agnolotti* out of the water and place into a shallow pan. Sprinkle in the truffle and reserved favas and add some of the *burro fuso*. Toss gently to coat, heat through, and season with salt to taste.

To serve, spoon 12 to 15 pieces of *agnolotti* onto warmed plates. Spoon some of the favas and *burro fuso* over each serving. Garnish with mint leaves and finish with a grating of pecorino.

TAGLIATELLE D'ORO *with* Chicken Livers, Mushrooms, *and* Black Truffle

A yolk-rich pasta paired with black truffles sounds extravagant, but in Umbria it's not necessarily so. Many families have backyard chickens, and black truffles can also be considered something of a backyard crop. Pasta made with a lot of egg yolks is much more supple than pasta made solely with flour and water or whole eggs. The soft texture of the pasta is complemented by a sauce made with a silky purée of chicken livers. Sautéed mushrooms, grated truffles, and fresh thyme echo the earthy decadence of the dish. Leftover egg whites can be saved for making a clarifying raft for consommé (page 182) or coconut macaroons (page 269).

SERVES 6

Tagliatelle

250 grams • scant 2 cups 00 flour

2 grams • ¹/₂ teaspoon kosher salt

120 grams • 6 egg yolks

50 grams • 1 egg

4 grams • 1 teaspoon extra virgin olive oil

150 grams • 5¹/₄ ounces (about 1 cup) chicken livers

kosher salt and black pepper

extra virgin olive oil

57 grams • 2 ounces mixed mushrooms, such as chanterelle, black trumpet, oyster, and hen of the woods, sliced lengthwise into 4 to 6 pieces each (about 1 cup)

1 shallot, minced

1 garlic clove

1 gram • ¹/₂ teaspoon minced thyme leaves, plus whole leaves to serve

15 grams • 1 tablespoon chopped black truffle

40 grams • 3 tablespoons unsalted butter

2 grams • 1 tablespoon chopped Italian parsley

a block of truffle-infused sheep's milk cheese, such as pecorino tartufo, for grating

To make the tagliatelle: In a stand mixer fitted with the paddle attachment, mix together the flour and salt. In a bowl, whisk together the egg yolks, egg, and oil. With the mixer on low, drizzle in the egg mixture. Mix the dough for 2 to 3 minutes, then turn onto the counter and knead for several minutes by hand; it will feel firm and dry. Flatten the dough into a rectangle, wrap in plastic wrap, and leave on the counter for 30 minutes.

Roll out the dough according to the instructions for laminated pasta on page 273. Cut the pasta into 12-inch sheets and dust with flour. Remove the pasta machine rollers and replace with the tagliatelle cutters. (If you don't have tagliatelle cutters, use the narrowest noodle cutters.) With one hand, feed the sheets through the cutter one at at time. As the noodles emerge from the cutter, catch them with your other hand. Shake the noodles loose from each other, place on a lightly floured baking sheet, and cover.

Trim away any discolored parts or visible veins from the livers. Cut into 1-inch pieces and soak in ice water for 2 hours to remove any blood or impurities. Rinse, pat dry, and season with salt and pepper. Heat a film of olive oil in a large sauté pan over medium-high heat. Sear the livers on each side until lightly browned on the outside but still pink in the center, 1 minute per side. Transfer two-thirds of the livers to a blender and purée until smooth.

Wipe the pan clean and return to medium-high heat. Coat the pan with a film of olive oil. Sear the mushrooms until they begin to brown, about 1 minute. Stir in the shallot, garlic, and minced thyme and cook for 2 minutes, or until the mushrooms are cooked through. Season with salt and pepper, transfer to a bowl, and stir in the truffle and the remaining third of the seared livers.

Bring a large pot of salted water to a boil, add pasta and cook until al dente, 3 to 4 minutes. Drain, reserving about ¹/₂ cup of the cooking water, and return the pasta to the same pot. Stir in the liver purée and a few tablespoons of the pasta water until the purée lightly coats the pasta. Season with salt and pepper, then add the butter, parsley, mushrooms, and chicken livers. Grate about ¹/₄ cup of cheese into the pot and mix to combine. Divide the pasta among 6 warmed plates and finish with more grated cheese and a sprinkle of thyme leaves.

LINGUINE AL COCOA
with Venison Ragù

Deer run wild all over Umbria's hillsides. The meat itself is flavorful but lean, with a rich minerality that melds well with unsweetened cocoa. This gently cooked ragù is made with ground shoulder meat. After the meat simmers with tomato, chiles, and spices, it is finished with cream to bring the flavors together. Instead of relying on imported Italian cheeses, I often turn to Italian-inspired domestic cheesemakers, such as Sartori, a family-owned creamery in Wisconsin. For this pasta, I opt for BellaVitano, Sartori's mild, buttery, and slightly sweet cow's milk cheese for grating.

SERVES 6 TO 8

Linguine

225 grams • 1¹/₂ cups 00 flour

115 grams • 1¹/₄ cups durum flour

14 grams • 1 tablespoon plus 1 teaspoon unsweetened cocoa powder

2 grams • ¹/₂ teaspoon kosher salt

100 grams • 2 eggs

70 grams • 5 tablespoons warm water

extra virgin olive oil

360 grams • 13 ounces ground venison, preferably shoulder meat

kosher salt and black pepper

150 grams • ¹/₂ yellow onion, finely chopped

20 grams • 4 garlic cloves, minced

65 grams • scant ¹/₄ cup tomato paste

60 grams • ¹/₄ cup soffritto (page 282)

a pinch of dried red pepper flakes

5 grams • 1 teaspoon Calabrian chile oil (page 278)

300 grams • 1¹/₂ cups red wine

300 grams • 1¹/₂ cups white stock (page 282)

a sachet with 4 sprigs thyme, 1 sprig sage, 10 black peppercorns, and 4 cloves (see page 282)

50 grams • scant ¹/₄ cup heavy cream

1 gram • ¹/₂ teaspoon quatre épices

80 grams • 2 cups baby spinach leaves

1 to 2 tablespoons unsalted butter

a block of BellaVitano or Parmigiano-Reggiano cheese for grating

To make the linguine: In a stand mixer with the paddle attachment, mix together the flours, cocoa powder, and salt. In a bowl, whisk together the eggs and water. With the mixer running on low speed, drizzle in the egg mixture. Mix the dough for 2 to 3 minutes, then turn onto the counter and knead by hand for several minutes; the dough will feel firm and dry. Flatten the dough into a flat rectangle, wrap in plastic wrap, and leave on the counter for 30 minutes to soften and hydrate.

Roll out the dough according to the instructions for laminated pasta on page 273. Cut the pasta into 12-inch sheets and dust with flour. Remove the pasta machine rollers and replace with the linguine cutters. (If you don't have linguine cutters, use the narrowest noodle cutters.) With one hand, feed the sheets through the cutter one at a time. As the noodles emerge from the cutter, catch them with your other hand. Shake the noodles loose from each other, place on a lightly floured baking sheet, and keep on the counter.

Heat a thin film of olive oil in a large Dutch oven or heavy-bottomed pot over medium-high heat. Stir in the venison and brown well, 5 to 7 minutes. Season with salt and pepper, then stir in the onion and garlic. Cook until the onion has softened, about 3 minutes. Stir in the tomato paste, soffritto, and red pepper flakes and simmer, stirring often, until the tomato paste has darkened to brick red. Stir in the chile oil, then pour in the wine. Bring the ragù to a simmer, then lower the heat to a very slow simmer and cook until the red wine has reduced to about 2 ounces, about 30 minutes. Pour in the stock and add the sachet. Simmer the ragù over very low heat until the liquid has reduced by at least half, 30 minutes more. Pour in the cream and season with *quatre épices*. Simmer until the ragù has thickened and has a velvety texture, another 15 minutes, seasoning with more salt and pepper if needed. If making the day before, cool the ragù with the sachet. Before serving, remove the sachet, pressing on it to extract liquid.

{continued}

Bring a large pot of salted water to a boil. Stir in the pasta and cook until al dente, 3 to 4 minutes. Drain, reserving about ¹/₂ cup of the pasta cooking water, and return the pasta to the same pot. Meanwhile, simmer the ragù. Add spoonfuls of the ragù to the linguine until sauce clings to the noodles. Cook over medium heat, thinning with a splash or two of the saved pasta water if the pot becomes too dry. Stir in the spinach and the butter, seasoning with more salt and pepper if needed. Serve the pasta in warmed bowls and grate cheese over the top.

FARRO-STUFFED QUAIL
with Chestnuts, Persimmons, *and* Dandelion Greens

Although quail isn't difficult to find at a good butcher shop or grocery store, it is often overlooked. This is a missed opportunity—quail are rich in flavor and perfectly portioned for individual servings. Butchers sell them semiboneless, with the ribcage and spines removed. I stuff them with a chestnut and bread stuffing to ensure they stay moist when roasting and to infuse the meat with the earthy sweetness of chestnuts, persimmon, and sage. Dried persimmons are available at farmers' markets in the winter and spring. They have a pleasant, mild sweetness that pairs well with chestnuts. If you have extra stuffing, bake it in a small casserole and serve alongside the quail.

SERVES 6

Stuffing and Quail

100 grams • ¹/₂ cup farro

100 grams • about 2 cups cubed day-old country bread

75 grams • ¹/₃ cup soffritto (page 282)

63 grams • ¹/₄ cup diced dried persimmon

27 grams • about 1 cup grated Parmigiano-Reggiano

5 grams • 1 clove garlic confitura (page 279)

100 grams • 2 eggs, beaten

24 cooked and peeled chestnuts

10 grams • 10 to 15 chopped sage leaves

2 grams • ¹/₂ teaspoon kosher salt

black pepper

955 grams • 6 quail (2 pounds, 4 ounces), semiboned (rib cages and spines removed)

Chestnut Purée

extra virgin olive oil

18 grams • 1 shallot, sliced

4 grams • 1 garlic clove, sliced

165 grams • 1 cup cooked and peeled chestnuts

30 grams • 2 tablespoons white wine

180 grams • 3/4 cup heavy cream

57 grams • 1/4 cup water

kosher salt

extra virgin olive oil

57 grams • 6 cooked and peeled chestnuts, sliced into coins

kosher salt and black pepper

14 to 28 grams • 1 to 2 tablespoons unsalted butter

36 grams • 2 tablespoons simple syrup (page 281)

160 grams • 2 firm Fuyu persimmons, peeled

27 grams • about 1 cup baby dandelion greens

1 dried persimmon slice, cut into thin strips

To stuff the quail: Rinse the farro until the water runs clear, then drain. Gently simmer the farro in salted water until tender, about 15 to 18 minutes, then drain. You will have about 1 cup cooked farro. Cool to room temperature. Using your hands, combine the farro, bread, soffritto, dried persimmon, cheese, and garlic confitura, breaking up the pieces of bread as you mix the stuffing. Mix in the egg, chestnuts, sage, salt, and about 5 grindings of pepper. Roll the stuffing into 6 balls slightly bigger than golf balls and tuck 1 into each quail.

To truss the quail: with a paring knife, make a small slit just above the lower leg joint of one leg. Slide the other leg into the slit so the quail looks cross-legged. Tuck the wings back, then loop a piece of butcher's twine around the sides, wings, and legs, tying it tightly at the back of the quail.

To make the chestnut purée: Heat a film of olive oil in a medium pot over medium-low heat. Gently sweat the shallot and garlic until soft but not caramelized, about 2 minutes. Stir in the chestnuts and cook for a few more minutes. Pour in the wine and simmer briefly until reduced by half. Add the cream and water, cover, and cook over low heat until the chestnuts are tender, about 10 minutes. Strain, reserve the liquid, and place the solids in a blender. Purée, adding back the liquid gradually until smooth. Season with salt and a drizzle of olive oil. If the purée is dry, add another splash of cream.

To prepare the persimmons: Place the persimmons in a vacuum pouch with the simple syrup. Vacuum seal to compress, then remove, drain, and cut into wedges.

Preheat the oven to 375°F. Warm a large sauté pan in the oven as it preheats.

Heat a thick film of oil in another sauté pan over high heat until nearly smoking. Scatter the chestnuts in one even layer and season with salt and pepper. Swirl in a pat of butter and cook until the chestnuts are golden brown. Drain the chestnuts on paper towels and sprinkle lightly with more salt.

Place the preheated pan on the stove over medium heat. Pour in about a tablespoon of oil. Season the quail with salt and pepper, then sear until golden on all sides, about 1 minute per side. Return the pan to the oven and roast 8 to 10 minutes, or until the thigh meat is pink and the stuffing is hot. Transfer the pan to the stove and add a pat of butter. Baste the quail in the butter and pan juices for about 2 minutes, then transfer to a platter and let rest for a few minutes. Remove the butcher's twine.

Spoon a dollop of chestnut purée onto each plate. Put a quail on top of the purée. In a small bowl, mix together the persimmon wedges and dandelion greens with salt, pepper, and olive oil. Scatter over the plate, then sprinkle a few dried persimmon strips over the top.

PISTACHIO TORTA *with* Meyer Lemon Curd, Pistachio Crema, *and* Brown Butter

Citrus and pistachios are a classic combination. The pistachio torta and crema draw out the savory pistachio flavors while the curd emphasizes the sweet side of Meyer lemons. I love the nutty sweetness of brown butter. With the help of liquid glucose (see page 280), I capture the flavor of brown butter in a sweet emulsion, the dessert equivalent of mayonnaise. Made from finely ground pistachios, pistachio flour also is often called pistachio meal. You can grind your own pistachio flour in a food processor, but avoid over working it or you'll have pistachio butter instead. Cocoa butter is the pure fat from the cacao bean. It adds texture to the pistachio crema and can be found at natural foods stores.

SERVES 8

Torta

150 grams • 1 cup all-purpose flour, sifted

67 grams • 2/3 cup pistachio flour

5 grams • 1 teaspoon baking powder

3 grams • 3/4 teaspoon kosher salt

227 grams • 1 cup unsalted butter

100 grams • 1/2 cup sugar

60 grams • 1/3 cup brown sugar

4 grams • 1 teaspoon vanilla extract

150 grams • 3 eggs

Lemon Curd

270 grams • scant 1 1/4 cups Meyer lemon juice

250 grams • 1 1/4 cups sugar

250 grams • 5 eggs

20 grams • 1 egg yolk

325 grams • 1 1/3 cups unsalted butter

15 grams • 1 tablespoon heavy cream

Brown Butter

130 grams • 1 1/2 cup plus 1 tablespoon unsalted butter

50 grams • 1 tablespoon plus 2 teaspoons liquid glucose (see page 280)

20 grams • 1 egg yolk

5 grams • 1 teaspoon lemon juice

2 grams • 1/2 teaspoon kosher salt

Pistachio Crema

45 grams • 1/2 cup pistachios

100 grams • 3 1/2 ounces simple syrup (see page 281)

100 grams • 1/3 cup plus 2 tablespoons heavy cream

20 grams • 2 tablespoons whole milk

9 grams • 1 teaspoon liquid glucose (see page 280)

125 grams • 4 1/2 ounces white chocolate, finely chopped

20 grams/ 2/3 ounces cocoa butter, finely chopped

a pinch of kosher salt

2 to 3 citrus, such as orange, blood orange or grapefruit, segmented

8 slices lemon confitura (page 279)

1 tablespoon toasted, chopped pistachios

To make the *torta*: Preheat the oven to 350°F. Lightly coat a 9 by 13-inch baking pan with nonstick spray. Cut a piece of parchment paper to fit the bottom of the pan, press it into the pan, and lightly coat with nonstick spray.

In a bowl, whisk together the flour, pistachio flour, baking powder, and salt. In a stand mixer fitted with the paddle attachment, cream the butter and sugars on medium speed until light and soft, about 3 minutes. Turn the mixer to low speed and beat in the vanilla, then the eggs one at a time. Gradually add the flour mixture and mix until just incorporated, about 2 minutes.

Pour the batter into the prepared pan and bake for 15 to 20 minutes or until a toothpick inserted in the cake comes out clean. Cool to a warm room temperature, about 20 minutes, then refrigerate for at least 2 hours or overnight. Once chilled, cut the cake in half lengthwise, then cut into 1 1/2-inch-wide rectangles crosswise. You should have about 16 rectangles.

{continued}

To make the lemon curd: Prepare an ice bath. Then, in a double boiler or heatproof bowl over (not in) a pot of barely simmering water, whisk together the lemon juice, sugar, eggs, and yolk until frothy. Continue to cook, whisking constantly, until the curd thickens, about 5 minutes. Remove the curd from the heat and whisk in the butter, then the cream. Strain the curd through a fine-mesh strainer and cool over an ice bath. You will have about 4 cups, which is more than you need for the recipe (leftover curd keeps for 1 week, refrigerated). Transfer the curd to a pastry bag fitted with a small round tip.

To make the brown butter: In a small pan over medium heat, melt the butter and cook, whisking, until it turns golden brown and smells nutty, about 3 minutes. Cool to room temperature. In a small pan over medium heat, heat the glucose until warm. Using a spatula, scrape the glucose into a blender. While the machine is running, add the egg yolk, followed by the lemon juice. Scrape down the sides of the blender. Drizzle in the brown butter gradually, as if you were adding oil to a mayonnaise. Season with a pinch of salt and refrigerate until ready to serve.

To make the pistachio crema: In a small pot over medium heat, bring the pistachios and simple syrup to a boil. Simmer for 3 to 4 minutes, then pour in a blender. Return the pot to the stove and bring the cream, milk, and liquid glucose to a simmer. Pour over the pistachios and purée. While still hot, pour the purée over the white chocolate and cocoa butter and let sit for a minute. Stir until the chocolate is melted, then season with a pinch of salt and let cool.

Preheat the broiler. Place the *torta* rectangles on a baking sheet and toast until the tops are golden, 2 to 3 minutes. Place a spoonful of brown butter on each serving plate. Put the *tortas* on the plates and place a few spoonfuls of the pistachio crema over and around them. Pipe the lemon curd around the *torta* and garnish with citrus segments, lemon confitura, and pistachios.

SUCKLING PIG

Throughout central Italy, suckling pig is spit-roasted whole with fennel and garlic until the skin is crispy and the meat is tender. The resulting preparation, *porchetta*, is sliced and stuffed into sandwiches by market vendors for one of the world's most satisfying forms of street food. In the north, especially Emilia-Romagna, Trentino–Alto Adige, and Friuli, pork (prosciutto, pancetta, sausage, and speck) comprises an important part of the local diet. Suckling pig adapts to both Italian and German-influenced flavors, from pasta and polenta to pickled vegetables and sauerkraut.

Instead of roasting the pig whole, I prefer to prepare the parts separately to showcase the combination of technique and ingredient. I braise the head and trotters until tender, pull the meat off the bone, and mix it with breadcrumbs and eggs to make *crocchette* (croquettes). I roll the rich belly meat into a roulade and cook it slowly, and I braise the legs in pork fat, serving them with squares of crispy skin. Compared with pork, suckling pig tastes lighter and sweeter; I complement it with the sweetness of dried fruit, the acidity of rhubarb, and the savory depth of prosciutto rendered into a sauce. I turn braised suckling pig into a ragù for *blécs*, a free-form pasta from Friuli (page 98). Whether its parts are served together for a large gathering or prepared as individual dishes, the suckling pig remains the star ingredient.

Traditionally, suckling pigs were available in the spring and fall, but they can now be had nearly year-round. You can buy suckling pigs as small as 10 pounds, but I prefer them larger, around 30 pounds—there's more meat to work with. For the following recipes, use one 25-to 30-pound suckling pig, broken down into primal cuts by your butcher. Use the bones to make brown pork stock (page 283).

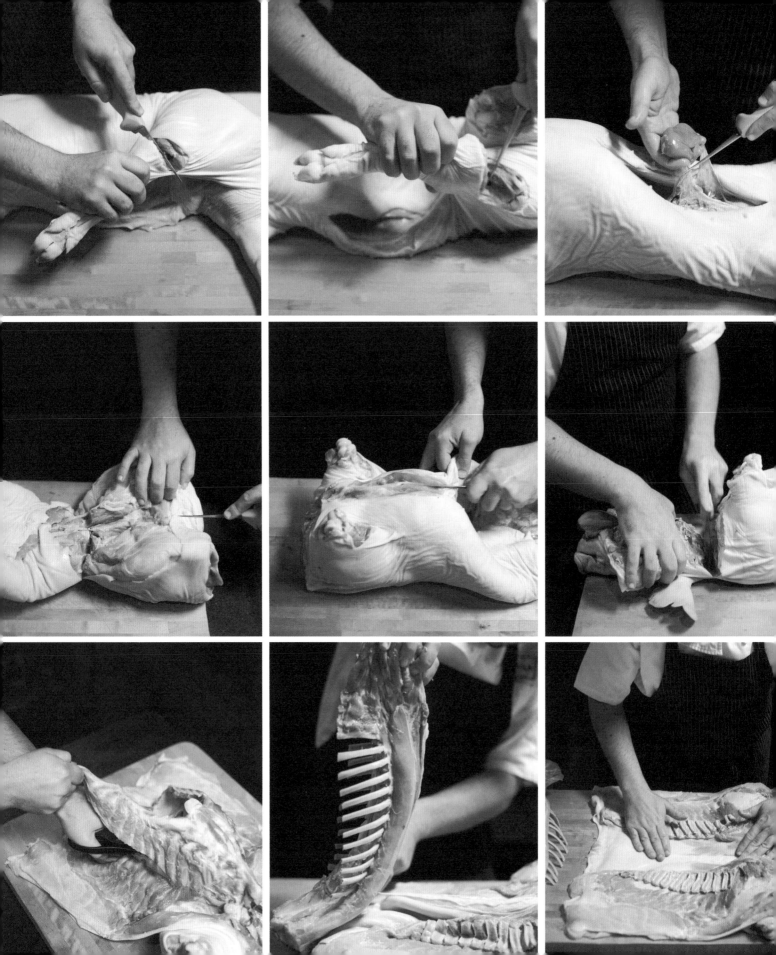

CROCCHETTE *with* Pickled Green Rhubarb *and* Apricots

A pig's head has a surprising amount of meat, from the tender cheeks to the tongue and the ears. Supplemented with trotters, the part of the leg below the knee, all this gelatinous meat binds together naturally for *crocchette*. Before I cook the meat, I brine it for two days. The brine has a touch of pink curing salt, which prevents the meat from losing its rosy color once cooked. Curing salt is available online, but butchers who make their own sausage might also sell you a small quantity.

SERVES 6 TO 8 AS AN APPETIZER

2956 grams • 3 quarts plus $1/2$ cup water

2 cups kosher salt, plus extra

1 tablespoon pink curing salt

scant $2/3$ cup sugar

10 thyme sprigs

1 teaspoon black peppercorns

1 teaspoon white peppercorns

1 teaspoon coriander seeds

1 teaspoon fennel seeds

1 star anise

1 bay leaf

1 garlic clove, smashed

1.5 kilograms • 1 ($3^1/2$-pound) suckling pig head

560 grams • 1 pound, 4 ounces (about 2) trotters (below the knee)

one 750 ml bottle neutral white wine, like Trebbiano

black pepper

2 to 4 tablespoons Dijon mustard

about 1 cup dried breadcrumbs

about $1/2$ cup chopped mixed herbs, such as parsley, sage, and chives

2 to 3 eggs

$1/2$ cup Wondra flour (see page 283)

extra virgin olive oil

To make the brine, combine the water, 2 cups of salt, pink salt, sugar, thyme, peppercorns, coriander, fennel, star anise, bay leaf, and garlic in a large pot. Bring to a boil and cook until the salt and sugar have dissolved.

Pour into a large storage container and cool completely over ice.

Pour the cooled brine over the head and trotters, ensuring that the meat is completely submerged. Cover and refrigerate for 2 days.

Transfer the head and trotters to a tall, narrow pot that fits the head snugly. Strain the brine, discarding the liquid and tying the aromatics in cheesecloth to make a sachet. Pour the wine into the pot and add enough water to cover the head and trotters completely. Bring to a brisk simmer over medium heat, lower to a gentle simmer, and add the sachet. Simmer for $2^1/2$ to 3 hours or until meltingly tender. Let the head and trotters rest in the cooking liquid for 2 hours.

Discard the sachet. Gently lift the head and trotters out of the pot. Carefully pick through the meat, discarding the bones, glands, and cartilage. Using your fingers or a paring knife, peel the skin from the tongue and discard. Coarsely chop the tongue, skin, ears, and meat and place in a bowl. Season with salt and pepper and stir in mustard to taste. Mix in $1/2$ cup of the breadcrumbs and the herbs, then mix in one egg. The mixture should feel slightly tacky. If it seems dry, add another egg. Refrigerate until slightly chilled, about 15 minutes.

Prepare an ice bath. Shape a third of the mixture on a long piece of plastic wrap into a long cylinder. Roll the meat into a 1-inch-thick log according to the instructions on page 272. Repeat with the remaining mixture until you have three cylinders. Float the cylinders in the ice bath to chill completely. If you see any air pockets, use a cake tester or other small skewer to poke the plastic and release the air. When completely cold, remove the cylinders from the ice bath and cut off the plastic. Slice the rolls into 1-inch croquettes.

Blend the remaining $1/2$ cup of breadcrumbs in a blender to ensure the crumbs are very fine and place in a shallow bowl. Put the Wondra flour in a separate shallow bowl. Purée the remaining egg with a splash of water in a third shallow bowl. Dredge each croquette in the flour, then the egg, then the breadcrumbs.

{continued}

Heat a thick film of olive oil in a large sauté pan over medium-high heat. Pan-fry the *crocchette* in batches until browned on all sides and hot all the way through. Blot the pieces on paper towels, season with salt, and transfer to a serving platter.

....

LEGS *and* BELLY
with Thyme, Lemon, *and* Fennel Pollen

I cure the leg and belly meat before cooking them *sous vide* (see page 271). Before serving, I cut the belly into medallions and sear them. For the leg meat, shred it, pressing it back into its skin. You may serve the pork belly with the leg pieces, the *crocchette* (see page 95), the rack (see page 97), any combination will work.

SERVES 6

3/4 cup kosher salt

1/4 cup brown sugar

2 garlic cloves, smashed

2 thyme sprigs, picked

1/2 teaspoon black peppercorns

1/2 teaspoon white peppercorns

1/2 teaspoon coriander seeds

1/2 teaspoon fennel seeds

2260 grams • 2 (2¹/₂-pound) suckling pig legs (above the knee and the foreshank)

1/4 cup rendered pork fat, duck fat, or olive oil

1135 grams • 1 (2¹/₂ pound) suckling pig belly

ground black pepper

a few pinches of fennel pollen

1 tablespoon chopped thyme

1 lemon for zesting

To make the cure: Mix the ³/₄ cup of salt and the sugar together. In a mortar with a pestle, coarsely crush the garlic, thyme, peppercorns, coriander, and fennel, then combine with the salt-sugar cure. Rub the legs generously with the cure. Cover and refrigerate for 6 to 8 hours.

Fill a large, rectangular water bath fitted with an immersion circulator and heat to 155°F (see *Sous Vide*, page 271).

Rinse the legs well with water and pat dry. On the inside of each leg, make a shallow incision along the bone just through the skin. (This will help you remove the skin later.) Put the legs in separate vacuum pouches, spoon equal portions of the pork fat into each, and vacuum seal.

Season the belly on both sides with salt and pepper. Sprinkle with fennel pollen and thyme, then grate lemon zest over the top. Roll the belly crosswise into a tight roll and wrap in plastic as directed on page 272. Place the legs and the belly in the preheated water bath and cook for 20 to 24 hours. Carefully pull the belly and legs from the water and let cool for 2 hours.

Prepare an ice bath. Cut off the plastic ends off the belly roll, leaving the rest of the plastic in place. Drain out the juices that have accumulated, then wrap a few fresh layers of plastic over the roll, twisting the ends using the same process as before. Plunge the meat into an ice bath to chill. Once cold, remove from the ice bath and refrigerate until ready to serve.

Cut open the leg pouches and drain, reserving any liquid. Put the legs on a cutting board and carefully peel away the skin, trying to keep it in one rectangular piece. Line a 9 by 13-inch rimmed baking sheet with plastic wrap. Put the skin on the lined tray with the outer side facing down, trim the skin to fit the baking sheet, scraping any fat and sinew off with a spoon. Pick the leg meat off the bone, taking care not to shred it too finely and place it in a bowl. Adjust the seasoning with salt and pepper and mix in enough braising liquid to moisten, about ¹/₄ cup. Pack the meat over the skin until it reaches about ³/₄-inch thickness. Cover the pan with plastic wrap and place an equal-sized baking pan on top. Weigh down the meat with a couple of cans and refrigerate overnight or until completely cold.

Remove the cans and the top pan. Peel off the plastic wrap and invert the pressed meat onto a cutting board.

Cut the meat through the skin into squares or rectangles. Transfer to a clean sheet pan, cover, and refrigerate until ready to cook.

To cook the pork leg pieces, preheat the oven to 350°F. Heat a thin film of olive oil in a large sauté pan over medium-high heat. Season the pieces lightly with salt and pepper. Put the pieces skin side down in the pan and sear until the skin begins to crisp, about 3 minutes. Transfer to the oven and cook until just warmed through, 5 to 7 minutes. Carefully lift the pieces from the pan and serve skin side up.

Slice the belly through the plastic wrap into ¹/₂- to ³/₄-inch rounds. Discard the plastic wrap. Heat a thin film of olive oil in a large sauté pan over medium-high heat. Sear the medallions until brown and crispy, about 3 to 4 minutes per side. Blot the pieces on a paper towel and transfer to a serving platter.

....

CHOPS *with* Prosciutto Sauce

The rack of any animal offers the most tender cuts, which are best when simply prepared. I either roast suckling pig loin and rack whole and carve them at the table, or I cut them into double-thick portions before roasting. The meat is so special that I am careful not to overcook it. I roast it to 135°F and allow carryover heat to bring the internal temperature to about 140°F.

SERVES 4 TO 6

   1135 grams • 2¹/₂ pound suckling pig rack and loin
   kosher salt and black pepper
   extra virgin olive oil
   2 to 3 tablespoons unsalted butter
   2 or 3 sprigs freshly picked herbs, such as thyme and rosemary

Preheat the oven to 375°F. Tie butcher's twine crosswise around each piece of pork. Season the meat with salt and pepper. Heat a thin film of olive oil in a large sauté pan over medium-high heat. Sear the pork in batches until

the pieces have evenly caramelized on all sides, about 4 minutes. Transfer the sauté pan to the oven and roast until the meat is medium rare with an internal temperature of about 130°F, 8 to 10 minutes. Remove the pan from the oven and place over high heat. Add the butter and herbs to the pan and baste the meat with the butter and pan juices, about 2 minutes. Transfer the meat to a cooling rack to rest for 10 minutes. To serve, cut off the butcher's twine and slice the pork into individual portions.

BLÉCS *with* Suckling Pig Ragù *and* Rapini

A classic buckwheat pasta called *blécs* in Friuli and *maltagliati* elsewhere, this is one of the more free-form pasta shapes. *Blécs* require no molds—simply slice them into triangles or strips, cook them, and toss them with ragù. You can even roll the dough out by hand if you prefer. *Blécs* are made with buckwheat flour, which carries a natural sweetness echoed by the suckling pig. To counter that sweetness, I add rapini leaves right before serving, letting them wilt into the pasta.

SERVES 4 TO 6

Ragù

1530 grams • about 3 pounds, 6 ounces bone-in, suckling pig, probably shoulder, cut into large pieces

55 grams • 1/3 cup plus 1 tablespoon basic meat cure (page 276)

extra virgin olive oil

2 or 3 carrots, cut into large dice

1 yellow onion, thinly cut into large dice

2 celery stalks, cut into large dice

kosher salt

2 cups white wine

5 1/2 cups brown stock (page 283)

a sachet with 4 sprigs thyme, 2 sprigs rosemary, 2 bay leaves, 5 black peppercorns, 2 cloves, and 1/2 teaspoon fennel seeds

1/2 yellow onion, thinly sliced

80 grams • 1/2 cup diced thick-cut bacon

35 grams • 1/4 cup golden raisins, soaked and drained

black pepper

Blécs

107 grams • 3/4 cup 00 flour

107 grams • 3/4 cup durum flour

35 grams • 1/3 cup buckwheat flour

2 grams • 1/2 teaspoon kosher salt

140 grams • 3/4 cup warm water

1 cup rapini leaves

1 to 2 tablespoons unsalted butter

a block of Parmigiano-Reggiano for grating

To make the ragù: Trim off any visible excess fat from the suckling pork and season with the cure. Cover and refrigerate for 2 to 3 hours, then rinse and pat dry.

Preheat the oven to 325°F. Heat a thin film of olive oil in a Dutch oven over medium heat. Stir in the carrots, onion, and celery and sweat with a pinch of salt until softened, about 3 minutes. Add the pig pieces and 1 1/2 cups of the wine and bring to a simmer. Pour in the stock, add the sachet, and return to a simmer. Cover the pot and transfer to the oven. Braise until the meat is meltingly tender, about 3 1/2 hours. Uncover and cool for 2 hours.

Using a slotted spoon, scoop the meat from the braising liquid and pull it apart, discarding the skin, fat, and connective tissue. Run a knife through the meat to break it into smaller pieces. Strain the braising liquid into a clean pot and discard the vegetables. Skim the fat off the top of the liquid with a ladle, then place over medium heat and reduce by half, 8 to 10 minutes.

In a dry Dutch oven or heavy-bottomed pot over medium heat, sweat the thinly sliced onion until slightly softened, about 2 minutes. Stir in the bacon and render until browned and crisp, about 4 minutes. Pour in the remaining 1/2 cup of wine, bring to a simmer, and reduce by about two-thirds. Pour in the pork braising liquid, return to a simmer, and reduce another third. Stir in the suckling pig meat and the raisins and simmer for a minute more. Season with salt and pepper if needed. Keep warm if serving soon, or refrigerate.

To make the *blécs*: In a stand mixer fitted with the paddle attachment, mix together the flours and salt. With the mixer running on low speed, drizzle in the water and mix for 2 to 3 minutes. Turn the dough onto a floured counter and knead for several minutes by hand; the dough will feel dry and firm. Flatten the dough into a rectangle, wrap in plastic wrap, and leave on the counter for 30 minutes to soften and hydrate.

Roll out the dough according to the instructions for laminated pasta on page 273. With a knife or fluted pasta wheel, cut the sheets into irregular but even-sized shapes no longer than 3 inches. Place the pasta on a lightly floured baking sheet.

{continued}

Bring a large pot of salted water to a boil. Stir in the *blécs* and cook until al dente, 4 to 5 minutes. Drain, reserving about 1 cup of pasta cooking water, and return the blécs to the pot. Bring the ragù to a simmer. Spoon enough ragù into the pot to cover the noodles, then cook the ragù and pasta together over medium heat until the ragù clings to the noodles. Stir in the rapini leaves and a spoonful of butter, then season to taste with salt and pepper. Spoon into bowls and grate Parmigiano-Reggiano over each portion of pasta.

PICKLED RHUBARB
and Dried Apricots

When a local farmer came in with green rhubarb that had been picked by mistake, I accepted the challenge of figuring out what to do with it. After a few less-succesful ideas, I landed on the concept of using sweet to tame rhubarb's intense sour flavor. It is pickling in reverse: instead of adding acid, I sweeten already acidic underripe rhubarb by vacuum-sealing it with simple syrup. This technique works well for other tart fruits, like green apples, strawberries, or peaches. Dried apricots underscore the pig's natural sweetness and also make this dish wine-friendly.

MAKES 2¹/₂ CUPS

227 grams • 4 stalks green rhubarb

130 grams • ¹/₂ cup plus 2 tablespoons simple syrup (page 281)

113 grams • ¹/₂ cup white verjus (see page 283)

120 grams • ¹/₂ cup dried apricot slices

Prepare an ice bath. In a pot of boiling, salted water, quickly blanch the rhubarb, then stick in an ice bath. Place the rhubarb in a vacuum pouch and add 2 tablespoons of simple syrup, seal, wait a couple of minutes, then cut open the bag and drain. Slice rhubarb into ¹/₂ inch pieces.

In a small pot over medium heat, mix together the remaining ¹/₂ cup of simple syrup and the verjus. Add the apricots and simmer until soft, about 5 minutes. Let the apricots cool in the syrup, then drain before serving.

PROSCIUTTO SAUCE

Prosciutto sauce is an ideal way to use up prosciutto trimmings, the inevitable ends and sides left behind after the center part of the leg has been sliced into thin sheets; it doesn't take very much to flavor the sauce. Served with roasted chops—or any of the other suckling pig preparations—the sauce adds depth and maturity to the meat. Before grinding the prosciutto, look for and remove any metal bits that might be embedded in the meat.

MAKES ABOUT 1¹/₂ CUPS

680 grams • 3 cups brown stock (page 283)

28 grams • 1 ounce prosciutto trimmings

a pinch of sugar

a few drops of balsamic vinegar

salt and black pepper

In a small pot over medium heat, reduce the stock by half. With a meat grinder, grind (or by hand, finely chop) the prosciutto trimmings finely. In a sauté pan over medium-low heat, render the prosciutto until it becomes crisp, 5 to 10 minutes. Pour the rendered prosciutto onto paper towels to remove excess fat. Wipe out the pot and return the prosciutto to it. Sprinkle with the sugar and, over medium-low heat, caramelize lightly, 2 to 3 minutes. Pour in the reduced stock, bring to a simmer, and season with vinegar and pepper, but taste before seasoning with salt—the prosciutto is salty. Simmer to reduce slightly, and keep warm to serve.

VIA POSTUMIA—
VENETO AND
FRIULI-VENEZIA GIULIA

Veneto wine
production areas

Lugana
Bianco
di Custoza
Breganze
Prosecco di
Conegliano
Valdobbiadene
Montello/
Colli Asolani
Piave
Lison -
Pramaggiore
Valpolicella
Lessini
Durello
Gambellara
Bardolino
Soave
Classico
Colli
Berici
Verona
Venezia
Colli
Euganei

Friuli-Venezia Giulia
wine production areas

Colli Orientali del Friuli
Udine
Friuli Grave
Collio
Lison - Pramaggiore
Friuli
Latisana
Friuli
Isonzo
Friuli
Aquileia
Friuli
Ànnia
Carso
Trieste

VIA POSTUMIA—VENETO AND FRIULI-VENEZIA GIULIA

Veneto

It was early Saturday morning and already the Autogrill off the *autostrada* to Verona was jammed with travelers waiting for espresso. Yet when a short, graying man in a sweater vest ordered a glass of Prosecco, the overworked barista didn't miss a beat, pouring out a tall glass before pivoting back to the endless stream of cappuccino orders. A glass of Prosecco served before ten in the morning in the Veneto barely raises an eyebrow.

Verona is the hub of the Veneto's prolific wine region. When the city hosts Vinitaly, the largest annual trade show dedicated to Italian wine, it also becomes the acting capital of the Italian wine industry. Vinitaly started in the 1960s, as a show for farming and cellar equipment. Now it's a weeklong event in which winemakers and distillers from every corner of Italy showcase their wares and mingle with importers, journalists, equipment manufacturers, sommeliers, and salespeople. If there's any place where you can get a sense of the concerns and aspirations within the entire Italian wine community, it's here.

Verona is a forward-thinking city that embraces innovation, a characteristic of the Veneto as a whole and of the region's winemaking styles. Unlike areas that relied on the quality in their native fruit to make good wine, vintners in the Veneto have always had a knack for manipulating local grapes to surpass expectations. Prosecco, for instance, emerged as a way to leverage the acidity in the Glera grape, while *appassimento*, the practice of drying grapes before making voluptuous wines like Amarone, raised the profile of a motley assortment of red grapes. In between easygoing Prosecco and meditative Amarone, the Veneto has become adept at producing wines with attractive price-value ratios, such as Soave and Valpolicella.

But sometimes, grape manipulation and value pricing go too far. With about 220 million gallons of wine made annually, the Veneto is the most productive region in Italy, a distinction that elicits grumbles from its artisan winemakers. Some winemakers in the Veneto have become serious about defining their wine, using the region's significant clout to rack up several new DOCG zones: these now number in the dozens. While some of the newer appointments have been controversial, the overall message seems to be a call for quality in a zone where quality hasn't always come first.

Part of the reason for the region's high yields is its terrain. With the exception of the prealpine slopes of classic Prosecco growing areas in the Treviso province, most of the Veneto's growing regions are flat or gently hilly. The Po River valley, which covers nearly half of the region, provides a fertile blanket of soil for agriculture. In the humid weather of the plains, grapes grow easily in high pergola trellises that accommodate mechanical harvesting. While the Veneto's top Valpolicella and Soave vineyards surrounding Verona and up-and-coming areas like Colli Euganei near Padova are hilly, gallons of nondescript wines flow from the plains.

Wine has played an important role in the economy of northeastern Italy since Roman times. The name Valpolicella comes from *vallis polis cellae*, Latin for the valley with many cellars. Grapes were dried before being pressed into a sweet, concentrated wine capable of withstanding shipping without spoiling. This ancient sweet style was the precursor to Port-like Recioto, which in turn led to Amarone. While wine production declined in post-Roman times, it picked up in the late Middle Ages, when making wine became an aristocratic and ecclesiastic endeavor.

By its peak in the sixteenth century, the Venetian Republic brought ample wealth to the region. Spices flowed into Venice from the eastern Mediterranean and wealthy families moved west toward Padua and set up farming estates and hunting lodges. Venice itself was a big market for local wines. During the Venetian Republic, vendors would set up stalls in the shadow of the Campanile, earning the nickname *ombra*, meaning shadow or shade. In Venice today, *ombra* also means "glass of wine." The wine consumed in Venice was made with local grapes until Napoleon conquered the area in the late eighteenth century, bringing Merlot and Cabernet vines with him. Today producers in central and eastern Veneto make convincing wines with Bordeaux varieties. But the biggest story in the Veneto hinges on native grapes—and their manipulation, for better and for worse.

For white grapes, the most striking examples reside with Prosecco and Soave. In the case of Prosecco, human intervention has been a good thing. While *frizzante* field wines had always been made in the Treviso province, Prosecco's modern incarnation started in the nineteenth century when Antonio Carpenè and his partners founded the Carpenè Malvolti firm with the aim to bring sparkling wine production to the region. Instead of using the classic method employed in Champagne production, in which wines carry out their secondary fermentation in the bottle, Carpenè made wine that passed through its second fermentation in pressurized tanks before being bottled under pressure. (The same method is used to make Asti Spumante.) For Glera, the grape used in Prosecco, tank fermentation captured its fleeting stone-fruit aromatics and crisp acidity, allowing the grape's best qualities to shine through. The Charmat method, as the technique is now called, was embraced as the ideal method for making wine with this grape.

It's been a good couple of decades for Prosecco producers. Prosecco is effortlessly cool, and its appealing price tag has turned it into an international star. Today the area between Conegliano and Valdobbiadene, a dramatic series of slopes covered in vines, has changed from a chain of farming communities into a wealthy enclave. Within this area, Cartizze, with its moraine, sandstone, and clay soils, is considered the top vineyard for Prosecco. Sparkling wines made from Cartizze fruit carry a distinct mineral backbone with a delicate nose of peaches and cream. But with one hectare valued at 2.5 million euros in 2011—one of the highest for vineyard land in Italy—Cartizze's prestige raises the question of just how easygoing Prosecco can afford to stay.

The wine's global success also has led to a host of imitators. Because Prosecco was once the name of both the grape and the wine, anyone using the grape could call his sparkling wine Prosecco. Producers from Treviso, including Conegliano, Valdobbiadene, and Asolo, another classic area of Prosecco production, lobbied to restrict the use of the label Prosecco to wines made in the classic zones and succeeded. Now wines made with Glera grapes grown outside classic Prosecco areas cannot be called Prosecco.

In Soave, winemakers also have struggled to defend the quality of their wine brand. When Garganega, the main grape in Soave, is planted on the stony terraced hillsides of Soave Classico near Verona, it turns ripe and slightly savory with a nutty, lemony flavor. The same grape, however, becomes lean and bland when planted in the fertile plains, where the zone's boundaries were inexplicably extended. As volumes rose, quality became diluted and the mix of grapes changed to include more Trebbiano Toscano and less Garganega.

The best bet when buying Soave is to look for names of makers that have focused on Garganega. In 1971, Leonildo Pieropan released Il Calvarino, the first single-vineyard Soave, soon followed by a more steely single-vineyard wine, La Rocca. Both wines remain top performers in the region. Graziano Prà, a gentleman farmer and local winemaking hero, produces complex, well-structured Soaves as well, especially his Monte Grande bottling. Aged in its lees in thirty-hectoliter casks, this Soave Classico brings out the natural luster of Garganega with accents of lemon peel, wax bean, and stone fruit.

The region's other white wines are a similar mix of grapes found in Soave. Made in Vincenza, Gambellara is Soave's lesser-known twin. On the southern shores of Lake Garda on the border of Lombardia, Trebbiano di Soave is the main grape of Lugana, a flinty, aromatic wine.

While more than 60 percent of the wine produced in the Veneto is white, red wine production remains significant, nearing 70 million gallons in 2010. The main red wines come from western Verona, a temperate region insulated by Lake Garda and the Adige River and the cooling alpine breezes from the Lessinia Mountains. Rather than being famous for certain grapes, however, the red wines made around Verona are known for their style, from bright, medium-bodied Bardolino, refreshing Chiaretto, and black cherry–hued Valpolicella to inmitable Amarone and sweet, Port-like Recioto. Most of these wines are a near-endless combination of local grapes.

Valpolicella, the Veneto's most important red wine area, is an extremely profitable place for vintners, mainly because of one wine: Amarone. This wine enchants me in the glass, offering intense fruit and acidity curbed by the idea of sweetness; it also takes a romantic to make it. While most vintners can stop worrying about grape quality after harvest, makers of Amarone (and Recioto, the sweet *passito* wine made from the same blend of grapes, and Amarone's predecessor) monitor grape quality for several more months while the bunches dry and the grapes raisin. During this lengthy *appassimento* process, which typically takes place in temperature- and humidity-controlled drying rooms, bunches are monitored for broken berries and mold growth. By the time the grapes are crushed (anywhere between sixty to a hundred days after harvest), they have lost nearly half of their weight. Between harvest and the time the grapes are ready to be crushed, winemakers walk a fine line between dried grapes and those that are on the verge of spoiling.

The first Amarone likely emerged from a barrel of Recioto that somehow fermented itself dry. Until fairly recently, Recioto was more esteemed than Amarone. For this reason, Amarone once was called Recioto Amaro, or bitter Recioto. In the 1950s, the Bolla family began bottling this dry wine as Recioto della Valpolicella Amarone, but the wine was not a commercial success until recently. Until 1996, barely 1.5 million bottles of Amarone were made each year. By 2005, production surpassed 5 million, and estimates for the future are more than double those of 2005. The affect of the Amarone boom on the Valpolicella growing region has been significant. In 1997, 8.2 million kilograms of Valpolicella-grown grapes were used for *appassimento* wines. By 2007, the amount of grapes had ballooned to 25.7 million kilograms.

The growth in Amarone production has popularized *ripasso*-style wines, which are made by filtering Valpolicella wine through the pressed skins of Amarone grapes, imparting the wine with the sugars and yeast remaining from Amarone. At their best, *ripasso* wines are stronger and weightier wines than Valpolicella made with fresh grapes alone. On the label, they are distinguished from other Valpolicella wines as Valpolicella Superiore Ripasso. A favorite of mine is Tommaso Bussola's Ca' del Laito, a *ripasso* wine imbued with dark cherry fruit balanced by acidity.

Like Prosecco and Soave, Amarone's international popularity, coupled with a huge leap in output, has vintners worried that the wine may become a victim of its own success. Some winemakers fear that the light, cherry style of regular Valpolicella could be eclipsed by *ripasso* wines. Others are frustrated with the lack of definitive style for Amarone: no one seems to know exactly what it is supposed to taste like. But when you think about how young the wine is compared to other classic Italian wines such as Chianti or Barolo, it's clear that it's still figuring out what it needs to be.

Like sipping Moscato d'Asti after a day of tasting Barolo, the intensity of Amarone requires relief with a low-alcohol sparkler. My favorite selection is Fior d'Arancio Spumante from La Montecchia, a winery owned by Count Giordano Emo Capodilista. I have been pouring this elegant, sweet, and uplifting wine made with an aromatic variety of Moscato for years, and I especially like serving it with goat cheese. The easygoing nature of Fior d'Arancio is an extension of Giordano, who instantly makes guests feel comfortable with his warm handshake and occasional invitation to a round of karaoke. This perspective is reflected in his wines. While Giordano feels that special-occasion wines have their place, he prefers making wines that can be enjoyed with less ceremony. If we're lucky, Giordano—and the Veneto as a whole—will never lose the ability to delight us with a bright, breezy sparkler or two. —SL

White Grapes

GARGANEGA

The main grape of Soave is a vigorous, thick-skinned, and late-ripening variety also used in the wines of Gambellara, Bianco di Custoza, Colli Berici and Colli Euganei DOCs. At its best, Garganega produces elegant, well-structured wines with wax bean and peach notes. Some of the benchmark examples come from around Monteforte d'Alpone, such as Prà and Gini. In San Bonifacio, Stefano Inama makes a straw-hued, fruity Soave from organically farmed grapes. While Roberto Anselmi dropped the Soave name from his label, his nutty, rich wine is a benchmark example of Garganega. The popular grape has several clones, the latest discovery being Dorona on Mazzorbo, an island in the Venetian lagoon.

RECOMMENDED PRODUCERS: Prà, Suavia, Anselmi, Inama, Gini, Pieropan, Coffele, Ca' Rugate, Vicentini Agostino, Nardello

GLERA

The origins of the main grape of Prosecco are not clear. Most sources point to the town of Prosecco, near Trieste in Friuli-Venezia Giulia, and until recently, the grape was called Prosecco. While light green, tart Glera isn't well known as a still wine, as Prosecco it attains celebrity status, especially in the winemaking area of Conegliano and Valdobbiadene. Conegliano has fewer craggy hills than Valdobbiadene and tends to produce slightly richer wines, while the Valdobbiadene wine is more mineral, racy, and crisp on the finish. In addition to Prosecco, a few producers are also trying their hand at making bottle-fermented (Champagne-style) sparkling wines with Glera. It's too early to tell whether these experiments will outshine the tank-fermented wine that made the area famous, but the impulse to make bottle-fermented wines seems to be part of a strategy to promote the quality of Glera, suggesting that it is capable of more than providing bubbles for bellinis.

RECOMMENDED PRODUCERS: Le Vigne di Alice, Adami, Bisol, Ruggeri, Nino Franco, Sorelle Bronca, Col de' Salici, Casa Coste Piane, Trevisiol

RIESLING ITALICO

Grown throughout the Veneto and Friuli, this grape may be distantly related to Riesling from Germany (called Riesling Renano in Italy). While some discount it for being less nuanced than German Riesling, it can be a delightful floral, light *aperitivo* wine.

RECOMMENDED PRODUCERS: Torresella, Cecilia Beretta, Mille

VESPAIOLA

This sharp, local grape (*vespe* means wasp in Italian) is rendered into sweet nectar in Torcolato, the *passito* wine of the Breganze DOC in the Dolomite foothills. Unlike the grapes that are dried for Amarone and Recioto in crates, Torcolato is made by braiding the vine branches together and suspending the grapes from the ceiling to dry. Still dry wines from producers such as Contrà Soarda are also becoming fashionable.

RECOMMENDED PRODUCERS: Maculan, Vigneto Due Santi, Contrà Soarda

SEE ALSO: Malvasia (page 14), Moscato (page 201), Verduzzo (page 117), Trebbiano (page 71)

Red Grapes

CORVINA

A thick-skinned, vigorous grape, Corvina is the main variety of Amarone, Recioto, Valpolicella, and Bardolino wines. On its own, it yields a ruby-hued, fragrant, and bright-tasting wine, but it is most often experienced when blended with other local grapes. Amarone producers, such as Allegrini and Dal Forno, often use the maximum amount of Corvina (about 70 percent) in their cuvees, the remaining percentage being any combination of other grapes, from Dindarella, Molinara, Negrara, Oseleta, and Rondinella to the occasional splash of Cabernet Sauvignon. When used for blending, Corvina provides perfume, body, and color. Allegrini's magestic La Poja, a wine made solely with Corvina, also demonstrates the potential of this grape on its own.

CORVINONE

Once thought to be a subvariety of Corvina, Corvinone is now known to be a separate variety. Its vigor and large grape size can make for diluted wines, but if yields are kept in check, Corvinone offers admirable color and tannin in blends and dries well for *appassimento* wines.

DINDARELLA

A very light, peppery, and acidic grape, Dindarella is a good candidate for rosé wines. Historically it was blended into the red wines of Valpolicella (including some Amarone bottlings), but a few producers, such as Brigaldara, have chosen to vinify it alone.

DURELLO

Made in the Lessini hills, Durello is one of the few native red grapes not used in the blended wines of Valpolicella and Bardolino. Instead, the highly acidic grape (said to be related to Prosecco's Glera) is used in sparkling wine and *passito* production. The Marcato family has long championed Durello, making both a bottle-fermented sparkling wine and a *passito*. Because of its apple-like nuances, I pour Dama del Rovere Lessini Durello Brut in the fall.

RECOMMENDED PRODUCERS: Dama del Rovere, Fongaro, Marcato

MOLINARA

While Corvina delivers aroma and fruit to the red wines of Valpolicella and Bardolino, Molinara brings acidity. The grape is otherwise lightly aromatic and light in color. A maximum of 25 percent of Molinara is permitted in Amarone, but most producers use it sparingly or leave it out completely.

NEGRARA

Grown in the Negrar district of Valpolicella, where some of the best Amarone wines come from, this minor grape is most often used for blending. It is a mild grape, with light tannins and deep color.

OSELETA

Recent interest in Oseleta has reinvigorated its standing in a crowded field of local red grapes. While the grape is still used primarily for blending, some vintners now make spice-driven wines with it. Wines made with solely Oseleta are dark, medium- to full-bodied, and fruity but firm with acidity.

RECOMMENDED PRODUCERS: Masi, Zymè

RABOSO

While most of Italy's grapes tend to carry a good amount of acidity, Raboso lands at the high end. "The angry one," as Giordano Emo Capodilista calls it, the native grape from the Piave River valley is harvested as late as November so its ripeness can counter some of the acidity. Giordano's family winery, La Montecchia in the Euganei hills, makes Forzatè, a deeply colored wine with a generous amount of black cherry and blueberry fruit. Other producers, like Col de' Salici, leverage its acidity into sparkling wines.

RECOMMENDED PRODUCERS: Col de' Salici, La Montecchia

In Amarone and other red blended wines, the job for this grape is to provide the tannins that are missing from Corvina and Molinara. Since it is a hearty grape that is resistant to mold, it is a good candidate for the long drying needed for *appassimento* production. On its own, it is modestly floral with a tart cherry taste.

SEE ALSO: Marzemino (page 144), Croatina (page 167)

Friuli-Venezia Guilia

In the wine business, it takes a big fortune to make a small fortune, or so goes the industry saying. To make great wine, however, time, skill, and dedication bordering on obsession are far more important. This is evident at the Vodopivec estate in the Carso, a plateau of limestone and evergreens in the southwest corner of Friuli-Venezia Giulia. The Carso is a land of opposites: while breezes from the Adriatic Sea bring relief on hot summer days, bone-chilling *bora* winds from eastern European mountains howl in the winter. People who live here tend to be resilient, and winemaker Paolo Vodopivec is no exception. His chiseled jaw, strong build, and suntan give him the look of a 1950s movie star, but he is more likely to be working in the vineyard than kicking back at the beach.

Paolo and his brother, Valter, started making wine in the 1990s, but even today, production remains tiny: Vodopivec produces fewer than 15,000 bottles annually, which has proven to be a tough way to make a living. To support his family, Valter has taken up full-time work in the nearby city of Trieste while Paolo forges on more or less as a one-man show. Vodopivec wines are made exclusively with Vitovska, a native white grape rarely found outside the Carso DOC. The vines are never irrigated. Instead, Paolo drills into the fossilized seabed to encourage roots to reach deep into the rock. This effort in the vineyard gives the Vitovska grapes a mineral edge that comes through in every glass of Vodopivec wine. But it is grueling work, and sometimes even the best-laid plans can be foiled. One year the deer ate half the crop. Paolo swallowed hard and built a taller fence.

Work continues in the cellar. What looks like nothing more than a small ring in the dirt is actually the lip of a large terra-cotta amphora buried in the ground—a storage tank that is naturally temperature-controlled by the soil. He ferments and macerates the wine in underground amphorae as well as in above-ground 790-gallon oak *botti*. His process is unusual in that he leaves the skins in contact with the grape juice for as long as six months. A long, slow maceration period on the skins gives the wine unexpected elegance, an unusual amber hue, and the capacity for long periods of aging. This is not your average glass of white wine.

Josko Gravner, a wine pioneer in Friuli-Venezia Giulia, paved the way for winemakers like Paolo to test the limits of what is possible in white wine production. In the 1980s, when everyone in Friuli was using temperature-controlled steel tanks for fermenting and aging white wine, Gravner began to use new French oak. When oak became overused, he traveled to Georgia, the former Soviet territory, where he encountered the ancient tradition of aging wine in amphorae. Believing that this method would allow him to express grapes and land better than more modern techniques, Gravner returned to his hometown of Oslavia within the Colli Orientali del Friuli growing region and built a room to age wine in underground amphorae. He released his first vintage of amphora-aged wine in 2001.

When I visited Gravner's amphora room, I felt as if I had entered a temple, a place where you feel you must speak in a whisper to avoid disrupting the wine. This isn't far from the truth. For Gravner, wine is a living, breathing entity. He even avoids entering the room when in a bad mood. It may sound a tad mystical, but the alchemy of grapes, terra-cotta, soil, and good vibes works: Gravner's wines are unlike anything I have tasted. I found Gravner's Anfora, a wine made with local Ribolla Gialla grapes, took some getting used to. It was a contrarian wine: honeyed and nutty, yet dry and distinctly savory. Then I tried it with food. Immediately my mind began to open up to the food-wine pairing possibilities.

Bordering Slovenia to the east, Austria to the north, and the Veneto to the west, Friuli-Venezia Giulia region draws on Slovene, Germanic, and Italian cultures, a collective heritage derived from borders that have been fluid since Roman times. Even the region's hyphenated name (which I habitually shorten to Friuli) is itself a

result of redrawn borders. The larger northwestern area, Friuli, and smaller, southeastern portion, Venezia Giulia, merged only in 1964. The foods of Friuli reflect its patchwork heritage. Polenta, traditionally served from a cauldron suspended over the *fogolâr* (a hearth in the center of the room) is a staple starch. Coastal cities have Venetian-style risotto and *sarde in saor*, while inland menus reflect Germanic influences with pork, game, and sauerkraut made from turnips and wine. Meanwhile, Trieste is Italy's coffee capital, and its cafés serve *torta Sacher* in a Viennese spirit. There are also wholly Friulian indulgences, like *frico*, a toasted cheese crisp made with grated Montasio cheese. And in the eastern alpine foothills of the Collio and Colli Orientali—Friuli's premier wine zones—meals often start with a plate of mildly smoky prosciutto and a glass of flinty Friulano.

The Collio and Colli Orientali del Friuli are two of the top appellations in Italy for white wine. Collio looks like a horizontal half-moon hugging the Slovenian border while the Colli Orientali runs north to south. Parts of these hills feel more Slovenian than Italian, but that is natural to Ales Kristancic. The winemaker of Movia has vineyards spanning from the Collio into the Slovenian Brda growing zone. But Movia, an estate that has produced wine for three centuries, is as much a part of Friuli's wine heritage as any estate on the Italian side of the border. In this corner of the world, politics may shift, but a culture of winemaking remains constant.

The Collio and Colli Orientali del Friuli are well suited for white wine. Though the vineyards are no more than an hour's drive from the sea, the Collio has an alpine aura. Even in late spring, snow-dusted peaks are visible from Collio producer Venica & Venica's legendary Sauvignon vineyard, Ronco delle Mele. During the day, the vines enjoy warm breezes that blow in from the Venetian lagoon while at night the alpine air cools the fruit, preserving aromatic compounds. Meanwhile, the splintery *ponca* soil derived from a fossilized seabed imparts acidity to the grapes, giving Friuli white wines their characteristic freshness.

Even though the region produces red wine, Friuli means white wine to most consumers. From 2005 to 2009, white wine production consistently hovered around 60 percent. The sheer variety of white grapes that grow here encourages experimentation. Native grapes Friulano (formerly Tocai Friulano), Ribolla Gialla, Malvasia Istriana, Verduzzo, and Picolit commingle with Pinot Grigio, Pinot Bianco, and Sauvignon (the Italian synonym for Sauvignon Blanc). Felluga's elegant Terre Alte, a blend of Sauvigon, Friulano, and Pinot Bianco, and Silvio Jermann's fresh Vintage Tunina are benchmarks for the region. So are the wines from the producer Edi Keber, whose Collio Bianco is a blend of Friulano and other local grapes.

Friuli's modern-day successes with white wine started in the 1960s, when winemakers such as Mario Schiopetto and Livio and Marco Felluga started making white wines in a style previously unknown in Italy. Instead of the oxidized white wines typical in Italy during the first half of the twentieth century, these pioneers applied new technology—slick, temperature-controlled steel tanks used by some French and German winemakers. By controlling the temperature of fermentation and treating grapes with care, Schiopetto, Felluga, Venica & Venica, and others started producing light, fresh, and aromatic wines that became known as the Friuli style: a crisp, mineral-tinged wine uninhibited by oak or malolactic fermentation.

The process of making these wines is exactly opposite of Gravner's amphora approach. Instead of prolonging skin contact, the entire process is about minimizing it. When you eat a grape, "the pulp is what gives you the most satisfaction," explains Giorgio Venica, who runs the family's namesake estate with his brother, Gianni. "When you keep chewing, you release more flavors. And if you keep chewing, the flavors become bitter. We try to take away all of the grape that we can without extracting much bitterness."

In contrast to the thoroughly modern Friuli whites, the region's white wine history resides in *passito* wines made with the amber Verduzzo grape and Picolit, formerly Friuli's most fashionable native grape. Abbazia di Rosazzo, a monastery-turned-art center for humanities, has also played a crucial role in Friulian wine history, acting as a seed bank for native grapes since the thirteenth century. Efforts by the Benedictines have saved several native grapes from extinction, including red grapes Pignolo and Schioppettino, which were wiped out

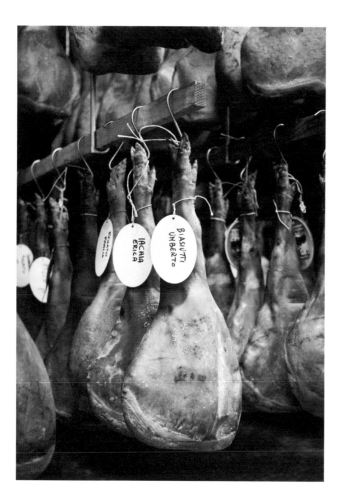

The best place to reflect on Friuli's current state of enology is in the dining room at La Subida, a large farmhouse that was converted into a sophisticated restaurant in Cormòns, a town in the center of the Collio. I always order the locally made D'Osvaldo prosciutto, which is wheeled out to the table and sliced by hand tableside while everyone at the table nibbles on *frico*. I'm also drawn to the wine selection: La Subida has the deepest cellar I've encountered in Friuli. The sommelier, Michele Paiano, keeps better tabs on the wine industry here than possibly anyone else. With so many Friuli wines to choose from—from modern thirst quenchers to cuvees inspired by the ancients—it's impossible to ever be satiated. —SL

FRIULANO

Despite the grape variety's long history in the region (it's been grown there for more than eight centuries), Friulano is more recognized by the confusion over its former name, Tocai Friulano, than its characteristics. When called Tocai, it was often confused with the Hungarian wine Tokaji, prompting the European Union to pressure Italy to change the grape's name. Yet Friulano has never been remotely similar to Hungary's prized dessert wine. Some Friulano wines have a funky, cave-like aroma, while others emit robust doses of chalk, wet stone, and flint. Still others can taste tart and green, like green apples or gooseberries. The reason for variation comes down to transparency: Friulano is an expert at showcasing the conditions of the vintage from which it was produced.

RECOMMENDED PRODUCERS: Venica & Venica, Livio Felluga, Bastianich, Schiopetto, Miani, Villa Russiz, Lis Neris, Isidoro Polencic, Zuani, Pighin, Oscar Sturm, Skerk

PICOLIT

Most known for a DOCG *passito* wine from Colli Orientali del Friuli, Picolit is an extremely low yielding variety, at times producing as few as ten grapes per bunch. This is one of the reasons that plantings have declined. Yet Picolit was once one of the region's most fashionable wines, favored among Austrian royals in the eighteenth and nineteenth centuries for its aroma and delicate sweetness. Several years ago, a scandal involving inferior wines falsely labeled as Picolit further hurt

elsewhere in Friuli during the phylloxera blight of the nineteenth century.

Apart from the Collio, Colli Orientali, and the Carso, Fruili's growing regions spread across the plains to the south and west. Grave, a main growing area for Merlot, stretches across the river plains toward Veneto. Along the coast, the Aquiliea, Latisana, and Friuli Annia DOCs have sandy, loamy soils, yielding softer white wines and lively reds with the native Refosco grape. Near the coast, the Isonzo DOC's well-draining, iron-rich red clay soil is ideal for more powerful white and red wines. Vie di Romans produces several sophisticated white wines here, including a cider-hued, oaked Pinot Grigio, Dessimis, that could convert anyone who thought that the ubiquitous grape was incapable of producing anything more than simple white wine. Another producer, Fulvio Bressan, is trying to harness the potential within native red grapes Pignolo and Schioppettino.

the variety's popularity, but after the Ramandolo Picolit garnered DOCG status in 2006, the variety has been revitalized. Today Picolit comes two ways: either crisp and dry or in a *passito* style with notes of hulled walnuts, dried apricot, ginger, and rose petals. Piculit Neri, the grape's red twin, makes a rare but delightful medium-bodied wine with accents of pepper and raspberry.

RECOMMENDED PRODUCERS: La Roncaia, Moschioni, Marco Cecchini, Ronchi di Cialla, Rocca Bernarda, Maurizio Zaccomer, Bastianich, Livio Felluga, Ermacora, Le Vigne di Zamò

PINOT GRIGIO
Even though it originated in Burgundy (where it goes by Pinot Gris), Pinot Grigio is one of Italy's most grown grapes. It is grown extensively in northern Italy, including Valle d'Aosta (where a local mutation is called Malvoisie) and in Trentino–Alto Adige (where best-selling Santa Margherita is made). It reaches some of its best expressions in the *ponca* and sandy soils of Friuli. Here the grape takes on a copper hue from darker skins, and vintners leverage the fruit in handcrafted wines, which vary in style from the honey-infused mountain-fresh Jesera from Venica & Venica to the rich oak-aged Dessimis from Vie di Romans.

RECOMMENDED PRODUCERS: Doro Princic, Scarbolo, Livon, Comelli, Zuani, Damijan Podversic, Villa Russiz, Roberto Scubla, I Clivi, Castello d'Albola, Albola, Lis Neris, Venica & Venica

RIBOLLA GIALLA
Phylloxera dealt Ribolla Gialla a blow in the nineteenth century, and it was on the decline before getting attention in the last few decades from winemakers who make white wines like red wines: aged on their skins. Ribolla Gialla's ground zero is Oslavia, a town near the Slovenia border, where Gravner makes amphora-aged wines. The grape itself has a burnt-orange color with defining tannins and acidity. When made in a more conventional style for white wines, its medium- to full-body texture—like the wines from Eugenio Collavini and Filiputti—offer a great Italian alternative for Chardonnay lovers.

RECOMMENDED PRODUCERS: Gravner, Radikon, La Castellada, Movia, Eugenio Collavini, Dorigo,

Filiputti, Schiopetto, Gradis'ciutta, Abbazia di Rosazzo, Cantarutti, Ronchi di Cialla

SAUVIGNON
There is hardly a wine-producing country that doesn't grow the French grape Sauvignon Blanc. In Friuli, where the grape is called Sauvignonasse or Sauvignon Vert, it can make extraordinary wines. When Sauvignon grows in poor, *ponca* soil in the Collio's prealpine climate, it sheds the more overtly herbal and grassy components normally associated with the grape and mellows, while still retaining its tropical aromas and acidity. Venica & Venica's famous Ronco delle Mele vineyard brings forth a Sauvignon that has a tart finish and notes of passion fruit and green apple. The elegant Sauvignon wines from Vie di Romans and Villa Russiz are also benchmarks for the region.

RECOMMENDED PRODUCERS: Vie di Romans, Venica & Venica, Ronco del Gnemiz, Villa Russiz, Schiopetto, Livon

VERDUZZO
The savory, honeyed *passito* wines made in the Ramandolo hills of the Collio offer a taste of historic Verduzzo, and pair well with blue cheeses. In the Friulian plains, however, the grape makes a drier, crisper wine that captures the grape's natural honey and apple flavors. Fulvio Bressan's dry, oak-aged, Verduzzo is a great match for delicate stuffed pastas, heirloom tomatoes, and meat dishes. While there are a few subvarieties cultivated, Verduzzo Friulano is the best for quality wine.

RECOMMENDED PRODUCERS: Bressan, Marco Felluga, La Tunella, Lis Neris, Dario Coos, Ronchi di Cialla, San Lorenzo, Specogna

VITOVSKA
The rare Vitovska grape grows along the limestone plateau of the Carso, and rarely anywhere else. In the glass, Vitovska emits delicate aromas of orange blossom, jasmine, and pear. There also can be a honeyed richness and tannic sturdiness that is unique for a white wine. Perhaps that's why Paolo Vodopivec, who produces a rich, amber-colored rendition of Vitovska, insists that the name derives from the term *vino od vitez*, Slovenian for

"wine of the knight." Edi Kante produces a more delicate perfumed Vitovska. It is a perfect match for the incredible seafood of the Adriatic.

RECOMMENDED PRODUCERS: Vodopivec, Edi Kante, Elena Parovel, Zidarich

SEE ALSO: Malvasia (page 14), Pinot Bianco (page 143)

PIGNOLO

Recognized by the pinecone shape of its grape bunches, Pignolo has grown in the Colli Orientali for centuries. Like most of Friuli's native red grapes such as Tazzelenghe and Schioppettino, the difficult-to-cultivate grape fell out of favor, and only recently have winemakers taken to revitalizing the variety. While early experiments with Pignolo could be overly austere, winemakers have learned to tame the grape's tannins by aging the wine in oak. Pignolo wines offer plenty of jammy, blackberry fruit balanced with pleasant tartness. As producers such as Moschioni, Le Vigne di Zamò, and Dorigo turn out bold, rich wine that can age ten years, the variety is fast becoming a rising star red in a white grape haven.

RECOMMENDED PRODUCERS: I Comelli, Le Vigne di Zamò, Moschioni, Gigante, Abbazia di Rosazzo, Bressan, Girolamo Dorigo, Walter Filiputti, Sant'Elena

REFOSCO

Sturdy and tannic Refosco grows in Colli Orientali del Friuli and in the Carso, where it is called Terrano. Local interest in this variety started in the 1980s, and some great renditions of aged Refosco are available today, especially from producers like Dorigo in Colli Orientali. (Dorigo grows Refosco dal Peduncolo Rosso, a subvariety with a reddish vine.) Most Refosco wines are deep purple to black in color, yet they also have delicate flavors of red plum, cardamom, and cinnamon.

RECOMMENDED PRODUCERS: Miani, Edi Kante, Girolamo Dorigo, Livio Felluga, Bastianich, La Roncaia, Le Vigna di Zamò

SCHIOPPETTINO

Thought to have originated in the Colli Orientali del Friuli, this grape was nearly extinct after the nineteenth-century phylloxera blight. Its existence today is due to the research into native grapes carried out at Abbazia di Rosazzo. Its name, which means gunshot or "little crack" in local dialect, reflects the burst of juice held within its small, thick-skinned black grapes. Some producers, like Bressan, make Schioppettino wines that resemble Cabernet Franc; others, such as Dorigo, produce it in a style that mimics the black pepper and blackberries of northern Rhône wines.

RECOMMENDED PRODUCERS: Bressan, Girolamo Dorigo, Ronco del Gnemiz, Petrussa, Le Vigne di Zamò, Antico Broilo

TAZZELENGHE

Native to the Colli Orientali, Tazzelenghe's elevated tannins and acidity are an accurate reflection of its name, which translates to tongue cutter in the local dialect. Like other local red grape varieties, Tazzelenghe fell into decline after the phylloxera blight of the nineteenth century. Recently, however, it has piqued the interest of a handful of Friulian winemakers, especially Girolamo Dorigo, who believes it has the potential as a long-aging wine. Tazzelenghe is a vigorous vine that produces thick-skinned grapes, yet it can be difficult to manage in the vineyard, requiring green harvesting (cutting away unripe grapes) to get grape bunches to ripen evenly. At least five years of aging are needed to soften the grape's tannins.

RECOMMENDED PRODUCERS: Dorigo, Beltrame, Conte d'Attimis-Maniago

Con Niente

NORTHEAST OF the Venetian lagoon, Friuli's Grado lagoon is a calm, shallow stretch of salt water. Its name-sake city, which was once part of the Venetian Republic, shares the architecture, colorful facades, and canals of Venice. But this is not a world of idle gondolas—Grado has more pluck and swagger. On a bright Saturday morning in the spring, ruddy fishermen had already finished cleaning squid in the Cooperativa Pescatori di Grado, the local fishing co-op that sends its catch directly through the back door of Zero Miglia, a restaurant serving seafood that has traveled "zero miles" before hitting the pan. This is a macho world, with a twist: Grado men fish during the day and cook at night—proudly, simply. One of my most memorable meals in Friuli came at the hands of one such fisherman.

Arriving dockside, I met red-cheeked Roberto Camotto, a local fisherman, by the side of the canal next to the fishing co-op. He had invited us to his *casone*, a simple fisherman's hut out on the lagoon accessible only by boat, where we were going to cook lunch. En route, we stopped to pull up traps of fresh seafood from the lagoon: *gamberetti* (tiny shrimp) no bigger than a finger and guppy-sized silver fish, all of which Roberto dumped into a cooler.

When we arrived at his *casone*, Roberto soaked the catch in salt water, explaining that this makes the fish rise to the top, the shrimp fall to the bottom. Then he got to work. From the beyond-rustic looks of his kitchen, a *casone* is the Grado version of the man cave. These traditional fishing huts, which dot the lagoon, are leased through the local government with terms that span generations. Yet it had everything Roberto needed: a stove, a pot for pasta water, a large sauté pan, a food mill, a stove-top espresso maker, and several mismatched glasses for when friends from nearby *casoni* stopped by for grappa. Soon a plate of lightly breaded fried shrimp landed on the well-worn picnic table. A bottle of Vodopivec Vitovska also appeared. Before long, I was churning out a paste of shrimp and tomato through a metal food mill. This would be our sauce for spaghetti. It was nothing more than shrimp and tomato, a few crumbled grissini, some coarsely chopped parsley. By the time the grappa came out, a few weathered gentlemen had arrived, settled into lawn chairs, and begun sharing jokes.

By the end of the meal, as a light breeze came off the calm lagoon, there was nothing to distract our attention from where we were in that moment; we were a captive audience. And although the meal was, as Roberto put it, *con niente*—of nothing, with nothing—it was more than I could have asked for. —MA

SPAGHETTI *with* Shrimp *and* Tomato Passatina

This is a pasta born from my experience of *con niente*, a meal created from nothing more than the few ingredients we managed to find around us. With this pasta, I've striven to recreate the simplicity of the meal we made at Roberto's *casone* on the lagoon. The shrimp—*gamberetti*—were simply cooked with tomato, then sent through a food mill, shells and all. This rich, pink sauce became the *condimento* for the store-bought spaghetti that Roberto had on hand.

SERVES 4 TO 6

extra virgin olive oil

150 grams • ½ yellow onion, finely diced

12 grams • 3 garlic cloves, minced

150 grams • 1 carrot, cut into ¼-inch pieces

454 grams • 1 pound shell-on raw baby shrimp

kosher salt and black pepper

a pinch of dried red pepper flakes

115 grams • ½ cup white wine

240 grams • 1½ cups canned tomatoes

50 grams • 4 breadsticks, like grissini, broken up

2 grams • 2 teaspoons chopped parsley

340 grams • 12 ounces fresh spaghetti (page 264) or dried

Heat a thin film of olive oil in a large, wide pot over medium heat. Stir in the onion and sweat until softened, 3 minutes. Stir in the garlic and sweat 1 to 2 minutes more until aromatic. Add the carrot and sweat until softened, 3 to 4 minutes.

Turn up the heat to medium-high, stir in the shrimp, and season with salt, pepper, and pepper flakes. Pour in the wine and bring to a simmer. Stir in the tomato and return to a simmer. Pour in 1 cup of water, lower the heat, and cook for 8 to 10 minutes or until the shrimp are soft enough to break up with a wooden spoon if pressed. Stir the broken grissini pieces into the pot, remove from the heat, and stir in the parsley.

Place a food mill fitted with a coarse plate over a clean pot. In batches, pass the shrimp and broth through the food mill. You will have a coarse paste. (If it's too dry to go through the food mill, stir in more water). Taste the shrimp paste and season with salt and pepper.

Bring a pot of salted water to a boil. Cook the spaghetti for 4 minutes if using fresh, and as directed on the package if using dry. Drain the spaghetti, reserving a cup of pasta water, and return the spaghetti to the pasta pot. Stir spoonfuls of the shrimp paste into the spaghetti until evenly coated, adding a few spoonfuls of water if the pasta looks dry, and simmer for one more minute before serving.

SARDINES *in* Saor *with* Peperonata Jam

Served at wine bars throughout Venice, *sarde in saor* is the classic Venetian version of Mediterranean *escabeche*: fish that is first fried, then soaked in a sharp marinade. I take guidance from tradition, incorporating saffron, coriander, and fennel—spices made common long ago in northern Italy when Venetian merchants controlled the spice trade—in the marinade. But rather than panfry the whole fish, I butterfly it, lightly searing the flesh side but leaving the skin alone. I also serve it skin side up, amplifying the dramatic look of the raw skin with basil leaves adhered with a lightly spiced vinegar gel.

The sweet-savory *peperonata* jam that accompanies the sardines can be served as a condiment for antipasti. To thicken the jam, I add powdered pectin, which is easy to find at grocery stores.

SERVES 4

Sardines

600 grams • 1 pound, 4 ounces (8 to 12) sardines, scaled, gutted, and butterflied

kosher salt

extra virgin olive oil

1 baby carrot, thinly sliced

3 white pearl onions, peeled and sliced crosswise into rings

1 gram • $1/2$ teaspoon toasted and crushed fennel seeds

1 gram • $1/2$ teaspoon toasted and crushed coriander seeds

a pinch of saffron

4 grams • 1 teaspoon sugar

60 grams • scant $1/4$ cup white balsamic or white wine vinegar

Peperonata Jam

400 grams • 2 sweet peppers (preferably 1 red and 1 yellow)

extra virgin olive oil

15 grams • 2 tablespoons minced red onion

kosher salt

2 grams • $1/2$ garlic clove, minced and smashed into a paste

15 grams • 1 tablespoon chopped capers

8 grams • 2 teaspoons sugar

30 grams • 3 tablespoons red wine vinegar

6 grams • $11/2$ teaspoons powdered pectin

Vinegar Gel

180 grams • $3/4$ cup water

4 grams • 2 teaspoons agar-agar (see page 276)

20 grams • 1 tablespoon plus 1 teaspoon sugar

20 grams • 2 teaspoons liquid glucose (see page 280)

4 leaves minced opal basil

a pinch of ground fennel

a pinch of ground coriander

a few drops of white balsamic or white wine vinegar

extra virgin olive oil

4 to 6 slices of country bread

1 garlic clove

flaky sea salt

10 to 15 small basil leaves

Season the flesh side of the sardines lightly with salt and set aside for 10 minutes to let the salt firm up the flesh. Pat dry. Heat a film of oil in a large sauté pan over medium-low heat. Working with one at a time, place a sardine flesh side down in the sauté pan and drag it across the pan. Repeat a couple of times until the flesh is lightly seared. Transfer the sardine to a platter, and repeat with the remaining fish.

Wipe the pan out and heat a fresh film of oil over medium heat. Sweat the carrot and onions with a pinch of salt until soft, about 3 minutes. Stir in the fennel, coriander, and saffron, turn the heat to low, and cook for a moment until the spices smell fragrant. Sprinkle in the sugar, turn off the heat, and pour in the vinegar. Swirl to combine, then pour into a long rectangular storage container. Lay the sardines flesh side down in the marinade. Cover and refrigerate for at least 2 hours or as long as 8 hours before serving.

To make the *peperonata* jam: Preheat the oven to 400°F and line a baking sheet with foil. Cut the peppers in half and coat lightly in olive oil. Place the peppers skin side down in the oven and roast until their skins have started to loosen, 15 to 20 minutes. When cool enough to handle, peel the peppers, discard the skins, seeds, and membrane, and finely dice.

Heat a film of olive oil in a pot over medium heat. Stir in the onion and sweat with a pinch of salt. Stir in the garlic and cook until aromatic, about 1 minute. Add the peppers, raise the temperature to medium-high, and season with a pinch of salt. Stir in the capers and sprinkle with 1¹/₂ teaspoons of the sugar. When the sugar has dissolved, pour in the vinegar. Mix the remaining ¹/₂ teaspoon of sugar into the pectin and stir it into the jam. Continue to cook until thick, about 2 minutes. You will have about 1 cup. Refrigerate until needed.

To make the vinegar gel: In a small pot over medium heat, whisk together the water, agar-agar, sugar, and glucose and bring to a simmer. Pour into a heatproof bowl and refrigerate until set, 5 to 7 minutes. Once set, scrape

into a food processor (a small one works better than a standard-size model). Blend with the basil, spices, and a few drops of vinegar. It will be tacky and thick. Transfer to a small bowl or small pastry bag and refrigerate until needed.

Brush olive oil on each slice of bread, then grill or broil until toasted and lightly charred. Rub each piece with garlic.

Drain the sardines (reserving the vegetables and marinade) and arrange on a platter. Drizzle olive oil over the top. Pipe or spoon a few small dots of gel onto the sardines, then press a basil leaf onto each of the gel dots. Sprinkle a pinch of sea salt over each sardine. Add the vegetables and some of the marinade around the fish. Spoon *peperonata* jam alongside and serve with the bread.

ASPARAGUS *with* Lardo-Wrapped Rye Dumplings, Goat Cheese, *and* Sprouting Greens

Asparagus is a harbinger of spring, helping to bridge the gap between the rich foods of late winter and the lighter fare that follows. In the snowy mountains of Friuli and the Veneto, it is an especially welcome vegetable. Asparagus shakes off the grip of winter, adding lightness to the table.

A few technical tips: Instead of peeling the asparagus, I push a pastry tip up the stalk, removing the tough green skin. The dumplings are like savory bread pudding that I poach in plastic wrap to give it an attractive shape. Tapioca maltodextrin, a modified food starch, turns ingredients like rendered fats and oils into a powder that melts on your tongue. Though optional, it adds visual and textural interest.

SERVES 6

Rye Dumplings

extra virgin olive oil

1 garlic clove, minced

kosher salt

2 grams • 1/2 teaspoon minced sage leaves

60 grams • 1/8 cup soffritto (page 282)

120 grams • 1 1/4 cups cubed pumpernickel bread

60 grams • 1 cup cubed pain de mie (white bread), crusts removed

92 grams • 6 tablespoons heavy cream

50 grams • 1 egg

Lardo

70 grams • 2 1/2 ounces lardo (page 221)

1 allspice berry

1 clove

1 juniper berry

kosher salt

black pepper

21 grams • 2 tablespoons tapioca maltodextrin powder (see page 283)

142 grams • 5 ounces fresh goat cheese at room temperature

60 grams • 4 tablespoons heavy cream

5 grams • 1 clove garlic confitura (page 279), chopped

a pinch of espelette pepper

1 gram • 1/4 teaspoon minced thyme leaves

1 gram • 1/4 teaspoon minced rosemary leaves

1 gram • 1/4 teaspoon minced sage leaves, plus 4 to 6 whole leaves

2 to 3 tablespoons unsalted butter

400 grams • 18 to 24 jumbo asparagus spears (3 or 4 per person)

kosher salt and black pepper

extra virgin olive oil

1 to 2 tablespoons lemon juice

6 quail eggs

about 1 cup buckwheat or sunflower sprouts

6 to 12 onion or calendula flowers (optional)

To make the dumplings: Heat a film of olive oil in a sauté pan over medium heat. Sweat the garlic with a pinch of salt until softened, 1 to 2 minutes. Add the sage, then stir in the soffritto. Cook until heated through.

Put the bread cubes in a medium bowl. Mix in the soffritto mixture and cool to room temperature. Whisk the cream and egg together. Pour over the bread and let the cream soak into the bread for 5 to 10 minutes. Stir the bread and cream together and season with a pinch of salt.

Extend a long piece of plastic wrap on a work surface. Shape half of the bread mixture into a 10-inch log and wrap in plastic around according to the instructions on page 272. Repeat with the remaining bread mixture. You should end up with two 10-inch logs about 3/4 inch in diameter. Tie each end with butcher's twine.

Prepare an ice bath. Bring a pot of water to a simmer. Poach the bread pudding in the plastic wrap for 20 to 25 minutes or until cooked through. Remove from the water and cool in the ice bath. Once chilled, refrigerate at least a few hours or overnight. When cool, slice the log into 3- to 4-inch dumplings and peel away the plastic wrap.

Cut the lardo into 3 paper-thin slices per serving, and set aside. Transfer any trimmings to a small pot and render it down over medium-how heat until melted (you'll want about 20 grams). Strain and cool to room temperature.

Meanwhile, grind together the allspice, clove, and juniper. In a small bowl, whisk together the spice blend, a pinch of salt, and few gratings of pepper, and the maltodextrin. Whisk in the rendered lardo and continue to whisk until the mixture forms a powder.

In a bowl, mix together the cheese and cream. Fold in the garlic confitura, espelette pepper, thyme, rosemary, and minced sage.

In a large sauté pan over medium-high heat, melt a pat of butter. Brown the dumplings on one side, turn over, and add the whole sage leaves. Cook until the dumplings are warmed through. Divide the dumplings among the plates. While they're still warm, wrap three pieces of lardo around each dumpling.

Trim off the dry ends of the asparagus spears (about 1 inch). With a paring knife, remove the spikes just below the asparagus tips (they can hold dirt). Push a pastry tip or small biscuit cutter up the base of the stalk to remove some of the fibrous skin. Meanwhile, bring a large pot of salted water to a boil. Blanch the asparagus for 2 to 3 minutes or until the stalks barely give when pressed. Season the asparagus with salt, pepper, olive oil, and lemon juice and divide among the plates.

In a sauté pan over medium heat, cook the quail eggs sunny-side up and season with salt and pepper. With a spatula, slide the eggs on top of the asparagus. Sprinkle the seasoned goat cheese over the top and dust with powdered lardo. Scatter sprouts and flowers across the plates. Drizzle more olive oil and lemon juice over the top to finish.

SQUID INK LINGUINE
with Braised Squid, Sea Urchin, Broccoli Crema, *and* Pan Grattato

This pasta reflects the sea, and changes as you eat it: the first bite could be briny, the next creamy, the next crunchy. Squid ink is mildly salty, complementing the inherent brininess of sea urchin. I prefer using frozen squid ink, though the shelf-stable kind does the trick in a pinch. Broccoli and squid both have mineral-rich flavors that also tie in well with sea urchin. While it is unusual to pair creamy béchamel with briny flavors, I find that the sauce's richness grounds the pasta and adds balance.

Soft, orange-hued sea urchin roe is a favorite ingredient both in Japan and throughout the Mediterranean where it is tossed in pasta. It is also abundant in California. You can find it at Japanese markets and wholesale fish markets. The delicate ingredient is best scooped onto the pasta right before serving. Pan grattato—sometimes called the poor man's Parmesan—is breadcrumbs toasted and sprinkled over pasta.

SERVES 6

Linguine

227 grams • 1 1/2 cups semolina flour
113 grams • 1 cup durum flour
2 grams • 1/2 teaspoon kosher salt
100 grams • 2 eggs
49 grams • scant 1/4 cup warm water
7 grams • 1 teaspoon squid ink

Squid

extra virgin olive oil
454 grams • 1 pound cleaned whole squid
kosher salt
8 grams • 2 garlic cloves, thinly sliced
a pinch of dried red pepper flakes
40 grams • 2 1/2 tablespoons white wine
266 grams • 1 cup juice from canned San Marzano tomatoes
280 grams • about 6 canned San Marzano tomatoes, sliced
4 grams • 1 teaspoon sugar
15 grams • 1 tablespoon capers, rinsed and drained
12 grams • 6 black olives, sliced off the pit
8 grams • 1 white anchovy, minced
black pepper

Broccoli Crema

140 grams • 2 cups small broccoli florets
33 grams • 2 1/2 tablespoons unsalted butter
38 grams • 1/4 cup all-purpose flour
208 grams • 3/4 cup whole milk
2 grams • 1/2 teaspoons kosher salt
a pinch of white pepper
1 nutmeg for grating

40 grams • 1/4 cup dried breadcrumbs
14 grams • 1 tablespoon extra virgin olive oil
a pinch of kosher salt
1 gram • 1/2 teaspoon lemon zest
22 grams • 1/4 cup half-inch broccoli florets
about 114 grams • 3 to 4 ounces sea urchin roe
5 to 8 mint leaves, thinly sliced

To make the linguine: In a stand mixer fitted with the paddle attachment, mix together the flours and salt. In a bowl, whisk together the eggs, water, and squid ink. With the mixer running on low speed, drizzle in the egg mixture. Mix the dough for 2 to 3 minutes, then turn it onto the counter and knead for several minutes; the dough will feel dry and firm. Flatten the dough into a rectangle, wrap in plastic wrap, and leave on the counter for 30 minutes to soften and hydrate.

Roll out the dough according to the instructions for laminated pasta on page 273. Cut the pasta into 12-inch sheets and dust with flour. Remove the pasta machine rollers and replace with the linguine cutters. (If you don't have linguine cutters, use the narrowest noodle cutters, or cut the pasta by hand. With one hand, feed the sheets through the cutter one at a time. As the noodles emerge from the cutter, catch them with your other hand. Shake the noodles loose from each other, place the nests on a lightly floured baking sheet and keep on the counter.

{continued}

To cook the squid: Heat a film of olive oil in a heavy-bottomed pot over medium heat. Season the squid lightly with salt and sear briefly. Add the garlic and sweat with a pinch of salt until softened, 1 minute. Return the squid to the pot and season with the pepper flakes. Let the red pepper flakes fry in the oil briefly, then pour in the wine. Simmer until the pan is nearly dry, then stir in the tomato juice and cover the pot. Reduce the heat to low and cook until the squid is nearly tender, about 25 minutes. Remove the lid and stir in the sliced tomatoes and sugar. Cook 10 to 15 minutes more on low heat. Stir in the capers, olives ,and anchovy and season with salt and pepper.

To make the broccoli *crema*: Prepare an ice bath. Bring a pot of water to a boil and season with salt. Blanch 2 cups of broccoli florets until tender, 1 to 2 minutes. Shock in ice water. Once chilled, drain well and finely chop. In a saucepan over medium heat, melt the butter. Stir in the flour and cook for 3 minutes. Before it starts to color, whisk in the milk and continue to cook, whisking constantly, until the sauce boils. Turn the heat to a low simmer and continue to cook for about 5 minutes. Season with salt, white pepper, and 6 gratings of nutmeg.

The sauce will be thick, but it will thin slightly when the broccoli is mixed in. Cover with a lid to prevent a skin from forming on the sauce. Keep warm.

In a small pan over low heat, mix the breadcrumbs with olive oil and toast, frequently stirring, until golden-brown. Remove from heat and season with a pinch of salt and lemon zest. Bring a large pot of water to a boil and season with salt. Stir in the pasta and cook until al dente, 3 to 4 minutes. In the last minute of the cooking time, add the raw broccoli florets. Drain, reserving about $1/2$ cup of cooking water. Return the pasta to the pot and add spoonfuls of the braised squid until the pasta is evenly coated. Warm the pasta and squid together, adding a splash of reserved cooking water if needed. Taste, adjust the seasoning, and add the sea urchin roe, breaking it up into the pasta.

Stir the blanched broccoli into the broccoli *crema*. Spread a spoonful of *crema* on each of 6 warmed plates. Pile the linguine mixture on top of the *crema*. Scatter pan grattato and mint on top to finish.

FARRO PASTA *with* Speck, Green Onions, *and* Poppy Seeds

The menu at Valter Scarbolo's La Frasca, an always-busy *osteria* in the middle of Friuli-Venezia Giulia, offers a quick study of the region's cultural influences. Poppy seeds, an ingredient used more often in Austria than in Italy, accent plates of pasta while sauerkraut is as natural on the menu as tagliatelle. Yet the ingredients are wholly local, down to the wheel of Montasio cheese used in *frico*, the ever-present crisps of cheese served in Friuli, and the platters of speck and prosciutto. In this Friuli-inspired dish, ridged noodles made with ground farro are a hearty backdrop for slices of speck and green onions in a buttery sauce.

SERVES 6

Pasta

300 grams • 2 1/3 cups 00 flour

200 grams • 1 3/4 cups farro flour or whole wheat flour

2 grams • 1/2 teaspoon kosher salt

200 grams • 4 eggs

115 grams • 1/2 cup butter

57 grams • 1/4 cup white wine

115 grams • 1/2 cup heavy cream

1 gram • 1 1/2 teaspoons poppy seeds

40 grams • 2 green onions, sliced thinly on an angle

83 grams • 3 ounces (1/2 cup) thinly sliced speck

kosher salt and black pepper

a block of grana padano for grating

To make the pasta: In a stand mixer fitted with the paddle attachment, mix together the flours and salt on low speed. Drizzle in the eggs and mix the dough for 2 to 3 minutes, then turn it onto the counter and knead for several minutes by hand; it will feel dry and firm. Flatten the dough into a rectangle, wrap in plastic wrap, and leave on the counter for 30 minutes to soften and hydrate.

Unwrap the dough and roll it out following the instructions for laminated pasta on page 273. Cut the pasta into 10-inch sheets and dust with flour. Lay the sheets on a work surface and, using a fluted pasta cutter or a knife, cut them into 1/2-inch-wide ribbons, and place on a lightly floured baking sheet until ready to cook.

With the butter and 2 tablespoons of water, make *burro fuso* according to the instructions on page 276; keep warm. In a large sauté pan with straight sides, bring the wine to a simmer over medium heat. Reduce until almost dry, then pour in the cream and reduce until the pan is nearly dry again. Mix in the *burro fuso* and keep warm. Bring a large pot of salted water to a boil. Cook the noodles for 5 to 6 minutes or until al dente. Drain pasta, return it to the pot, and pour in the sauce. Sprinkle with poppy seeds, green onions, and speck, and toss to combine. Season to taste with salt and pepper and grate cheese over the top. Divide the pasta among 6 warm plates and finish with more grated cheese over the top.

DUCK RAVIOLI *with* Sour Cherries *and* Candied Pecans

In addition to their meat, ducks offer something perhaps even more valuable: duck fat, which adds a fragrant sweetness to meat. Although it takes fat from several ducks to accumulate enough to cook with. You can also buy duck fat. After cooking with it, strain and refrigerate for future use. Since we buy whole ducks, we also get the rich duck liver, which adds complexity to the ravioli filling. If you are buying duck legs only, you can substitute with either chicken livers or foie gras. After the legs have been cooked, I like to pull off the duck skin and fry it until crisp. Then I chop it and either fold it into the filling or sprinkle it over the pasta right before serving. I also confit duck legs *sous vide* because it uses less fat. To do so, heat an immersion circulator to 155°F. Vacuum seal duck legs with cold duck fat and cook for 2½ to 3 hours (see page 271).

SERVES 4 TO 6

Duck

100 grams • ¾ cup kosher salt, plus extra for seasoning

42 grams • ¼ cup brown sugar

10 black peppercorns

4 allspice berries

2 star anise

8 sprigs thyme

3 sprigs rosemary

8 grams • 2 garlic cloves, smashed

525 grams • 1 pound, 2 ounces (3 or 4) duck legs

330 grams • 2 cups duck fat

65 grams • 4½ tablespoons softened unsalted butter

80 grams • ⅓ cup soffritto (page 282)

8 grams • 2 tablespoons chopped mint

8 grams • 3 tablespoons chopped parsley

30 grams • ⅛ cup chopped dried sour cherries

70 grams • 2½ ounces (½ cup) chopped duck liver

40 grams • ⅛ cup grated Asiago

black pepper

Ravioli

250 grams • 2 cups 00 flour

2 grams • ½ teaspoon kosher salt

100 grams • 2 eggs

9 grams • 2 teaspoons water

Candied Pecans

25 grams • ¼ cup chopped pecans

15 grams • 1 tablespoon simple syrup (page 281)

kosher salt

24 grams • 2 tablespoons red verjus (see page 283)

12 grams • 1 tablespoon red wine

12 grams • 1 tablespoon water

12 grams • 1 tablespoon sugar

1 star anise

45 grams • ¼ cup pitted sour cherries (fresh or brandied)

14 to 28 grams • 1 to 2 tablespoons softened unsalted butter

12 sage leaves

kosher salt and black pepper

To make the duck: In a large bowl, mix together the salt, sugar, peppercorns, allspice, star anise, 4 sprigs of thyme, 2 sprigs of rosemary, and 1 garlic clove. Coat the duck legs with this cure and sprinkle an even layer of the cure in a nonreactive food storage container. Tuck the duck legs into the cure and top with the remaining cure. Refrigerate for 2 hours. Remove the duck from the cure, rinse, and pat dry.

Preheat the oven to 300°F. Heat the duck fat in a heavy-bottomed pot or Dutch oven over medium heat until melted and translucent. Nestle the duck legs into the pot and add the remaining 4 sprigs of thyme, sprig of rosemary, and garlic clove. Cook over medium heat for 5 minutes, then cover and transfer to the oven. Confit the legs for 2½ to 3 hours or until tender when pierced with a fork. Remove from the oven, uncover, and cool for 1 hour. Pick the duck meat from the bones and skin. (Save the skin to fry and mix into the filling, if desired. Discard the bones.) Strain the duck fat, cool, and save for another use. Cut the duck meat into ½-inch pieces and place in a medium bowl. Mix in the butter, followed by the soffritto, mint, parsley, and dried cherries. Carefully fold in the duck liver and cheese. Taste and adjust the seasoning with salt and pepper if necessary. Refrigerate until needed. You will have just over 2 cups of filling.

To make the ravioli: In a stand mixer fitted with the paddle attachment, mix together the flour and salt on low speed. In a bowl, whisk together the eggs and water. With the mixer running on medium speed, drizzle in the egg mixture. Mix the dough for 2 to 3 minutes, then turn the dough onto the counter and knead by hand for several minutes; it will feel dry and firm. Flatten the dough into a flat rectangle, wrap in plastic wrap, and leave on the counter for 30 minutes to soften and hydrate.

Unwrap the dough, and roll out according to the instructions for laminated pasta on page 273. Lay the sheets out on the counter and punch out 3-inch rounds, using as much of the pasta surface area as possible. Lightly flour the rounds and stack them. (At this point, the pasta rounds can be stored in a covered container.) Gather up the remaining trim and reroll through the machine to yield a total of about 50 rounds.

Fill a few ravioli at a time. Lay a few rounds down on a work surface. With a spray bottle, lightly mist the pasta with water. Add a spoonful of duck filling to the center of each ravioli round. Cover the filling with another round and seal the edges, expelling as much air as possible by running your fingertips gently around the filling as you pinch the edges together. Place the filled pasta on a baking sheet lightly dusted with flour.

To make the candied pecans: Preheat the oven to 325°F. Line a baking sheet with parchment paper. Mix the pecans in a bowl with the simple syrup and a pinch of salt. Distribute the nuts on the baking sheet and bake until toasted, and slightly shiny, 20 to 25 minutes.

In a small pot over medium heat, simmer the verjus, wine, water, sugar, and star anise together until reduced slightly, 1 to 2 minutes. Stir in the cherries. Cool to room temperature. Discard the star anise before serving.

Bring a large pot of salted water to a boil. Add the ravioli and cook until al dente, 3 to 4 minutes. While the pasta cooks, melt the butter in a large sauté pan over medium heat. Swirl in the sage leaves and cook until the butter just begins to brown. Using a slotted spoon, lift the ravioli from the pasta water and slide into the butter. Season the pasta with salt and pepper and toss until evenly coated in the brown butter.

Divide the ravioli among 4 to 6 warmed plates. Spoon the brown butter and sage leaves over the top. Drizzle a few cherries in syrup over the ravioli, followed by a grating of cheese and a sprinkling of candied pecans.

CHOCOLATE TORTA
with Vanilla Mascarpone

This chocolate *torta* is decadent, but it is not too sweet. The filling is essentially the same as a flourless chocolate cake—chocolate, butter, eggs—and very little sugar. Mascarpone adds richness; mixed with yogurt it also brings freshness to the plate.

This *torta* is made in one 10-inch tart shell; you can also use six individual tartlet shells. Since the *torta* will need time for the chocolate to set up, plan on making the dessert well before you intend to serve it. The bit of liquid glucose keeps the ganache pliable, even after it has cooled. Without it, the ganache hardens substantially. For a bright accent, I like to garnish this *torta* with dehydrated strawberries. They're easy to make in a food dehydrator or 175°F oven: Slice the strawberries 1/8 inch thick, lay them on a silicon baking sheet, sprinkle them with sugar, and dehydrate for about four hours until they are as pliable as fruit leather.

SERVES 8 OR MORE

Crust

200 grams • scant 1 1/2 cups all-purpose flour

35 grams • 1/8 cup cocoa powder

1 gram • 1/4 teaspoon kosher salt

113 grams • 8 tablespoons unsalted butter, softened

57 grams • 1/2 cup confectioner's sugar

25 grams • 1/2 whisked egg (use remaining half in the filling)

Filling

170 grams • 6 ounces bittersweet chocolate

170 grams • 12 tablespoons unsalted butter

57 grams • 1/4 cup crème fraîche

1 gram • 1/4 teaspoon kosher salt

30 grams • 1/4 cup sugar

75 grams • 1 1/2 eggs (use the 1/2 egg left over from the crust)

1 gram • 1/4 teaspoon coffee extract

Ganache

113 grams • 1/2 cup heavy cream

10 grams • 1 teaspoon liquid glucose

113 grams • 4 ounces bittersweet chocolate, chopped

coarse sea salt

Vanilla Mascarpone

150 grams • 1/2 cup mascarpone

100 grams • 1/4 cup heavy cream

50 grams • 1/8 cup whole milk yogurt

15 grams • 1 tablespoon sugar

1/2 vanilla bean

dried strawberries, to garnish

To make the crust: In a medium bowl, sift together the flour, cocoa powder, and salt. In a stand mixer fitted with the paddle attachment, mix together the butter and confectioner's sugar on medium speed until light and smooth. Stir in the 1/2 egg. On low speed, stir in the dry ingredients until the dough just comes together. Pat the dough into a 6-inch disk, then cover and refrigerate until chilled, at least 1 hour and up to 4 days.

On a lightly floured work surface or between two sheets of parchment paper, roll the disk into a 13-inch round. Drape the round over and into a 10-inch tart pan. Gently press the dough into the bottom of the pan, trying not to stretch it to make it fit. (If the round is too small, remove it from the pan and roll it out a little more). The dough is delicate, so handle it carefully and work with it while it's cold. Fold the overhanging dough into the sides of the pan so the sides are thicker than the bottom. With a paring knife, trim away any excess dough on the sides and refrigerate for 15 minutes.

Preheat the oven to 350°F. Bake the crust for 10 to 15 minutes or until it just starts to set. Cool completely before pouring in the filling.

To make the filling: Preheat the oven to 275°F. Melt the chocolate and butter in separate bowls. In a mixing bowl, whisk the chocolate and butter together, then whisk in the crème fraîche and the salt, then the sugar, eggs, and coffee extract. Pour the filling into the prebaked crust and bake for about 20 minutes or until the edges begin to set. (You do not want the center to be completely set.) Cool to room temperature.

To make the ganache: In a small pot, bring the cream and glucose to a simmer. Put the chocolate in a heatproof bowl. Pour the hot cream over the chocolate and stir until smooth. Pour the ganache over the torta and sprinkle with a few pinches of sea salt. Let set for about 1 hour.

To make the vanilla mascarpone: In a bowl whisk together the mascarpone, cream, yogurt, and sugar. Using the tip of a spoon, scrape out the seeds from the vanilla bean and stir them into the mascarpone. (Reserve the vanilla bean for another use.)

Slice the *torta* into serving portions. Spoon a dollop of mascarpone on top of each serving. Garnish with dried strawberries.

VIA CLAUDIA AUGUSTA—
TRENTINO–ALTO ADIGE

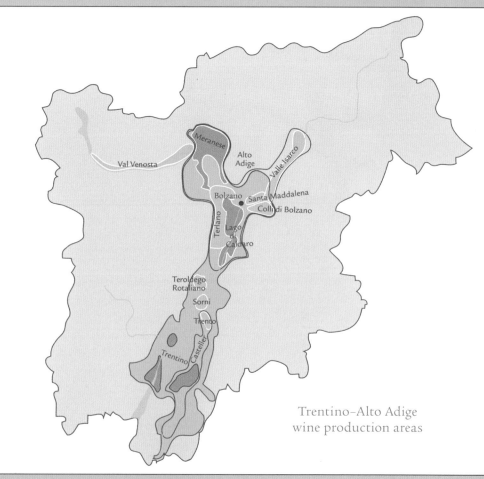

Trentino–Alto Adige
wine production areas

VIA CLAUDIA AUGUSTA—
TRENTINO–ALTO ADIGE

When driving across the border from Austria into Italy's alpine Trentino-Alto Adige region, you need to keep a firm grip on the steering wheel. Here the autobahn merges with the *autostrada*, and there's not a lot of room for timid drivers. On one of my trips, I marveled at how German and Italian speedsters wound around mountainsides, skimmed across bridges, and plunged through tunnels with apparent ease, while for me every turn seemed to bring a rush of adrenaline. It was like surfing, but instead of waves, we were riding the Brenner Pass, a historic mountain passage turned modern highway.

The Brenner Pass provides a crucial link between northern and southern Europe. It has existed, in one form or another, since the second century, yet it wasn't the first mountain crossing in the area. The Roman road Via Claudia Augusta, which stretched from the Po Valley to Germany, beat it by nearly two centuries. (It still exists today, more often trafficked with cyclists and hikers than cars and trucks.) No matter the route taken into the region, however, there is little risk of missing the breathtaking scenery. Trentino-Alto Adige borders the Dolomites to the east and the Alps to the north. Most of the region is mountainous, with the notable exception of the Adige Valley, which runs down its center. Insulated from colder northern air by the mountain ranges and warmed by the Ora winds from the south, the valley was once a haven for prehistoric humans. Today it is a productive agricultural area. Apple orchards blanket the valley floor while vineyards flourish on the hillsides. In the summer, it turns into a cyclist's paradise, with bikes moving *en masse* along the apple roads.

The climate so favorable to apples also benefits grapes. Historically Trentino-Alto Adige vintners put more emphasis on red grapes than white, with light red Schiava (also called Vernatsch) the most planted variety. Yet lately favor has shifted strongly toward white grapes. Both Alto Adige in the north and Trentino in the south have a diverse selection of white grapes. In Alto Adige, winemakers deftly juggle German grapes like Gewürztraminer, Kerner, and Veltliner with Sauvignon and Pinot Bianco (which is also called Weissburgunder here). Farther south in Trentino, Müller-Thurgau and the local Nosiola grape make memorable wines in both dry and *passito* styles. Both sides put out buckets of Pinot Grigio—some of it memorable, some of it less so. But taken all together, the white wines of Trentino-Alto Adige are as diverse as heritage apples: some are crisp and flinty, others fragrant and mildly spiced. In Alto Adige, the cool, sunny climate, long growing season, and volcanic porphyry and limestone soils produce grapes with high levels of acidity. As a result, some of Alto Adige's white wines taste astonishingly fresh, even after a few decades of aging.

Red wines in the region are also experiencing a revival. While Schiava plantings are down, the variety is evolving into a more refined style, especially when the fruit comes from the Santa Maddalena hills northeast of Bolzano. The same area is revered for the native red grape Lagrein. The alluvial soils of the valley floor around Bolzano—where temperatures in the summer can soar higher than anywhere else in Italy—is ideal for ripening the plummy, slightly bitter native grape. South of Bolzano in the northern corner of Trentino, significant

improvements have been made with the local Teroldego grape as well, which is starting to generate interest in the wine community as a grape variety on the rise. And Marzemino, a lighter red grape, produces a refreshing cherry-like tart wine—the perfect picnic wine.

Bordeaux grapes have also found footing in Trentino, most notably at Tenuta San Leonardo, a historic estate in the small town of Avio along the Adige River. Once a monastery, it is now owned the noble Gonzaga family. With the aid of Giacomo Tachis, the same enologist who created Toscana's famous Sassicaia wine, the Gonzaga family released its Bordeaux blend in the early 1980s. To me, Tenuta San Leonardo is exceptionally elegant, with accents of cocoa nibs, black currant, and black cherries. Trentino also excels at producing classic-method (Champagne-style) sparkling wines with Pinot Noir and Chardonnay. A tried-and-true producer in the area is Ferrari, a winery founded by Giulio Ferrari in 1902 in Trento and now run by the Lunelli family.

Trentino–Alto Adige isn't a culturally homogenous mix of apples and wine, though. Trentino, the southern half, feels like Italy; Alto Adige was part of Austria's Tyrol state until after World War I (it is just as often called Südtirol—South Tyrol), and some of the locals feel only remotely linked to Rome. The culture shift—in language and in architecure—is evident as soon as you leave Trentino. Yet both Italy and Austria are represented at the table. Spaetzle and *canederli*, dumplings made with old bread and flour, are served, but so is polenta and pasta. Cured pork, especially speck, and braised beef make frequent appearances, while both lard and olive oil are used for cooking. And baked apples are eaten everywhere.

My longtime friend Martin Foradori, who runs the J. Hofstätter winery south of Bolzano in the Alto Adige town of Termeno, embodies this hybrid identity. While he was growing up, his mother, Sieglinde Oberhofer, spoke German to him, while his father, Paolo Foradori, spoke Italian. Both sides of the family were fluent in winemaking. The Hofstätter winery was started by Martin's great-uncle, Josef Hofstätter, and later was run by his father, who was the first in the area to start bottling wine instead of shipping it in tanks. South of Bolzano in Trentino, his cousin Elisabetta Foradori makes some of region's best Teroldego at her namesake winery.

Martin, who took over operations in 1997, has maintained J. Hofstätter's reputation as an innovator in the region. His round-the-clock work ethic and exacting nature seem to be Germanic, but his pride in his wine feels *cento per cento* Italian. J. Hofstätter consistently is singled out for making two of Alto Adige's best wines: Pinot Nero Barthenau Vigna Sant'Urbano and Gewürztraminer Kolbenhof. Barthenau is often described as one of Italy's standout examples of Pinot Noir. (The grape has grown in Alto Adige since the nineteenth century.) But because Pinot Noir is produced in so many corners of the world, it's Kolbenhof that shows true regional identity. Made from burnt-orange, fragrant Gewürztraminer grapes, Kolbenhof strikes an elegant balance among aroma, minerals, and acid. Somewhat unusual for Gewürztraminer, it is also bone-dry on the finish.

While most of Alto Adige's winemaking occurs south of Bolzano, interest is growing in the Venosta and Isarco valleys north of Bolzano, where the altitude is higher, the climate cooler, and the terrain steeper. On my visit to the Isarco Valley, I met Brigitte Pliger and her sheep dog at a gas station. After a friendly greeting, she beckoned me to follow her Volkswagen van up the hillside to Kuenhof, the estate that Brigitte runs with her husband, Peter. The couple are dedicated to Sylvaner, Veltliner, and Riesling. With vines grown organically at altitudes ranging from 1,800 to 2,300 feet above sea level, the Kuenhof wines demonstrate pure, steely renditions of each grape. Kuenhof Sylvaner is flinty, with orange blossom and pear notes, while the Veltliner and Riesling manage to integrate iron and acidity into floral and spicy flavor notes. The high levels of acidity in all of the Pligers' wines not only allow them to age but also enable them to pair well with a range of foods, from asparagus with speck to braised pork with *mostarda*.

Just south of the Alto Adige around the Trentino city of Mezzocorona, the terrain flattens out into the stony, alluvial plains of the Campo Rotaliano. This soil, warmed by heat-absorbing rocks in a dry riverbed, is home to the native Teroldego grape. In the 1980s, the deep purple, moderately tannic grape was subjected to industrial farming, yielding forgettable wine. This changed once Martin's cousin Elisabetta Foradori decided to prove that the grape deserved more attention. Taking over the estate in 1985 after her father died unexpectedly, Elisabetta began revitalizing Teroldego by choosing better clones. Instead of singling out vines that were the most vigorous, as had been done in the past, she selected vines that produced the best fruit. In the meantime, she gradually turned over her vineyard to biodynamic farming.

Her efforts have brought forth two outstanding wines made with the grape. Teroldego Rotaliano, the less expensive of the two, is earthy and fresh, with a bright, acidic finish. Granato, which is aged in oak barrels, tends to be more peppery, savory, and reserved. I think of the two Teroldego wines as the Trentino version of Rosso Montalcino and Brunello del Montalcino—the former is to be consumed while the latter ages in the cellar. Elisabetta has not stopped at Teroldego, though. She also makes a natural white wine with Nosiola. Grapes are left on their skins to ferment and macerate for eight months in terra-cotta amphora vessels, akin to the style used for the wines of Josko Gravner in Friuli-Venezia Giulia.

As privately owned wineries, J. Hofstätter, Kuenhof, and Foradori are outliers in Trentino–Alto Adige, a region in which the majority of production comes from co-operatives. Yet here—especially in Alto Adige—co-ops are quality leaders, producing wines that are not only technically proficient but also expressive of place. Names like Terlano, San Michele-Appiano, and Abbazia di Novacella make some of the area's most recognizable wines. One of my most memorable Alto Adige moments came from tasting a wine from Abbazia di Novacella, one of the oldest continually operating wineries in the world, with wine production dating back to 1142. The wine was made with Kerner, a hybrid of Riesling and Schiava grapes. Yet its taste was a revelation, emitting a delicate balance of fruit, with a lean backbone and zesty finish.

In Alto Adige, co-ops often buy from growers who farm less than a hectare of land, and as a result, the vines tend to be looked after. The objective for the co-ops—rather, for co-ops and independent producers alike—has never been about quantity over quality, for good reason: they can't compete in volume. Trentino–Alto Adige's output of nearly 30 million gallons of wine made annually, while not insignificant, is dwarfed by neighboring Veneto's 220 million gallons. Give thanks to that gorgeous alpine terrain and all of those apple orchards for limiting this region's land for vines. But more importantly, thank the co-ops that maintain high-quality standards, the aristocratic producers who continue their wine heritage, and the small operations that take chances on overlooked grapes. In Trentino–Alto Adige, winemakers are some of the most progressive in Italy, and they are dedicated to maintaining a healthy approach to growing grapes, not only for the vines but also for the community. —SL

White Grapes

GEWÜRZTRAMINER
Although it's unlikely that it originated there, Gewürztraminer takes its name from the Alto Adige town of Termino (Tramin, in German). One of the oldest grapes in the species *Vitis vinifera*, Gewürztraminer is said to be the progenitor of Cabernet Franc and Pinot Noir, though it shares few characteristics with its offspring. When grown in the limestone-rich soils of Alto Adige, Gewürztraminer exhibits the distinctive aromas of lychee, rose petal, and honeysuckle as well as clove. Unlike Gewürztraminer produced in Alsace, Italian versions are made crisp and dry in most cases, except for *vendemmia tardiva*—late harvest—style.

RECOMMENDED PRODUCERS: Elena Walch, J. Hofstätter, Terlan, Tiefenbrunner, Nussbaumer

KERNER
Developed in the 1920s as a cross between Riesling and the local red Schiava grape, Kerner was loved primarily for its high yields. Yet over time, winemakers in Alto Adige learned how to tease nuance out of this hybrid grape. At small, biodynamic Niklas winery in the village of St. Nikolaus, Dieter Sölva and his father make Kerner with an incredible piercing acidity made with fruit harvested from Alto Adige's the oldest Kerner vines. Kerner from Niklas is world-class, full of Bartlett pear, green almond, grapefruit, lime, and flinty pencil lead.

RECOMMENDED PRODUCERS: Abbazia di Novacella, Cantine Valle Isarco, Kofererhof, Niklas

MÜLLER-THURGAU

A German hybrid developed in the late nineteenth century, Müller-Thurgau was once the most planted grape in Germany. In Alto Adige, Müller-Thurgau thrives on the steep hillsides and cooler climates, yielding light, crisp wines. Yet when it is grown on the high plateau of Fennberg, the grape becomes more complex. The flagship Müller-Thurgau, Feldmarschall von Fenner, from Tiefenbrunner, has refined aromas of sage, marjoram, and white flowers.

RECOMMENDED PRODUCERS: Alois Lageder, Elena Walch, Köfererhof, Muri-Gries, Terlan, Tiefenbrunner, Widmann

NOSIOLA

Nosiola may just surprise us all and emerge as Trentino's most interesting local grape. Once grown throughout the region, its plantings are now concentrated to the Valle dei Laghi and the hills above Trento and Pressano. Nosiola has a hazelnut or green walnut flavor. While it tends to yield light wines when aged in stainless steel, it can turn rich when aged in oak. Winemaker Elisabetta Foradori has been experimenting with a natural Nosiola wine fermented and macerated on the grape skins in amphorae then aged in acacia-wood casks. The method produces an exquisite balance of the pure fruit with savory flavors.

RECOMMENDED PRODUCERS: Elisabetta Foradori, Pojer e Sandri, Endrizzi

PINOT BIANCO

The Italian term for Pinot Blanc, Pinot Bianco grows throughout northern Italy, including in Lombardia where it is used in Franciacorta's sparkling wines. As a still wine, it comes into its own in the prealpine hills of Alto Adige (where it's also called Weissburgunder). Co-ops like Terlan have shown that Pinot Bianco ages astonishingly well. The temperature fluctuations between night and day and the altitude encourage the grapes to retain a substantial amount of acidity without diminishing any richness.

RECOMMENDED PRODUCERS: Terlan, J. Hofstätter, Niedrist, St. Michael-Eppan, Andriano, Colterenzio, Cortaccia, Alois Lageder, Sölva & Söhne, Nals Margreid

RIESLING

Widely planted in Alto Adige, Riesling grows throughout the Adige Valley. These wines tend to be closer in style to Austria than Germany, and they also have higher levels of alcohol than most German Riesling. Alto Adige Riesling offers sweet notes of apricot, Granny Smith apple, and guava balanced by racy acidity.

RECOMMENDED PRODUCERS: Kuenhof, Köfererhof, Castel Juval, Franz Pratzner, Eastine, Valle Isarco

SEE ALSO: Pinot Grigio (page 117), Sauvignon (page 117)

SYLVANER

Some may raise an eyebrow at the idea that Sylvaner can make good wine. But in Alto Adige, it is gaining traction for quality. Most of the vines planted at Abbazia di Novacella—the oldest continuously operated winery in Italy—are Sylvaner. The Pligers, the couple behind Kuenhof wines, sold their grapes to Abbazia di Novacella until 1990, when they started producing their own wine. Their lean, racy Kuenhof Sylvaner has since garnered the prestigious Tre Bicchieri award. The light straw color of wines made with Sylvaner is deceptive: within the glass there is a world of white peach, mandarin, wild baby greens, and minerality. Taken together, they make for complex, lively food pairings.

RECOMMENDED PRODUCERS: Abbazia di Novacella, Cantine Valle Isarco, Köfererhof, Kuenhof, Pacherhof, Garlider

VELTLINER

Being so close to the border of Austria, it would make sense that Veltliner in Alto Adige would be synonymous with Grüner Veltliner, but it's unrelated. With cardamom, white pepper, green bean, and key lime, and a stark minerality and verve, Veltliner complements acidic and grassy vegetables, like asparagus that grow wild in the Dolomites and the *mostarda* found in many dishes.

RECOMMENDED PRODUCERS: Kuenhof, Köfererhof, Nössing, Cantine Valle Isarco, Pacherhof, Garlider, Strasserhof, Hoandlhof

Red Grapes

LAGREIN

Rooted in the Alto Adige province of Bolzano, bright, spicy Lagrein rarely grows elsewhere. Even within the region, it is not widespread. Yet its lack of vineyard plantings belies how well the grape has taken to Bolzano's gravelly, sandy soils and blistering summers. When ripe, the grapes are nearly black in color, foreshadowing the flavors in the wine, which exhibits blackberries, blueberries, red currants, leather, and iodine. A well-made glass of Lagrein exhibits a wonderful balance of fruit and earth, whether it's made to be mineral-rich, like Niklas Lagrein, or in a firm, Bordeaux-like style Steinraffler from J. Hofstätter. Lagrein is generally best after aging in oak, which gives the tannins time to integrate, but there are also stylish, slightly herbaceous *rosato* (rosé) Lagreins that showcase flavors of raspberry and cherry tomatoes.

RECOMMENDED PRODUCERS: Alois Lageder, Elena Walch, J. Hofstätter, Muri-Gries, Niedrist, Niklas, Terlan, Tiefenbrunner, Waldgries, Scuro Mirell

MARZEMINO

Versa il vina! Eccellente Marzemino! That's how Mozart started his opera *Don Giovanni*. Grape geneticists connect Trentino's Marzemino with the region's other native red, Teroldego, but Marzemino is much lighter. Late-ripening Marzemino produces a medium-bodied, cheerful wine that expresses accents of red cherry, strawberry, and cinnamon. It grows just south of Trento, and in Veneto where it used as a blending grape.

RECOMMENDED PRODUCERS: De Tarczal, La Cadalora, Terre di Gioia

PINOT NERO

Pinot Nero—Italian for Pinot Noir—is a difficult grape to grow in Italy. With a few notable exceptions (like the Mancini Pinot vineyard on the coast of Le Marche, Pinot Nero is mostly grown in Italy's northern regions—in Trentino and neighboring Lombardia for sparkling wine production and Alto Adige for still wines. On the western side of the Adige Valley, the grape has adapted well to the porphyry soils, climate, and sun exposure. Pinot Nero offers great depth of fruit and complexity, whether it is

meant to be consumed young, like cranberry-hued, sage-accented Krafuss from Alois Lageder to the ageworthy Barthenau Vigna S. Urbano from J. Hofstätter, a wine rich with red currants, raspberry, and cedar.

RECOMMENDED PRODUCERS: Alois Lageder, Colterenzio, Cantina Tramin, J. Hofstätter, Terlan (still); Ferrari, Letrari, Balter, Altemasi Graal (sparkling)

SCHIAVA

Although it has ceded some ground to Lagrein, for centuries Schiava (also called Vernatsch or Trollinger) has been one of Alto Adige's most grown grapes. The vigorous vine's fruit mostly makes everyday wines, but when planted around Santa Maddalena and Lake Caldaro, where it has grown since the thirteenth century, it produces wines that have boosted the profile of the variety. With minimal tannins, pleasant acidity, and fruit character, Schiava is best consumed within three years of bottling.

RECOMMENDED PRODUCERS: Cantina Santa Maddalena, Castel Sallegg, Niedermayr, Nusserhof, Cantina di Caldaro, St. Michael-Eppan, Terlan, Widmann

TEROLDEGO

Teroldego thrives around the commune of Mezzocorona, especially in Campo Rotaliano. The grape was all but forgotten until the 1980s, when Elisabetta Foradori took an interest in the native vines on her property and raised the variety's profile. Teroldego reaches its apex with Foradori's inky, rich Granato Teroldego, which can age for ten years or longer and match Syrah's intense color and tannins. Not all Teroldego is meant to be aged, however. It also lends itself to fresh, spicy wines that don't require a special occasion to pour. In general, Teroldego wines exhibit ripe red plums, licorice, juniper, and blackberries.

RECOMMENDED PRODUCERS: Elisabetta Foradori, Endrizzi, Cavit

Natural Fusion

GEOLOGICALLY the Adige Valley is remarkable. The cliffs on one side of the valley are red, the other side stark white—and it's a kind of metaphor for the cultural change that occurs when you travel from Trentino to Alto Adige. Road signs change from Italian to German; lederhosen, beer, and bratwurst coexist alongside pasta.

But even the pasta here is different, hearty with butter and speck rather than olive oil and tomatoes. I found that in Alto Adige, Germanic influences added additional layers of sharpness to dishes—tang from sauerkraut, heat from *mostarda*, the piquant Italian fruit preserve. In the dead of winter, when the Dolomites are covered in snow, strong flavors like mustard and horseradish are meant to warm you from the inside, bringing a rush of blood to your head. These elements seem necessary to balance the richness of sausages, potatoes, and braised pork and beef dishes.

Seeing elements from Austria and Germany on the menus in Alto Adige made me think about the broader cultural influences that impact food all over Italy, from the French and Swiss dishes recreated in Valle d'Aosta and Piemonte to the Arab spices and citrus used throughout Sicily. Cooking anywhere is a collection of ideas and sensibilities. Like our translation of Italian food in America, the greatest infuence on cuisine tend to be geographic. —MA

CHILLED ASPARAGUS SOUP *with* Meyer Lemon Yogurt *and* Fish Roe

Chilled soups are a great way to start a springtime meal. Asparagus grows well in both northern Italy and northern California, and its appearance indicates that other fresh, green produce—spring garlic, baby leeks, peas—will soon follow. I mix Meyer lemon juice with yogurt, which I then lighten by placing it in a canister charged with compressed gas, the same device used for whipped cream. This heightens the flavors and allows the yogurt to float on top of the light soup. But a spoonful of yogurt will taste just as good. For a briny finish: American sturgeon caviar, salmon roe, or trout roe.

SERVES 4 TO 6

Asparagus Soup

800 grams • 1 pound, 12 ounces asparagus

kosher salt

126 grams • 4 cups spinach or nettles

40 grams • 2 cups Italian parsley

extra virgin olive oil

300 grams • 1 yellow onion, thinly sliced

140 grams • 1 leek, white and light green part only, sliced thinly crosswise

65 grams • 2 stalks spring garlic, minced

700 grams • 3 cups heavy cream

black pepper

Meyer Lemon Yogurt

3 grams • 1 sheet gelatin (see page 279)

155 grams • 2/3 cup heavy cream

250 grams • 1 cup whole-milk plain yogurt

57 grams • 1/4 cup Meyer lemon juice

22 grams • 1 1/2 tablespoons extra virgin olive oil

kosher salt

extra virgin olive oil

1 lemon for zesting

kosher salt

28 grams • 1 ounce fish roe of your choice

To make the soup: Prepare an ice bath. Trim the tips and ends off the asparagus stalks, discarding the ends and reserving the tips. Slice the remaining stalks into 1/2-inch-thick disks. Bring a large pot of salted water to a boil. Blanch the asparagus tips (not the stalks) until al dente, 1 to 2 minutes. With a slotted spoon, remove the tips and plunge into the ice bath. Chill completely. Refrigerate until ready to serve.

In the same pot, blanch the spinach and parsley until soft, 1 to 2 minutes. Using a slotted spoon, remove the greens and plunge into the ice bath lined with a mesh strainer. When cold, remove them from the ice bath and squeeze out the excess water.

Heat a film of olive oil in a wide pot over medium-low heat. Gently sweat the onion, leek, and spring garlic, taking care not to caramelize them, about 3 to 5 minutes. Stir in the asparagus and cook until softened. Turn off the heat and pour in the cream and add the blanched greens. Season with salt and pepper. In a blender, purée the soup until smooth. Be patient—it will take a few minutes. With a rubber spatula, push the purée through a fine-mesh strainer, extracting as much liquid as possible. Chill the strained soup over an ice bath. (If the soup seems thick, add a couple of tablespoons water or cream.) Once cold, taste the soup and season with salt if needed. You should have about 6 cups. Refrigerate until ready to serve.

To make the yogurt: Soak the gelatin sheet in ice water for about 2 minutes or until softened. In a small pot, bring the cream to a simmer and remove from heat. Squeeze out any excess water from the gelatin and dissolve it in the cream. Let cool to room temperature. In a bowl, whisk together the yogurt, lemon juice, and a pinch of salt. Whisk in the cream and refrigerate until ready to serve. If using a canister, pour in the yogurt and charge the canister; shake well and refrigerate.

Pour the soup into 4 to 6 chilled bowls. In a bowl, dress the asparagus tips with olive oil and grated lemon zest. Season with a pinch of salt and toss until evenly coated. Place a small pile of dressed asparagus into the center of the bowls. Float a dollop of yogurt on top, then garnish with a spoonful of roe.

MUSTARD SPAETZLE
with Chanterelle Mushrooms *and* Stridoli

Spaetzle is a forgiving recipe. Designed to drip into a pot of boiling water, it's not supposed to look uniform. An inexpensive spaetzle maker, in which you guide the batter across a set of holes, is a dependable way to control the size of the spaetzle. I also like to use another method common in northern Italy: I spread a thin layer of batter across a cutting board and then shave it into ribbons with a palette knife into a pot of simmering water. Spaetzle is hard to overcook—an extra minute here or there won't make much of a difference. Even so, I recommend shocking it in ice water after boiling to rinse off any excess starch. This lessens the chances of pieces sticking to the pan when browning. I serve the spaetzle with chanterelle mushrooms as an accent. *Stridoli*, a lemony, wild mountain green, offers a foil to the richness of the spaetzle and mushrooms. A few small farmers in northern California have started cultivating *stridoli*, but if it is unavailable, sorrel or baby spinach can be used instead.

SERVES 6

Spaetzle

430 grams • 2 cups yogurt

300 grams • 6 eggs, lightly beaten

30 grams • 1 egg white

30 grams • 2 tablespoons whole grain mustard

16 grams • 1 tablespoon Dijon mustard

300 grams • 2$\frac{1}{3}$ cups all-purpose flour

2 grams • $\frac{1}{2}$ teaspoon kosher salt

1 gram • $\frac{1}{4}$ teaspoon black pepper

extra virgin olive oil

300 grams • 10$\frac{1}{2}$ ounces (about 3 cups) chanterelles, sliced lengthwise into 4 to 6 pieces each

kosher salt and black pepper

2 tablespoons unsalted butter

1 green onion, sliced into thin rounds, white and light green parts only

75 grams • 2 cups stridoli or baby spinach leaves

a block of grana padano for grating

To make the spaetzle: Prepare an ice bath. In a large bowl, combine the yogurt, eggs, egg white, and mustards. Sift in the flour in three additions, whisking until smooth between additions. Stir in the salt and pepper and let the batter rest at least 10 minutes or up to 6 hours in the refrigerator.

Bring a large pot of salted water to a boil. Oil 2 baking sheets. Fill the well of the spaetzle maker with a small ladleful of batter, hold the spaetzle over the pot, and slide the batter over the holes into the water. Let the spaetzle bob to the surface and cook for another minute or two. Using a skimmer or slotted spoon, lift the spaetzle out of the pot and plunge into the ice bath. Repeat until all of the batter is used. Spread the spaetzle on the prepared baking sheets and coat lightly with olive oil. You will have about 6$\frac{1}{2}$ cups.

To cook the mushrooms: Heat a thin film of olive oil in a large sauté pan over high heat until almost smoking. Scatter the chanterelles in an even layer and sear without moving them until they begin to brown, about 1 minute. Give the pan a stir, season with salt and pepper, and drain on paper towels.

Heat a thin film of olive oil in a large sauté pan over high heat. (If the pan isn't hot enough, the spaetzle will stick.) In uncrowded batches, brown the spaetzle until golden. Swirl in a pat of butter, season lightly with salt, and drain on paper towels. Repeat until all the spaetzle is browned.

Return the spaetzle to the pan and add another pat of butter. Stir in the chanterelles and green onion and toss to combine. Right before serving, wilt the *stridoli* into the spaetzle. Divide the spaetzle among 6 warmed plates. Finish with a generous grating of grana padano.

RYE GNOCCHI *with* Savoy Cabbage, Potatoes, *and* Crispy Speck

With potatoes, caraway seeds, and *burro fuso*, this is a rich mountain dish with German influences. For a contrast to the soft, rich potatoes and gnocchi, I stir in sliced cabbage cooked with speck. Like the gnocchi I make with semolina flour (page 34), here I turn to *pâte à choux*, the same dough used to make éclairs and cream puffs. The protein in the eggs helps hold together the rye flour, which is low in gluten. To make the gnocchi, I pipe the batter in pieces directly into boiling water and then cook them until the gnocchi float to the surface.

SERVES 4 TO 6

Rye Gnocchi

155 grams • ²/₃ cup water

88 grams • 6 tablespoons unsalted butter

kosher salt

75 grams • ³/₄ cup rye flour

43 grams • ¹/₃ cup all-purpose flour

150 grams • 3 eggs

20 grams • ¹/₃ cup grated grana padano

370 grams • 13 ounces (about 12 small) fingerling potatoes

kosher salt

10 black peppercorns

2 parsley stems

1 thyme sprig

370 grams • 13 ounces (1 head) savoy cabbage

extra virgin olive oil

100 grams • ¹/₃ cup plus 1 tablespoon unsalted butter

4 grams • 1 garlic clove

140 grams • ¹/₂ yellow onion

black pepper

12 ounces (12 slices) speck

about 1¹/₂ cups blended oil (see page 278)

10 caraway seeds

57 grams • ¹/₄ cup white wine

a block of grana padano for shaving

To make the gnocchi: In a medium pot, bring the water and butter to a boil. Add a few pinches of salt and stir in the flours. Cook over medium heat, stirring constantly with a wooden spoon, until the dough has thickened and turns slightly shiny, about 2 minutes. Transfer the dough to a stand mixer fitted with the paddle attachment and mix on low speed for 1 minute so the dough cools slightly. Turn the mixer to medium speed and add the eggs one at a time, mixing well between each addition. On low speed, mix in the grana just until incorporated. Transfer the batter to a pastry bag fitted with a medium tip.

Bring a large pot of salted water to a boil. Oil a large baking sheet. With one hand, position the pasty bag over the water. Holding a butter knife in your other hand, slowly pipe out the batter, cutting it into 1-inch pieces as it comes out of the pastry bag, and let the pieces fall into the water. Poach the gnocchi for about 2 minutes after they bob to the surface. Using a skimmer or slotted spoon, scoop up the gnocchi and spread them in a single layer on the baking sheet to cool. Repeat in batches until all the gnocchi batter is cooked. If not serving in a few hours, cover the gnocchi with plastic wrap and refrigerate. You should have 4¹/₂ cups of gnocchi.

To make the potatoes: Put the potatoes in a medium pot and cover with about an inch of water. Bring the pot to a simmer over medium heat, then season with a few pinches of salt. Mix in the peppercorns, parsley, and thyme and cook until the potatoes are cooked through but not falling apart, about 15 minutes (they should yield to pressing like a ripe avocado). Remove the pot from the heat and let the potatoes cool in the cooking water. Once cool, drain the potatoes, peel if you like, and slice into ¹/₄-inch coins.

While the potatoes cook, prepare the cabbage. Discard the outer leaves. Cut out the core and separate the head into individual leaves. Cut out the thick vein that runs

{continued}

through the center of the leaves, then slice the leaves into 2-inch pieces.

Heat a thin film of olive oil in a high-sided medium pot over medium heat, then add 1 tablespoon of the butter. Once the butter has melted, stir in the garlic and cook until slightly soft, 1 minute. Stir in the onion, season lightly with salt, and sweat gently until soft, about 3 minutes. Mix in the cabbage, season lightly with salt and pepper, and cook, adding a splash of water to the pan to prevent the bottom from scorching, for about 5 more minutes. Chop 2 slices of the speck, stir it in, and cook until warmed through, about 1 minute. Taste, seasoning with salt and pepper if needed. Remove the garlic clove and discard. Keep the cabbage warm.

With the remaining 1/3 cup of butter and 2 tablespoons of water, make *burro fuso* according to the instructions on page 276; keep warm.

In a medium pot, heat the blended oil to 350°F. Tear the remaining 10 speck slices in half or in quarters and fry, keeping pieces from overlapping or folding, until crisp, about 20 seconds. Using a skimmer or slotted spoon, drain the speck chips on paper towels and season with pepper.

Heat a thin film of olive oil in a large sauté pan over medium-high heat. Sear the gnocchi on all sides, swirling the pan occasionally, until lightly golden. Lower the heat to medium-low and add the caraway seeds. Remove the pan from the heat and pour in the wine. When the wine has finished sputtering, return the pan to the heat and stir in the cabbage and potatoes.

Cook until warmed through, then add some of the *burro fuso* and toss to combine. If the pan looks dry, add more *burro fuso* until the gnocchi and cabbage looks glossy and evenly coated. Taste and season with salt and a few grindings of pepper if needed.

MUSHROOM RISOTTO

Risotto is best when made and then immediately served. Cooking risotto from start to finish takes a while. I rarely serve it in restaurants because it's hard to get the timing right. Yet the place where I ate risotto the most happened to be in a restaurant. When I worked for chef Antonello Colonna in Labico, we ate risotto for our staff meal—sometimes more than a few times a week. When made with just enough broth, risotto should spread on the plate *all'onda*, like a wave crashing on the shore and gently spreading. As long as you monitor the consistency of the rice as it cooks, it is not difficult to achieve *all'onda*. There are a few varieties of risotto rice to choose from; I prefer Vialone Nano, a short-grain variety that yields a creamy risotto. The broth for the risotto is made from the mushroom trimmings (mainly stems) remaining from the mushrooms in the risotto. The addition of fermented black garlic at the end reinforces earthiness of the mushrooms.

SERVES 4 TO 6

300 grams • 11 ounces mixed foraged and cultivated mushrooms, such as chanterelle, black trumpet, oyster, and yellowfoot

400 grams • 1 1/2 yellow onions

100 grams • 1 small carrot, diced

30 grams • 1/2 celery stalk, diced

50 grams • 1 3/4 ounces (1 1/2 cups) dried porcini

3 sprigs thyme, 1 whole, and leaves picked from remaining 2

8 cups water

extra virgin olive oil

kosher salt

250 grams • 1 cup Vialone Nano rice

50 grams • scant 1/4 cup Marsala

100 grams • scant 1/2 cup white wine

15 grams • 1 head fermented black garlic, cloves peeled and minced

1 block grana padano for grating

black pepper

15 to 30 grams • 1 to 2 tablespoons unsalted butter

Clean, trim, and slice the mushrooms into even-sized pieces, saving stems and trimmings for the broth. Chop ³/₄ onion coarsely for the stock and finely chop the remaining ³/₄ onion for the risotto.

To make the broth: In a dry pot over medium heat, sweat the coarsely chopped onion, carrot, and celery until slightly softened, about 3 minutes. Add the mushroom trimmings and continue to cook until the mushrooms begin to release water. Pour in the dried porcini, then add a sprig of thyme and the water. Bring to a simmer and cook for 50 minutes, then turn off the heat and keep warm.

Heat a thin film of olive oil in a large, heavy-bottomed pot over medium heat. Stir in the finely chopped onion and sweat until softened, about 3 minutes. Stir in the sliced mushrooms and a pinch of salt and cook until the mushrooms start to soften, about 2 minutes. Add the rice and toast, stirring, until the grains start to look translucent around the edges, about 1 minute. Pour in the Marsala and white wine and simmer, stirring often, until the pot is nearly dry, about 5 minutes.

Ladle the broth through a strainer into the pot in three increments, cooking the risotto until nearly dry between each addition. Once the rice has a firm texture but no crunch, adjust the quantity of broth until the risotto self-levels—spreads on its own if spooned on a plate. Stir in the black garlic, grate about ¹/₄ cup of grana padano over the pot, and finish with pepper, a drizzle of olive oil, and a pat or two of butter. Taste, seasoning with more salt and pepper if needed. Divide the risotto among 6 shallow bowls. Shave more grana padano over each portion and sprinkle with thyme leaves.

BEER-BRAISED PORK CHEEKS *with* Escarole

Pork cheeks are an inherently rustic cut excellent for braising. They become very tender after cooking for just a few hours. For this recipe, I take an equally rustic approach. To enhance the natural pork flavor, I season and marinate the cheeks in beer the day before braising them. Polenta is a classic match for the rich braised meat; see baked polenta (page 226) or buckwheat polenta (page 190).

SERVES 6

740 grams • 1 pound, 10 ounces (10 to 12) pork cheeks

kosher salt and black pepper

40 grams • ¼ cup Wondra flour

extra virgin olive oil

150 grams • ½ yellow onion, sliced

150 grams • 1 carrot, sliced into disks

100 grams • 2 celery stalks

12 grams • 3 garlic cloves, smashed

12 grams • 1 tablespoon plus 2 teaspoons smoked paprika

680 grams • 2 (12-ounce) bottles amber beer

960 grams • 4 cups brown stock (page 283)

4 grams • 1 garlic clove, thinly sliced

a pinch of dried red pepper flakes

340 grams • 12 ounces (1 head) escarole, cored, leaves sliced

3 slices bacon, diced into lardons

170 grams • 6 ounces baby vegetables (any combination of
    carrots, cippollini onions, turnips, or celery) trimmed, peeled
    if necessary, and cut to the same size (about 1½ cups)

sea salt

Trim the cheeks of any visible silver skin. Pat dry, season with salt and pepper, and dredge in Wondra, shaking off any excess. Heat a film of olive oil in a large pan over medium-high heat. Sear the cheeks until evenly caramelized on all sides. (You may need to do this in two batches.) In a large storage container or bowl, season the onion, carrot, celery, and garlic with the paprika and a pinch each of salt and pepper. Nestle the seared cheeks into the vegetables and cover them with the beer. Cover the container and refrigerate overnight.

Preheat the oven to 300°F. Strain the beer into a pot and transfer the cheeks and the vegetables to a Dutch oven. Bring the beer to a simmer and cook for 10 minutes, skimming the surface to remove impurities and coagulated proteins.

Strain the beer broth into the Dutch oven and pour in the stock. Bring to a simmer over medium heat, until barely simmering, then cover and transfer to the oven. Braise for 2½ to 3 hours or until the cheeks yield when pressed but aren't falling apart. Let cool for 2 hours in the braising liquid. Skim away any fat from the top of the cooled braising liquid and put the cheeks in a roasting pan. Strain the liquid and discard the vegetables. Transfer the liquid to a pot and reduce by one-third to one-half to intensify the flavor. Strain and pour back over the pork cheeks.

Heat a film of olive oil in a pot over low heat. Sweat the garlic and red pepper flakes until the garlic barely begins to brown. Stir in the escarole, increase the heat to medium, and cook until the escarole wilts and becomes tender, about 4 minutes. Season with salt. In a sauté pan over medium heat, render the bacon lardons for about 2 minutes. Add a splash of olive oil, increase the heat to medium, and mix in the baby vegetables. Sauté until the vegetables are al dente and glazed in bacon fat and oil, then season with salt and pepper.

Preheat the oven to 300°F. Place the pan with the pork cheeks on the stove top and warm over medium heat, transfer to the oven for 25 to 30 minutes, basting the pork cheeks every 8 to 10 minutes to lightly glaze them.

In the center of each of six serving bowls, place a spoonful of escarole. Place two cheeks over the escarole and spoon some of the braising liquid over the cheeks. Top with the baby vegetables. Garnish with a drizzle of extra virgin olive oil, sea salt, and black pepper.

VENISON LOIN *with* Parsnips *and* Huckleberry Vinaigrette

Sometimes a recipe can transport you. The feel of this dish conjures a visit to the Italian Alps, a place where meat and game rule menus and evergreens dominate the landscape. On the plate, sweet parsnips and huckleberry vinaigrette give way to the distinct flavor of venison loin. A spritz of Douglas fir hydrosol, an unexpected touch, evokes the woods. I buy whole sides of venison, which allows me to cook the meat on the bone, and also use trimmings to make venison ragù (page 85).

SERVES 4 TO 6

Venison Loin

100 grams • ⅓ cup balsamic vinegar

100 grams • ½ cup red wine

150 grams • ½ onion, diced

12 grams • 3 garlic cloves

2 bay leaves, crushed

1 rosemary sprig

15 black peppercorns

4 juniper berries

1000 grams • 1 pound, 8 ounce venison loin, trimmed, or 2 pounds, 4 ounces bone-in venison, trimmed

Parsnip Purée

265 grams • 9 ounces (about 3) parsnips, peeled and diced

227 grams • 1 cup water

240 grams • 1 cup heavy cream

10 grams • 2 teaspoons kosher salt

30 to 45 grams • 2 to 3 tablespoons unsalted butter

Vinaigrette

40 grams • ⅓ cup fresh or frozen huckleberries

30 grams • 3 to 4 blackberries

16 grams • 4 to 5 raspberries

1 egg yolk or 1 gram xantham gum (page 283)

12 grams • 1 tablespoon minced shallot

11 grams • 1 tablespoon Dijon mustard

17 grams • ⅛ cup red wine vinegar

16 grams • 1½ tablespoons sugar

65 grams • ⅓ cup canola oil

4 grams • 1 teaspoon kosher salt

extra virgin olive oil

kosher salt

Douglas fir branches for roasting (optional)

150 grams • 5 ounces (about 1) parsnip, peeled and cut on the bias

230 grams • 8 ounces (10 to 16) small cipollini onions, blanched and peeled

1 or 2 juniper berries, crushed and chopped finely

coarse sea salt and finely ground pepper

1 tablespoon butter

Douglas fir hydrosol (optional, see page 65)

onion or chive flowers (optional)

To make the marinade: In a small pot, simmer the balsamic vinegar until it has the consistency of syrup. Let cool completely. In a large bowl, whisk together the wine and balsamic vinegar. Mix in the onion, garlic, bay leaves, rosemary, peppercorns, and juniper berries. Coat the venison in the marinade, cover, and refrigerate for 2 hours.

To make the parsnip purée: In a medium pot, mix together the parsnips, water, cream, and a pinch of salt over medium-high heat. Bring the mixture to a simmer, then lower the heat to low, cover, and cook until the parsnips are falling apart, 10 to 15 minutes. Pour the parsnips and half of the cooking liquid into a blender and purée until smooth. If the purée looks dry, add a little more cooking liquid. Blend in a few pats of butter and taste, adjusting with more salt if needed. The purée should be very smooth and creamy, but not soupy.

{continued}

To make the vinaigrette: In a blender, combine the huckleberries, blackberries, raspberries, egg yolk or xantham gum, shallot, mustard, vinegar, and the sugar. Blend together briefly, then drizzle in the oil while the blender is running. Season with salt.

Preheat the oven to 350°F. Remove the venison from the marinade and pat dry, discarding the marinade. Coat the venison in olive oil and season with salt and pepper. In a sauté pan over high heat, sear the venison on all sides, then place on a roasting pan lined with Douglas fir branches and transfer to the oven. Roast until the venison is medium-rare, 10 to 12 minutes for loins and 30 to 40 minutes for saddle, and an internal temperature of 130–135°F. Let the meat rest for 5 to 10 minutes.

In a large sauté pan over medium heat, sauté the parsnips in olive oil until the edges start to caramelize, about 5 minutes. Stir in the onions and cook until lightly caramelized and heated through, about 10 to 15 minutes. Swirl in a pat of butter and season with salt and pepper.

To serve, slice the venison loin crosswise into 1/4-inch-thick pieces. Serve with the parsnip purée, huckleberry vinaigrette, and vegetables. Mix a few pinches of coarse salt with the juniper berries and sprinkle over the venison loin. Spritz with hydrosol and finish with onion blossoms.

RICOTTA BAVARESE *with* Verjus-Poached Rhubarb, Orange Confitura, *and* Powdered Olive Oil

While Italy generally is known for taking a restrained approach to dessert, in Alto Adige, with its Germanic influences, sweets are more decadent. A Bavarian cream of custard and whipped cream is a prime example of a Tyrolean treat. This one tastes light, with a fresh sweet-tart accent from the rhubarb and candied orange. While not essential, the powdered olive oil is a simple, modern twist that brings out the oil's floral flavor without an oily texture. You'll need to keep a double boiler simmering to prepare three different elements of the *bavarese*. I chill the cream in individual molds, then serve it with a crunchy crust made with biscotti crumbs. Since you can hold the *bavarese* in the freezer for a few days before serving, it's a good make-ahead dessert.

SERVES 8

Ricotta Bavarese

275 grams • 2 cups drained ricotta (see page 281)
175 grams • ³/₄ cup sour cream
3 grams • 1 sheet gelatin (see page 279)
57 grams • ¹/₄ cup orange juice
1 lemon for juice and zest
50 grams • 1 egg
80 grams • ¹/₃ cup sugar
230 grams • 1 cup heavy cream
¹/₂ teaspoon vanilla paste
a pinch of kosher salt
150 grams • 1 cup crushed biscotti (page 64)
50 grams • ¹/₄ cup brown sugar
112 grams • ¹/₂ cup melted butter

Rhubarb

150 grams • ³/₄ cup sugar
113 grams • ¹/₂ cup water
57 grams • ¹/₄ cup red verjus (see page 283)
200 grams • 7 ounces rhubarb, cut on an angle into ¹/₄-inch pieces (about 2 cups)

Orange Confitura

1 orange
100 grams • ¹/₂ cup sugar
55 grams • ¹/₄ cup water

Powdered Olive Oil

15 grams • 1 tablespoon tapioca maltodextrin powder (see page 283)
8 grams • 1 tablespoon confectioner's sugar
a pinch of kosher salt
19 grams • 1 tablespoon plus 1 teaspoon extra virgin olive oil

1 lemon for zest

To make the *bavarese*: In a heatproof bowl over a pot of barely simmering water (ensure that the water doesn't touch the bottom of the bowl), whisk together the ricotta and sour cream until most of the ricotta curds are broken up and the mixture is smooth. Remove the bowl but keep the pot of water simmering.

Soak the gelatin sheet in ice water until softened. Place a new bowl over the pot of simmering water and add the orange juice and 1 tablespoon of lemon juice. Squeeze out any excess water from the gelatin and stir it into the orange juice mixture until dissolved. Remove from the heat. Place a third bowl over the pot of simmering water and whisk the egg and 2 tablespoons of the sugar until light and frothy, 3 or 4 minutes. Remove the bowl from the heat and turn the pot of water off.

In a stand mixer fitted with the whisk attachment, whip the cream, the remaining sugar, and the vanilla paste until the cream holds medium peaks when the whisk is removed. Stir the orange juice mixture into the ricotta, then gently fold in the whipped cream and the whisked egg. Grate lemon zest directly into the bowl and stir to combine. Pour the bavarese into eight 4-ounce ramekins or 8 large silicone muffin cups, cover tightly, and freeze overnight.

Preheat the oven to 325°F. In a food processor, blend the biscotti to fine crumbs. Pulse in the brown sugar, then drizzle in the butter and pulse to combine. Press into a thin layer on a parchment-lined baking sheet and bake for 8 to 10 minutes or until set. Cool completely, then break into chunks.

To make the rhubarb: In a medium pot, bring the sugar, water, and verjus to a simmer over medium heat. Stir in the rhubarb, lower the heat, and poach until the rhubarb just starts to soften, 2 to 3 minutes. Strain the poaching liquid and set aside the rhubarb. Return the poaching liquid to the pot and cook until slightly syrupy, 5 to 8 minutes. Pour over the rhubarb and let cool. Refrigerate until needed.

To make the *confitura*: Using a vegetable peeler, peel away the orange zest in strips. Blanch the strips in boiling water for 2 minutes and then rinse under cold running water until cool, about 2 minutes. Dab the blanched strips dry and slice into slivers. Segment the orange: With a paring knife, cut between the white pith to release the orange segments. In a small saucepan, bring the sugar and water to a boil over medium-high heat. Turn to a low simmer and add the zest slivers and poach until tender and lightly candied, 6 to 8 minutes. Cool the zest in the syrup and refrigerate until needed.

To make the powdered olive oil: In a small bowl, whisk together the tapioca powder, confectioner's sugar, and salt. Whisk in the olive oil and mix until a waxy powder forms. This will take a few minutes. Keep covered tightly at room temperature for up to two weeks.

For each serving, unmold the *bavarese* into a chilled bowl. Spoon the poached rhubarb and some of its syrup over the top. Garnish with crushed biscotti, a few pieces of orange zest and segments. Add a dusting of powdered olive oil on the side and grate lemon zest over the top to finish.

VIA AEMILIA—
EMILIA-ROMAGNA
AND LOMBARDIA

Emilia-Romagna
wine production areas

Colli Piacentini
Parma
Colli di Parma
Reggiano
Salamino di
Santa Croce
Colli di Scandiano
e di Canossa
Sorbara
Modena
Gasparosa
di Castelvetro
Reno
Bologna
Colli
Bolognesi
Bosco Eliceo
Sangiovese di
Romagna
Albana di Romagna
Pagadebit di
Romagna
Rimini

Lombardia wine
production areas

Valtellina
Valcalepio
Franciacorta
Garda
Cellatica
Milano
Brescia
Botticino
Capriano
del Colle
Lugana
Garda Colli
Mantovani
San Colombano
al Lambro
Pavia
Mantova
Oltrepò Pavese
Lambrusco Mantovano

VIA AEMILIA—EMILIA-ROMAGNA AND LOMBARDIA

Women have made wine in Italy for a long time, but not always with the same kind of recognition as they do today. As estates are handed down to younger generations, daughters are now filling the ranks of the family business. Some develop a knack for running a cellar, others for running the entire business. Elena Pantaleoni is one of the talented women who have opened the doors for the next generation of women in Emilia and beyond.

Elena runs biodynamic La Stoppa in the gently rolling hills of Colli Piacentini. She modestly tells me that many women now make wine in this western corner of Emilia south of Piacenza, but this only goes to show how La Stoppa's influence has spread through the local winemaking community. Bordering the Oltrepò Pavese DOC in Lombardia, Colli Piacentini produces similar wines. Yet as an estate dedicated to making natural wines, La Stoppa is a standout. In 1973, the Pantaleoni family took over the century-old winery, which historically had focused on French varieties. Elena joined the family business in 1991 and took over operations in 1997. Today she works with winemaker Giulio Armani to hone the estate's singular style. While La Stoppa makes Bordeaux-style wines such as a smoky Cabernet, as well as a couple of rich blends of Barbera and Croatina , it's Elena's dedication to Malvasia di Candia aromatica—the primary grape in La Stoppa's Ageno—that has catapulted her into the pioneering realm of natural wines.

The calcareous soils and warm climate of Colli Piacentini are ideal for Malvasia di Candia aromatica, an ancient strain of Malvasia thought to have originated in Crete. Malvasia grows all over northern Italy, and its renditions made in Emilia vary widely. They can be crisp, dry, and floral. Or they can be aromatic sparklers—some are even nicknamed *champagnino* for a display of yeasty aromatics. Camillo Donati, a winery outside of Parma, makes a sparkling Malvasia that is as refreshing as a cold beer, with natural yeasts that impart a malty, almond character to each glass. Ageno, however, is altogether different. Inspired by the farmhouse tradition in which red and white wines were made in the same way—left to macerate on the skins before fermentation—it resembles the amphorae wines in Friuli-Venezia Giulia. To make the wine, Malvasia, Trebbiano, and Ortrugo grapes are left on their skins for about a month, a process that extracts tannins, curbs Malvasia's natural sweetness, and amplifies aromas while imparting the wine with a deep amber hue. Then the wine takes a contemporary turn, being aged in a combination of stainless steel and used *barrique* barrels. The result: an unfiltered, savory wine with a nose of dried flowers. It is also an unusually versatile food wine, effortlessly able to transition from sea urchin to braised pork in the same meal.

That a wine can complement a meal is nothing new in Italy, but perhaps nowhere else is it more important than in Emilia-Romagna, a place defined by food. The wealthy north-central region counts not only prosciutto di Parma and Parmigiano-Reggiano as its own but also leads the country in pasta manufacturing and *aceto balsamico* production. Even its capital city, Bologna, is emblematic of a rich bowl of ribbon-like noodles glazed with a meaty, slow-cooked ragù. I was not surprised when

I learned that the historic term of endearment for the city is La Grassa, the fat.

Yet when it comes to the local wines, there is still a lot left to study. It is not because wine from Emilia-Romagna is rare. With more than 166 million gallons produced in 2011, the region had the third largest output in Italy after Veneto and Puglia. A common complaint is that these wines taste like they could have been made anywhere. Yet anonymous wines are no longer driving the Emilia-Romagna story. Producers are learning how to reinterpret terroir in meaningful ways. And with pioneering estates such as La Stoppa, Emilia-Romagna's overlooked wine industry offers a lot to get excited about.

What's less clear is just how winemakers will define the region's styles. Emilia-Romagna offers an extremely broad collection of wines. Most of its DOCs resemble Russian nesting dolls: open one up and you'll find several more versions beneath the surface. DOC subzones (like the Colli Piacentini's Gutturnio, for instance) range from wines made with several grapes to wines made with a single variety. They can be still or sparkling, and they can vary in sweetness, from *asciutto* and *secco*, bone dry and dry, to *amabile*, semisweet, and *dolce*, sweet. And yet they all fit snugly inside the same DOC.

Also at issue is the region's hybrid wine identity. Even though the two halves of the region are married through history—nearly every important city in Emilia-Romagna arose along the ancient Via Aemilia route, and Emilia itself was named after the road—they are culturally distinct from one another, and so are their wines. Sangiovese and Albana are the calling cards of the hills of Romagna. Emilia also has hills, but the Po River plains, where miles of pergola-trained vines thrive, cover half of it. These plains are the main source of fruit for Lambrusco, the most famous wine of the region.

In preindustrial times, Lambrusco became effervescent naturally when it refermented in the bottle or cask. Depending on how it fermented, the wine could be dry, sweet, or somewhere in between. But in the 1970s and 1980s, sweet won out and producers hit export-market pay dirt with a style more poised to compete with Coca-Cola than with other wines. After spending the past few decades exiled to bulk production, however, Lambrusco is regaining attention from wine lovers. This is due in part to the staunch devotion to Lambrusco in Emilia, where the wine is served everywhere, from local cafés to top-flight restaurants like Osteria Francescana in Modena. Meanwhile, growing interest in salumi in America has boosted popularity for the wine, whose fizzy acidity is tailored to cut through porcine richness.

It's fun to get excited about Lambrusco. It fizzes on contact with the glass, creating a pink, beer-like head. When sipped, it prickles pleasantly on the tongue while an undercurrent of acidity tames its berry flavors. Purple Lambrusco is only one option; I also like to pour *rosato* and white Lambrusco by the glass at SPQR to demonstrate the range that exists within this style.

If Emilia feels at times like an extension of Lombardia, the same can be said for Romagna and Toscana. Like its southern neighbor, Romagna's primary grape is Sangiovese. As the quantity of Bordeaux blends produced here increases, it may only be a matter of time until parts of Romagna rival Toscana's coastal Bolgheri growing area. Even the environment—the rolling hills, the maritime climate, the cypress trees—feels more like central Italy than like the regions north of the Po. Yet Romagna also has its own traditions, such as Albana di Romagna.

Grown for centuries around the Bertinoro hills, the Albana vine arrived in Romagna from the Colli Albani, a cluster of hills outside of Rome. Like many of Italy's classic white wines, Albana's modern reputation has been less than gilded. Even though the robust wine was upgraded to a DOCG in 1987—the first white wine to earn the promotion—many grumbled its quality was too variable to be categorized among Italy's top-tier bottles. Yet just as white wines throughout Italy evolve, Albana di Romagna is finding its footing in both its dry and *passito* styles.

What's helped Albana's reputation is better cellar technology. Albana grape skins contain a lot of tannins, nearly as many as a red grape. To decrease bitterness, producers like Tre Monti minimize skin contact as much as possible. Yet Tre Monti, which cultivates grapes in the Imola and Forlì hills, also stays true to the grape's natural qualities, like its intrinsic nuttiness. The winery's Albana Vigna Rocca, a wine aged on its lees in stainless steel exclusively, expresses a fruity nose with hints of apricots and bitter almonds typical of the Albana wine. In cold seasons, Tre Monti's proprietor Roberta Navacchia explained to me, Albana takes on a delicate elegance. In hotter years, the grape yields a more rustic personality.

Dry Albana di Romagna is actually less traditional than its *passito* version, with this sweeter style dating back to the forth or fifth century. Albana classically expresses raw honey and apricot flavors wrapped within a light floral perfume, and these characteristics are emphasized in *passito*. Led by another talented woman, Christina Giminiani, Fattoria Zerbina makes Albana wines that have long been favorites of mine. I always stock the estate's Arrocco, a refined, slightly petrol-accented *passito*. Meanwhile, Zerbina's decadent AR Riserva is one of Italy's most-lauded sweet wines.

Grown in the same hills as Albana, Pagadebit is another white grape with a local, if less glamorous, history. Farmers used to grow the hardy, disease-resistant grape, whose reliable harvest would help them pay back debts. For similar reasons, central Italy's Trebbiano is planted throughout Romagna and parts of Emilia as well. Trebbiano from Romagna offers notes of yellow wax bean with a hefty dose of acidity. Yet these white workhorse grapes tend to take a backseat to the area's main red, Sangiovese.

Grown in the same areas as Albana (and produced by many of the same estates), Sangiovese thrives in Romagna, where it has adapted to the hilly terrain and heavier soils. The thick-skinned, blue-black grape has numerous clones and because of the endless stylistic choices that winemakers can make in the cellar, it is hard to generalize about the differences between Romagna and Toscana Sangiovese. Still, there are a few characteristics that I encounter. Compared with Tuscan styles, the Sangiovese wines from Romagna are darker, have riper tannins, and tend to linger like velvet on the palate.

After that, the generalizations end. In Romagna, variations in soil composition and climate make for wide style differences among Sangiovese wines. Fattoria Zerbina's Pietramora combines ripe tannins with plush fruit and acidity while the warmer Rimini coast, where soils boast a desirable mix of clay and limestone, yield wines with more Mediterranean-style flavors. Avi, a Sangiovese di Romagna produced by San Patrignano

outside of Rimini, is a masculine wine perfumed with spices and scrub brush.

But the best thing about Sangiovese di Romagna—indeed, many of the bottlings from Emilia-Romagna—is that these wines are still under the radar. For that reason, they offer great value, not just in price but also in potential. This is a region that only recently recognized that its wines deserve just as much attention as its ragù, and I'm excited to stay tuned. —SL

White Grapes

ALBANA

The grape of Albana di Romagna, the first white Italian wine to attain DOCG status, Albana is also Romagna's most historic white grape. One legend attributes Albana's popularity to the daughter of Roman Emperor Theodosius II, who declared that it was so good it should only be consumed from gold goblets. For this reason, the story goes, the hills surrounding Albana's premier growing area are called Bertinoro, which roughly translates to "drunk in gold."

Here, between the coastal city of Rimini and Bologna, the hills and maritime climate from the Adriatic provide a perfect microclimate for the grape. Classic Albana di Romagna exhibits notes of raw honey, apricot, white flowers, and, on occasion, a hint of evergreen. Some styles are reminiscent of wines made with Veneto's Garganega grape, to which it might be related. As a dry wine, it is aged in stainless steel tanks for a clean, bright wine or *barrique* for a rounder, richer style. As a *passito* wine, Albana di Romagna is a concentrated version of its dry style, making it one of Italy's most-prized *vini dolce*.

In addition to straight *passito*, there are also hybrid styles of Albana. Fattoria Monticino Rosso, a producer in Imola, makes a dry wine with a glycerine richness, as if some of the grapes caught a bit of botrytis before they were harvested. I pair Albana with everything from winter squash and mushrooms to squid ink pasta.

RECOMMENDED PRODUCERS: Baciami, Fattoria Monticino Rosso, Leone Conti, Tre Monti, Umberto Cesari, Zerbina

ORTRUGO

Allegedly introduced into Emilia's Colli Piacentini hills by a barbarian who brought cuttings in his horse's saddlebags, Ortrugo can be sparkling or still, sweet or dry. The delicate nature of Ortrugo allows it to express terroir; it also exhibits orange blossom, green apple, lime, and, on occasion, petrol. As a sparkling wine, it can taste almost creamy, but it finishes refreshingly dry.

RECOMMENDED PRODUCERS: Castelli del Duca, Ferrari e Perini, Loschi, Mainetti, Torretta, Villa Rosa

PAGADEBIT

Derived from a phrase in the local Romagnolo dialect, Pagadebit means to pay debts. The name came from farmers who valued the robust, prolific vine, which yielded consistently large harvests that allowed them to pay back lenders. Today it's used in Pagadebit di Romagna DOC, a wine made around Forlì and Cesena that come in various forms: dry, semidry, and *frizzante*. Pagadebit is a derivative of the Bombino Bianco grape from Puglia and Lazio, but it has a lighter, more aromatic style. In the glass, it carries a straw color with a greenish tinge and offers notes of pea shoots and flowers.

RECOMMENDED PRODUCERS: Campodelsole, Celli, Guarini, Monsignore, Paradiso

PIGNOLETTO

Named "little pine cone" for the shape of its grape clusters, this indigenous green grape is at its best when grown in the limestone and clay soils of the Colli Bolognesi. Colli Bolognesi Classico Pignoletto is a fresh, light wine at its best when young. Like other wines in the region, it is also made in a *frizzante* style. Yet in the hands of a few producers, the grapes take on a smoky, malty flavor and deep golden color, which complements Bologna's famous *tortellini en brodo*. Alberto Tedeschi's Spungola Bellaria, an amber wine fermented with the skins and stems, shows the serious side of Pignoletto.

RECOMMENDED PRODUCERS: Alberto Tedeschi, Zucchi, Branchini, Montalcino Rosso, Orsi
SEE ALSO: Trebbiano (page 71)

Red Grapes

ANCELLOTTA

The inky, juicy Ancellotta grape is planted in Romagna around the cities of Forlì, Cesana, and Ravenna and in Emilia in the same areas used to grow Lambrusco. Ancellotta is most often blended with Sangiovese and Lambrusco for color, but the grape comes into its own around Reggio Emilia, where some producers vinify it alone. Outside of Emilia-Romagna, Luigi Mancini, a winemaker in northern Marche, makes Blu, a single-varietal wine named after the dark stain the grape makes.

RECOMMENDED PRODUCERS: Lini 910, Medici Ermete, Prato, San Martino, Masone-Campogalliano (Emilia-Romagna), Luigi Mancini (Le Marche)

LAMBRUSCO

Lambrusco is both the name of the grape and the style of wine produced in Emilia. Most Lambrusco grows within the pergola-trained vines planted in the plains of the Po River near Modena, but higher quality fruit is coming from the Emilian hills. A small amount also grows around Mantua in Lombardia. While the Lambrusco grape has myriad clones, only a handful are used for wine production. Lambrusco di Sorbara tends to be the lightest and fruitiest, while Lambrusco Salamino di Santa Croce is more medium-bodied. Lambrusco di Grasparossa di Castelvetro yields the most full-bodied styles. Meanwhile, the most planted clone, Lambrusco Reggiano, is behind most of the light-bodied wines made for the export market but also is used in more serious wines.

What all the clones have in common is a high level of acidity—which makes it ideal for *frizzante* wine. Lambrusco comes in shades from white to rosé to dark purple, and all levels of sweetness. While up to 15 percent of Ancellotta is allowed to be blended into Lambrusco, most wines are composed entirely of Lambrusco.

RECOMMENDED PRODUCERS: Albinea Canali, Barbolini, Camillo Donati, Ceci La Luna, Chiarli, Donelli, Francesco Vezzelli, Giacobazzi, Lini 910, Ca' Montanari, Medici Ermete, Pederzana, Saetti, Vittorio Graziano
SEE ALSO: Barbera (page 205), Bonarda (page 205), Sangiovese (page 248)

Lombardia

When most of us fly into the Milan airport, the first thing on our minds is usually not local wine. While Rome is the political and religious capital of Italy, Milan is its economic center, an urban engine that drives the country's industry. It is a place of art and design, of industry and finance, and of Michelin-starred restaurants that source the best food and wine from around the world. There are still local favorites, like *risotto milanese* (gilded with gold leaf at its most elaborate), but there are also jet-fresh tropical fruit plates and take-out counters of prepared food dressed with aspic. It is all part of the city's cultured persona.

Milan's suburbs sprawl, and until you travel to the lake country thirty miles northwest of Milan or drive south across the Po River to the gentle hills of Oltrepò Pavese, Lombardia presents itself as a place for work, not leisure. Perhaps because it competes for attention with Milan's high-profile industries, the wine business in Lombardia flies under the radar, rarely receiving the same kind of attention granted to the wines within regions where viticulture and enology form important revenue streams. Or perhaps the Milanese just want to keep local finds for themselves.

Lombardia's hills, lakes, plains, and mountains create pockets of wine styles that are impressive in their variety. A good many of those wines are classic-method sparklers—Lombardia is the only region in Italy claiming two DOCGs dedicated to wine made like Champagne. Northeast of Milan, Franciacorta is Italy's leading classic-method sparkling wine region. On the southwest border, the prolific growing zone Oltrepò Pavese also has a DOCG classic-method sparkling wine and also produces several other *frizzante* and still styles. Still wines from other growing areas also can be remarkable, both for bargains and splurges. From Lake Garda, we get cherry-accented red wines and understated white wines made with Trebbiano di Lugana. And then there is Valtellina, an island of Nebbiolo (called Chiavennasca locally) cultivated against the backdrop of the Swiss Alps. Valtellina's awe-inspiring setting—and the literal heights that vintners scale to make their wines—make it one of Italy's most dramatic wine areas.

Compared with the tangle of grapes and histories found in other regions, Lombardia wine is more straightforward. The region's annual output is less than 40 million gallons of wine, far short of the robust yields of neighboring Veneto and Emilia-Romagna. With the exception of a few local grapes (and a few confusing synonyms), the vines cultivated in this region have familiar names. French varieties, such as Chardonnay, Pinot Blanc (Bianco), and Pinot Noir (Nero) trip off winemakers' tongues. So do Italian grapes from neighboring regions, like Barbera from Piemonte and Trebbiano from Veneto. Around Mantua, Lombardia even has its own sparkling Lambrusco. These wines, whether sparkling or still, complement both the sophistication of Milan and the region's rich country fare, from smoked lake trout to local cheese to risotto and polenta dishes.

The most visible flagship of quality wine in the region is Franciacorta, the gold standard for classic-method sparkling wine in Italy. As in most of Italy's growing zones, vine cultivation here dates to pre-Roman times, but the history of Franciacorta is a lot younger. In 1961, local enologist Franco Ziliani convinced his friends Guido Berlucchi and Giorgio Lanciani to referment one thousand bottles of Pinot Nero using the same techniques used to make Champagne. The wine, Pinot di Franciacorta, started the region's significant shift toward sparkling wines, and the growing zone took off, today producing an average of 10 million bottles annually.

In Franciacorta, vines grow along the south banks of subalpine Lake Iseo around the city of Erbusco. Lake breezes cool the vines in the summer while hills protect the area from the warm, humid air that settles around Milan. In the winter, the lake works in reverse, warming the air and insulating its shores. The soil also is conducive to sparkling wine production: the vines (predominantly Chardonnay and Pinot Bianco but also Pinot Nero) grow in rocky glacial moraine with very little clay, yielding lean fruit with plenty of acidity.

The other side of the success story in Franciacorta comes down to skill and investment. With Zilani's urging, Berlucchi was the first producer to dedicate itself to classic-method sparkling wine, and the name remains a leading producer of Franciacorta. Others soon followed. For some, it was a matter of shifting priorities on existing family property. The striking mustard-colored Il Mosnel estate dates back to the sixteenth century, but the Barboglio family didn't plant Chardonnay, Pinot Nero, and Pinot Bianco vines until 1968. Today run by sister-brother team Lucia and Giulio Barzanò, Il Mosnel is outfitted with top-level equipment, producing an elegant Franciacorta Brut with toasty sweet notes of brioche, apple, and crème brûlée balanced by fine bubbles and long finish. The legendary estate of Ca' del Bosco also started on family property. Winemaker Maurizio Zanella's mother, Annamaria Clementi, bought a farmhouse in Erbusco. Zanella converted the estate into a winery, planting Chardonnay and Pinot Nero in the middle of what used to be a chestnut forest. Zanella makes one of Franciacorta's best wines, Annamaria Clementi Rosé, one of the quintessential sparkling rosé wines in the world, full of rose petals and strawberries with a refined texture and poised balance.

Not all estates were built upon existing property. Vittorio Moretti, a wealthy businessman, arrived in Erbusco in the 1970s and founded Bellavista, turning it into one of Franciacorta's most important estates. On the other side of heavy wooden doors from the retro-modern tasting room, stainless steel tanks for blending tower over the wooden barrels used for aging the nearly ninety different base wines. Classic-style sparkling wine is one of the labor-intensive styles of wines to produce, so it's also one of the most expensive. One look at the elaborate security gates and sophisticated tasting rooms of the leading estates—Bellavista included—makes it clear Franciacorta is not for *garagistes*, semiprofessional hobbyists making wine at home.

Because their tradition has been adapted from France, Franciacorta producers use a hybrid of French-Italian phrases to describe their process. Like Champagne production, the base wines for Franciacorta are aged—sometimes in used oak—for a year or so. After aging, they are blended with other base wines, bottled, and inoculated with a combination of wine and yeast that kickstarts the secondary fermentation—the *presa di spuma*. After the bottles rest in the cellar for at least two years but more likely several more, the spent yeast cells are disgorged (removed), and the bottle is corked. Depending on the style of wine, bottles may get a splash of *dosage*,

reserved wine mixed with sugar, in varied amounts before they are corked. This isn't typically intended to make the wine sweet but rather to add balance. Here the terms indicating level of sweetness diverge slightly from the French system. While *brut* written on the bottle indicates a very dry wine, a wine without any *dosage* is labeled *pas dose* or *pas operé*. (In France, it might be called *ultra brut*.) These wines are exceedingly dry, but their verve and balance can be addicting. One of my favorite examples is Bellavista's Gran Cuvée Pas Operé, an masculine sparkler with well-integrated acidity. In contrast to this bone-dry style, *satèn*, a creamier style of sparkling wine, offers a softer side of Franciacorta.

Compared with Franciacorta, Oltrepò Pavese strikes a more laid-back tone. Giovannella Fugazza's Castello di Luzzano sits perched at the end of one of the many narrow rural roads that serpentine the gentle hills of the growing region. Once a Roman castle, the estate became property of the church before coming into the care of the Fugazza family. Today it is a winery and an *agritourismo*. In contrast to the white-tablecloth restaurants in Franciacorta, here a casual restaurant down the hill in what used to be the customs house offers country food, like hand-shaped pasta and roasted pork with apples.

The Fugazza family's estate stretches across the border to Emilia, occupying growing zones in both regions, Oltrepò Pavese and Emilia's Colli Piacentini. Rows of Barbera and Croatina vines grow in even rows down the slopes overlooking a narrow valley where several years ago archaeologists unearthered Roman terra-cotta amphorae. As the largest growing zone in Lombardia, Oltrepò Pavese produces more than half of the region's DOC wines (Franciacorta makes about 17 percent). The wines themselves vary, from Malvasia and Riesling to still and sparkling Pinot Nero wines. Oltrepò Pavese also makes gallons of everyday drinking wines, which might be the best expression of juicy grapes like Croatina and Barbera. One of my go-to wines from Castello di Luzzano is Romeo, a plush, floral blend of Barbera and Croatina that was named for a faithful farmhand who once lived on the property.

Lake Garda is also a significant source of Lombardia wines. The climate around the lake is warm enough to support lemon trees and olive groves, and vines also benefit from the temperate weather. Made with Trebbiano di Lugana grapes (which are thought to be a clone of Umbria's Trebbiano Spoletino vine), Lugana DOC white wines are subtle, with hints of lemon zest and nuts. Lake Garda winemakers also deliver some captivating red wines. Gropello makes a bright, spicy cherry-hued wine in the Valtenesi hills on the western shores of the lake, and it also is often blended with Marzemino, Barbera, and Sangiovese for the area's *rosso* DOC wine. Additionally, the local perfumed Chiaretto is one of Italy's best under-the-radar *rosé* wines.

For the ultimate red wine from Lombardia, however, Valtellina takes top billing. Starting near the tip of Lake Como, the Adda Valley runs west to east, with vines planted on south-facing vineyards. In the summer, the stone walls that support the trellises amplify the sun's rays and scorching heat (for this reason, one main vineyard is called Inferno). Yet with the Swiss Alps looming to the north, cold air is never far away. By September and October, temperatures can swing twenty degrees or more from night to day. Despite the threat of frost and snow, however, harvest often does not occur until November.

Extremes are exactly what gives the wines from Valtellina their nerve. Historic producer Nino Negri, whose namesake founder started selling local wine to the Swiss from the small town of Chiuro in 1897, is one of Valtellina's best producers. The company makes both Valtellina Superiore, a wine made from the Adda Valley's top vineyards, and Sforzato (also called Sfursat), a rare, intense wine described as the Amarone of the Alps. Like Amarone, grapes go through the *appassimento* process, drying in crates after harvest until around December or January, when they are then crushed, vinified, and aged in barrels for a year or more. The resulting wine is concentrated Nebbiolo with notes of balsamic vinegar, flowers, and ripe cherries. Another classic producer, Mamete Prevostini, makes a Sforzato called Albareda, a muscular, aromatic wine with notes of dried fruit. Prevostini also produces fragrant and fresh *cru* wines from Valtellina's top vineyards, which offer a good way to experience the range of mountain Nebbiolo

No wine made with Nebbiolo can avoid comparisons to Barolo and Barbaresco. Valtellina's rockier soils give the non-Sforzato wines a more reserved profile than their counterparts in the Langhe, but I'd argue that it is hardly a compromise. What Valtellina lacks in weight it makes up for it in nervous intensity complemented by a nose of rose petals and leather. Every well-made glass from this small growing zone is a complete counterpoint to the hustle of Milan, directly reflecting the rocky soil, clean air, and robust health so intrinsic to mountain life. —SL

White Grapes

SEE: MALVASIA (page 14), Pinot Bianco (page 143), Trebbiano (page 71)

Red Grapes

CROATINA
Confusingly referred to as Bonarda (a different grape in Piemonte), Croatina is one of the main grapes of the southern Oltrepò Pavese growing zone. Grown in Lombardia and Piemonte since the Middle Ages, Croatina is a durable vine that resists mildew. Its name comes from *croatti*, the tie worn on holidays when the wine traditionally would be served. In Oltrepò Pavese and in Gutturnio in Emilia, it is blended with Barbera. Croatina is often compared to Dolcetto because it is tart and has fresh berry and plum flavors. It is a medium-bodied wine best consumed within a few years of being released.

RECOMMENDED PRODUCERS: Albani, Bruno Verdi, Castello di Luzzano, Francesco Montagna, La Stoppa, Martilde, Torti

GROPELLO
Native to Lombardia, Gropello grows around the shores of Lake Garda near Brescia. Within the same vine, the color and size of the individual grapes vary from white to red, but together they produce a juicy, medium-bodied red wine with notes of black pepper and spices. It is also often blended with Marzemino, Barbera, and Sangiovese for Chiaretto, a wine made in a *rosato* style.

RECOMMENDED PRODUCERS: Provenza, Trevisani, Zuliani
SEE ALSO: Barbera (page 205), Lambrusco (page 164), Nebbiolo (page 206), Pinot Nero (page 144)

Progressive Italian

IN PUGLIA, where my extended family lives, small boats still go out to fish in the Adriatic every morning, returning each afternoon with an array of seafood. If you want to be alone, you need only drive five minutes out of town to be in the middle of a grove of olive trees with not another soul in shouting distance. It is a postcard of life in the classically envisioned Italian countryside, yet it doesn't tell us the whole story. In contrast to Puglia and the rest of the southern peninsula, northern Italy churns with industry and business. It has a greater concentration of cities—and affluence—and it carries closer ties in food and culture to its European neighbors than the rest of Italy. At the center of it all is Milan, a dense city with the energy of New York and the sprawl of Los Angeles. At the table, modern sensibilities meet tradition head on.

On my first visit to Milan many years ago, I experienced meals that offered takes on traditional ideas infused with contemporary sensibilities. Classics, like pork prepared *milanese*-style (pounded thin, breaded, and panfried) were on the menu, but cubed rather than pounded. There might be pasta made from mozzarella or tofu skins. In these restaurants, cuisine was progressive and elegant, striving to ask the question what it meant to be cooking and living in Italy today. This trip was the first time that I saw how Italian cuisine didn't always mean traditional and homey—and how I could infuse Italian cooking with my own Italian and American heritage.

This progressive dialogue occurs alongside a culture that still supports small fishing boats that bring in the daily catch and cheesemakers who make cheese from the milk of their own herd. Tradition is never very far away, a fact that informs the work of even the most creative Italian chefs. At Da Vittorio, a three-star Michelin restaurant outside of Milan near Bergamo, chocolate spheres with saffron and gold leaf bookends the same meal that included a bowl of wide-noodle, chewy *paccheri* buried in a creamy tomato sauce. In an unexpected way, dining in such a restaurant can increase excitement in tradition.

The recipes in this chapter pay tribute to traditional but polished Italian dishes, from *erbazzone*, a classic Emilian Italian pie, to *tortellini en brodo,* a classic consommé preparation from Bologna. Though I might update or change the preparation of some of the ingredients, these dishes and others like them form the foundation of my perspective on traditional Italian cooking, giving me a perspective from which to move forward.
—MA

FRITTO MISTO

This classic recipe from Emilia-Romagna makes use of nearly every part of the animal, and offal is frequently highlighted in the region's classic *fritto misto*. From pig ears to tripe, chicken livers to rabbit kidneys, I've dipped them all in this basic beer batter. So mix and match the offal to suite your tastes. If you've made sweetbreads for the crayfish risotto on page 220 or are braising pig ears for the appetizer on page 20, save some for the *fritto misto*. Likewise, if you plan to cook tripe, make extra and reserve it for this recipe (or buy cooked tripe). You could also use one type of offal, like chicken livers, and supplement the remaining misto with vegetables. And even if offal isn't your thing, I urge you not to ignore this recipe. The batter works wonders with all kinds of vegetables, and the lemon confitura (page 279) complements animal and vegetable equally.

Success in *fritto misto* lies in the details. Only mix the batter after you have assembled all of the ingredients for frying. To prevent ingredients from clumping together, fry in batches. To avoid frying with too much batter, use tweezers to remove the ingredients from the batter and gingerly drop them into the oil. Offal splatters when it fries: place a mesh splatter guard over the pot. Serve *fritto misto* as soon as the last pieces come out of the oil.

The mix of dry ingredients makes more batter than you'll need for a single frying session, but this way it's easy to whip up a new batch of batter if you're getting low. I advise you to mix half of the batter with half the beer and half the mustard, to start, then mix the remainder if you start to run low.

255 grams • 9 ounces veal sweetbreads

28 grams • 1/8 cup white vinegar

kosher salt

207 grams • 12 chicken livers (about 1 cup)

250 grams • 12 rabbit kidneys (about 1 cup)

450 grams • 2 cooked pig ears (page 20)

227 grams • 8 ounces cooked tripe

225 grams • (7 1/2-ounce) delicata squash, peeled

225 grams • 1 (7 1/2-ounce) sweet potato, peeled

20 grams • 3 green onions

5 grams • 12 slices lemon confitura (page 279)

Batter

300 grams • 2 cups Wondra flour

200 grams • 1 1/2 cups cornstarch

14 grams • 2 teaspoons baking soda

4 grams • 1 teaspoon kosher salt

2 grams • 1 teaspoon paprika

2 grams • 1 teaspoon onion powder

2 grams • 1 teaspoon cayenne

2 grams • 1 teaspoon fennel pollen (see page 279)

650 grams • 3 cups Pilsner-style beer, such as Menabrea

40 grams • 4 tablespoons Dijon mustard

blended oil for frying (see page 278)

kosher salt and white pepper

1 sprig sage leaves, stemmed

1 sprig rosemary

1 lemon, cut into wedges and seeded

coarse salt

Soak the sweetbreads in ice water for at least 3 hours but preferably overnight. Drain the sweetbreads and rinse. If the water is pink, soak again until the water is clear. Prepare an ice bath. Bring 8 cups of water to a boil with the vinegar and a pinch of salt. Poach the sweetbreads at a gentle simmer until the membrane has turned from translucent to opaque, 2 to 3 minutes. Transfer the sweetbreads to the ice bath. Once cool enough to handle, peel away the outer membrane and any visible fat. (They will still be rare.)

Lay the sweetbreads on a parchment-lined baking sheet, cover with another piece of parchment paper, and place a baking sheet on top. Put a few cans or other heavy items to weight down the sheet and flatten the sweetbreads as they cool. Refrigerate until chilled and firm, at least 2 hours but preferably overnight. Once cool, cut the sweetbreads into 1-inch cubes. You should have about 12 pieces.

Meanwhile, trim away any discolored parts or visible veins from the livers and rabbit kidneys. Soak each offal variety separately in ice water for 2 hours. Rinse and pat dry. Slice the pig ears into triangles or strips. Slice the tripe crosswise into strips. You should have about 12 pieces each of pig ears and tripe.

Slice the delicata squash crosswise into 1/4-inch rounds (you should have at least 12). Scrape out the seeds from the center of each round. Slice the sweet potato into 1/4-inch rounds (you should have at least 12). Trim the root and the green tips off of the green onions and slice into 2-inch pieces.

To make the batter: In a large bowl, whisk together the Wondra flour, cornstarch, baking soda, salt, paprika, onion powder, cayenne, and fennel pollen. Gradually whisk in the beer, mixing well between additions to avoid forming lumps in the batter, then whisk in the mustard.

In a large, tall pot, heat 4 inches of oil to 360°F. Place a cooling rack over a baking sheet and line with paper towels. Fry the *fritto misto* in batches, starting with the offal. Season the sweetbreads, livers, kidneys, and tripe with salt and white pepper. Mix the offal into the batter. Using a pair of kitchen tweezers or small tongs, drag each piece one at a time up the side of the bowl, then gingerly drop into the oil (adding the pieces individually into the oil avoids frying them in one clump). Fry until crisp, about 2 minutes. With a skimmer or a slotted spoon, lift the pieces out of the oil and drain on the paper towels. Season immediately with salt and white pepper.

Once the offal is fried, mix the squash, sweet potato, green onions, and lemon *confitura* in the batter (you do not need to season the vegetables first). Using the tweezers or small tongs, drag each vegetable one at a time up the side of the bowl, then gingerly drop into the oil. Fry until crisp, 1 to 2 minutes and skim out of the oil, drain on the paper towels, and season immediately with salt and white pepper.

Fry the sage and rosemary for a few seconds until crisp. Drain on paper towels and season with a pinch of salt. When cool enough to handle, pull the rosemary leaves off the stem. Arrange the offal and vegetables on a large platter. Sprinkle with the fried herbs and serve with lemon wedges and coarse salt.

CHESTNUT-FILLED PASTA *with* Broccoli di Cicco, Guanciale, *and* Burnt-Orange Sauce

The flavors of bitter and sweet are inherent to the fall season. With creamy sweet chestnuts balanced by bitter *broccoli di cicco* (an Italian variety with smaller florets than conventional broccoli), this pasta gently transitions toward hearty winter fare. Once used to stretch the supply of more expensive wheat flour, chestnut flour is common throughout Italy. I use it in the pasta dough to reflect the chestnut filling. Tying the sweet-tart elements together is the burnt-orange sauce made by blackening orange halves and then adding the burnt halves to a caramelized sauce. *Guanciale* (cured pork jowl) rounds out the flavors with salty richness. Sold in jars or vacuum packed, cooked, cleaned chestnuts are often available in the fall. I recommend them for cooking at home as they will save you quite a bit of prep time.

SERVES 4 TO 6

Filling

extra virgin olive oil
50 grams • 1 shallot, sliced
140 grams • 18 cooked, peeled chestnuts
kosher salt
50 grams • 1/4 cup white wine
115 grams • 1/2 cup heavy cream
40 grams • 3 tablespoons mascarpone

Pasta

200 grams • scant 1 2/3 cups 00 flour
50 grams • 1/4 cup chestnut flour
3 grams • 1/2 teaspoon kosher salt
100 grams • 2 eggs
semolina flour for dusting

Sauce

1 orange, halved
11 grams • 1 tablespoon sugar
39 grams • 3 tablespoons sherry
225 grams • 1 cup brown stock (page 283)
1 thyme sprig
kosher salt and black pepper

48 grams • 6 chestnuts
55 grams • 4 tablespoons butter
kosher salt
extra virgin olive oil
95 grams • 3 1/2 ounces (12 strips) guanciale
65 grams • 1 cup broccoli di cicco, trimmed into small florets
1 orange for zesting
a block of Parmigiano-Reggiano for grating

To make the filling: Heat a thin film of olive oil in a wide sauté pan or pot over medium-high heat. Sweat the shallot until soft, about 1 minute. Stir in the chestnuts, season with salt, and cook to warm through, about 2 minutes. Pour in the wine and reduce until the pan is almost dry. Add the cream, reduce the heat to medium-low, and cook until the chestnuts are soft enough to be broken apart with a spoon, about 7 minutes. Put the filling in a blender and purée into a paste. Pour into a bowl and fold in the mascarpone until completely incorporated. You should have about 1 cup. Taste, seasoning with more salt if needed. Cool completely, then transfer the filling to a pastry bag fitted with a medium tip and refrigerate until needed.

To make the pasta: In a stand mixer fitted with the paddle attachment, mix together the flours and salt. In a bowl, whisk together the eggs. With the mixer running on medium speed, drizzle in the eggs. Mix the dough for 2 to 3 minutes, then turn onto the counter and knead several times by hand; it will feel dry and firm. With your hands, flatten the dough into a rectangle. Wrap in plastic wrap and leave on the counter for 30 minutes to soften and hydrate.

Roll out the dough according to the instructions for laminated pasta on page 273. Lay the sheets of pasta out

{continued}

on the work surface and, with a knife, cut into 3-inch squares. Cut each square diagonally to form triangles. Pipe about 1 teaspoon of filling into the center of each triangle. Lightly mist water over the squares or dab the edges with a damp pastry brush. Pinch the two corners along the long side of the triangle together and fold the remaining corner in to form a pyramid. Using your fingertips, pinch the edges of the pyramid together to seal in the filling. Repeat until all of the dough and filling is used. You will have about 45 pieces. Place the filled pasta on a baking sheet lightly sprinkled with semolina flour.

To make the sauce: In a dry pan over medium heat, char the cut side of the orange until evenly blackened, 6 to 8 minutes. In a heavy-bottomed pot over low heat, melt the sugar until it forms a light caramel. Carefully add the orange halves (the caramel will start to seize up and sputter) and pour in the sherry. Stir until the caramel has dissolved, then cook until the pan is nearly dry, about 3 minutes. Pour in the stock, then simmer gently until the stock has reduced by three-quarters, about 10 minutes. Add the thyme and let steep for a few

minutes. Strain the sauce through a fine-mesh strainer, pushing on the orange halves with a spoon so they release all of their juice. Season with salt and pepper and keep warm.

Slice the chestnuts into disks. In a sauté pan over medium heat, melt 1 tablespoon of butter. Brown the chestnuts in the butter until nearly crisp, then drain on paper towels and season lightly with salt. Wipe the sauté pan clean and heat a thin film of olive oil over medium heat. Fry the *guanciale* strips until crisp, then drain on paper towels.

Bring a large pot of salted water to a boil. Drop in the pasta, and cook until al dente, 4 to 5 minutes. In the last minute of cooking, add the broccoli and cook until softened. Using a strainer or slotted spoon, lift the pasta and broccoli out of the water and into a sauté pan with straight sides or a wide, shallot pot. Swirl in about 3 tablespoons of butter and simmer over low heat until the pasta is lightly coated. If the sauce is too thick, moisten the pan with a couple of drops of pasta cooking water.

To serve, divide the pasta and broccoli among 4 to 6 warmed plates. Top with a few chestnut slices and *guanciale* strips and grate orange zest over the top. Spoon a few tablespoons of the sauce over the pasta and grate Parmigiano-Reggiano over the plate to finish.

SQUASH CAPPELLACCI
with Medjool Dates, Rosemary Brown Butter, *and* Saba

In the world of filled pasta, *tortelli di zucca*, the classic winter squash–filled pasta in brown butter, is a polarizing dish. Some say it's a favorite, others find it too sweet. I like it because it is all about emphasizing the naturally rich flavor of mature winter squash. In this filled pasta, which takes the shape of the pope's hat, I pair the squash with complementary flavors such as dates and *saba*, a syrup made from reduced grape must. Fresh rosemary replaces traditional sage leaves, giving the brown butter sauce a more savory edge. After I roast winter squash or pumpkin, I scoop out the pulp and let it drain, preferably overnight. If the pulp releases a lot of water, I simmer it to concentrate the flavors and then mix it back into the squash.

SERVES 6 TO 8

Filling

500 grams • 1 pound, 2 ounces butternut squash

45 grams • 3 tablespoons unsalted butter, divided

8 grams • 1 teaspoon honey, preferably acacia, divided

kosher salt and black pepper

35 grams • 2 tablespoons mascarpone

Pasta

250 grams • scant 2 cups 00 flour

2 grams • 1/2 teaspoon kosher salt

100 grams • 2 eggs

20 grams • 1 egg yolk

30 to 40 grams • 24 to 32 almonds

127 grams • 8 medjool dates

105 grams • 7 tablespoons unsalted butter

1 sprig rosemary, stemmed

kosher salt

a block of Parmigiano-Reggiano for grating

saba for serving

To make the filling: Preheat the oven to 350°F. Cut the squash in half and scoop the seeds out and discard. Place the squash face up in a baking pan. In the hollowed-out cavity, divide 1 tablespoon of the butter and 1/2 teaspoon of the honey between the two halfs. Season with salt and pepper, then cover with aluminum foil and bake for 45 minutes. Uncover and bake an additional 25 to 40 minutes or until completely soft and lightly caramelized. When it's cool enough to handle, scrape the cooked squash into a fine-mesh strainer placed over a bowl and drain overnight.

In a small sauté pan over medium-high heat, brown 1 tablespoon of butter until deep brown and nutty, about 1 minute. Measure out 250 grams of the drained squash (about 1 1/2 cups). Put the squash in a food processor with the remaining 1 tablespoon of butter, the brown butter, the remaining 1/2 teaspoon of honey, and the mascarpone. Season with about 1/2 teaspoon of salt and pulse until smooth. Taste and season with salt or pepper if needed. Cool completely. Once cold, transfer to a pastry bag fitted with a medium tip and refrigerate until needed.

To make the *cappellacci*: In a stand mixer fitted with the paddle attachment, mix together the flour and salt on low speed. In a bowl, whisk together the eggs. With the mixer running on medium speed, drizzle in the eggs and yolks. Mix the dough for 2 to 3 minutes, turn the dough onto the counter and knead by hand for several minutes; the dough will feel dry and firm. Flatten the dough into a flat rectangle, wrap in plastic wrap, and leave on the counter for 30 minutes to soften and hydrate.

Roll out the dough according to the instructions for laminated pasta on page 273. Lay the sheets of pasta out on a work surface and cut into 2-inch squares. Pipe about 1/2 teaspoon of filling into the center of each square. Lightly mist water over the squares or dab the edges with water with a pastry brush. Fold one corner over to the opposite corner to form a triangle and pinch the edges to seal. With the tip of the triangle facing upward, fold the two corners over each other and pinch to seal (it will look like a pope's hat). Repeat until all of the dough and filling is used. You will have about 75 pieces. Place the filled pasta on a baking sheet lightly dusted with flour.

{continued}

Preheat the oven to 350°F. In a sauté pan over medium-high heat, warm the almonds until they begin to toast. Put the pan in the oven and bake the almonds for 10 to 12 minutes or until light brown in the center (starting the nuts on the stove will lower the time it takes to toast the almonds). Once they're cool enough to handle, take the tip of a paring knife and pierce each nut in half crosswise: it should divide into two equal pieces. Peel, pit, and quarter the dates and roll the pieces into balls resembling marbles.

Bring a large pot of salted water to a boil. Add the *cappellacci* and cook until al dente, 4 to 5 minutes. Meanwhile, in a large sauté pan or shallow, wide pot over medium heat, melt the butter until it begins to bubble. Stir in the rosemary and fry until the rosemary is aromatic and the butter has begun to brown, about 3 minutes. Add the date balls and almonds and swirl the pan. If the butter is becoming too brown, remove from the heat and add a small splash of pasta water. Drain the *cappellacci* and add the pasta to the brown-butter sauce. Toss gently to coat and season with salt to taste.

To serve, spoon the *cappellacci* onto 6 or 8 warmed plates. Spoon a few almond pieces and date balls and a few tablespoons of sauce over the pasta and grate Parmigiano-Reggiano over each plate. Drizzle the pasta with a few drops of *saba* to finish.

RICOTTA *and* QUAIL EGG RAVIOLI *with* Wild Greens *and* Fontina

Decadent, with a rich yolk center that breaks on contact, the plate-sized raviolo is a contemporary menu favorite. The original rendition comes from San Domenico, a landmark fine dining restaurant in Imola, a town built along the Via Aemilia. The restaurant's late chef, Nino Bergese, devised a raviolo filled with spinach and one raw egg yolk, serving it adorned solely with shavings of white truffle and a dusting of Parmigiano-Reggiano. I've drawn on the inspiration for smaller ravioli, some of which are filled with quail egg yolks (you may omit the yolks and fill them only with the ricotta mixture). To balance the dish, I add wild greens—essentially edible weeds that grow everywhere from meadows to the side of the road. Spring is an ideal time to look for them and to gather their edible flowers. Cultivated greens and chicories work well too, but if they are large, run your knife through them before cooking.

SERVES 6

Filling

150 grams • ³/₄ cup drained ricotta (see page 281)

50 grams • 1 egg

50 grams • ¹/₂ cup finely grated fontina cheese

¹/₂ teaspoon kosher salt

black pepper

nutmeg, for grating

12 quail egg yolks

Pasta

250 grams • scant 2 cups 00 flour

2 grams • ¹/₂ teaspoon kosher salt

100 grams • 2 eggs

9 grams • 2 teaspoons water

extra virgin olive oil

150 grams • ¹/₂ yellow onion, thinly sliced

kosher salt

3 grams • 1 garlic clove

120 grams • 6 cups mixed wild greens, such as dandelion, mustard, and kale, tough ends removed

85 grams • ¹/₃ cup unsalted butter

50 grams • ¹/₂ cup finely grated fontina

black pepper

To make the filling: In a large bowl, mix together the ricotta, regular egg, and fontina. Season with salt, pepper, and a few gratings of nutmeg. Transfer to a pastry bag fitted with a small tip.

To make the pasta: In a stand mixer fitted with the paddle attachment, mix together the flour and salt on low speed. In a bowl, whisk together the eggs and water. With the mixer running on medium speed, drizzle in the egg mixture. Mix the dough for 2 to 3 minutes, turn onto the counter and knead by hand for several minutes; it will feel dry and firm. Flatten the dough into a flat rectangle, wrap in plastic wrap, and leave on the counter for 30 minutes to soften and hydrate.

Roll out the dough according to the instructions for laminated pasta on page 273. Lay the sheets of pasta out on a work surface and punch out 3-inch rounds, using as much of the pasta surface area as possible. Lightly flour the rounds and stack them. (At this point, the rounds of pasta can be placed in a storage container and refrigerated.) Gather up the trimmings and reroll to yield a total of about 50 rounds.

Fill a few ravioli at a time. Lay a few rounds down on a work surface. Pipe a small ring of filling in the center of each piece, leaving a hole in the center. Lightly mist the pasta with water. For each egg-filled ravioli, slide a quail egg yolk into the center of the ring; otherwise, add a dab more ricotta to the center. Cover the pasta with another round and seal the edges, expelling as much air as possible by running your fingertips gently around the filling as you pinch the edges together. You should have about 25 pieces (keep the egg and the cheese ravioli separate so

{continued}

everyone gets some of each). Place the filled pasta on a baking sheet lightly dusted with flour.

Heat a thin film of olive oil in a medium Dutch oven over low heat. Sweat the onion until softened, about 3 minutes. Season with salt and then stir in the garlic and cook until it begins to soften, about 1 minute. Add the greens and cook until wilted and soft, 5 to 8 minutes. Keep warm. Make the butter and 2 tablespoons of water into *burro fuso* according to the instructions on page 276; keep warm.

Preheat the broiler. Bring a large pot of salted water to a boil. Add the cheese ravioli and cook until al dente, 2 to 3 minutes. Skim them out and add the quail egg ravioli to the boiling water, cooking for 2 to 3 minutes so the yolk remains runny. Transfer the ravioli to a large oven-proof platter. Scatter the greens on top, then sprinkle with the fontina. Place under a broiler for just long enough to melt the fontina, about 2 minutes. Spoon some *burro fuso* over the top. Finish with black pepper and a drizzle of olive oil.

VEAL *and* MORTADELLA TORTELLINI *en* Consommé

Since there is no hiding behind a sauce, serving delicate tortellini in a crystal-clear consommé is an ultimate expression of hand-crafted pasta. After many years of practice, I can turn just about anything into consommé. Give me the murkiest bucket of rainwater and I'll make it as clear as a mountain stream. I say this not to boast but rather to suggest that clarifying broth with a paste of egg whites, ground meat, and vegetables—the classic method to make consommé—is not as difficult as some imagine it to be. A broth becomes clear when it bubbles through a raft of protein that floats on top of the pot, pulling away impurities from the broth. The temperature needs to be gentle and steady to ensure that all the stock filters through the raft, but other than that, there isn't much to worry about. I start making consommé with the stock and the clarifying ingredients at room temperature. Before the raft forms, I stir the paste into the stock a few times, add a bit more stock, and then let the raft rise to the surface. Once most of the raft has risen and I know that no pieces of egg have stuck to the bottom of the pot to scorch, I can leave the pot at a lazy simmer, confident that the broth will be clear in the end.

SERVES 6

Filling

680 grams • 1½ pounds bone-in veal breast

kosher salt and black pepper

extra virgin olive oil

150 grams • 1 carrot, diced

150 grams • ½ yellow onion, diced

50 grams • 1 celery stalk, diced

454 grams • 2 cups white wine

2800 grams • 12 cups brown stock (page 283)

a sachet with 2 sprigs thyme, 1 sprig rosemary, 1 or 2 bay leaves, 5 black peppercorns, ¼ teaspoon fennel seeds, and 2 cloves (see page 282)

75 grams • ⅓ cup drained ricotta (see page 281)

35 grams • ¼ cup finely diced mortadella

10 grams • 2 tablespoons grated Parmigiano-Reggiano

2 grams • 2 teaspoons thyme leaves

Pasta

250 grams • scant 2 cups 00 flour

2 grams • ½ teaspoon kosher salt

100 grams • 2 eggs

20 grams • 1 yolk

Consommé

28 grams • 1 ounce (¾ cup) dried porcini

112 grams • 1 leek, white and light green parts only, chopped

125 grams • 1 carrot, diced

135 grams • ½ small yellow onion, diced

75 grams • 2 small celery stalks, diced

6 sprigs Italian parsley

6 sprigs thyme

100 grams • 3 egg whites

227 grams • 8 ounces ground veal

940 grams • 4 cups veal breast braising liquid

28 grams • 3 green onions, sliced thinly (about ¼ cup)

28 grams • 3 or 4 button mushrooms, sliced thinly (about ¼ cup)

To make the filling: Preheat the oven to 325°F. Season the veal with salt and pepper. Heat a thin film of olive oil in a large Dutch oven over medium-high heat. Sear the veal until golden brown on all sides, about 3 minutes. Transfer the veal to a plate and wipe out the bottom of the pot. Over medium heat, add a couple of drops of olive oil to the pot and stir in the carrot, onion, and celery. Sweat until soft, 2 to 3 minutes. Nestle the veal into the center of the vegetables, pour in the wine, and bring to a simmer. Add the stock and return to a simmer. (You are using more stock than you might for other braises because you will need the liquid to make the consommé.) Cover the pot and transfer to the oven. Cook the veal for 3 hours or until tender, pulling apart easily when pierced with a fork. Let the veal cool in the braising liquid for 2 hours.

Place the cooled veal on a cutting board. Pull away and discard any bones or connective tissue, then finely chop. Strain the braising liquid through a fine-mesh strainer and discard the vegetables and sachet. Skim the fat off the top of the liquid with a ladle. Set aside 4 cups of braising liquid for the consommé (if you don't have 4 cups, top off with water).

In a large bowl, mix together the chopped veal, ricotta, mortadella, Parmigiano-Reggiano, and thyme. Season to taste with salt and pepper, if needed. Transfer to a pastry bag fitted with a medium tip and refrigerate.

To make the pasta: In a stand mixer fitted with the paddle attachment, mix together the flour and salt. In a bowl, whisk together the eggs and yolk. With the mixer running on low speed, drizzle in the eggs. Mix the dough for 2 to 3 minutes, then turn onto the counter and knead several times by hand; it will feel dry and firm. Flatten the dough into a rectangle, wrap in plastic wrap, and leave on the counter for 30 minutes to soften and hydrate.

Roll out the dough according to the instructions for laminated pasta on page 273. Lay the sheets of pasta out on a work surface. With a 2-inch round cutter, punch out circles of pasta, using as much of the pasta surface area as possible. Lightly flour the rounds and stack them. (At this point, the rounds of pasta can be placed in a storage container and refrigerated.)

Pipe a dab of filling into the center of each circle. Lightly mist water over the rounds or dampen the edges with water using a pastry brush. Fold the circles in half and pinch together the edges until firmly sealed, expelling any extra air from inside the pasta while doing so. For each piece, hold the half-moon shape in both hands with the arched side facing up. Bring the ends together and pinch to seal. You will have 80 to 90 tortellini and leftover filling. Place the tortellini on a baking sheet lightly dusted with flour. If not cooking right away, cover and refrigerate.

To make the consommé: Soak the porcini in 1 cup of hot water for 5 minutes or until soft and hydrated. In a food processor, pulse together the porcini with its soaking water, leek, carrot, onion, celery, parsley, thyme, egg whites, and ground veal until it forms a coarse paste.

Pour 2 cups of the veal braising liquid into a 4- to 6-quart pot over medium heat. While the broth is still on the cool side of room temperature, stir in the paste with a spoon until well mixed. (The key is evenly distributing the egg proteins into the broth.) Pour in the remaining 2 cups of braising liquid. Increase the heat to medium-high and monitor the pot, stirring occasionally, until the particles float to the surface and form a dense raft. Do not stir the pot after the raft has formed. Lower the heat to a gentle simmer. With a ladle, poke a hole in the center of the raft. The broth will flow into the hole and up the sides, and then filter back through the raft. Simmer gently for 40 to 60 minutes or until the consommé is deep amber brown and tastes rich but not overreduced. If the raft starts to sink, this can also indicate the consommé is ready.

Line a fine-mesh strainer with a paper coffee filter and place over a fresh pot. Gently press the bottom of a ladle against the hole in the raft until it fills with consommé, then pour the consommé through the strainer. (Do not try to remove the raft first: this will stir up particles and result in a cloudy consommé.) Continue ladling the consommé out until all that remains in the pot is the raft; discard the raft. Bring the consommé in its new pot to a simmer and reduce until the liquid yields a deep, well-rounded flavor. Season with salt to taste.

Bring a large pot of water to a boil and season with salt. Add the tortellini and cook until al dente, about 3 minutes. Meanwhile, bring the consommé to a simmer. Pour the consommé into a large soup terrine. Drain the tortellini and add to the soup terrine. Garnish with green onion and mushroom slices. To serve, ladle tortellini and consommé into bowls at the table.

BOLOGNESE *with* Egg Noodles

As its popularity has spread internationally, bolognese might be the most famous—and maligned—example of a regional Italian ragù. I revisit the bolognese tradition, with a detour or two. I return the focus to the meat (ground pork shoulder), with a dab of tomato paste to offset its richness. I also use pig skin, which adds an unctuous texture that is characteristic of good bolognese. However, I also stir in a spoonful of minced chipotle peppers in adobo. Not only does it add a subtle smokiness to the ragù, it also offers a hint of unexpected flavor, balancing the richness in the ragù and making it more interesting to eat. In addition, I add soffritto at the end so that the vegetables don't taste tired and overcooked. I pair wide, silky egg noodles with the ragù, which complement the richness of the sauce. I salt the meat (using 5 grams of salt per pound of meat) before grinding it, which helps integrate the salt. The ragù is best prepared a day before serving.

SERVES 4 TO 6

Egg Noodles

250 grams • scant 2 cups 00 flour

2 grams • ¹/₂ teaspoon kosher salt

220 grams • 11 egg yolks

5 grams • 1 teaspoon extra virgin olive oil

Bolognese

600 grams • 1 pound, 5 ounces boneless pork shoulder, cubed

kosher salt

200 grams • 7 ounces pig skin (optional)

extra virgin olive oil

300 grams • 1 onion, chopped finely

30 grams • 6 garlic cloves, sliced

75 grams • ¹/₄ cup tomato paste

10 grams • 1 tablespoon chopped canned chipotle peppers in adobo

a pinch of dried red pepper flakes

300 grams • 1¹/₃ cups red wine

285 grams • 1¹/₄ cups water

nutmeg for grating

a sachet with 2 thyme sprigs, 1 rosemary sprig, 1 sage sprig, and 10 cloves (see page 282)

250 grams • 1¹/₂ cups soffritto (page 282)

75 grams • ¹/₃ cup heavy cream

red wine vinegar, to taste

kosher salt and black pepper

2 to 4 tablespoons unsalted butter

a block of Parmigiano-Reggiano for grating

To make the egg noodles: In a stand mixer fitted with the paddle attachment, mix together the flour and salt. In a bowl, whisk together the egg yolks and olive oil. With the mixer running on low speed, drizzle in the egg-oil mixture. Mix the dough for 2 to 3 minutes, then turn onto the counter and knead by hand for several minutes; it should look bright yellow and feel firm. Flatten the dough into a rectangle, wrap in plastic wrap and leave on the counter for 30 minutes to soften and hydrate.

Roll out the dough according to the instructions for laminated pasta on page 273. Cut the pasta into 12-inch sheets and dust generously with flour. In stacks of 2 or 3 sheets, roll both short sides until the rolls meet in the center (like a pair of binoculars). Slice the rolls into wide, ¹/₃-inch-thick noodles. Put a knife or stick into the center of the binoculars and lift to shake the noodles loose. Lay the noodles on a baking sheet dusted with flour and keep covered until ready to cook.

To make the bolognese: In a large bowl, season the pork with 2 teaspoons of salt. Cover and refrigerate for 2 hours. Fit a stand mixer with the meat grinder attachment fitted with the medium plate (or use a hand-crank meat grinder) and grind the pork and pig skin.

Preheat the oven to 325°F. Heat a thin film of olive oil in a large Dutch oven or heavy-bottomed pot over medium-high heat. Stir in the ground pork and brown well, 5 to 7 minutes. Transfer the pork and juices to a bowl. In the same pot, heat another film of olive oil over medium heat. Stir in the onion and a pinch of salt and sweat, stirring occasionally, until softened, about 3 minutes. If the bottom of the pan is beginning to get too dark, add a splash of water to deglaze. Mix in the garlic and sweat

{continued}

1 minute more. Stir in the tomato paste, chipotle, and red pepper flakes and cook until the tomato paste begins to brown, about 3 minutes. Return the pork and juices to the pot, and pour in the wine. Bring to a simmer and reduce the liquid by about a third, 3 to 5 minutes. Add the water and return to a simmer. Grate the nutmeg into the pot and submerge the sachet. Cover, transfer to the oven, and cook for $1^1/_2$ hours. Uncover the pot and taste the bolognese, skimming away excess fat. The meat and skin should be tender and the sauce noticeably thicker. Over low heat, stir in the soffritto and cream and simmer until the sauce has a velvety texture, 7 to 10 minutes. Taste, seasoning with salt and pepper if needed. Add a few drops of red wine vinegar to brighten the flavors. With a slotted spoon, remove the sachet, pressing on it to extract as much liquid as possible.

Bring a large pot of salted water to a boil. Stir in the pasta and cook until al dente, 3 to 4 minutes. Drain the pasta, reserving about 1 cup of pasta cooking water, and return the pasta to the pot. Meanwhile, simmer the bolognese. Add spoonfuls of the bolognese to the noodles until enough sauce clings to the noodles without covering them entirely. (You might have extra bolognese.) Cook over medium heat, thinning with a splash or two of the saved pasta water if the pot becomes too dry. Stir in a pat of butter and adjust salt and pepper if needed. Serve the pasta in warmed bowls and grate Parmigiano-Reggiano over the top.

ERBAZZONE TORTA *with* Braised Greens, Prosciutto Cotto, *and* Eggs

I grew up eating *erbazzone*, a savory, home-style Italian pie. Consisting of hearty braising greens, hard-boiled eggs, *prosciutto cotto*, and ricotta encased within a sturdy crust, *erbazzone* is at its best at room temperature, making it the perfect do-ahead recipe for a picnic or family meal. Rather than butter or lard, the crust for this pie is made with flour, olive oil, and wine, yielding a sturdy, more forgiving crust than the flaky crusts favored in American pie making. To counter the rich flavors of the *erbazzone*, I serve raw cardoon stalks dressed lightly in garlicky *bagna cauda*, a traditional vegetable dip from Piemonte.

SERVES 8

Dough

250 grams • scant 2 cups 00 flour

160 grams • 1 1/3 cups durum flour

2 grams • 1/2 teaspoon kosher salt

108 grams • 1/2 cup white wine

108 grams • 1/2 cup hot water

108 grams • 1/2 cup extra virgin olive oil

Filling

300 grams • 6 eggs

25 grams • 2 tablespoons extra virgin olive oil

25 grams • 2 tablespoons unsalted butter

75 grams • 1/4 yellow onion, finely chopped

600 grams • 1 pound, 5 ounces mixed braising greens, such as kale, mustard, chard, and dandelion, stemmed (about 12 cups)

2 grams • 1/2 teaspoon kosher salt

black pepper

100 grams • 1/2 cup soffritto (page 282)

200 grams • 1 cup drained ricotta (see page 281)

75 grams • 2 1/2 ounces prosciutto cotto, diced finely (a generous 1/2 cup)

50 grams • 2 ounces (3/4 cup) finely grated ricotta salata

nutmeg for grating

a pinch of sea salt

300 grams • 11 ounces (3 to 5 stalks) cardoon

1 lemon, cut into wedges

55 grams • 1/4 cup extra virgin olive oil

14 grams • 1 tablespoon unsalted butter

10 grams • 2 anchovies, minced

8 grams • 2 garlic cloves, minced

a pinch of dried red pepper flakes

1 gram • 1 teaspoon minced dill

kosher salt and black pepper

To make the dough: In a stand mixer with the paddle attachment, mix together the flours and salt on low speed. In a bowl, whisk together the wine, water, and oil. With the mixer on medium speed, drizzle in the liquid. Mix for 2 to 3 minutes or until a coarse dough forms, then turn onto the counter and knead several times by hand until the dough comes together and feels elastic. Wrap in plastic wrap and let rest for 30 minutes to soften and hydrate.

Preheat the oven to 325°F. Lightly oil a round casserole or pie dish.

Put 4 eggs in a small pot and cover with 1 to 2 inches of cold water. Bring the pot to a boil for 1 minute. Turn off the heat and let the eggs stand in the water for 8 minutes. Prepare an ice bath. Shock the eggs in the ice bath, then peel.

Heat the olive oil in a large, wide pot. Add the butter and onion and sweat until softened, about 2 minutes. Stir in the greens, season with salt and pepper, and cover. Cook until the greens are very soft, about 8 minutes. Pour the vegetables into a colander and let them drain. When cool enough to handle, chop the greens and place in a mixing bowl. Stir in the soffritto, ricotta, *prosciutto cotto*, and ricotta salata, and season with a few gratings of nutmeg, salt, and pepper. In a small bowl, whisk together the remaining 2 eggs and fold into the greens.

Clear a large work surface for rolling out the dough. Unwrap the dough and cut off a piece just slightly bigger than half of the total. With a rolling pin, roll the larger piece of dough on a lightly floured surface until it is about as thick as piecrust. Line the prepared dish with

{continued}

the dough. Spread half of the filling in the base of the pan, then nestle in the hard-boiled eggs. Cover the eggs with the remaining filling. With your fingertips or a pastry brush, brush water along the edge of the crust.

On a lightly floured surface, roll out the remaining half of the dough to the thickness of a piecrust. Drape the dough over the *torta*. Using your fingers, pinch the top and bottom crusts together, and crimp the edges, trimming away any excess dough. Using a paring knife, cut slits on the top of the *torta* so steam can escape. Brush the top with olive oil and sprinkle lightly with sea salt. Place the *torta* on a baking sheet and transfer to the oven. Bake for 65 to 70 minutes or until golden brown. Cool for at least 15 minutes before serving.

With a vegetable peeler, peel the stringy external layer off the cardoons. Slice the cardoons into 2-inch pieces, then soak in water with the juice from 1 or 2 lemon wedges. For the *bagna cauda*, in a small pot over very low heat warm the olive oil and butter. Add the anchovies and garlic and let infuse for 30 minutes. Stir in the red pepper flakes and remove from the heat. Drain the cardoons. Toss in a bowl with enough *bagna cauda* to coat. Season with dill, salt, pepper, and a few squeezes of lemon juice. Serve the *torta* in slices and spoon the dressed cardoons alongside.

PORK MILANESE, Pickled Cabbage Salad, Anchovy, *and* Lemon Brown Butter

By interpreting recognizable dishes in a new way, chefs can play with diners' emotional responses to food. This dish is a balancing act between contemporary and traditional: I keep the classic preparation intact while freshening up the accompaniments, including a raw cabbage salad quickly pickled with the help of a vacuum sealer. The pressure from the vacuum speeds up osmosis, forcing the pickling liquid to infuse into the vegetables faster than if they were left to soak in the brine. Alternatively, marinate the cabbage salad with the pickling liquid for at least a couple of hours or overnight. Since the salad is meant to be more of an accent than a side, the recipe makes only a small quantity. If you prefer serving a more generous portion, consider doubling it.

SERVES 4

Cabbage Salad

75 grams • 1 cup finely sliced brussels sprouts

65 grams • 1 cup finely sliced green cabbage

kosher salt

75 grams • 1 cup finely sliced red cabbage

30 grams • 1/4 cup julienned carrot

120 grams • 1/2 cup pickling liquid (page 281)

a pinch of caraway seeds, toasted

a pinch of mustard seeds, toasted

454 grams • 4 (4-ounce) or 8 (2-ounce) pork cutlets from loin, tenderloin, or leg

kosher salt and black pepper

2 eggs

about 1/2 cup Wondra flour

about 1/2 cup dried, finely ground breadcrumbs

blended oil for frying (page 278)

extra virgin olive oil

20 grams • 1 1/2 tablespoons sliced lemon confitura (page 279)

15 grams • 3 tablespoons finely sliced mint leaves

50 grams • 4 tablespoons unsalted butter

6 sage leaves

2 grams • 1/2 minced garlic clove

4 grams • 1/2 white anchovy, minced

15 grams • 1 tablespoon lemon juice

10 grams • 2 teaspoons chopped parsley

coarse sea salt

lemon wedges

In a colander, toss the brussels sprouts and green cabbage together with a generous pinch of salt. In a separate colander, mix the red cabbage with a generous pinch of salt. Let both mixes sit for 10 minutes. Pat both cabbage mixes dry, then combine in a bowl with the carrot. Transfer to a vacuum-seal bag, add the pickling liquid, the toasted caraway and mustard seeds, and vacuum-seal the bag. When ready to serve, cut open the bag and drain the salad.

Trim any sinew off the cutlets. Place them on a sheet of parchment paper and cover with an additional sheet. With a mallet, pound to 1/4 inch thick. Season with salt and pepper. Blend the eggs with a splash of water and pour into a shallow bowl. Put the flour on one plate and the breadcrumbs on another. Dredge each piece of pork in the flour, followed by egg wash, followed by the breadcrumbs.

In a large sauté pan, heat a thick film of blended oil over medium heat. In 2 batches to avoid crowding the pan, panfry the pork until golden brown and cooked through, about 2 minutes per side. In between batches, wipe the pan clean and add additional oil. Place the cutlets on paper towels and season with salt. Divide among 4 plates. Wipe the pan clean and set aside.

Toss the cabbage salad with enough olive oil to lightly coat, 1/2 tablespoon of the lemon confitura, and the mint. Taste and season with more salt or pickling liquid if needed, then divide the salad among the plates.

For the pan sauce, melt the butter in the sauté pan over medium heat. When the butter starts to foam, swirl in the sage leaves, followed by the garlic. Stir in the parsley, anchovy, and remaining 1 tablespoon lemon confitura and remove from the heat. Add the lemon juice and spoon the sauce over and around the pork. Season with coarse sea salt and serve lemon wedges alongside.

BUCKWHEAT POLENTA TARAGNA, Rabbit Stufato, Cherry Tomato, *and* Mimolette

Inhabitants of Lombardia's Adda Valley near the border of Switzerland, use buckwheat extensively in their hearty mountain cooking. It's especially common to add the dark, speckled flour to cornmeal for *polenta taragna*, a more savory alternative to classic polenta. Coarse, freshly ground cornmeal has a much more convincing corn flavor and better texture. (Since freshly ground polenta can be perishable, I buy it in small quantities and store it in the refrigerator.) But it does require longer cooking times. To avoid having the polenta dry out before it is fully cooked, I keep the pot covered until the very end, stirring it now and again to prevent scorching. The rich, soft polenta is an excellent foil for the simple braised rabbit legs.

In Lombardia, it is more traditional to finish *polenta taragna* with the local Bitto cheese. Mimolette, a deep-orange French cow's milk cheese colored with annatto, also makes a compelling flavor pairing with the polenta.

SERVES 4

Rabbit Stufato

extra virgin olive oil

710 grams • 4 (6-ounce) rabbit legs

kosher salt and black pepper

about ¼ cup Wondra flour

150 grams • ½ yellow onion, finely chopped

8 grams • 2 garlic cloves, sliced thinly

115 grams • ¾ cup soffritto (page 282)

1 teaspoon smoked paprika

a pinch of dried red pepper flakes

a pinch of cumin seeds

30 grams • 2 tablespoons tomato paste

100 grams • ¾ cup white wine

790 grams • 2 (14-ounce) cans canned cherry tomatoes

a sachet with 4 sprigs thyme, 2 sprigs rosemary, and 1 sprig sage (see page 282)

Polenta

200 grams • 1½ cups coarse cornmeal

50 grams • ½ cup buckwheat flour

680 grams • 3 cups water

480 grams • 2 cups whole milk

kosher salt

50 grams • 1¾ ounces unsalted butter

extra virgin olive oil

a block of Mimolette cheese

20 grams • 2 tablespoons minced pitted olives (green or black)

2 tablespoons chopped parsley

1 lemon for zesting

To make the rabbit: Preheat the oven to 325°F. Heat a film of olive oil in a Dutch oven or heavy-bottomed pot over medium-high heat. Season the rabbit legs on both sides with salt and pepper. Coat the legs lightly in Wondra, shaking off any excess. Brown the legs lightly on all sides, about 2 minutes per side, then transfer to a platter.

Wipe out the pot and heat a film of olive oil over medium heat. Stir in the onion and garlic, season with a pinch of salt, and sweat until softened, about 3 minutes. Stir in the soffritto, paprika, red pepper flakes, and cumin and cook for about 2 minutes more. Add the tomato paste and cook until lightly browned, 1 to 2 minutes. Pour in the wine and simmer until the wine has reduced by half. Pour in the tomatoes and their canning juices with 1 cup of water. Add the sachet and bring to a simmer. Nestle the legs into the pot, cover, and transfer to the oven. Braise for 1 hour. Remove the lid and cook for 15 minutes longer or until the rabbit legs are tender, yielding when pressed but not completely falling off the bone. Let cool for about 15 minutes. Taste the sauce, adding more salt and pepper if needed.

To make the polenta: In a bowl, mix together the cornmeal and flour. In a large Dutch oven or heavy-bottomed pot, bring the water and milk to a simmer. Season with a few pinches of salt. Whisk in the cornmeal-flour mixture and return to a boil. Whisk again, then turn the heat down to a very low simmer and cover the pot. Cook the polenta, removing the lid only to stir the pot every

10 minutes or so, for 35 minutes. Remove the lid and cook until the grains are completely cooked through, about 10 more minutes. If the polenta dries out at any point before the grains are cooked through, add a splash of water. To finish the polenta, stir in the butter and a splash of olive oil. Grate about 1/2 cup of Mimolette directly into the pot. Taste, adding more salt and cheese as needed. Keep hot until ready to serve.

Spoon the polenta into 4 warmed bowls. Place a rabbit leg in each bowl and sprinkle with olives and parsley. Drizzle some of the sauce over the legs. Grate lemon zest directly over the bowls and drizzle olive oil over the top. Finish with shavings of Mimolette.

FRIED QUINCE PIES
with Truffle Honey *and* Aged Balsamic

Emilia-Romagna's appetite for richness continues to dessert. Fried rosemary and sage leaves give the pies a sweet-and-savory flavor profile that lends well to wine pairings. I make these pies in several shapes, from half-moon turnovers to mini pies. Before frying, I freeze the pies so the filling is firm when it hits the oil. I also poke a hole into each pie to release steam and prevent them from bursting in the oil. I especially like the fragrance and tang of quince for this recipe, but apples are a fine substitute (you would need about 4 apples total for this recipe). Truffle honey makes good use of leftover truffle trimmings. Once made, it will keep for weeks, although the truffle flavor will become more pronounced over time.

MAKES 16 TO 20 PIES; SERVES 8 TO 10

Filling

215 grams • 2 quince (7 1/2 ounces)

75 grams • 1 small apple (2 3/4 ounces)

5 grams • 2 1/2 tablespoons unsalted butter

1 sprig rosemary

80 grams • scant 1/3 cup sweet wine, such as Moscato

7 grams • 2 teaspoons cornstarch

50 grams • 1/4 cup plus 3 tablespoons sugar

2 grams • 1/2 teaspoon kosher salt

1 gram • 1/2 teaspoon cinnamon

Dough

415 grams • 3 cups plus 1 tablespoon all-purpose flour

8 grams • 2 teaspoons baking powder

4 grams • 1 teaspoon kosher salt

40 grams • 3 tablespoons cold unsalted butter, cubed

40 grams • 3 tablespoons plus 1 teaspoon shortening

50 grams • 1 egg, lightly beaten

90 grams • 1/4 cup plus 1 tablespoon ice water

{continued}

2 sprigs rosemary, stemmed

1 egg

115 grams • ⅓ cup honey

2 grams • 1 tablespoon chopped black truffle, fresh or canned

3 grams • 1 teaspoon truffle oil

kosher salt

blended oil for frying (see page 278)

1 sprig sage, stemmed

confectioner's sugar

aged balsamic vinegar

To make the filling: Peel, core, and dice the quince, removing the fibrous white membrane in the center. Peel, core, and dice the apple. Melt the butter in a large, heavy-bottomed pot over medium heat until it bubbles and starts to brown. Stir in the quince and apple and cook until the fruit begins to soften, about 5 minutes. Stir in the rosemary sprig and continue to simmer.

In a small bowl, whisk together the wine and the cornstarch. Whisk the slurry into the fruit, followed by the sugar, salt, and cinnamon. Continue to simmer on medium to medium-low heat until the fruit is soft but still has texture, about 8 minutes. Cool to room temperature and remove the rosemary sprig. You should have about 1¼ cups of filling. Refrigerate until needed.

To make the dough: In a food processor, pulse together the flour, baking powder, and salt. Pulse in the butter and shortening until the fats form pea-sized pieces. Add the egg and the water. The dough will look crumbly, but should start to come together when kneaded on a lightly floured work surface. Form the dough into an 8-inch disk and cover in plastic wrap. Refrigerate for at least 1 hour or overnight.

On a lightly floured work surface, roll the dough into a large sheet about ⅛-inch thick. Using a 4-inch round cookie cutter, punch the dough into rounds. Gather the remaining trimmings and roll out again to make more rounds. You should have 16 to 20 rounds. Blend the egg and a splash of water to make an egg wash.

To shape each pie, place a heaping tablespoon of filling in the center of a round and embed with a couple of rosemary leaves. Brush the edges with an egg wash and fold the dough over to form a half-moon. Press the edges together to seal. With a skewer, punch a hole in the center of each pie to let the steam escape. Place the pies on a parchment-lined baking sheet, cover in plastic wrap, and freeze until ready to fry, at least 1 hour.

In a small bowl, mix together the honey, truffle, truffle oil, and a pinch of salt. In a large, wide pot, heat about 3 inches of oil to 360°F. Fry the remaining rosemary and sage until the leaves become crisp, about 20 seconds. Drain the leaves on a paper towel–lined plate. Using a skimmer or slotted spoon carefully lower the pies into the oil in batches. Fry until golden on all sides, 3 to 5 minutes. Drain the pies on paper towels and season with a pinch of salt. Dust with confectioner's sugar and serve, drizzling the tops of the pies with truffle honey and a scattering of crushed fried herbs. Finish with dots of balsamic vinegar.

VIA FRANCIGENA—
PIEDMONTE AND
VALLE D'AOSTA

Piemonte wine production areas

Boca
Gattinara
Bramaterra
Ghemme
Lessona
Colline Novaresi
Carema
Coste
della Sesia
Sizzano
Fara
Erbaluce di Caluso
Canavese
Valsusa
Gabiano
Torino
Collina Torinese
Chieri
Castelnuovo
Ruché
Asti
Monferrato
Colli
Tortonesi
Pinerolo
Roero
Moscato
d' Asti
Gavi
Barbaresco
Colline
Saluzzesi
Alba
Barolo
Langhe

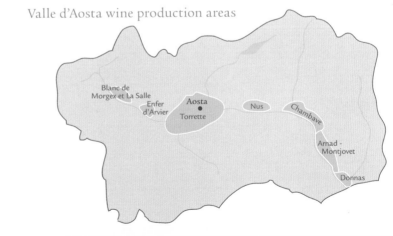

Valle d'Aosta wine production areas

Blanc de
Morgex et La Salle
Enfer
d'Arvier
Aosta
Nus
Chambave
Torrette
Arnad -
Montjovet
Donnas

VIA FRANCIGENA—PIEMONTE AND VALLE D'AOSTA

Piemonte

Tasting a wine made from an unfamiliar grape for the first time is to taste without preconceptions. Wading through Piemontese wines is an entirely different experience. Mention Barolo and Barbaresco and expectations rise. These two names, the calling cards of Piemonte's southeastern Langhe growing region, evoke mystique. This can be a good thing when looking to impress friends with a special-occasion bottle. It is less helpful when trying to encourage more casual consumers to venture into the very special—and surprisingly diverse—world of Piemonte wines. When the stakes are this high, everyone has an opinion.

With more DOC and DOCG zones than any other region, Piemonte is often considered Italy's top corner for quality wine production and grape diversity. When made with Nebbiolo, the wines from this mountainous northwest corner of Italy have long been compared to wines from Burgundy. Like top Burgundy bottles, Piemonte's Barolo and Barbaresco wines, with their enticing bouquets of rose petal, tar, and leather, require devotion and deep pockets from their enthusiasts. And while Piemonte's top *crus* (single-vineyard wines) aren't yet officially classified like they are in Burgundy, producers unofficially know where the best vineyards lie. In Piemonte, every last bit of limestone seems to be accounted for, making regions like Le Marche feel like uncharted territory in comparison. Connoisseurs can dedicate years to learning the differences among Barolos from the numerous subzones, such as La Morra and Monforte d'Alba, and still feel as if they barely have a handle on the nuances. For me, the trick has been finding a toehold in the region from which to learn, and then letting the wine do the talking.

Piemonte rests in the top western corner of Italy, sharing borders with France and Switzerland and abutting Valle d'Aosta, Lombardia, and Emilia-Romagna. I first visited the region in the fall, a time of year when Piemonte whirls with activity as harvest converges with the beginning of white truffle season. I had traveled to Torino for Terra Madre, the international Slow Food conference that occurs every other year. While artisans gathered to share culinary techniques from every corner of the world, *Gambero Rosso*, the prestigious Italian food and wine publication, held its annual Tre Bicchiere awards to the year's top wines. After the awards, I made my first trip to the Langhe hills, the epicenter of Piemonte's wine production. Lying east and south of the Tanaro River, it not only comprises Barolo and Barbaresco but also Alba (home to Barbera d'Alba), Dogliani (noted for Dolcetto), and countless more significant growing areas. Standing at the Castiglione Falletto on the road to Alba, I took in the panoramic view of the Barolo hills, each one tightly packed with manicured vineyards, and each one undoubtedly famous. These hills represent the highest concentration of quality viticulture in Italy, and healthy competition among neighbors guarantees that Piemontese wines keep getting better.

After walking through the aromatic autumn truffle festival in Alba, I headed west across the Tanaro River to Roero, an area that yields beautifully aromatic wines from grapes grown in sandy soils. There I met Mario Roagna, the proprietor of Cascina Val del Prete. Mario cultivates Nebbiolo, Barbera, and Arneis grapes using biodynamic methods, and his easygoing demeanor can be a breath of fresh air in a region that takes its wine so seriously. I mentioned the truffles I saw in Alba and Mario just shrugged his shoulders and unveiled a tennis ball–sized truffle that he had unearthed while out with his yellow Labrador. The pungent prize seemed to parallel what I was starting to discover about Piemonte: for all of the well-documented cellars in this wine region, there were still plenty of buried treasures.

Truffles' woodsy, autumnal perfume is a natural fit with Piemonte's sturdy cuisine. Ristorante Il Centro near Alba serves renditions of rich Piemontese dishes, like truffle-infused *fonduta*, the Italian answer to fondue. There is also *bagna cauda*, the buttery anchovy-infused dipping sauce served with cardoons, and risotto traditionally made with the rice grown in the Po Valley. These dishes beg for a wine with enough acid to cut through the richness, and Piemonte delivers. Nearly every kind of wine produced here, no matter the style, contains noticable acidity. Across the street, the mother of the owner of Il Centro runs an *aperitivo* bar pouring glasses of *spumante* in a casual place incongruously lined with bottles of Gaja, one of the region's best-known producers. Despite the famous bottles and decadent food, the whole scene feels down-to-earth, a mother and son running complementary businesses. The same can be said of Piemonte's pioneering vintners. No matter how grand the name, Piemonte winemaking is very much rooted in agriculture and community.

Walled off from the sea by the Ligurian Appenines, Piemonte has a classic continental climate. Temperatures drop in autumn and snow falls in winter. In inland winemaking regions, rivers hold high importance for their ability to temper climate extremes. Around the famous Langhe growing region, the Tanaro River serves this purpose, warming the air in the winter and cooling it in the summer. The cooling breezes from the mountains and the alkaline soil, a combination of clay, calcareous

marl, and limestone, allow for the development of grapes with high acidity. For naturally acidic Nebbiolo, which blossoms early and ripens late, the sunniest south-facing vineyard sites are ideal.

It's hard to talk about Piemonte without talking about Nebbiolo. While no one knows exactly when Nebbiolo arrived in the Langhe, the grape is mentioned as an established vine in the statutes of the La Morra commune as early as 1431. Years ago, the story goes, farmers studied the hills around Asti and Alba. They documented the slopes where the snow melted first, and these slopes became prime vineyard land for Nebbiolo. Today the south-facing vineyard land in the Barolo and Barbaresco zones is planted with Nebbiolo, while north-facing vineyards tend to be planted with Barbera and Dolcetto. Local vintners not only can date the soil of Barolo and Barbaresco—the late Miocene epoch—but also describe pitch of the slope and sun exposure. The Barolo zone alone comprises eleven subzones (Barolo, Castiglione Falletto, Cherasco, Diano d'Alba, Grinzane Cavour, La Morra, Monforte d'Alba, Novello, Roddi, Serralunga d'Alba, Verduno), and each subzone has its own vineyards. When you see "Cannubi" on a label, for instance, it's an indication that the wine was produced with grapes from the Cannubi vineyard in the Barolo subzone. For connoisseurs, this is an important detail: Cannubi is considered a prized *cru* in Barolo.

The history of Piemonte wines has both noble and humble roots. Many credit the estate of the Marchesi Falletti for linking the town name of Barolo with top-quality wine made with Nebbiolo grapes. The Falletti castle is in Barolo, but the Falletti estate covered neighboring communes La Morra, Serralunga, and Castiglione Falletto. After her husband died in 1838, the Marchesa Giuletta Falletti met French enologist Louis Oudart through her friend Camillo Benso di Cavour, who later became Piemonte's powerful prime minister. With Cavour's suggestion, she asked Oudart to make a modern wine from Barolo in the style of Burgundy. For Piemonte, this represented a significant break in tradition. Before Oudart, Nebbiolo wines were vinified sweet, never finishing fermentation. Through Oudart's guidance, winemakers soon shifted to a tradition that defined Piemonte's Nebbiolo wines until the 1970s and 80s: picking grapes late, fermenting the juices dry, and aging wine endlessly in large oak casks.

A much smaller area than Barolo with only three subzones (Barbaresco, Neive, and Treiso), Barbaresco used to be overshadowed by its neighbor. But like Barolo, the town of Barbaresco had long been recognized for wine. By the 1890s, it had became an official wine designation. Made with the same grape and using similar methods, both wines were often lumped together as one entity, and as their fame rose, makers of the wines sought to protect themselves from imitators. In 1966, Barolo and Barbaresco were granted DOC status, followed by DOCG status in 1980.

Piemonte's recent wine history has been far humbler, shaped by the people who worked in the cellars and vineyards themselves. The 1950s and 60s were not an easy time for Piemonte's rural areas, and young people moved to Torino to look for work. Around the Langhe, farmers with small plots of land cultivated grapes to sell to cellars for wine production. Vintners produced Barolo and Barbaresco from blends from several vineyards. That started to change in the 1970s. Some vintners began

buying up vineyard land to better control grape quality. Meanwhile, some of the great Nebbiolo growers, tired of selling quality fruit for low prices, started making their own wine. The changes converged in a period of unheralded prosperity in the Langhe, during which Barolo and Barbaresco gained international acclaim, property values ballooned, and winemakers became stars.

When people talk about the turning point in the region, the name Angelo Gaja inevitably comes up. Around the turn of the twentieth century, Gaja's grandparents ran a simple *osteria* in Barbaresco. The family maintained a modest winemaking operation on the side, selling wine to wealthy families. Their son Giovanni became the mayor of Barbaresco, and he ensured that his family's cellar continued to produce quality wine with the idea that he could pass the business on to his son. In the mid-twentieth century, the Gaja family began buying up plots of prime land in Barbaresco. When Angelo joined the family's wine operation in 1961, he started to see the value in changing the habitual approach to making wine. Against his father's wishes, Angelo started aging the wines in French *barrique* and encouraging malolactic fermentation, a process by which harsher malic acid is converted into softer lactic acid. The true turning point came in 1967, when Angelo released Barbaresco *cru*, Sorì San Lorenzo. The result: A wine that not only gave gravitas to Barbaresco—a designation that some used to dismiss as less-serious Barolo—but also changed the way that Piemonte vintners made and marketed wine by defining the vineyard on the label. (Angelo Gaja is just as legendary for his international outreach efforts to promote Italian wines as he is for making wine.) A few other famous producers, such as Bruno Giacosa in Barbaresco and Renato Ratti in Barolo, were also early to the game of *cru* Nebbiolo, which has now become common in the Langhe. The La Spinetta estate owned by the Rivetti brothers offers three distinctly different Barbarescos (Starderi, Gallina, and Valeirano) and one Barolo (Vursu Vigneto Campe), all designed to reflect the nuance of each wine's namesake vineyard.

In tandem with the shift that turned growers into vintners, significant changes to cellar management started thirty years ago. It was a time of debate between the so-called modernists, people like Angelo Gaja,

Giorgio Rivetti, and Roberto Voerzio, who saw temperature controlled fermentation and *barrique* aging as a way to advance the quality of their wines, and traditionalists, like Giuseppe Rinaldi, who eschewed new practices. Even today Rinaldi's cellar looks about the same as it did decades ago. Wines are fermented in open-topped wooden vats without temperature control and aged in large Slavonian oak casks.

Since the 1990s, American Barolo and Barbaresco consumers have been trained to take sides—choosing between traditional and modern styles—as if they are aligning themselves with a political party. Generally traditional-style wines are thought to be earthier wines imbued with leather, tobacco, and dried roses, while modern-style wines carry softer tannins and fruit-forward accents of black currant and sour cherry. Those who favor the modernists believe the harsh tannins of traditional-style wines make them undrinkable, even after decades of bottle aging. Modernists, the traditionalists argue, like their wines too sleek and international to be true expressions of the land. The reality in Piemonte is more nuanced. After years of argument and experimentation, Langhe winemakers are now making wine in a postmodern time, adapting both new and old techniques to suit their styles. "There isn't any discussion about *tradizionalista* or *modernista* any more," explains Silvia Altare, the oldest daughter of Elio Altare, one of the first in Piemonte to experiment with *barrique* aging (the decision caused his father to disinherit him). "Today we think that if a wine is objectively good, it can be good in any style," she says. "My dad always says that tradition is innovation that turned out well."

The most significant changes recently have been in the vineyards. Most top producers are continuing to reduce yields and implement biodynamic or organic farming practices. This postmodern style is evident among winemakers like Chiara Boschis, one of the only female producers of Barolo. Chiara, who studied economics, took over the historic E. Pira & Figli cellar in 1990. In contrast to the late legendary late enologist Luigi Pira, a staunch traditionalist who favored crushing grapes by foot, Chiara relies on shorter fermentations, malolactic fermentation, and *barrique* aging for her wines. Yet Chiara's sophisticated Barolo, made from organic grapes

from the famous Cannubi vineyard, convey all the power and complexity of the Nebbiolo grape.

Piemonte wine production does not stop at the banks of the Tanaro River. Barbera and Dolcetto, long designated as the table wines one drinks while waiting for Barolo to age, have been taken more seriously throughout southern Piemonte. The wines from Roero, a relatively new DOCG, are more accessible and aromatic than those from Barolo or Barbaresco because of sandier soils in the vineyards. For newcomers to Nebbiolo, these wines are an excellent place to start tasting. North of the rice fields surrounding the Po River, growers cultivate vines on remote, rugged terrain comprising alpine foothills, volcanic rock, and poor sandy soils. Grapes work harder to ripen here than they do in the Langhe. As a result, DOCG wines Gattinara and Ghemme as well as DOC wines Lessona and Carema produce nervy, lean Nebbiolos rounded out with other local grapes. One of my favorite summertime wines is Costa della Sesia Rosato Majoli, an aromatic *rosato* blend of Nebbiolo, Bonarda, Vespolina, and Barbera from Sella in Lessona.

MOSCATO

Grown in Greece, Italy, France, and far beyond, Moscato (Muscat) may be the original wine grapevine with one of the most diverse family trees in the *Vitis vinifera* species. While it is most often known as a white grape, it also grows red or black, sometimes on the same vine. As for the styles of wine that the grape produces, those too are seemingly endless—from dry to sweet, still to sparkling.

Golden-hued Moscato Bianco, called Moscato Canelli in Piemonte, is one of the most floral and aromatic subvarieties of Moscato grown in Italy. It is one of the most planted grapes in Piemonte, where it is grown extensively for sparkling Asti Spumante and Moscato d'Asti, effervescent, lightly sweet, low alcohol wines that can be perfect refreshers after a rich Piemontese meal. With its floral aromas and palate-cleansing bubbles, Asti provides a great match for goat cheese and fruit desserts.

Moscato also grows all over Italy, from Lazio, where jasmine-inflected Moscato di Terracina pairs well with seafood eaten along the Tyrhennian coast to Trentino–Alto Adige, where Moscato Rosa (Rosenmuskateller) yields a rosy, rose-scented still wine. Meanwhile, Moscato Giallo is a high-quality, golden Moscato subvariety that grows in Trentino–Alto Adige and Friuli. It has also taken to the Colli Euganei hills near Padua in Veneto, where it is used in Fior d'Arancio, a wine redolent of orange blossoms.

MOSCATO PRODUCERS

- **Piemonte:** Paolo Saracco, La Spinetta, Braida, La Morandina, Tre Donne, Bava, Traversa, Massolino, La Crotta di Vegneron, Il Falchetto
- **Veneto:** La Montecchia
- **Trentino-Alto Adige:** Alois Lageder, Zeni
- **Valle d'Aosta:** La Crotta di Vegneron
- **Le Marche:** Montecappone
- **Umbria:** Barberani
- **Lazio:** Cantine Sant'Andrea, Villa Gianna

Even though red wines get most of the attention in this region, Piemonte's treasures are just as likely to be white wines. In the right hands, Arneis, Erbaluce, and Cortese make more than thirst quenchers. Rescued from obscurity by Walter Massa, the Timorasso grape also has piqued interest. One of my personal favorite white wine discoveries in Piemonte is not made with a native grape at all. Sergio Germano, who makes Barolo under the Ettore Germano label, started planting Riesling in a vineyard surrounded by Dolcetto vines—a move that many called crazy. They took back their words when his fresh, mineral-tinged Langhe Bianco Hérzu went on to win a *Gambero Rosso* Tre Bicchieri award.

Despite the other wines produced in Piemonte, it's *spumante* that truly keep the lights on. Asti is easily the largest-producing DOCG in Piemonte. Comprising mainly Moscato Canelli grapes, Asti Spumante and Moscato d'Asti are the area's two best-selling sparklers, ranging from dry and off-dry to very sweet. The best versions are delightfully refreshing, with tangy apricot and peach notes. After a day of tasting through Barolo or Barbaresco or eating a rich *piemontese* meal, a glass of *spumante* can be the perfect palate refresher. La Spinetta first produced its fresh yet honeyed Moscato d'Asti Bricco Quaglia—the region's first *cru* Moscato—in 1977. More recently La Spinetta acquired Contratto, Piemonte's oldest producer of classic-method sparkling wines. With the historic property in Canelli now owned by the forward-thinking Rivetti family, perhaps we're in for another story of what was old is new again in Italian wine. —SL

White Grapes

ARNEIS

Once used mainly as a blending grape to cut Nebbiolo's intensity, Arneis came into its own a couple of decades ago to become one of Piemonte's most recognizable white grapes. Arneis means "little rascal" in the Piemontese dialect, a suitable name given the vine's tendency to be ornery and difficult to cultivate. By the 1970s, few producers grew the low-acid grape, which produced low yields in the vineyard, attracted mildew, and oxidized easily. After a few producers took an interest in the grape, notably Barolo producers Bruno Giacosa and Alfredo Currado, production grew, spurred by the development of a thirsty international market for Piemontese wines. Arneis is at its most aromatic when cultivated in the sandy soils of Roero, where it has DOCG status. The best renditions are delicate and aromatic with notes of jasmine, pear, almond, and apricot. Arneis can be lean, as in the renditions from Corregia and Giacosa, or it can be honeyed and rich, like the versions from Brovia and Cornarea.

RECOMMENDED PRODUCERS: Brovia, Bruno Giacosa, Castello di Neive, Ceretto, Cornarea, Deltetto, Giovanni Almondo, Malvirà, Matteo Correggia, Michele Chiarlo

CORTESE

The main grape of the Gavi DOCG, Cortese classically makes crisp, mineral-rich, and moderately acidic wines with notes of wax bean. Grown in southwestern Piemonte and parts of Lombardia for centuries, Cortese is a tough, disease-resistent variety that is able to produce high yields while still maintaining quality. Cortese also makes wonderful *spumante* wines, as evident by Villa Sparina Brut.

RECOMMENDED PRODUCERS: Villa Sparina, La Scolca, Broglia, Marchesi di Barolo, Nicola Bergaglio, Coppo La Rocca, La Giustiniana Lugarara, Bava, Contratto Arnelle, Cascina degli Ulivi, Michele Chiarlo

ERBALUCE

Ancient Erbaluce is an all-purpose grape. Grown in Piemonte for centuries, it was traditionally made as *passito* in the Canavese growing area near the border of Valle d'Aosta. But the sweet, dried-grape version is becoming increasingly rare as more producers vinify it dry. In this style, Erbaluce is a lean, aromatic wine with accents of wildflowers, almonds, and evergreen freshness. Luigi Ferrando's Erbaluce di Caluso Cariola is benchmark Erbaluce.

RECOMMENDED PRODUCERS: Ferrando, Orsolani, Antoniolo, Colombaio

FAVORITA

Favorita may be yet another branch on the tangled Vermentino vine's family tree. A traditional table wine of the Langhe hills and Roero, Favorita grapes are large and make good eating grapes. In the past, the grape was either blended with Nebbiolo to soften the red grape's tannins or made into a simple farmhouse white. More recently, Arneis and Chardonnay vines have replaced Favorita, but ongoing exploration of native grapes has encouraged some to revisit its potential. As a wine, Favorita is delicate but high in acidity, with mild notes of pear and stone fruit.

RECOMMENDED PRODUCERS: Deltetto, Gianni Gagliardo, Malvirà, Monchiero Carbone

TIMORASSO

Once common throughout Piemonte's Alessandria province, in recent years all that was left of Timorasso were a few hectares owned by Walter Massa near the city of Tortona. After several years of vineyard experiments, Massa landed on a winning formula, winning the *Gambero Rosso* grower of the year award in 2011. Today the pleasantly weighty, thick-skinned grape is made in both stainless steel and oaked styles. With its richness, high acidity, and flavor notes of graphite and stone fruit, Timorasso is a great food wine. When it is aged in oak, it takes on more buttery tones similar to Chardonnay.

RECOMMENDED PRODUCERS: Claudio Mariotto, Fontanassa, La Colombera, Ricci, Terralba, Vigneti Massa

Red Grapes

BARBERA

One of the most grown red grapes in Italy, Barbera accounts for almost half of the DOC wines in Piemonte, with Barbera d'Alba and Barbera d'Asti its best-known wines. With its low tannins and plump, juicy fruit, the grape makes accessible, versatile wines. It's often said that while the Piemontese wait for Barolo to age, they drink Barbera. Yet while a good deal of Barbera is light and fruit-forward, some can age up to ten years. While lower in tannins than Nebbiolo, Barbera carries a notable amount of acidity, which balances its plush fruit. In the 1980s, Giacomo Bologna of Braida was first modern producer to take Barbera seriously by aging it in *barrique*—an extravagance unheard of for the variety. Braida's Bricco dell'Uccellone elevated the status of the variety, inspiring other winemakers to do the same. Outside of Piemonte, Barbera shows up in several wines, such as the Croatina-Barbera blends of Gutturnio in Emilia and Oltrepò Pavese in Lombardia.

RECOMMENDED PRODUCERS: Braida, Matteo Correggia, Domenico Clerico, Elio Grasso, Grimaldi, Bava, Ceretto, Giovanni Rosso, Ca'Viola, Cavallotto, Massolino, G. D. Vajra, Olim Bauda, Gianfranco Bovio, Accornero, Rocche dei Manzoni

BONARDA

The Bonarda that grows in Piemonte is unrelated to the Bonarda in Lombardia's Oltrepò Pavese area (that grape is Croatina, page 167). Rather, Bonarda in Piemonte is a similar but separate fruity grape. It is low in tannins and, like Vespolina, is sometimes blended into the wines of Gattinara and Ghemme to add body and color to Nebbiolo. Confusingly, in Piemonte and beyond, the grape is also called Uva Rara.

RECOMMENDED PRODUCERS: Ioppa, Sella, Cantine Sociale Sizzano e Ghemme, Produttori di Govone, Il Vino dei Padri

BRACHETTO

The grape of one of Piemonte's more traditional wines, Brachetto d'Acqui, Brachetto was once thought to have aphrodisiacal qualities. The grape has a natural sweetness, an attribute emphasized in the off-dry styles of this wine. Brachetto d'Acqui is a *frizzante*, low-alcohol wine with flavors of strawberry, rose petal, and violets. As a postprandial beverage, it is often paired with chocolate or hazelnut-infused *gianduja*.

RECOMMENDED PRODUCERS: Marenco, Traversa, Malvirà, Icardi, Monchiero, Casa Sant'Orsola, Cascina Ca'Rossa, Tosti, Marchesi di Barolo, Matteo Correggia

DOLCETTO

The translation of this grape's name, "little sweet one," can be deceptive. It comes from the sweet character of the grape eaten out of hand, not the wine that it becomes. While deep-purple Dolcetto carries bright acidity, it doesn't offer much in the way of sweetness, although the tannins can have a sweet character when made in a riper style. The grape, which is related to Liguria's Ormeasco, has evolved into a bright, youthful wine that tends to be aged in stainless steel tanks to showcase the fruit. Top Dolcetto comes from Dogliani, a DOCG zone since 2005, especially from producers such as Pecchenino, though Alba also has also has a rich history of Dolcetto cultivation with producers like Elio Altare consistently releasing beautiful expressions of the wine.

RECOMMENDED PRODUCERS: Elio Altare, Roagna, E. Pira & Figli, Chionetti, Pecchenino, Massolino, Mascarello, Marziano Abbona, Anna Maria Abbona, Albino Rocca, Ca'Viola, Mauro Molino, Bruno Rocca, Villa Sparina, Brovia, Bricco Maiolica

FREISA

Once grown extensively throughout northern Italy for everyday wines, Freisa plantings today are most common in Piemonte. The grape is native to the region; DNA analysis has shown that Freisa is an offspring of Nebbiolo. Even though it has blue-black grapes, Freisa produces a medium-bodied red wine with floral, strawberry-like aromatics paired with slightly bitter tannins. It is used often in *rosato* wines.

RECOMMENDED PRODUCERS: Giacomo Borgogno, Cascina Gilli, Marchesi di Barolo, Cavallero, Lo Spaventapasseri

GRIGNOLINO

Indigenous to the Monferrato hills, Grignolino is a pale, orange-red grape; the wine carries hints of anise, black pepper, and cardamom. Its name means "many pips" because of the large number of seeds in each grape, which make it difficult to press. So the grape's seeds are removed early in the winemaking process, yielding a light-bodied, high-acid wine. Grown in two DOCs, Grignolino d'Asti and Grignolino del Monferrato Casalese, the variety is best consumed young.

RECOMMENDED PRODUCERS: La Casaccia, Luca Ferraris, Rinaldi, Tavijn, Damilano, Contratto,

NEBBIOLO

Nebbiolo emits an alluring aroma of rose petal and leather and can taste like everything from sour cherries to tar and iodine. It first draws you in with aroma and hooks you with complexity.

Nebbiolo is among Italy's most celebrated indigenous red grapes. Its name derives from the word *nebbia*, fog, which rolls into Piemonte every September and October in time for harvest. Nebbiolo has extremely high levels of tannin and acidity, which makes it an ideal candidate for long periods of aging. Indeed, the best Nebbiolo wines, whether they are from Barolo, Barbaresco, Roero, or farther afield—including Gattinara and Ghemme north of the Langhe, Carema and Donnas along the Valle d'Aosta border, and alpine Valtellina in Lombardia— are meant to age, sometimes for decades. Like Pinot Noir, Nebbiolo is prone to genetic mutation. It is likely that Nebbiolo is the parent grape of Freisa, Vespolina, and Viognier, among others. Of the countless clones of Nebbiolo that exist, Lampia and Michet are the most common, with lighter colored Rosé a distant third. Away from the Langhe, Nebbiolo goes by one of its several synonyms. In the Vercelli and Novara hills of northern Piemonte, it is called Spanna. In Valle d'Aosta, it is called Picotendro. And in Valtellina, it goes by Chiavennasca. These mountain Nebbiolo plantings yield lighter, medium-bodied wines compared with Nebbiolo from the Langhe, but they lack none of Nebbiolo's floral aromatics, intensity, or verve. For those looking for under-the-radar Nebbiolo, these mountain wines—when you can find them—are worth exploring.

RECOMMENDED PRODUCERS THROUGHOUT NORTHERN ITALY

- **Barbaresco:** Ca' del Baio, Ceretto, Cigliuti, Gaja, Icardi, Moccagata, Produttori del Barbaresco, Bruno Giacosa, La Spinetta, Paitin di Pasquero-Elia, Prunotto, Marchesi di Grésy, Albino Rocca, Enrico Serafino, Coppo, Pelissero
- **Barolo:** Aldo Conterno, Armando Parusso, Brovia, Bruno Giacosa, Castello di Verduno, Gianfranco Bovio, Giacomo Borgogno, Giacomo Conterno, Giuseppe Rinaldi, Paolo Scavino, Luciano Sandrone, Elvio Cogno, Schiavenza, Vietti, Renato Ratti, Pio Cesare, Oddero, E. Pira & Figli, Elio Altare, Renato Corino, Azelia, Boroli, Elio Grasso, Conterno Fantino, Michele Chiarlo, Fontanafredda, Germano Ettore

- **Roero:** Ca' Prete, Ca' Rossa
- **Gattinara:** Travaglini, Antoniolo, Anzivino, Umberto Fiore, Antonio Vallana, Dessilani, Nervi
- **Lessona:** Sella
- **Ghemme:** Antichi Vigneti, Dessilani, Umberto Fiore, Giuseppe Bianchi, Ioppa
- **Carema:** Ferrando, Orsolani
- **Boca:** Le Piane, Castello di Conti, Antonio Vallana
- **Valtellina:** Nino Negri, Conti Sertoli Salis, ArPePe, Aldo Rainoldi, Sandro Fay, Mamete Prevostini
- **Donnas:** Caves Cooperatives de Donnas, Cooperativa La Kiuva, Arnad-Montjovet

Prunotto, Braida, Castello di Neive, Olek Bondonio, Cavallotto, Villa Fiorita, Marchesi Incisa della Rocchetta

PELAVERGA

The Burlotto family has been instrumental in the recent revival of this noble vine. Light red Pelaverga is cultivated in the same areas used grow Nebbiolo, such as La Morra, Roddi, and Verduno. (Pelaverga from Verduno became a DOC in 1995.) Pelaverga wine carries strawberries and cranberries on the nose, accented with white pepper. Local folklore attributed aphrodisiacal properties to Pelaverga, and it is occasionally referred to as "Baciadonne," lady kisser.

RECOMMENDED PRODUCERS: G. B. Burlotto, Castello di Verduno, Giacomo Ascheri, Alessandria

RUCHÉ

Along with Lacrima di Morro d'Alba and Moscato Rosso, Ruché is one of Italy's most aromatic reds. Like those reds, Ruché's classic flavors skew floral, from violet to rose petal, but Ruché tends to carry more acidity and have undertones of spices like white pepper and clove. The sparsely grown, deep-purple grape has a peppery bite, making it a wonderful wine to pair with braises, rabbit, and bitter greens. The *passito* versions are hard to find, but when they're available I like to pair them with buttery cow's milk cheeses or nutty *gianduja*.

RECOMMENDED PRODUCERS: Tavijn, Sant'Agata, Luca Ferraris, Montalbera Laccento, Osel, Bava, Dacapo, Gitton Francesco, Dezzani, Crivelli

VESPOLINA

Most common in the northern Piemonte areas of Gattinara and Ghemme, Vespolina is a workhorse grape that is often blended with Nebbiolo for color and body. Many historic producers, like Tenute Sella, have Vespolina vines dating back to the mid-twentieth century. Blended into wines, such as Sella's Costa della Sesia Rosato Majoli in Lessona, it lends a round, spicy note to the *rosato* wine.

RECOMMENDED PRODUCERS: Ioppa, Sella, Antoniolo, Dessilani, Nervi, Travaglini, Umberto Fiore, Alessandro Antonelli, Rovellotti

Valle d'Aosta

Nearly any time I come across a wine region where production is naturally limited because of short growing seasons, space restrictions, or topographical challenges, I find good wine. When producers stubbornly persevere year after year despite challenges, the care and effort tends to shine forth in the glass. This is one of the reasons that, long before I ever visited, I started to seek out the wines of the tiny, alpine region of Valle d'Aosta.

Lying north of Piemonte, south of Switzerland, and east of France, Valle d'Aosta is truly alpine territory, a place more conducive to hiking and skiing than to agriculture. Yet wine has been made here for centuries, and some of the most historic vineyards are found at elevations higher than any other growing region in Europe. When I finally visited, my first stop was in Quart, a hillside commune close to Aosta, the region's capital city. There I piled into Vincent Grosjean's white van and together we ambled up to his family's vineyard. Vincent and his brothers run the Grosjean label, one of the most respected in the area. The vines, which have been farmed organically for decades, stood in neat rows perpendicular to the steep incline, the face of Mont Blanc looming large on the western horizon.

The Grosjeans produce an impressive range of wines. The family makes wine with Fumin, a dark-red, spicy native grape; Cornalin, a red variety better known in Switzerland; and Petite Arvine, a local white grape quickly becoming a favorite in the region, as well as a handful of others. I like to pair the Grosjean's Petite Arvine with Matthew's food because of the way the wine stimulates the palate with an unexpected mix of pine, walnut shell, and Golden Delicious apple.

Vincent poured me a glass of wine made with Premetta, a native grape rarely found outside of the region. At first I thought I was tasting *rosato*—Italian rosé—technically a red wine vinified without skin contact. But the wine undergoes eight days of fermentation and maceration on the skins—because Premetta is such a light, thin-skinned grape, its skins do not have much color to extract. I was instantly hooked on the light, spicy Premetta. These are the kinds of finds that make Italy so exciting for wine geeks.

Valle d'Aosta is by far the smallest region in Italy, and its wine production is similarly diminutive. In 2010, the region produced slightly more than 580,000 gallons—less than 1 percent of Italy's total output. Yet winemaking here predates Roman times. The Romans, who founded the city of Aosta around 25 BC, built roads leading out of the Aosta valley by cutting into the rocky sides of the mountains. These strategic pathways through the Alps remained important for centuries after Roman rule. Some roads, later cobbled together in the Middle Ages as the Via Francigena, became the main thoroughfare for northern European pilgrims on their way to Rome. Other roads encouraged settlement in temperate Donnas in the southeastern corner of Valle d'Aosta, which became known for its Nebbiolo-based wine. (The main cooperative in the area, Caves Cooperatives de Donnas, is located on Via Roma.) In addition to roads, the Romans carved trellises into hillsides, dividing vineyard parcels with stones. Some of these trellises are still in use. Meanwhile, the stones, which conduct heat throughout the day, are relied upon to keep vines warm on cold alpine nights.

While grape cultivation continued for centuries after the Roman occupation, it started to decline in the twentieth century. Vineyards were abandoned as *valdostani* emigrated to France or Switzerland or left to work in booming northern Italian cities such as Torino. By the late 1960s, less than 500 acres of vineyard remained in use. There were a few blips of fame that temporarily reinvigorated local viticulture until, in 1983, local growers founded the cooperative Cave du Vin Blanc de Morgex et de La Salle at the foot of Mont Blanc, which soon set the standard for quality in Valle d'Aosta. Today, led by enologist Gianluca Telloli, the cooperative has become most known for its nervy sparklers and still wine made with Prié Blanc grapes. The late Ezio Voyat also received attention from Italian wine aficionados and sommeliers for his small-production, idiosyncratic wines. His 1961 Chambave Rouge, an electrifying red wine made with local Petite Rouge, became a cult classic, its tart and ripe flavors offering the unusual combination of a wine that was at once vibrant and jammy, with high-toned aromatics such as freesia and rose petals. Today a neighbor makes wine for the Voyat family.

At the end of the twentieth century, few bottles were exported from Valle d'Aosta—if you wanted to try the region's wines, you had to visit. The one individual who was able to break onto the international scene early on—and stay there—is Constantino Charrère of Les Crêtes. Inspired by the white wines of Burgundy, Charrère started making *barrique*-aged wine from locally grown Chardonnay. Grown in mountainside vineyards near the base of Mont Blanc, Charrère's Chardonnay kept the rich, tropical flavors of the grape in check with toasty notes of hazelnut supported with a firm mineral backbone. Today Les Crêtes is the largest privately owned winery in Valle d'Aosta. Consequently it tends to be the easiest Valle d'Aosta wine to find domestically, delivering a level of quality and integrity representative of the area.

Today the market for Valle d'Aosta wines has opened up—somewhat. The region now has about 870 acres in vine, nearly double what it had a few decades ago. As interest in native grapes continues to grow throughout Italy, Valle d'Aosta has proven to be full of treasures. Since the phylloxera insect never took hold in the cold climate or sandy soil of the Blanc de Morgex vineyards, Prié Blanc vines were spared from the devastating vineyard disease that affected most of Europe's wine-production zones. Some Prié Blanc vines planted with original rootstocks are more than ninety years old.

Outside of the best-known producers, like Les Crêtes, and the handful of cooperatives, most vintners make wine on the scale of a *garagiste*, the French term for someone who makes wine at home. One such producer, Franco Noussan, lives near Aosta in a hillside town of Saint-Christophe. After inheriting old Fumin, Petite Rouge, Mayolet, and Pinot Gris vines, he started making wine at home, releasing the wine under his own label in 2005. With only five thousand bottles produced annually, winemaking isn't a full-time pursuit for Franco (he also teaches at a local university). Yet his Torrette, a wine made mainly with Petite Rouge, was one of the best reds I tried in the region, a subtle, medium-bodied wine of red plum and dark chocolate with a pleasant, velvety texture. Similar alpine reds are extremely versatile food wines. Some are acidic and aromatic enough to pair well with seafood dishes, but they are best tasted alongside Valle d'Aosta's fontina cheeses and braised beef dishes.

Valle d'Aosta wines have a way of feeling as impenetrable as the wall of mountains that surrounds the region. Naming conventions range from varietal names (Valle d'Aosta Petite Rouge is made with Petite Rouge) to place names (Torrette, named for the town of Torrette, is based on Petite Rouge but also can include other red grapes). In addition, the area already has an eclectic mix of grapes and wine names. Some grapes are Piemontese, some are French, some are Swiss, and some are native to Valle d'Aosta. Pinot Grigio is more commonly known as Pinot Gris, yet a local mutation of Pinot Gris is called Malvoisie. Nebbiolo is grown, but it's called Picotendro—some of the time. And even native grapes have more than one name. Prié Blanc is also called Blanc de Morgex, after the town it grows around.

All these grapes are made into wines under the region's eponymous DOC, which accounts for more than two dozen styles of wine. Most of the vineyard land in the growing area shares the same semifertile glacial moraine. The western corner of the DOC near Mont Blanc, where Morgex is located, has the highest, coldest vineyards while Donnas, the narrow southeastern corner that borders Piemonte, is nearly Mediterranean in comparison. Here, Caves Cooperatives de Donnas produces aromatic, bright acidic mountain Nebbiolo that shares some similarities to the Nebbiolo grown around Piemonte's Caluso commune just across the border. The center of the DOC, which includes Nus, Torrette, and Chambave, tends to offer the most variety: medium-bodied reds in any combination of Petite Rouge, Fumin, and Gamay grapes as well as dry and sweet wines with Moscato and Malvoisie. While the region continues to produce more red wine than white, its successes with Chardonnay, Pinot Gris, Prié Blanc, and local Petite Arvine indicate that the mountain soils and crisp climate are effective at drawing out notes of nuts and stone fruit wrapped in an attractive, mineral-tinged package.

The growing season in Valle d'Aosta is short. Some vines blossom as late as June and harvest often starts around mid-September so growers can avoid snowfall. The steeply pitched slopes make mechanical harvesting impossible, and the vines themselves are physically difficult to maintain. Vines are trained close to the ground in a traditional *pergola bassa*—low pergola—trellis system

used here for centuries, which forces the vines to lie low to the ground so they can absorb heat generated from the soil and rock. Vines trellised this way are also strong, able to withstand damage due to heavy snowfall. Yet low vines means that harvest often requires a great deal of kneeling. It's a true communal effort to get the grapes picked, but the effort is well worth it. Italians have a term for this kind of demanding vine cultivation: *viticoltura eroica*, heroic viticulture. To this kind of heroism, I raise my glass. —SL

White Grapes

NUS MALVOISIE

The local name for Pinot Grigio (page 117), Nus Malvoisie is a traditional white in the Valle d'Aosta village of Nus. Traditionally consumed before a meal, it is a delicate wine imbued with stone fruits. Even though it is a strain of Pinot Grigio, it carries more of an evergreen and hazelnut character than classic Pinot Grigio.

RECOMMEDED PRODUCERS: 4000 Mètres, Les Crêtes, La Crotta di Vegneron, Les Granges

PETITE ARVINE

While the origin of Petite Arvine is unknown, the grape has been grown in Switzerland and Valle d'Aosta for centuries. Its name comes from the small berries and concentrated flavors, which yield nervy, ageworthy wines. In the steep slopes of Valle d'Aosta, the grape gains mineral structure and flavor notes of evergreens, Golden Delicious apples, and honey.

RECOMMENDED PRODUCERS: Les Crêtes, Grosjean, Ottin

PRIÉ BLANC

Primarily known for the Blanc de Morgex et de La Salle DOC, Prié Blanc is a high altitude–loving white grape grown at the base of Mont Blanc. Its refreshing acidity provides a great backbone for the flinty, slate-like, and green apple character of Prié Blanc, which also makes it a good grape for sparkling wines. Prié Blanc is farmed by small growers and most of the production is made at La Cave, a cooperative that unites about ninety growers. The grape is traditionally planted in the *pergola bassa* method near the stone walls that surround each vineyard and capture as much heat as possible. Some harvesters pick the grapes either on their knees or laying on their backs, leaving a small quantity of grapes on the vines for late-harvest ice wine Chaudelune. For this wine, grapes can only be picked after the vines have experienced a few significant freezes—a style that emerged in the early nineteenth century during an extremely harsh stretch of winters.

RECOMMENDED PRODUCERS: Cave du Vin Blanc, Vevey, Ezio Voyat, 4000 Mètres, Ermes Pavese

Red Grapes

CORNALIN

While this grape may have originated in Valle d'Aosta, it is better known in Switzerland's Valais wine region. Cornalin performs well in the alpine climate, reaching higher levels of ripeness, color, and tannins in the region's short growing season. Blended with other red grapes, it creates some of the best wines of Valle d'Aosta.

RECOMMENDED PRODUCERS: Grosjean, Anselmet, Les Crêtes

FUMIN

This almost extinct *valdostani* native grape—meaty and Syrah-like, with rustic charm—is experiencing a renaissance. Fumin wines offer wonderful depth of fruit flavor with deep, inky color and fresh acidity. While it is made into a stand-alone wine, it is often blended with other grapes for color and body.

RECOMMENDED PRODUCERS: La Crotta di Vegneron, Les Crêtes, Ottin, Di Barró, Feudo di San Maurizio, Grosjean

SEE ALSO: Dolcetto (page 205), Pinot Nero (page 144), Nebbiolo (page 206)

MAYOLET

A cross between Cornalin and Petite Rouge, Mayolet is a difficult grape to propagate because of its tendency to ripen unevenly. Yet its piercing acidity can make it an ideal red wine for food pairings, like shellfish, that usually are matched with richer white wines. Mayolet carries a subtle spiciness, with white pepper and cardamom, balanced by red berry fruits.

RECOMMENDED PRODUCERS: L'Enfer d'Arvier, Coenfer, Di Barró, Noussan, Les Crêtes

PETITE ROUGE

Known for its compact berries and thick purple skins, Petite Rouge accounts for most of the red wine production in Valle d'Aosta and is planted throughout the region. Compared with other alpine red grapes, Petite Rouge can offer a rounded wine imbued with blackberry fruits. While most wines in Valle d'Aosta contain blends of grapes, vintners have started to shift to producing premium wines with single varieties, and Petite Rouge is one of the grapes leading the way.

RECOMMENDED PRODUCERS: Ezio Voyat, Grosjean, Noussan, Les Crêtes, L'Enfer d'Arvier, Anselmet, Didier Gerbelle, Château Feuillet

PREMETTA

This is hands down the lightest red grape that I've encountered. While made like a red wine, it's the same blush color of France's Bandol rosé. The grape's skin has little color to extract, and the grapes are large, which dilutes the skin-to-pulp ratio. Grown around the towns of Aosta and Avise, early-ripening Premetta is rare, although growers like Grosjean are working on reviving it. As a red wine, it has beautiful strawberry and cranberry accents with tomato leaf aromatics and an orange-red, coral color. The wine carries slight tannins and finishes refreshingly dry.

RECOMMENDED PRODUCERS: Grosjean, Les Crêtes

Slowing Down

THE FIRST TIME I visited Valle d'Aosta, it was spring, just after the close of ski season. Apart from the small number of year-round residents, the alpine towns had emptied. With the throngs of French and Italian skiers gone, even finding an open restaurant proved challenging. It was as if the local economy that had sprinted to keep up with the winter tourists instinctually had shifted into a slower gear.

Capped by the imposing Mont Blanc, the Aosta Valley is really only accessible by the well-maintained A5 *autostrada*, which winds by fortified mountain towns that once served as an early warning system for northern invasion. This geographic protection has kept the valley and many of its traditions intact, even in the twenty-first century. Molded by the mountains, the people of Valle d'Aosta are hardy and proud. The cuisine in the region also reflects these surroundings. When I think of Valle d'Aosta, I think of hills carpeted with wildflowers, which perfume the local honey. I remember dairy cows that roam the mountainsides with their clanging bells and I can taste the deep-yellow cheeses made from their milk. In this alpine valley, I most often enjoyed hearty, unfussy meals, like slow-cooked beef served over polenta.

Another hearty cuisine is served south of Valle d'Aosta, although it is one with a few more famous ingredients. The Piemonte region is home to the white truffles of Alba and chocolate of Turin, and the piemontese town of Bra plays host to the headquarters of the Slow Food movement. On a visit to Bra, the menu at Osteria del Boccondivino, the restaurant located at the headquarters, reflected an obsession with ingredients—and tradition. A plate of lardo, salsiccia di Bra, and carne cruda battuta was presented in stark simplicity: slices of snowy white fat, a timbale of chopped pink meat, and a link of raw, rosy sausage (yes, you could eat it raw). I ate it just like it was served, and it was amazingly good.

The concept of slowing down to consider the providence of ingredients and flavor is integral to contemporary cooking. For me, ingredients offer a place from which to start. From good ingredients, we can spring forward with technique and creativity. The recipes in this chapter are inspired from instances when time slows down. From childhood, I remember eating egg in a hole and my grandmother's stuffed artichokes. From traveling in Italy, I hearken back to hearty flavors evocative of this inland corner of Italy, from fontina and mushrooms, to chestnuts and veal, beef and red wine, and—of course—truffles. —MA

EGG "IN THE HOLE"
with Mushrooms
and Miner's Lettuce

There is an irresistible whimsy in an egg cooked in the center of a piece of bread. With earthy mushrooms and rutabaga, this version is evocative of a brisk fall walk through the woods. I would serve it as a savory weekend lunch dish or, topped with shaved white truffles, a decadent first course. To add even more decadence, I occasionally make homemade butter. It is surprisingly easy to do: pour good cream in a stand mixer and whip it long enough that the butterfat breaks free of the buttermilk. Drain the buttermilk away, mix the butterfat with a pinch of salt, and it is ready to use.

SERVES 4

60 grams • 2 ounces rutabaga, peeled and cut in small dice ($1/2$ cup)

extra virgin olive oil

160 grams • $5^1/2$ ounces (2 cups) mushrooms, preferably hen of the woods

kosher salt

60 grams • $1/4$ cup finely diced bacon

40 grams • 3 tablespoons white wine

115 grams • $1/2$ cup brown stock (page 283)

4 ($3/4$-inch) slices brioche

about 4 tablespoons unsalted butter, plus more to finish

4 eggs

15 grams • $1/2$ shallot, minced

1 gram • 1 teaspoon chopped tarragon

a handful of miner's lettuce or chickweed

In a small pot of boiling, salted water, blanch the diced rutabaga until al dente, about 2 minutes. Drain well. Heat a film of olive oil in a large sauté pan over high heat until almost smoking. Scatter the mushrooms in an even layer and sear without moving them until they begin to brown, about 1 minute. Turn the heat down, give the mushrooms a stir, and season with salt. Sauté until the mushrooms are cooked through, 1 to 2 minutes more. Drain the mushrooms on paper towels and return the pan to the stove over medium heat. Add the bacon and cook until the fat has nearly fully rendered, about 3 minutes. Stir in the rutabaga and cook until the bacon is fully rendered and the rutabaga edges have started to caramelize, about 2 minutes. Drain the bacon and rutabaga on paper towels. Return the pan to the stove over medium-high heat. Pour in the wine and simmer until reduced by half, about 1 minute. Pour in the stock and simmer until reduced by half, about 3 minutes. Keep warm.

Preheat the oven to 350°F. Using a 2-inch round cutter, punch holes in the center of each slice of bread but keep the punched out pieces in the slices. To toast the bread, heat a large, ovenproof skillet over medium heat. (If the skillet can't accommodate all the bread, work in batches.) Add a few pats of butter to the pan and swirl until melted. Place the bread in the pan, pressing down lightly to ensure it browns evenly. Brown one side, about 2 minutes and flip the slices over. Remove the centers and place in the pan to toast alongside the slices.

Crack the eggs and slide one egg into each hole. Cook the eggs for a minute to set, then transfer the skillet to the oven. Bake the eggs until the whites are fully cooked but the yolks are still runny, about 6 minutes. Divide the egg toasts among 4 plates.

Return the pan with the stock to medium heat. Swirl in the shallot and tarragon and stir back in the mushrooms, rutabaga, and bacon. Season with salt and swirl in a pat of butter. Spoon the sauce over the eggs, then place a toast round askew over each egg. Garnish each plate with a few pieces of miner's lettuce.

BONE MARROW SFORMATO *with* Stuffed Baby Artichokes

Popular since Roman times when it was slathered on bread for a snack, bone marrow is the foie gras of beef. The first time I fell in love with its decadence was at the original Blue Ribbon on Sullivan Street in New York City, a restaurant known for its late-night menu and for its pairing of bone marrow with oxtail marmalade. In this recipe, I pay a small tribute to that memory by adding a drizzle of braising liquid from the Barolo Beef (page 228) or another other meaty braise that I happen to have on hand.

Here I use bone marrow fat in two places: rendered for *sformato*, a molded custard, and baked into the stuffed artichokes. To prepare the marrow, you need to soak the bones in ice water overnight to leach out excess blood. Scraping out the marrow fat from the bone is easier to do if you ask the butcher to split the bone lengthwise. To render the fat, I vacuum-seal it in a bag and cook it in a water bath at 180°F to 190°F for an hour. After an hour, I remove the bag, cut it open, and pour the rendered fat off the top. (This is a great way to render any small amount of animal fat.) Or scrape the fat into a pot, add a splash of water, and let it slowly melt over low heat until the water has evaporated. Whichever method you use, strain the rendered fat before using it.

When making the *sformato*, be prepared to bake it as soon as you've puréed the custard base. If it sits too long, the fat will separate and leave you with an unappetizing layer of fat on top. Anchoring the *sformato* on the plate is a simple purée of sweet onions thickened with rice, which can be made ahead and reheated.

SERVES 4

Stuffed Baby Artichokes

1 or 2 lemons, halved

400 grams • 12 to 16 baby artichokes

extra virgin olive oil

kosher salt

8 pearl or baby onions, peeled

15 grams • 1 tablespoon finely diced bacon

40 grams • 3 tablespoons bone marrow fat, diced

black pepper

55 grams • 1/2 cup breadcrumbs

15 grams • 1 tablespoon soffritto (page 282)

15 grams • 2 tablespoons finely grated fontina cheese

1 teaspoon chopped parsley

1 gram • 1/2 teaspoon chopped tarragon

1 gram • 1/2 teaspoon chopped thyme

1 egg yolk

Sweet Onion Purée

125 grams • 1/2 sweet onion, such as Walla Walla, quartered, cored, and separated into individual layers

10 grams • 1 1/2 teaspoons Arborio rice

kosher salt

57 grams • 4 tablespoons unsalted butter

extra virgin olive oil

Sformato

150 grams • 2/3 cup heavy cream

45 grams • 1/4 cup crème fraîche

2 eggs

54 grams • 1/4 cup rendered bone marrow fat (see headnote)

2 grams • 1/2 teaspoon kosher salt

2 slices bacon

a handful of watercress

1 horseradish root for grating

black pepper

90 to 120 grams • 1/4 to 1/2 cup braising liquid from Barolo Beef (page 228), or brown stock (page 283)

To make the artichokes: Heat a large, water bath fitted with an immersion circulator to 185°F (see *Sous Vide*, page 271). Prepare a bowl of cold water mixed with the juice of half a lemon. Working with one artichoke at a time, snap off the tough outer leaves, stopping once you reach the softer, inner leaves. Cut off about 1 inch from the top of the leaves. Trim off the very end of the stem. If the stem is long, use a paring knife to strip away the skin, leaving as much of the inner stem intact as possible. With the tip of a spoon, scrape out the prickly, fibrous choke from the top of the artichoke. (You will fill this gap with the breadcrumb stuffing.) Submerge the artichoke in the lemon water while you clean the remaining artichokes.

Put the artichokes in a vacuum pouch. Drizzle with 1 tablespoon of lemon juice and 1 tablespoon of olive oil. Season with a pinch of salt and vacuum-seal. Put the baby onions in a vacuum pouch. Season with salt, add about 1 tablespoon of olive oil, and vacuum-seal. Cook the pouches in the water bath for 45 to 60 minutes or until the vegetables feel somewhat soft when squeezed through the bags. Prepare an ice bath. Remove both bags and plunge in a large ice bath to chill completely.

Meanwhile, in a small sauté pan over medium-low heat, render the bacon until crispy. Preheat the oven to 350°F. Open the bags and drain. Finely chop the onions and transfer to a bowl. Trim the bases of the artichokes so they will stand on a plate. Chop the stem trimmings and add to the bowl with the onions. Stir in almost all of the breadcrumbs, leaving about 2 tablespoons for sprinkling over the top of the artichokes when they bake. Stir in the rendered bacon, chopped marrow fat, soffritto, fontina, parsley, tarragon, and thyme. Mix in the yolk and stir into the breadcrumbs. Season with salt and pepper. Fill the artichokes with a spoonful of stuffing and place, face up, in a baking dish. (You may have stuffing left over: you can bake it in a ramekin to serve on the side.) Sprinkle the remaining breadcrumbs over the top. Cover with aluminum foil and bake for 15 minutes or until warmed through. Uncover and bake 10 more minutes or until golden on top.

To make the onion purée: Put the onions and rice in a small pot. Add 1/4 cup of water and season with salt. Place over low heat, cover, and steam gently, avoiding scorching, until the onion layers are completely soft and the rice is cooked through, about 25 minutes. Transfer to a blender and purée with butter and about 1 tablespoon of olive oil. Season with salt and purée until smooth.

To make the *sformato*: Preheat the oven to 325°F. Coat four 3-ounce ramekins with nonstick cooking spray. In a small saucepan over low heat, warm the cream and crème fraîche. In a blender, purée the eggs. With the blender running on low speed, gradually pour in the cream mixture. Blend in the marrow fat and salt. You will have about 1 1/2 cups of *sformato* base. Skim off any air bubbles from the top. Pour into the prepared ramekins and set in a baking pan. Fill the pan with water halfway up the sides of the ramekins and bake for about 18 minutes or until the custard has just set around the sides and is still slightly soft in the center.

Grill the bacon until lightly charred, then cut each into 2 or 3 pieces. Meanwhile, bring the braising liquid to a simmer and reduce slightly. Spoon the onion purée in the center of 4 plates. Unmold the *sformato* and place on top of the purée. Divide the artichokes among the plates and garnish with watercress and grilled bacon. Grate fresh horseradish over the top and finish with black pepper and a few spoonfuls of braising liquid.

FONTINA *and* MUSHROOM TORTELLI *with* Black Truffle Fonduta

In spring and early summer, the mountainsides of Valle d'Aosta overflow with wildflowers and bees, giving a new understanding of wildflower honey. Also from this terrain comes fontina, the complex, rich cow's-milk cheese used in *fonduta*, the northern Italian version of Swiss fondue. In Valle d'Aosta, it's served with bread, vegetables, meat, or firm pieces of polenta for dipping. Here I use *fonduta* as a sauce for a fontina-filled pasta. Be wary of fontal, an industrially produced, non-Italian version of fontina. Nutty, rich fontina makes much better, more complex *fonduta*. To season the *fonduta*, I use another prized local flavor—earthy black truffles.

SERVES 6

Filling

extra virgin olive oil

4 grams • 1 garlic clove, minced

15 grams • 1/2 shallot, minced

220 grams • 7 1/2 ounces mixed mushrooms, such as chanterelle, black trumpet, and oyster, cleaned and sliced lengthwise into 4 to 6 pieces (3 cups)

kosher salt and black pepper

150 grams • 3/4 cup mascarpone

212 grams • 1 1/4 cups finely grated fontina cheese

15 grams • 1 tablespoon chopped Italian parsley

15 grams • 1 tablespoon black truffle (optional)

Tortelli

250 grams • scant 2 cups 00 flour

2 grams • 1/2 teaspoon kosher salt

100 grams • 2 eggs

9 grams • 2 teaspoons water

Fonduta

60 grams • 3 egg yolks

7 grams • 2 teaspoons cornstarch

260 grams • 1 1/4 cups whole milk

300 grams • 2 cups firmly packed grated fontina cheese

kosher salt and white pepper

1 nutmeg for grating

12 grams • 2 teaspoons grated black truffle

2 to 3 tablespoons softened unsalted butter

kosher salt

black truffle for grating

parsley sprigs

a block of aged fontina cheese for shaving

To make the filling: Heat a thin film of olive oil in a large sauté pan over medium-high heat. Briefly sweat the garlic and shallot, then scatter the mushrooms into the pan in an even layer. Let the mushrooms sear without trying to move them until they begin to brown, 1 to 2 minutes. Give the mushrooms a stir, season with salt and pepper, and cook until soft, 1 to 2 minutes more. Transfer to a mixing bowl and let cool to room temperature.

Set aside a couple of spoonfuls of cooked mushrooms for the finished dish. Finely chop the remaining mushrooms and return to the mixing bowl. Stir in the mascarpone, fontina, parsley, and truffle. Taste, seasoning with salt and pepper until the mixture tastes well seasoned. Transfer to a pastry bag fitted with a medium tip and refrigerate until needed.

To make the *tortelli*: In a stand mixer fitted with the paddle attachment, mix together the flour and salt. In a bowl, whisk together the eggs and water. With the mixer running on low speed, drizzle in the egg mixture. Mix the dough for 2 to 3 minutes, then turn onto the counter and knead several times by hand; it will feel firm and dry. Flatten the dough into a rectangle, wrap in plastic wrap, and leave on the counter for 30 minutes to soften and hydrate.

Roll out the dough according to the instructions for laminated pasta on page 273. Lay the sheets out on the workspace. With a 2¹/₂- or 3-inch round or square cutter, punch out pieces of pasta, using as much of the pasta surface area as possible. Lightly flour the pieces and stack them. (At this point, the pieces of pasta can be placed in a storage container, covered, and refrigerated.) Roll out the trimmings and punch out more rounds until you have about 50 pieces.

Working with a few pieces of pasta at a time, pipe about ¹/₂ teaspoon of filling into the center of each piece. Lightly mist water over the pasta or dampen the edges using a pastry brush. Fold the circles in half and pinch the edges together until firmly sealed, expelling any extra air and thinning the edges while doing so. Wrap each piece around your index finger. Bring the ends together and pinch to seal. Place the *tortelli* on a baking sheet lightly dusted with flour. If not cooking right away, cover with plastic wrap and refrigerate.

To make the *fonduta:* In a small bowl, whisk together the yolks and cornstarch until smooth. In a saucepan, whisk the yolk slurry into the milk and warm over medium heat, whisking constantly until the milk reaches a boil and thickens. Remove from the heat and let the fontina melt into the milk. Once melted, stir the *fonduta* and season with salt, white pepper, and a few gratings of nutmeg. Using a blender, purée until smooth, then pour through a fine-mesh strainer into a clean pot. Stir in the truffle and keep warm.

Bring a large pot of salted water to a boil. Add the *tortelli* and cook until al dente, 4 to 5 minutes. Meanwhile, in a large, straight-sided sauté pan over medium heat, melt a large pat of butter. Add about 2 tablespoons of pasta cooking water and swirl the pan to form an emulsified butter sauce. Drain the pasta and add to the pan, stirring to coat the *tortelli* lightly in the sauce (if too dry, add another splash of pasta water, but not too much—you don't want the sauce to break). Season with a pinch of salt, add the reserved cooked mushrooms, and grate some truffle directly into the pan.

To serve, spoon a thin layer of *fonduta* at the base of 6 warmed bowls. Divide the *tortelli* and mushrooms among the bowls. Garnish with parsley sprigs and shavings of aged fontina.

RISOTTO *with* CRAYFISH *and* Sweetbreads

While risotto itself is not a luxury dish, this version, a surf-and-turf interpretation, takes an extravagant, American turn. The sweetbreads alone would make a delicious risotto, but I go a little over the top, serving crayfish—a nod to a brief time I spent working at Emeril's in New Orleans—in two styles: folding the cooked meat into the risotto and frying soft-shell crayfish for a crisp garnish. But if you can't find softshell crayfish, you can turn to soft-shell crab, the smaller in size the better. Or skip the crayfish and finish the risotto with lobster meat. With this dish, the key is timing: the components should come together at the same moment.

SERVES 4 TO 6

454 grams • 1 pound sweetbreads

white vinegar

kosher salt

680 grams • 1 1/2 pounds live crayfish, or lobster

90 grams • 5 lemon slices

Broth

115 grams • 1/3 yellow onion, chopped

75 grams • 1/2 carrot, chopped

25 grams • 1/2 celery stalk, chopped

kosher salt

400 grams • 14 ounces crayfish or lobster shells

130 grams • 1 scant cup chopped canned San Marzano tomatoes

30 grams • 2 tablespoons tomato paste

1 thyme sprig

1 tarragon sprig

Risotto

extra virgin olive oil

150 grams • 1/2 yellow onion, finely chopped

kosher salt

15 grams • 1 tablespoon tomato paste

205 grams • 1 cup Vialone Nano or other risotto-style rice

70 grams • 1/4 cup white wine, plus 1 tablespoon

57 grams • 1/4 cup sherry

1 block ricotta salata, for grating

50 grams • 3 1/2 tablespoons unsalted butter

8 grams • 1 tablespoon tarragon

black pepper

blended oil for frying (see page 278)

6 soft-shell crayfish

kosher salt and black pepper

about 1/2 cup Wondra flour

2 grams • 1/2 garlic clove, minced

1 gram • 1/2 teaspoon minced parsley

1 gram • 1/2 teaspoon minced tarragon

2 lemon wedges

whole tarragon leaves, for garnish

Prepare the sweetbreads according to the poaching instructions for Fritto Misto, page 170. Once cool, cut the sweetbreads into 1-inch cubes.

To prepare each crayfish, twist the center prong on the end of the tail and pull; the vein will come out with the prong. In a pot that can accommodate a steamer or perforated insert, bring a few inches of water to a boil. Add the lemons and place the steamer or insert into the pot. Prepare an ice bath. Place the crayfish in the steamer, cover, and steam for 8 to 10 minutes. Plunge the crayfish into an ice bath. Once cold, twist off the heads and claws and set aside. Using your hands, pull the tail meat out of the shell and reserve for the risotto. Clean the bodies: pop off the top of the head and discard the veins, gills, and sand sacs. Save the shells and claws for the broth.

To make the broth: In a dry pot over medium heat, sweat the onion, carrot, and celery with a pinch of salt until slightly softened, about 3 minutes. Add the crayfish shells and claws and sweat for a minute more. Stir in the tomato and tomato paste and cook, stirring frequently, until the tomatoes begin to brown. Pour in 5 cups of water and add the thyme and tarragon. Bring to a simmer and cook for 30 minutes. Turn off the heat and keep hot.

To make the risotto: Heat a thin film of olive oil in a large, heavy-bottomed pot over medium heat. Stir in the finely chopped onion and a pinch of salt and sweat until softened, about 3 minutes. Stir in the tomato paste and cook, stirring frequently, until lightly cooked, 1 minute. Stir in the rice and toast, stirring frequently until the grains start to look translucent around the edges, about 1 minute. Pour in the white wine and sherry and simmer, stirring often, until the pot is nearly dry, about 2 minutes.

Ladle the broth through a strainer into the pot in three increments. Cook the risotto until nearly dry between each addition. Once the grains of rice have been cooked to al dente and have reached the consistency that allows the risotto to spread out on its own if spooned on a plate, grate about 1/4 cup of ricotta salata over the pot, then finish with a drizzle of olive oil, the butter, tarragon, and pepper. Taste, seasoning with more salt and pepper if needed. Fold in the reserved crayfish tails and keep hot.

While the risotto cooks, in a narrow, tall pot, heat 2 inches of oil to 360°F. Place a cooling rack over a baking sheet and line with paper towels. Season the soft-shell crayfish with salt and pepper, then dredge in Wondra flour. Shake off any excess and fry the crayfish until crisp and red, about 1 minute. Drain on paper towels and season with salt.

Season the sweetbreads with salt and pepper, then dredge in Wondra, shaking off any excess. Fry the sweetbreads until crisp and cooked through, 3 minutes. Drain on paper towels, then toss in a bowl with garlic, parsley, and tarragon. Season with a pinch of salt and a squeeze of lemon. Divide the risotto between 6 shallow bowls. Top with sweetbread pieces and soft-shell crayfish and garnish with tarragon leaves.

SAVOY CABBAGE *with* Mushrooms, Lardo, *and* Crispy Prosciutto

The meaty flavor of mushrooms pairs well with other earthy ingredients like lardo, a cured pork fat, and cabbage. Like caramelized Brussels sprouts, cabbage roasted cut side down becomes sweet. The cabbages we buy are smaller than the heads sold at grocery stores, so weigh them first before starting this recipe. You may only need one head of cabbage. For crunch, I fry pieces of prosciutto, which crisp up like potato chips. They offer a pleasant salty counterpoint to the braised cabbage.

More butchers and delis now sell lardo, but I've also provided instructions on how to make your own. It takes twelve days for the pork fat to cure and one day for it to dry out in the refrigerator. This recipe makes more than you need, but save the extra for Asparagus with Lardo-Wrapped Rye Dumplings (page 124). I'm also partial to draping it over polenta or warm toast. If you buy lardo, you should get 4 ounces for 6 portions.

SERVES 6

Lardo

4 grams • 1 tablespoon black peppercorns

2 grams • 1 teaspoon fennel seeds

2 grams • 1 teaspoon coriander seeds

2 grams • 1 teaspoon juniper berries

40 grams • 3 tablespoons rock-style salt

40 grams • 3 tablespoons plus 1 teaspoon brown sugar

1/2 gram • 1/8 teaspoon pink curing salt

3 sprigs thyme

2 bay leaves

454 grams • 1 pound thick pork fatback, preferably in one piece, skin removed

{continued}

extra virgin olive oil

1120 grams • 2 pounds, 7 ounces (1½ heads) Savoy cabbage

28 grams • 2 tablespoons unsalted butter

515 grams • 2 small yellow onions, thinly sliced

kosher salt

85 grams • ½ apple, peeled, cored, and sliced

2 grams • ½ teaspoon caraway seeds

28 grams • 2 tablespoons cider vinegar

11 grams • 1½ teaspoons honey

220 grams • 7½ ounces mixed mushrooms, cleaned and sliced into
   ½-inch pieces (3 cups)

black pepper

1 garlic clove, minced

½ shallot, minced

1 tablespoon chopped Italian parsley

blended oil for frying (see page 278)

6 thin slices prosciutto

a block of ricotta salata for grating

To make the lardo: In a dry sauté pan over medium heat, toast the black peppercorns, fennel, coriander, and juniper berries until aromatic. Remove the juniper berries and crush. In a medium bowl, mix the toasted spices with the salt, sugar, pink salt, thyme, and bay leaves.

Rub the cure into the fatback. Scatter some of the cure on the bottom of a rectangular food storage container. Put the fatback on top, then coat with the remaining cure. Cover and refrigerate for 6 days. While the fatback cures, it will release water and gradually firm up. Remove the fatback from the refrigerator. Using your hands, scoop the sandy cure from the bottom of the storage container and pack it into a fresh container (leave the excess water behind). Transfer the fatback to the new container. Scoop more of the cure out of the old container and pack on top of the fatback, discarding any water. Cover and refrigerate for 6 more days.

Rinse the lardo and pat dry. Place on a drying rack set on a rimmed baking sheet. Refrigerate, uncovered, for 12 hours, then flip it over and let it dry in the refrigerator for another 12 hours. Once cured, wrap the fatback in plastic wrap and keep in the refrigerator until ready to slice. Or, if you have a large refrigerator or wine cooler,

you can hang the lardo: pierce a hole on one side and thread and knot butcher's twine through it, and hang.

Preheat the oven to 325°F. Heat a film of olive oil in a large sauté pan over medium-high heat. Place the cabbage, cut side down, in the pan and transfer to the oven. Roast until the bottoms are evenly caramelized, 25 to 30 minutes. Cool slightly.

Meanwhile, heat a film of olive oil and 1 tablespoon of butter in a large pot over medium-low heat. Sweat the onions with a pinch of salt until they start to caramelize, about 4 minutes. Stir in the apples and caraway seeds and season with a pinch of salt. Continue to cook over medium-low heat until the onions and apple are tender, about 5 minutes. Stir in the vinegar and honey and cook until the pan is almost dry, about 1 minute. Keep warm.

When the cabbage is cool enough to handle, discard the outer leaves. Cut out the core and the thick vein that runs through the center of the larger leaves. In stacks of 2 or 3, roll the leaves up and slice into ribbons about ¼-inch thick. Mix the cabbage leaves with the onions.

Heat a film of olive oil in a large sauté pan over medium-high heat. Scatter the mushrooms in the pan, season with salt and pepper, and sear, tossing the pan once or twice to evenly brown the mushrooms, about 3 minutes Stir in the garlic and shallot, add the remaining 1 tablespoon of butter, and cook for 1 more minute or until the garlic and shallots have softened. Sprinkle in the parsley and keep warm.

In a medium pot, heat 1 inch of oil to 360°F. Tear the prosciutto slices in half or in quarters and fry until crisp, about 20 seconds. Using a skimmer, drain the prosciutto on paper towels.

To serve: Portion the cabbage by spoonfuls on each plate. With a sharp knife, slice the lardo crosswise into thin strips, about 2 to 3 slices per plate. Drape over the cabbage, then spoon the mushrooms alongside. Scatter 1 or 2 pieces of fried prosciutto onto each plate, then grate ricotta salata over the top to finish.

CHESTNUT-STUFFED VEAL BREAST *with* Orzotto

Cima, stuffed veal breast, is a classic dish from the Ligurian mountains and southern Piemonte. *Orzotto*, a risotto made with barley, is a common whole-grain stand-in for rice in this part of Italy. I make use of nasturtiums, an herbaceous, peppery plant that grows wild all over the Bay Area. To brighten the rich earthy flavors in the dish, I finish each plate with a sprinkling of gremolata, a mix of garlic and citrus zest.

You will need just under 1000 grams of veal breast for this recipe: 660 grams for the veal breast and 330 grams in trimming for the filling. If you buy one large veal breast, simply cut it down and use the trimmings in the filling. If you have more trimmings than you need for this recipe, grind all of it and freeze the extra for other uses, such as Lasagna Vincisgrassi (page 58). For this recipe, plan on twenty hours of *sous vide* cooking (see page 271).

SERVES 4 TO 6

155 grams • 1/2 cup barley, rinsed

2 grams • 1/2 teaspoon kosher salt

370 grams • 1²/3 cups water

Stuffed Veal Breast

38 grams • 1/4 cup dried chestnuts

660 grams • 1 pound, 7 1/2 ounces boned veal breast

at least 330 grams • 11 1/2 ounces veal trimmings

40 grams • 4 dried figs, chopped

50 grams • 1/4 cup soffritto (page 282)

50 grams • 1 egg

8 grams • 2 tablespoons chopped parsley

3 grams • 2 teaspoons chopped sage

8 grams • 2 teaspoons kosher salt

black pepper

40 grams • 1/4 cup breadcrumbs

a pinch of dried red pepper flakes

Orzotto

50 grams • 1/4 cup soffritto (page 282)

2 to 3 tablespoons unsalted butter

a block of Parmigiano-Reggiano for grating

10 grams • 3 tablespoons chopped nasturtium leaves (or parsley)

kosher salt and black pepper

extra virgin olive oil

Gremolata

1/2 garlic clove, minced

1 orange, for zesting

2 tablespoons chopped nasturtium leaves (or parsley)

a pinch of kosher salt

50 grams • 1 egg

20 grams • 2 tablespoons Dijon mustard

55 grams • 1/2 cup breadcrumbs

extra virgin olive oil

a handful of small nasturtium leaves or flowers

Put the barley in a medium pot and cover with about 1 inch of water. Bring to a simmer, add a generous pinch of salt, and lower to a gentle simmer. Cook until tender, 20 to 25 minutes. Drain, reserving the cooking water for the orzotto. You should have 2 1/2 cups of cooked barley.

To make the veal breast: Preheat a large water bath fitted with an immersion circulator to 150°F (see *Sous Vide*, page 271). Cover the chestnuts with about 1 inch of hot water. Soak for 20 minutes, then drain. Put the meat grinder, 1/8-inch die, and the bowl into which you'll grind the meat into the freezer to chill.

Lay the veal breast on a cutting board and pound with a mallet to even out the thickness to about 3/4 inch. Cut away any visible sinew and discard. Trim the breast into a rectangle, saving the trimmings to grind for the filling. Make a pocket: with your knife parallel to the cutting board, make a deep incision on the long side of the veal breast, slicing from one end to the other, leaving an edge about 3/4-inch intact along all three sides of the pocket.

Cube the trimmings. Fit the meat grinder attachment to the stand mixer. With the mixer on low speed, feed the trimmings through the grinder into a chilled bowl. Reserve 330 grams or 1 3/4 cups for the stuffing (freeze the rest). Season both sides of the breast and inside the pocket with salt and pepper.

{continued}

In a large bowl, mix together the chestnuts, 1/2 cup barley, figs, soffritto, egg, parsley, and sage. Mix in the reserved ground veal, salt, and pepper, followed by the bread-crumbs and red pepper flakes. To check the seasoning, pinch off a small patty and fry in a nonstick pan; add more salt if needed.

Spoon the filling into the pocket, pressing lightly to even the filling and press out any air pockets. Wrap the breast in plastic wrap 12 times, folding over the sides each time. Tie a few loops of butcher's twine around the breast to hold it together. Place the veal breast in the preheated water bath and cook for 20 hours.

Pull the veal breast from the water and let it rest for 1 hour, then plunge into an ice bath for 5 minutes to cool. Remove the veal breast from the water and place it, still sealed in plastic, between two baking sheets. Put the sheets in the refrigerator and place a weight, like a can of tomatoes, on top to ensure that the breast cools in a flat, shape. Refrigerate overnight.

To make the *orzotto*: In a straight-sided sauté pan over medium-low heat, bring the remaining 2 cups of cooked barley and a few tablespoons of the reserved barley cook-ing water to a simmer. Stir in the soffritto and warm through. Swirl in the butter, then grate in a tablespoon or two of cheese. Cook until the barley has the consistency of risotto, then finish with nasturtiums, salt, pepper, and a drizzle of olive oil.

To make the *gremolata*: Preheat the oven to 375°F. Mix the garlic, zest, nasturtiums, and salt in a small bowl. In another small bowl, whisk together the egg and mustard. Cut the veal out of the plastic. Brush the top (the side with visible fat) with the egg wash, then dip that side into the breadcrumb mixture. Heat a thin film of olive oil in a large sauté pan over medium-high heat. Place the veal in the pan, breadcrumb side down, and transfer to the oven. Bake until the breadcrumbs are crispy and the veal is warmed through, 10 to 15 minutes. Remove the veal to a cutting board and let it rest for a few minutes.

Slice the veal into 1/4-inch slices. For each serving, place a spoonful of *orzotto* in the center of each plate. Place 4 to 5 slices of veal on top and sprinkle with *gremolata* and nasturtiums.

BAKED POLENTA *with* Beef Cheek Ragù, Eggs, *and* Fontina

Inspired by the *valdostani* tradition of braised beef served with polenta, I created my own rendition with beef cheeks and eggs. Dried chestnuts in the braising liquid impart a nutty perfume to the meat (they also hold their shape bet-ter than cooked, peeled chestnuts). As in most Northern Italian regions, polenta is an ever-present starch in Valle d'Aosta. The corn is dried after harvest and ground as needed throughout the year. Baked with eggs, as it is in this recipe, the polenta offers satisfying sustenance even without the beef. I use freshly ground coarse polenta, which retains a bit of moisture and has a more intense, fresh flavor. (It's perishable, so I buy it in small quantities and store it in the refrigerator.)

SERVES 6

Beef Cheek Ragù

1000 grams • 2 pounds, 2 ounces (5 or 6) beef cheeks

kosher salt and black pepper

about 1/4 cup Wondra flour

extra virgin olive oil

one 750 ml bottle red wine

an herb bundle with 5 parsley sprigs, 5 sage sprigs, 5 rosemary
   stems, and 5 thyme sprigs (see page 282)

a sachet with 6 peppercorns, 3 fennel seeds, and 1 clove
   (see page 282)

100 grams • 3 1/2 ounces pancetta, cut into 1/2-inch cubes
   (about 3/4 cup)

150 grams • 1/2 red onion, cut in medium dice

8 grams • 2 garlic cloves, sliced

a pinch of ground cloves

a pinch of dried red pepper flakes

a pinch of fennel seeds

60 grams • 1/4 cup tomato paste

40 grams • 10 dried chestnuts

750 grams • 3 1/3 cups brown stock (page 283)

Polenta

565 grams • 2¹/₂ cups water

240 grams • 1 cup whole milk

1 garlic clove, smashed

3 or 4 thyme sprigs

150 grams • 1 cup coarse cornmeal

kosher salt

35 grams • ¹/₄ cup grated fontina

57 grams • 4 tablespoons unsalted butter

black pepper

6 farm eggs

kosher salt and black pepper

about ¹/₄ cup grated fontina

125 grams • 1 small carrot, sliced on the bias

50 grams • 1 celery stalk, sliced into ¹/₂-inch pieces

To make the ragù: Trim the cheeks of any visible silver skin or connective tissue and cut into 1-inch cubes. Season with salt and pepper, then dredge in Wondra, shaking off any excess. Heat a film of olive oil in a large pan over medium-high heat. In batches to avoid crowding, sear the cheeks until evenly browned on all sides, about 2 minutes per side. Transfer the cheeks to a storage container or bowl.

Turn off the heat and pour the fat off the pan. Put the pan back over medium heat and deglaze with the wine, scraping the bottom with a wooden spoon. Pour the wine over the cheeks. Add the herb bundle and sachet, then cover and refrigerate for at least 4 hours or overnight.

Remove the cheeks from the wine and strain it into a small pot, reserving the herb bundle and sachet. Bring to a simmer and skim the surface to remove any coagulated proteins, then strain through a fine-mesh strainer.

Preheat the oven to 325°F. In a large Dutch oven or heavy-bottomed pot over medium-low heat, render the pancetta until light brown, about 3 minutes. Transfer the pancetta to a plate and reserve.

Stir the onion and garlic into the pancetta fat, add a pinch of salt, and sweat until softened, 3 minutes. Season with the cloves, red pepper flakes, and fennel. Stir in the tomato paste and cook 1 to 2 minutes. Add the chestnuts

and return the cheeks to the pot. Pour in the strained wine and the stock. Return the herb bundle and sachet to the pot and bring to a simmer. Cover, transfer to the oven, and braise for 1¹/₂ to 2 hours. Remove the lid and braise for another 15 to 20 minutes or until the meat is tender but not falling apart. Discard the herb bundle and sachet and let the cheeks cool to room temperature in the braising liquid, skimming any fat that rises to the surface.

To make the polenta: In a large Dutch oven or heavy-bottomed pot, bring the water and milk to a simmer with the garlic and thyme. Fish out the garlic and thyme, then whisk in the cornmeal. Season with a few pinches of salt, and return to a boil. Whisk again, then turn the heat down to a very low simmer and cover the pot. Cook the polenta, removing the lid only to stir the pot every 10 minutes or so, for 45 minutes or until the grains are completely cooked through. Remove the lid and stir in the fontina and butter. Taste, adding more salt as needed. Keep hot.

Preheat the oven to 350°F. Spoon the polenta into 6 individual (6-ounce) gratin dishes or 1 large (4 quart) gratin dish. Use the back of a large spoon to form an indentation for each egg. Crack the eggs one by one into a small bowl and slide into an indentation. Season the eggs with salt and pepper and sprinkle the gratin with fontina. Bake for 12 to 15 minutes or until the whites have started to set but the yolks are still runny. Turn the oven to broil and cook until the fontina is melted and slightly brown.

Meanwhile, in a sauté pan over medium heat, warm the reserved pancetta. Sweat the carrot and celery until soft, about 4 minutes. Season with salt and pepper.

If baking in one dish, spoon an egg and some polenta onto each plate. Spoon the ragù over or alongside the eggs, then top with the carrots, celery, and pancetta. If serving individual dishes, spoon the ragù on top of each egg and garnish with carrots, celery, and pancetta.

BAROLO BEEF *with* Carrots *and* New Potatoes

Nearly every wine-producing region in the world braises beef in red wine. It's a classic match: not only does the meat become sweet and tender when cooked in wine, but it also becomes extremely wine-friendly. In Piemonte, beef and red wine is a natural pairing. I've taken some liberty with the name of this recipe—I don't often get to cook with Barolo. Instead, I use deep red, low-tannin California wine. Even in the Langhe, the heart of Barolo and Barbaresco production, cooks are far more likely to cook with wines made from Barbera and Dolcetto than they are with ageworthy Barolo. As far as a food-and-wine pairing goes, however, the savory tannins of Barolo do well by braised beef.

When paired with tiny, waxy new potatoes, the dish is warming, well-rounded comfort food. If buying bone-in short ribs, start with 1700 grams: a lot of the weight will be lost once the bones and sinew are removed. Save the bones for adding to brown stock (page 283). This recipe requires 20 hours of sous-vide cooking, unless you opt to braise the short ribs in the oven (see page 230).

SERVES 4

Short Ribs

900 grams • 4 short ribs (2 pounds), boned and trimmed of sinew and excess fat

kosher salt and black pepper

extra virgin olive oil

150 grams • 1 yellow onion, diced

150 grams • 1 carrot, diced

50 grams • 1 celery stalk, diced

2 sachets, each with 10 sprigs parsley, 5 sprigs rosemary, 5 sprigs thyme, 6 black peppercorns, 3 star anise, and 1 clove (see page 282)

one 750 ml bottle red wine

460 grams • 2 cups brown stock (page 283)

Potatoes

325 grams • 11 ounces new potatoes the size of large marbles (2 cups)

8 grams • 2 garlic cloves, halved

3 or 4 sprigs thyme

kosher salt and black pepper

42 grams • 3 tablespoons extra virgin olive oil

30 grams • 2 tablespoons red wine vinegar

8 grams • 1 teaspoon Dijon mustard

20 grams • 1 tablespoon honey

3 grams • 2 tablespoons finely chopped dill

15 grams • 1 tablespoon minced shallot

Carrot Purée and Roasted Carrots

320 grams • 11 ounces (3) carrots, peeled and sliced into 1/8-inch rounds

380 grams • 1 1/2 cups carrot juice

kosher salt

2 to 3 tablespoons unsalted butter

1 to 2 tablespoons extra virgin olive oil

500 grams • 18 to 24 baby carrots, each about 4 inches long, with leafy tops intact

2 sprigs thyme

Season the short ribs with salt and pepper. Heat a thin film of olive oil in a sauté pan over medium-high heat. Brown the meat on all sides, 3 to 5 minutes per side. Transfer to a heatproof container and add the onion, carrot, celery, and sachets. Pour the excess oil from the sauté pan and pour in the red wine. Bring to a simmer, scraping any browned bits from the pan with a wooden spoon. Pour the wine over the meat, cool, and marinate overnight.

Preheat a large water bath filled nearly to the top, set an immersion circulator to 150°F (see *Sous Vide*, page 271). Strain the marinade into a pot and bring to a simmer over medium heat, using a ladle to skim away any scum that floats to the surface. Meanwhile, divide the meat, vegetables, and sachets between two large vacuum bags and set aside (don't seal yet). Using a fine-mesh strainer lined with cheesecloth, strain the marinade directly into a clean pot over medium heat and reduce by half. Add the brown stock and bring to a simmer. Strain the marinade

{continued}

again into a clean container and cool to room temperature over an ice bath. Divide the marinade between the bags and vacuum-seal them. Place them in the preheated water bath. Cook the short ribs for 20 to 24 hours or until the meat feels tender when pressed through the bag. Remove the bags from the water, let them rest at room temperature for 2 hours, and then soak in an ice bath to cool completely. (At this point, the meat can be refrigerated for a few days.)

Put the potatoes in a medium pot. Cover with about an inch of water and season with garlic, thyme, and salt. Bring the pot to a brisk simmer over medium-high heat, then lower the temperature and cook until the potatoes are cooked through but not falling apart, 15 minutes. Remove from the heat and let the potatoes rest in the cooking water for about 20 minutes. Drain the potatoes and discard the garlic and thyme. In a bowl, season the potatoes with salt and pepper, then mix in the olive oil, vinegar, mustard, honey, dill, and shallot.

In a small pot mix together the sliced carrots, carrot juice, and a pinch of salt over medium-high heat. Bring to a simmer, cover with a lid, then lower heat to low and cook until the carrots are falling apart, 10 to 15 minutes.

Pour the carrots and half of the liquid into a blender and purée until smooth, adjusting with more liquid if the purée looks too thick. The purée should be very smooth and creamy but not soupy. Blend in a few pats of butter and taste, adjusting with more salt if needed.

Set aside a few baby carrots with greens attached for garnish. In a large pot of boiling, salted water, blanch the remaining carrots for 2 minutes and shock in an ice bath. Drain the carrots and rub off the skins with your fingers. Heat a thin film of olive oil in an ovenproof sauté pan over medium heat. Add the carrots and sauté just until they start to color, 3 to 4 minutes. Season with salt and continue to cook until the carrots are just tender, about 5 more minutes. Swirl in a pat of butter and the thyme sprigs. Season with salt, if needed.

Preheat the oven to 300°F. Cut open the short rib bags and strain the liquid into a pot, discarding the vegetables and sachets. If the short ribs are larger, cut them into 4- to 6-ounce portions. Nestle the ribs into a snug-fitting roasting pan. Bring the braising liquid to a simmer over medium heat; cook until it begins to coat the back of a spoon, 15 to 20 minutes, skimming off any fat that rises to the surface. Pour the braise over the short ribs and transfer to the oven for 25 to 35 minutes.

Spoon carrot purée in the centers of 4 warmed plates. Slice and divide the short rib portions among the plates and spoon some of the braising liquid over the top. Spoon the potatoes and roasted carrots alongside. Dress the raw carrots with olive oil, salt, and place alongside the short ribs.

BRAISING SHORT RIBS IN THE OVEN

When braising short ribs, I prefer to use *sous vide* (see page 271). It requires less braising liquid and it cooks the ribs more evenly. They are tender throughout but can still be sliced for serving, without the dried-out corners that can occur when short ribs are cooked in the oven. Yet I acknowledge that many people like the aromas that come from beef stewing in the oven. If you'd prefer to cook this without *sous vide*, follow these instructions after the beef is marinated and before it is reheated to serve:

Preheat the oven to 325°F. Strain the marinade into a pot and bring to a simmer over medium heat, using a ladle to skim away any scum that floats to the surface. Transfer the meat and vegetables to a Dutch oven or heavy-bottomed pot. Using a fine-mesh strainer lined with cheesecloth, strain the marinade directly into the Dutch oven. Pour in the stock and water and bring to a simmer. Cover with a tight-fitting lid and transfer to the oven. Stew the short ribs for 3 hours or until the meat is tender when pierced with a fork but not completely falling apart. Let the short ribs cool in the braising liquid for 2 hours. At this point, the meat can be refrigerated in the braising liquid for up to 3 days.

CHOCOLATE SOUFFLÉS
with Milk Chocolate Gelato

Chocolate and Torino are intrinsically linked. Not only has this Piemontese city produced chocolate since the late Renaissance but it also invented *gianduja*, the classic chocolate-hazelnut blend. For this dessert, I harness the power of the favorite sweet ingredient in two classic ways: in soufflé and in gelato. I like to spoon the gelato on top of a hot soufflé, which gently collapses under the weight of the melting cream.

There is such a thing as a too-light soufflé. When you add too many egg whites, the texture might be airy but the flavor becomes diluted. Rather than classically light, these soufflés are slightly denser—and more forgiving, with more chocolate flavor.

SERVES 6

Milk Chocolate Gelato

$^1/_2$ vanilla bean

100 grams • $^1/_2$ cup sugar

240 grams • 1 cup whole milk

230 grams • 1 cup heavy cream

80 grams • 4 egg yolks

68 grams • 2$^1/_3$ ounces milk chocolate, chopped

a pinch of kosher salt

Soufflés

227 grams • 8 ounces bittersweet chocolate, chopped

60 grams • 3 egg yolks

75 grams • $^1/_3$ cup warm water

120 grams • 4 egg whites

40 grams • 3 tablespoons sugar, plus extra for dusting the ramekins

To make the gelato: With the tip of a spoon, scrape out the seeds from the vanilla bean and add them to a bowl with the sugar. (Reserve the vanilla bean for another use.) Using your hands, rub the vanilla into the sugar.

Heat the milk, cream, and $^1/_3$ cup of the vanilla sugar in a pot over medium heat. Bring to a boil and remove from the heat. In a large bowl, whisk together the yolks with the remaining sugar. Using a ladle, gradually whisk about $^1/_4$ cup of the hot milk into the yolks and stir until well blended. Gradually whisk in the remaining milk, then pour the custard base back into the pot. Cook the custard over medium heat, stirring constantly, until it is thick enough to coat the back of a spoon.

Put the chocolate and salt in a heatproof bowl. Pour the custard over the chocolate and stir until the chocolate has thoroughly melted and the custard is well mixed. Strain through a fine-mesh strainer into a clean bowl and chill thoroughly over an ice bath. Refrigerate for 2 hours or preferably overnight. Freeze the ice cream in an ice cream maker according to the manufacturer's instructions. Transfer to a chilled container and place in the freezer until ready to serve.

To make the soufflés: Preheat the oven to 350°F. Butter six 4-ounce ramekins and dust lightly with sugar; place on a rimmed baking sheet. In a heatproof bowl over a pot of barely simmering water (ensuring that the water doesn't touch the bottom of the bowl), melt the chocolate. Whisk in the yolks and water and remove from the heat. In a stand mixer fitted with the whisk attachment, whip the egg whites and sugar together until they form medium peaks. In three additions, fold the whites into the chocolate. Fill the ramekins with soufflé batter and bake for 12 minutes or until the batter has risen from the rim and has started to fall. Serve the soufflés with a spoonful of gelato on top.

VIA AURELIA—
LIGURIA AND TOSCANA

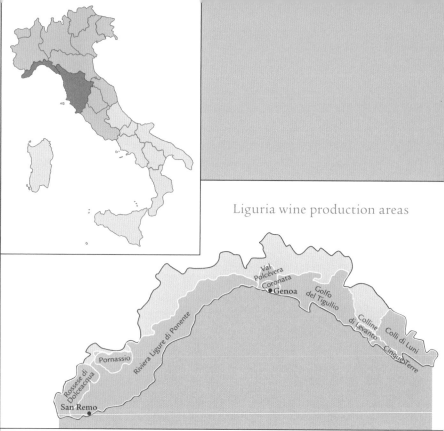

Liguria wine production areas

Val Polcèvera
Coronata
Genoa
Golfo del Tigullio
Colline di Levanto
Colli di Luni
Cinque Terre
Pornassio
Riviera Ligure di Ponente
Rossese di Dolceacqua
San Remo

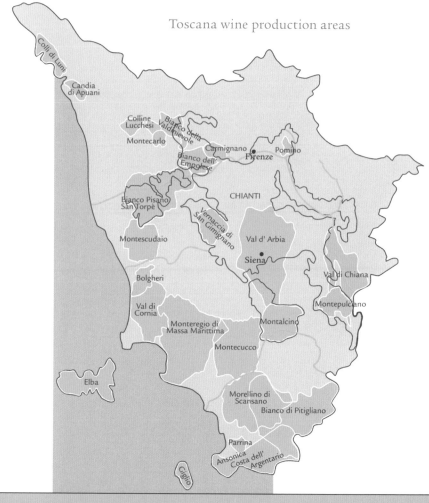

Toscana wine production areas

Colli di Luni
Candia di Apuani
Colline Lucchesi
Bianco della Valdinievole
Montecarlo
Carmignano
Firenze
Pomino
Bianco dell' Empolese
Bianco Pisano San Torpè
Vernaccia di San Gimignano
CHIANTI
Montescudaio
Val d' Arbia
Siena
Val di Chiana
Bolgheri
Montepulciano
Val di Cornia
Montalcino
Monteregio di Massa Marittima
Montecucco
Elba
Morellino di Scansano
Bianco di Pitigliano
Parrina
Giglio
Ansonica Costa dell' Argentario

VIA AURELIA—LIGURIA AND TOSCANA

It's easy to become hooked on the flavors of Liguria, from pesto, the region's famous fragrant basil paste to *farinata*, a savory chickpea crepe, both of which are complemented by a glass of invigorating Pigato. I have long harbored a soft spot for Liguria and its cuisine. For several years, I lived in San Francisco's North Beach neighborhood, an area that has held ties to the region since the nineteenth century, when most of the Italians arriving in San Francisco during the California gold rush came from Genoa, Liguria's capital city. Italian families soon spread beyond North Beach, running grocery stores and farms farther afield. Historians often credit the origins of cioppino, San Francisco's classic tomato-based seafood stew served on New Year's Eve, to Genoa's similar *ciuppin*. But while Genovese traditions have been part of San Francisco's Italian identity for more than a century, finding Ligurian wine in San Francisco (or anywhere outside of Liguria, for that matter) has rarely been easy.

There are two good reasons for the wines' scarcity. First, Liguria has limited land for farming. Shaped like a thin, craggy half-moon hugging the Gulf of Genoa, Liguria runs into France to the west and Toscana and Emilia-Romagna to the east, separating itself from Piemonte to the north with its crown, the Ligurian Alps. In contrast to neighboring regions, each of which produced more than 52 million gallons of wine in 2010, Liguria yielded less than 2 million gallons, making it the second lowest-producing region in Italy (after Valle d'Aosta). Bound by mountains, forests, and sea, Liguria's topography naturally limits its production. What land remains for vine cultivation is carved into ancient terraced hillsides called *fasce*. Pitched as steep as 45 degrees in some places, the vineyards are impossible to harvest using mechanical means. The poor, rocky soils also limit vine vigor. And yet, vintners here persevere, growing grapes in all kinds of inopportune places, including against cliffs and above highway tunnels.

The second reason these wines are hard to find is because most of the wine is consumed in Liguria. With the Italian Riviera and Cinque Terre, tourism is an important economic driver in the region. Tourists sunning in Portofino or hiking around Cinque Terre can absorb all of the region's white wines. Years ago, this was a fine arrangement. Demand for Ligurian wine didn't travel far beyond the region's azure coastline. Yet winemakers who have recognized the natural advantages of making wine here—the sandy limestone soil and maritime breezes that preserve aromas, the reliable drainage in the vineyards, the collection of idiosyncratic native grapes—are steadily proving that Liguria can make much more than simple vacation quaffs. Great wines are not only a possibility here; they have become a reality.

For centuries, Liguria has been a cosmopolitan point of trade within the Mediterranean. Before the Romans arrived, Genoa was an important port for trade among the Phoenicians, Etruscans, and Greeks. The Romans strengthened Genoa's position as a port by extending the Via Aurelia, which ran up the Tyrrhenian coast from Rome, to around the Gulf of Genoa and into France. They also commissioned a new consular road, the Via Postumia, which spanned the Italian peninsula, connecting Genoa to the Gulf of Venice. The extension of the Roman roads not only increased trade but also spurred development of Roman settlements in the area. The Colli di Luni DOC was named after the hills around the Roman settlement of Luni. The zone's fragrant lemon verbena–imbued Vermentino and cherry-hued Ciliegiolo have once again put this area back on the wine map. When visiting, you can also walk through the ruins of Luni, now an outdoor museum.

While Genoa was strategically important in Roman times, it came into its own between the fourteenth and sixteenth centuries, becoming one of the most important maritime republics and financial centers in the Mediterranean. The merchants of *La Superba*, as Genoa came to be called, built fortunes trading wheat, silk, and spices. After the city's native son Christopher Columbus returned from the New World, Genoa became the center of trade for American silver. Unlike its coastal rival Venice, which exported local wine, Genoa was better known as a wine importer, drawing in amphorae from as far away as the Levantine islands in the eastern Mediterranean. Yet wine was still made locally.

Situated in eastern Liguria—an area referred to as the Riviera di Levante—today's Cinque Terre vineyards probably don't look all that different than they did centuries ago. The terraced hillsides, scattered among the five villages of Riomaggiore, Vernazza, Manarola, Monterosso, and Corniglia, look ready to cascade into the sea. During harvest, pickers carry backpacks full of grapes to the monorails, which bring the grapes to the wineries. Harvest in Cinque Terre requires a crazy amount of endurance—the physically demanding nature of cultivating grapes in Cinque Terre has reduced its land in vine from more than 3,500 acres in the seventeenth century to 200 acres today. To make things more difficult, wild boars have taken to eating the fruit and trampling the terraces. Yet the historic nature of the area, its indigenous white grapes, especially Bosco and Albarola, and the critical need to lessen soil erosion, have inspired locals, such as Walter De Battè, to continue making wine.

Northwest of Cinque Terre and Colli di Luni is the Golfo del Tigullio DOC. Like Colli di Luni, this coastal growing area produces reds with Ciliegiolo and Granaccia, the local name for the Grenache grape, and whites with Vermentino. Golfo del Tigullio is also the home of the rare white grape Bianchetta Genovese, thanks largely to the efforts of Piero Lugano, the owner of Enoteca Bisson. Piero has made it his mission to preserve local grapes, and his fresh Ü Pastine, a sparkling Bianchetta, is one such result of his efforts. His other experiments with sparkling wine rival Friuli-Venezia Giulia's Josko Gravner in their unconventional nature. Rather than aging wine in amphorae buried in the ground, as Gravner does, Lugano plunges bottles filled with a blend of Bianchetta and Vermentino in the sea, relying on water to regulate temperature and the current to keep the lees swirling in the bottles. The wine is called Abissi.

Western Liguria—known as the Ponente—also grows Vermentino, which goes into a varietal wine in the Riviera Ligure di Ponente DOC zone, and Pigato, one of the most popular white wines that we pour by the glass at SPQR. Vermentino and Pigato are genetically identical, though this can be hard to believe when tasting through a selection of Vermentino and Pigato wines. Vermentino tends to veer more toward wild fennel and herbs with a nearly briny finish, while Pigato brings forth an overall richer style that can be spun several ways, from golden wines imbued with stone fruit and petrol to lighter, brighter *aperitivo* quaffs.

Laura Aschero, one of my favorite producers in Liguria, makes Pigato and Vermentino wines near Pontedassio, a commune near the French border. A doctor's wife, Laura was a pioneer when she started incorporating modern techniques in the cellar in the 1980s. While Laura has passed away, her son Marco Rizzo, his wife, Carla, and their daughter, Bianca, continue to run the operation. Both the Pigato and the Vermentino exhibit classic herbal and floral notes found in Ligurian white wines, but the Pigato is a personal favorite, with its savory granite and petrol edge and its tangy fruit qualities. Northeast of Imperia is Ortovero, a commune within the province of Savona, which also has long grown Pigato. Antonio Basso's Durin estate has some Pigato vines that are at least seventy years old. Durin produces leaner Pigato wines with decidedly herbal, citrus accents. Yet these are only two examples, and it feels as if almost every month I'm being tipped off to an excellent new Pigato producer.

White wine is what Liguria is best known for, but the region's red wines have made significant strides toward

quality and consistency. While producers in the Levante revive Ciliegiolo, a central Italian grape that has grown in eastern Liguria for decades, producers in the far west corner of the Ponente are rendering serious wine from the local Rossese grape. The Ortovero valley and the Rossese di Dolceacqua DOC zone produce some of Liguria's best Rossese wines. In the mountains around Pieve di Teco, Ormeasca, the local version of Dolcetto, also comes into its own. Some Ligurian reds are light, others carry spice notes like black pepper, cinnamon stick, and clove. Overall they tend to be medium-bodied and fruit-driven wines. They're aromatic, with notes of dried rose petals followed by the tanginess of red berry fruits.

Yet one of my favorite discoveries from Liguria wasn't a Pigato or a Rossese di Dolceacqua. Instead, it is a *vino da meditazione*, after-dinner meditation wine. Every New Year's Eve I open a few special wines that I have been waiting to sample. One year the wine was Sciacchetrà, a nectar from Cinque Terre made by only a few producers. The one I tried, a blend of Bosco, Albarola, and Vermentino, came from Cantine Cinque Terre, the local cooperative. Considering that making wine in Cinque Terre is challenging enough, making Sciacchetrà, which necessitates a lengthy drying period for the grapes,

demands uncommon dedication. Sciacchetrà is a deeply amber *passito* wine that is at once savory and sweet, with notes of almonds, herbs, and apricots. It is perfect with salty, nutty styles of cheeses, like aged pecorino. But the backbone of this lush wine is all acidity and resilience, a direct reflection of the hillside vineyards. —SL

White Grapes

ALBAROLA

Used with Bosco and Vermentino in the Cinque Terre DOC blend, Albarola one of Liguria's classic grapes. It also is blended into Sciacchetrà, the area's rare *passito* wine. On its own, Albarola makes a light, dry *aperitivo-*style wine.

RECOMMENDED PRODUCERS: Elio Altare, Walter de Battè, Bisson, Bonanni, Cantina Cinque Terre, Forlini Cappellini

BIANCHETTA

The grape's name translates to "little white one." Grown south of Genoa, the grape was pulled out of obscurity by Pierluigi Lugano, the owner of Bisson, who has strived to save native vines in Liguria that had fallen out of favor because of the labor required to harvest them. While Bianchetta was once used exclusively as a blending grape, Bisson started making still and sparkling wine with the grape. The winery's Ü Pastine is an ideal *aperitivo* with its delicate, light body and accent of snappy zest. As a sparkling wine, Bianchetta is made with the same Charmat method used for Prosecco. It makes a lighter bodied, dry sparkling wine that is a great palate cleanser. Lugano also has experimented with a bottle-fermented Bianchetta and Vermentino blend, aged at an ideal cellar temperature—under the sea.

RECOMMENDED PRODUCER: Bisson

BOSCO

Named after Liguria's numerous forests, Bosco joins Albarola and Vermentino as a key grape in Cinque Terre. Although the grape oxidizes easily, it adds a savory edge to Cinque Terre DOC wines and Sciacchetrà *passito*. While 100 percent Bosco wines are rare, Elio Altare, a producer

in Piemonte, has started showing the complexity possible in this underrated grape.

RECOMMENDED PRODUCERS: Cantina Cinque Terre, Elio Altare, Walter de Battè, Forlini Cappellini

BUZZETTO

Buzze means "unripe" in Italian, and it's an appropriate name for this tart grape. Grown in the terraced vineyards of the Quiliano DOC, Buzzetto might actually be a type of Trebbiano. If so, it is the lightest, driest version of Trebbiano out there. The delicate aromas this grape provides and its herbaceous and flinty quality makes this a great wine with which to begin a meal. It is also called Lumassina or Mataossu.

RECOMMENDED PRODUCER: Punta Crena

CORONATA

From Coronata, an ancient village that is now part of Genoa, this white grape yields a pale straw-hued wine that, centuries ago, was compared with Riesling from Germany. The area around Genoa has lost much of its farmland, and today only a few vineyards produce true Coronata, a subset of the Val Polcevera DOC; there aren't yet any producers exporting wines made with solely this grape.

PIGATO

Pigato is one of Italy's great white grapes. Top producers in western Liguria—the cradle of Pigato—like Laura Aschero and Durin make white wines of incredible complexity, with strong mineral notes and great verve all while emitting delicate stone fruit. The grape can also be lively and crisp in the hands of other producers. It's believed that golden, speckled Pigato came from Greece; it is genetically related to Vermentino and Favorita vines. Pigato wines with stone fruit aromatics and a lighter, *aperitivo* are perfect for Liguria's seafood, fresh green herbs like basil, olive oil, *ceci* bean, and pasta diet.

RECOMMENDED PRODUCERS: Laura Aschero, Durin, Terre Bianche, Bio Vio, Colle dei Bardellini, Bruna

VERMENTINO

This white grape flourishes along the Tyrrhenian coast and in Sardinia. In Liguria, Vermentino is best known in Ponente di Liguria. It is also important in the Colli di Luni growing region, which spills into Toscana, and it's often blended into the wines of Cinque Terre. Vermentino wines exude peach and jasmine blossoms and wet stone. Like Pigato, it is a classic pairing with seafood and herb-based dishes served along the Tyrrhenian coast. In addition to white Vermentino, some producers cultivate a red strain of the grape. Ivan Guiliani has championed this Vermentino variation at his Terenzuola vineyards on the Tuscan-Ligurian border in Colli di Luni, and when I can get it, I pour his wine by the glass.

RECOMMENDED PRODUCERS: Bruna, Walter de Batte, Bio Vio, Laura Aschero, Terenzuola, Lambruschi, Terre Bianche, Lunae Bosoni, Claudio Vio, Tenuta La Ghiaia

Red Grapes

GRANACCIA

Related to Cannonau, a Sardinian red grape, as well as French Grenache and Spanish Garnacha, Granaccia thrives in Liguria's Savona and Colli di Luni growing areas. (It also goes by its synonym, Alicante.) It has a bright ruby color with tinges of orange, yielding a velvety, medium-bodied red wine accented with baking spices. Like Pigato and Vermentino, it is the perfect foil for Liguria's herby local cuisine.

RECOMMENDED PRODUCERS: Bisson, Durin, Bruna

ORMEASCO

The grape may have been named after Ormea, a town known for a deep orange-red rosé wine called Sciac-tra, made by pressing Ormeasco grapes quickly and removing the skins soon after. Ormeasco is closely related to Piemonte's Dolcetto, but Ormeasco has reddish vines, smaller bunches, and thicker grape skins. As a wine, Ormeasco is lighter than Dolcetto and a touch spicier, with sweeter, less firm tannins. The flinty terroir of Liguria comes through in this wine, and expressions of currant, black pepper, and blueberry flavors are common. This wine pairs well with a wide variety of pasta, seafood, and bitter greens.

RECOMMENDED PRODUCERS: Durin, Lupi Le Braje, Bruna Pulin, Ramo

ROSSESSE

Cultivated in the Dolceacqua DOC along Liguria's western Riviera, Rossesse has high, aromatic qualities of rose petal, red berries, tangerines, and dried fruit. Its wines remind me of the classic light reds of the Valle d'Aosta. It offers a pleasant, medium-bodied wine with refreshing, slate-like minerality. The occasional bottle of Rossesse Bianco is a rare find.

RECOMMENDED PRODUCERS: Terre Bianche, Durin, Bio Vio, Altavia, Enzo Guglielmi

Toscana

With its cypress trees, storybook castles, vines, and olive groves, Toscana is iconic Italy. Even people who have never visited are familiar with its sites: the tower of Pisa, the Florence Duomo, the statue of David. Yet international popularity and subsequent clichés can obscure the contemporary picture of Toscana. Clichés also overshadow Toscana's dynamic wine industry, a region with the muscle to drive trends (and controversy) far beyond its borders. The real story of Toscana reads like a good novel, complete with heroes, plot twists, and scandal. To view the region with fresh eyes, I began my most recent trip to Toscana not in Florence but on the Via Aurelia, the Roman road that traces the Tyrrhenian coast from Rome to France. Crossing the border from Lazio in the morning, we headed north to Bolgheri.

Bolgheri is a walled medieval village next to the legendary Tenuta San Guido estate. It is so small that it doesn't permit visitors to drive through it. Instead, everyone parks in a lot outside of the sandy brick walls. From the number of cars already in the lot, it appeared as if everyone who wasn't at the beach in nearby Bibbona was in Bolgheri taking their *passeggiata*, the traditional postprandial stroll. While sipping Vermentino in a wine bar and snacking on salumi, pecorino pepato, and classically Tuscan salt-free bread, I spotted the bar's wines-by-the-glass list posted on the wall. Although the setting was casual, the list was not: Ornellaia, Guado al Tasso, Ca' Marcanda, and Sassicaia, the names of some of Toscana's most famous and expensive wines, jumped off the list. Soon after, Sebastiano Rosso, Sassicaia's director of operations, stopped in.

A graduate of the University of California, Davis viticulture program, Sebastiano has every reason to boast about Sassicaia, the wine produced at Tenuta San Guido that put Bolgheri on the wine map in the 1970s. Today, though, he was more concerned about the wild boars that terrorize his low-trained Cabernet Sauvignon vines. We arranged to meet at Tenuta San Guido in the morning so I could see the Sassicaia vines for myself. A bit later, we made the trip down the hill to Bibbona for dinner. To complement the array of fresh seafood dishes, I chose a bottle of Massa Vecchia Bianco from the list. Made from local Malvasia di Candia grapes but vinified like a red wine with extended contact with the grape skins, this wholly natural wine was exceptionally flexible, complementing both the lighter and the more intense seafood flavors of the meal.

Like that glass of *bianco*, Toscana can be full of contradictions and contrasts. When we expect simple, we get grand. When we anticipate pomp, we find humility. That night, even though we were a ten-minute drive from some of the most famous Cabernet and Merlot vineyards in the world, we contentedly swirled a local white wine in our glasses.

The Maremma cuts a generous swath along the Tuscan coast starting in northern Lazio and stretching up to Livorno. The now-trendy area used to be horse territory, the place where Italian gentlemen came to ride or hunt. Many kept prized racehorses on their Maremma estates. In the 1940s, it was not a place for winemaking. Yet the lack of a track record did not deter the Marchese Mario Incisa della Rocchetta from planting Bordeaux vines in the stony hillside six miles inland on the grounds of Tenuta San Guido, his estate. Not only was the choice in grape variety unusual but so was the selection of the vineyard site. Most of the vines growing in the Maremma were planted on the flat, sandy soils close to the coast, yielding simple, low-acid wines. The Marchese, a Bordeaux drinker, felt that planting late-ripening Cabernet Sauvignon vines on the gravelly soil and hillsides farther inland could produce consequential wine. He began bottling a red wine made with Cabernet Sauvignon and Cabernet Franc for friends, but word soon spread about the quality of the wine. Starting with the 1968 vintage, Sassicaia (which means "place with stones") became available commercially. By the mid-1970s, it was already famous.

Sassicaia kick-started the Super Tuscan movement, a trend that drove modern winemakers to make concentrated, *barrique*-aged wines that flouted DOC regulation for the sake of quality. The Marchese's nephews, Piero and Lodovico from the noble Chianti family Antinori, started experimenting with vineyard sites on the coast. In the 1980s, Lodovico Antinori introduced Ornellaia, a Cabernet Sauvigon, Merlot, and Petit Verdot blend, soon followed by Masseto, a Merlot. (Both wines are now made by Frescobaldi, another noble Tuscan family.) Meanwhile, Piero started Guado al Tasso, a large estate south of Ornellaia and Tenuta San Guido that produces a Cabernet and Merlot blend. The success of these wines led to a land rush of sorts, and producers from other regions, like Piemonte's Angelo Gaja, also started investing in vineyards. Super Tuscans weren't limited to the coast, but the style of wine—and penchant for Bordeaux grapes—has been most persistent there.

A visit to Tenuta San Guido shows that it is pure class, not flash, that fuels the philosophy. Old oak *barrique* are favored over new, so each barrel is reused several times. Unlike in most wine regions that experienced a boom, remarkably little of the estate is covered in vine. Sebastiano explained that his stepfather, the Marchese Nicolo Incisa della Rocchetta (Mario's son) only planted vines into parcels of his land that had the optimal stony soil and elevation. From the low-lying vines, pruned as carefully as bonsai trees, I could see the coast. Meanwhile, a *cinghiale* (wild boar) footprint stood out from the rocky soil, a distinct reminder that we were not the only ones who coveted these grapes. These environmental factors go into each glass of Sassicaia, an elegant wine that can show Bing cherries, blackberries, and even milk chocolate, countered by fennel and pepper.

The coast also produces some of Toscana's best white wines. Vermentino, the primary white grape of Sardinia and Liguria, has filtered down from Colli di Luni to Val di Cornia. Michele Satta produces Costa di Giulia, an aromatic Vermentino with a touch of Sauvignon, the perfect accompaniment to salty Tuscan salumi. Recently Massa Vecchia introduced Ariento, a natural wine made solely with Vermentino, an alternate to their lovely Bianco

bottling. One of my favorite white Tuscan wines from the coast comes from the granite soils of Isola del Giglio and the local Ansonica grape, which delivers a wine full of orange blossoms backed with pleasing acidity.

Still, at about 15 percent of total output, white wine production is considerably limited in Toscana. Yet its first DOC—in fact, Italy's first-ever DOC—went to the historic white wine of San Gimignano in 1966. Surrounded by Sangiovese vineyards (San Gimignano overlaps with the southeast Chianti subzone Colli Senesi), Vernaccia di San Gimignano remains Toscana's most famous white wine, a notoriety maintained by location. The Via Francigena, the main route for religious pilgrims traveling to Rome from northern Europe, passed directly through the center of the medieval city. On this heavily trafficked route, word spread about the quality of the wine from San Gimignano. Today Vernaccia is still sopped up by the busloads of visitors who arrive to admire the city's towers and medieval center.

Apart from San Gimignano's oasis of white wine, the northern and central part of Toscana is Sangiovese country. While the 1980s and 90s ushered in sexy Sangiovese-Merlot and Sangiovese–Cabernet Sauvignon blends, the call today is for Sangiovese to stand on its own. Through improved clonal selections and vineyard management methods, winemakers are finding less of a need to blend the challenging grape with international varieties for well-balanced wine. This isn't always easy: a damp harvest can prevent the late-ripening grape from ripening completely, yielding a green, acerbic wine. But in warm, dry harvests, the grape can produce a wine that reflects Tuscan character. At first austere and reserved, it becomes generous over longer acquaintance. The grape's most classic renditions come from three main areas: Chianti, Brunello di Montalcino, and Vino Nobile di Montepulciano.

While no wine is more synonymous with Italy than Chianti, the connotation has not always been a positive one. Contemporary producers would prefer that we all experienced collective amnesia and forgot about straw-wrapped *fiaschi* filled with tawny, tart grape juice. For these producers, the mass-produced *fiasco* wines, which took off in America during the post–World War II era, embodied the other meaning of the word: a total failure.

Yet the kitschy bottles have made Chianti one of the most familiar Italian words on American wine lists.

Chianti's classic producing area, which extends one hundred miles between Florence and Siena, is the oldest official wine zone in Italy. During the Renaissance, aristocratic families, such as Antinori and Frescobaldi, began to devote their estates to wine production, selling cuvees by the glass or jug from a small window on the bottom of the floor of their *cantine*. (In fact, the Antinori family built most of its wealth through wine sales.) The wine made during this time was called Vermillio until the fourteenth century when the Florentine republic conjured the name *Chianti*. The wine was packed away in straw-covered bottles (the predecessors of the mass-marketed *fiaschi*) because the straw helped steady the rounded base of blown glass. To keep dust out of the wine, vintners poured olive oil on top and then covered the bottles with pieces of paper. In the sixteenth century, a scandal involving *fiasco* bottles filled with lower-quality wine attached the *fiasco* with its more-notorious meaning. To prevent tampering, seals changed from oil to molten lead.

In 1716, Grand Duke Cosimo III officially delimited the Chianti growing area, including subzones Radda, Gaiole, and Castellina. Greve was folded in later. Today wines from these subzones are labeled Chianti Classico, distinguished by a black rooster, the *gallo nero,* on their labels. This distinction became crucially important in the early twentieth century when the government allowed the growing zone to expand well beyond its classic area. Soon Rufina, Colli Senesi, Colli Fiorentini, Pisane, Colli Aretini, and Montalbano could carry the Chianti name. Of these newer Chianti areas, Rufina is the most distinctive, ageworthy red wine, while the rest are often saddled with blame for driving down the quality with mass-produced wines. Even now the distinction "Chianti" doesn't tell you much. It could come from the higher slopes of Arezzo to the east or in the flat coastal land around Pisa.

Apart from the dramatic expansion of the Chianti growing area, quality problems came from grape choices. In the late nineteenth century, Baron Bettino Ricasoli began drafting a recipe for Chianti. He suggested adding white Malvasia grapes for lighter, fresh-tasting red wines to drink young, a forward-thinking idea at the time.

To the chagrin of winemakers in the twentieth century, Ricasoli's smart suggestion for alternative lighter wines became the 1963 DOC formula. For a wine to be labeled Chianti, it needed to include at least 10 percent white grapes and up to 30 percent. By this time, inexpensive Trebbiano Toscano had long taken over from Malvasia. In addition, Sangiovese clones in the 1960s were chosen for their productivity, not their quality. These factors concluded in the acrid, watery wine that flowed into *fiasco* bottles and out in Italian-American restaurants but were completely at odds with wines like the Ricasoli family's powerful Castello di Brolio and other Classico wines.

Prone to rain in the fall, the Chianti Classico zone has a cooler continental climate than other growing areas in Toscana. Uneven harvests may be one explanation for why blended wines have always been more preferred over pure Sangiovese wines. Yet south-facing vineyards in mineral-rich, well-draining soil, like limestone or galestro, a splintery schist soil, help preserve acidity and aromas in the fruit while allowing for the vine's extremely long growing season. In the years that nature cooperates, Chianti Classico yields a sophisticated, savory wine reminiscent of Tuscan austerity, one of the ultimate expressions of central Italy's most important grape.

Yet some of the best Sangiovese grown in the Chianti Classico zone isn't Chianti at all. Around the same time that the Super Tuscan movement was gaining momentum, a retired gentleman, Sergio Manetti took over Montevertine, a run-down estate in the heart of Radda, restoring the land by planting Sangiovese as well as local blending grapes Canaiolo and Colorino. However, his top wine, Le Pergole Torte, is all Sangiovese. Sharp, with dried petals and garnet fruit, it is a complex wine that unfolds gradually over the course of an evening.

Southwest of Chianti country is the Brunello di Montalcino zone. Although Montalcino has been inhabited since Etruscan times, the success of its Brunello wine is a modern phenomenon. In the last few decades, interest in Montalcino wines has placed this once-obscure hill town onto the international stage, and Brunello di Montalcino now ranks as one of Italy's most esteemed red wines. Success hasn't come without complications. Massive interest in the powerful, all-Sangiovese wines has led to massive spikes in plantings, bottles, and brands.

Unchecked growth reached a critical point in 2008 when international scandal struck, bringing into question whether any of these wines could live up to the hype.

There is no denying Montalcino's natural advantage for winemaking. Not only does the inland growing area have a warmer, drier climate than Chianti Classico, but it also has Chianti's rocky galestro soil in some select vineyard sites. The combination suits Sangiovese Grosso (locally known as Brunello) well, encouraging the grapes to achieve ripe sugars and tannins while keeping the vines' notorious vigor in check. This ideal environment yields robust, high-acid fruit for structured, masculine wine capable of long periods of aging. Some bottles go back a hundred years. It was the quality inherent in old vintages that drove modern interest in Brunello di Montalcino.

The story starts in the 1840s. Before Baron Ricasoli devised his formula for Chianti, Clemente Santi isolated the Brunello vine from other Sangiovese variations. For years afterward, the grape was called Brunello and considered unique to the area. (It has since been found to be a clone of Sangiovese Grosso.) When he took over the family estate, Tenuta Il Greppo, Santi's grandson, Ferruccio Bondi, replanted vineyards devastated by phylloxera with Brunello vines, releasing the first Brunello wine in 1888. The wine was formalized in 1968, when Brunello di Montalcino was granted a DOC and local growers formed a *consorzio*. Still the region stayed under the radar until the late 1970s. In 1980, Brunello became the first Italian wine to be awarded DOCG status, and the boom in vine plantings and wine production exploded. Tenuta Il Greppo was an early driver of faith in Brunello di Montalcino capacity to age. Reports circulated of the vibrancy remaining in the Biondi-Santi family's Brunello bottles from 1888, and vintages from the 1960s still carried resolute acidity. Even today collectors seek Brunello wines from Biondi-Santi and other proven, traditional producers, such as Gianfranco Soldera.

In the ensuing years, producers from other parts of Toscana and beyond bought up land and planted it with vines, growing the zone from barely 150 acres in 1960 to more than 5,000 acres today. The rapid growth not only put pressure on the supply of Sangiovese grapes grown in the zone but also pushed the style of Brunello in an international direction. Instead of austerity, some Brunello delivered mouthfuls of plush, round fruit. Soon rumors circulated about Brunello being doctored with Bordeaux grapes. This wouldn't raise an eyebrow in Chianti or Vino Nobile di Montepulciano, where blends were the norm, but in Montalcino, a designation synonymous with Sangiovese, it meant fraud. In 2008, Brunellogate (or *Brunellopoli*, as it was called in the Italian newspapers) broke as regulators found evidence that some wines contained other grapes. With the U.S. government threatening to ban imports until the mess was sorted out, in 2009 Italian authorities demoted 20 percent of the 6.7 million liters of Brunello to IGT status (IGT stands for *Indicazione Geografica Tipica*, a less prestigious wine classification).

Even without a scandal, a lot has changed here since the zone's early days. Traditional Brunello wines were made with long periods of maceration and fermentation, with aging carried out in Slavonian oak *botti*. Today's DOCG regulations require that it ages for two years in oak and less than one year in bottle. As in Barolo and Barbaresco production, French *barrique* are used interchangeably with the large *botti*. And nearly everyone makes a Rosso di Montalcino, a less-expensive wine to drink while the Brunellos age.

There are also notable differences in the growing region itself. In a slightly cooler climate, vineyards north of the city grow in galestro soil. The vineyards south of the city grow in heavier clay and stone soils, yielding wines that are can be more powerful though less acidic than Brunellos made from northern vineyards. Laura Brunelli, who owned Osteria de Logge and Le Chiuse di Sotto with her late husband, Gianni Brunelli, makes wine from naturally farmed vineyards both north and south of Montalcino. Laura's *botti*-aged wines are elegant and graceful, direct reflections of the land and the grape. At Le Chiuse di Sotto, the vineyards northeast of Montepulciano, she goes for freshness and elegance, breaking the rocky soil so the vines have to reach down into rocks to extract minerals. In her Podernovone vineyard, she protects the grapes from heat by turning the canopy of leaves into a wall, shielding the fruit from the sun. The vines reach a balance with their environment, between the rocks, grasses, and vines. And every day like clockwork, a warm, dry wind blows through the vineyard. While the word *Brunello* often conjures the image of a

SANGIOVESE

From Brunello di Montalcino to Chianti Classico, Sangiovese makes some of Italy's most famous, ageworthy red wines. It is also one of the most planted grapes in Italy, yielding wines that vary dramatically in quality and style. But when it's good, it's good—smacked with herbs and tart red fruit, like cranberries, all of which is backed by an undercurrent of tannin and acidity.

There is a great deal of genetic diversity found within the variety. For years, some strains of Sangiovese, like Morellino, grown in the Maremma, and Prugnolo Gentile, grown around Montepulciano, were believed to be separate grapes entirely. Despite its widespread growth, Sangiovese isn't an easy grape to propagate. It blossoms early but ripens late, and autumn rains can prevent the grape from fully ripening. It is also a vigorous vine, and needs to be carefully trellised and pruned to encourage even ripening. In Toscana, the southern growing area of Morellino di Scansano makes a softer style, while in the north around Lucca, an emerging area for Sangiovese production, wines exhibit tart cherry, spices, and ripe strawberry. When grown in Chianti Classico or Montalcino, the wine becomes austere, capable of aging for years.

Farther afield, Sangiovese grows around Forlì, Rimini, and Cesena in Romagna, producing meatier wines with a deeper color, riper tannins, and velvety texture. In Umbria, Sangiovese is most associated with the Lungarotti family's Torgiano Rosso Riserva. Sangiovese is also widely used for *rosso* wines throughout Umbria and Le Marche.

RECOMMENDED PRODUCERS FROM CENTRAL AND NORTHERN ITALY

TOSCANA
- **Brunello di Montalcino:** Poggio Antico, Poggio di Sotto, Brunelli, Tenimenti Ruffino, San Filippo, Castello Romitorio, Valdicava, Uccelliera, Banfi, Tenuta Il Greppo, Lisini, Capanna, Biondi Santi, Caprili, Sesti, Castello di Argiano, Vitanza, Canalicchio di Sopra, Pietranera, Casanova di Neri, Altesino, Talenti, Case Basse Soldera, Il Poggione, Le Chiuse, Fonterenza, La Gerla, Stella di Campalto
- **Chianti Classico:** Badia a Coltibuono, Ciacci, Barone Ricasoli, Antinori, Felsina, Volpaia, Cecchi, Castello di Radda, Fontodi, Rocca di Castagnoli, Poggio al Sole, Spadaio e Piecorto, Castello di Fonterutoli, Castello di Cacchiano, Rocca di Montegrossi, Querciabella, Geografico, Monte Bernardi, Castello di Ama, Aiola, Nittardi
- **Chianti:** Lavacchio, Poggio Capponi, Grignano, Basciano, Bagnolo, Casabianca
- **Vino Nobile di Montepulciano:** Avignonesi, Dei, Le Berne, Fattoria del Cerro, Nottola, Gattavecchi, Triacca, Salcheto, Le Casalte, Boscarelli, La Braccesca, Tenuta Il Faggeto, Tenimenti Angelini, Poliziano, Villa Sant'Anna, Terra Antica
- **Other Sangiovese:** Montevertine, Podere Le Boncie, Tenuta San Guido, Tenuta di Valgiano, La Mozza, Mantellassi, Le Pupille, Le Sorgenti, Fubbiano

UMBRIA
- Lungarotti, Antignano, Brogal Vini, Santa Caterina, Antonelli, Di Filippo, Milziade Antano, Perticaia, Scacciadiavoli, Paolo Bea, Moretti Omero

EMILIA-ROMAGNA
- Tre Monti, Paradiso, Zerbina, Castelluccio, San Patrignano, Drei Donà, Giovanna Madonia, Valli, Bissoni

LE MARCHE
- Selvagrossa, Mancini, Velenosi, Saladini Pilastri, Laila, Ciù Ciù, Boccadigabbia, La Monacesca, Boira, Castello Fageto, Dezi

castle or an international brand, Laura's wines show a return to the land.

The last in line among Toscana's historic three red Sangiovese wines is Vino Nobile di Montepulciano. Once the home of a wine-loving Etruscan king, Montepulciano has a viticulture history that's as noble as it is ancient. Since the Middle Ages, European gentry praised the wine made in the town's hillsides for its quality. Like much of agricultural Italy, Montepulciano's farmland was managed under the *mezzadria* system, an arrangement in which crops were divided between the landowners and those who worked the land. The nobles kept the best grapes for cellar-worthy wine, leaving the rest of the harvest to the share-croppers who used it to make everyday wine.

Despite its lofty name, the wine fell into the same fate of other Tuscan wines, lost in the mass market. But like Montalcino, fortunes shifted in the early 1980s. After the growing zone earned a DOCG designation in 1980, wines such as Poliziano's Asinone Vino Nobile became benchmarks for finesse and consistency, driving up the quality expectations for the area. Contemporary Vino Nobile di Montepulciano is slighly rustic, with a savory edge of balsamic vinegar entwined with red berries, baking spices, and a wisp of smoke.

Still, it is very hard to make style generalizations about Vino Nobile. Unlike Brunello, which has to be 100 percent Sangiovese, or Chianti, which has tightened its regulations on blending grapes, Montepulciano offers the chose-your-own-adventure option. To be called Vino Nobile, 70 percent of the wine must be Sangiovese. (Here it's called Prugnolo Gentile, the local synonym for Sangiovese Grosso.) From there it's a grab bag of grapes, from Canaiolo and Colorino to Mammolo, an aromatic though rare local variety. And like Chianti, a small percentage of white grapes are also allowed, though few producers incorporate them.

While Vino Nobile di Montepulciano has gained recognition as one of Toscana's most important red wines, the area's other historic wine, Vin Santo, has stayed in the shadows. Producers throughout Toscana make a Vin Santo meditation wine, but Montepulciano is the wine's true home. Made from dried grapes (anything from Malvasia to Sangiovese), Vin Santo is a completely natural wine. After the dried grapes are crushed, the concentrated must is siphoned into *caratelli*, small fifty-liter barrels and then is set aside in a *vinsantaio*, an aging room. In cool weather, fermentation stops. On warm days, it resumes. The wine is left alone until it stabilizes, three years for some, several more for others. Vin Santo can be a oxidized, sherry-like wine or it can have a sweeter, honeyed edge. Avignonesi, a renowned producer of Vin Santo, makes its rare Occhio di Pernice Vin Santo with all Sangiovese, aging the wine for ten years before bottling. The classic savory notes of Vin Santo are all present: aromas of fresh-hulled walnuts, dried nectarines, and earthy spices are coupled with a tanginess that makes your mouth water. To me, this is the ultimate *vino de meditazione.* —SL

White Grapes

ANSONICA

The Tuscan version of Sicily's Inzolia grape, Ansonica arrived in Elba in the sixteenth century from Sicily. While it was later planted on the Tuscan mainland, the low-yielding grape is still best known on Elba. Like Sicily's Inzolia, Ansonica offers aromas of orange blossoms mixed with hints of stone fruit and crisp green apple. At Testamatta, a producer based in Fiesole, owner Bibi Graetz makes two versions from Elba fruit: Bugia, a rich rendition aged in oak, and Gigliese, a traditional style that is aged in cement tanks.

RECOMMENDED PRODUCERS: Altura, Bibi Graetz, La Parrina, Cecilia

VERNACCIA DI SAN GIMIGNANO

Grown in the province of Siena around the medieval town of San Gimignano, Vernaccia makes crisp, lean wines with accents of Macintosh apple and lemon curd, though they become richer when aged on the lees or in oak. Panizzi's Vernaccia di San Gimignano Santa Margherita, a single-vineyard, oak-aged wine is at once crisp with minerals and round with toasted nuts.

RECOMMENDED PRODUCERS: Panizzi, Fontaleoni, San Quirico, Poggio Alloro, Cappella Sant'Andrea, Le Calcinaie
SEE ALSO: Vermentino (page 240), Malvasia (page 14), Trebbiano (page 71)

Red Grapes

CILIEGIOLO

Once used mainly for blending in central Italy, Ciliegiolo is growing in popularity as wine grape in its own right. Thought to be of Spanish origin, the grape was planted in Toscana before spreading to Liguria. Today it thrives in the maritime climate of Colli di Luni, a growing region that spans the border between Liguria and Toscana. As a wine, Ciliegiolo has a bright, light-bodied cherry-like character that lends itself to *rosato* styles in which the grape skins have very little contact with the juices. The grape's minty freshness, tart fruity quality, and herbaceous notes match well with the fish soups and pesto common along the Tyrrhenian coast.

RECOMMENDED PRODUCERS: Sassotondo, Rascioni & Cecconello, Grillesino, La Selva, Motta

COLORINO

Most often blended with Sangiovese, Colorino is recognized for its ability to impart deep color to wine. It is grown mostly in Toscana, but it also grows around Lake Corbara and Rosso Orvietano in Umbria. In central Italy, the grape variety is going through a resurgence in popularity as producers from Toscana and Umbria experiment with single-variety Colorino wines.

RECOMMENDED PRODUCERS: Poggiopiano, Testamatta, Fattoria del Cerro, Romitorio di Santedame

SEE ALSO: Aleatico (page 15), Canaiolo (page 71)

Local Catch

THERE WASN'T any shortage of signs to La Pineta, a restaurant in Marina di Bibbona, a beach town in Toscana's Maremma. Wooden posts guided us through a campsite and a grove of coastal pines before directing us down a narrow, one-way sandy drive. From the look of the signs and the casual atmosphere we had seen in Bibbona, I anticipated a no-frills seaside restaurant. But once we reached the restaurant, it was clear that there was no place to park, or even to turn our car around. The restaurant was similarly jammed, and our request for a table was sternly turned down. La Pineta was more than a casual place at the beach. It was a Michelin-starred restaurant known for serving local seafood caught that day. If we wanted to eat there, we would need to call ahead.

A few hours (and a phone call) later, our group finally settled in to a meal at the restaurant, which started with fried shrimp smaller than the prongs of our forks. Toscana is famous for inland specialties, from *bistecca fiorentina* to salt-free bread used in *panzanella* salads, but its coastal cuisine tends to get much less attention. Yet the Tyrrhenian Sea also fuels creativity for chefs on the coast from Genoa to Reggio Calabria on the tip of Italy's boot. At La Pineta, the chef-owner (and former fisherman) Luciano Zazzeri prepares the catch of the day simply but precisely. Squid ink gnocchi with crispy baby artichokes was unapologetically briny, while a platter of seafood pulled out of local waters came with a sharp *gelatina* and rich aïoli on the side so the seafood could shine on its own.

I always like to see how other chefs showcase seafood, which always tastes its best when eaten at the source. Now that I cook on the West Coast, I focus on the fish and shellfish available in the Pacific. While I still bring in seafood from farther afield, I make an effort to focus on what can be sustainably harvested from local waters—getting excited about experiments with red abalone, sea urchin roe, and Dungeness crab. Not all of the recipes in this chapter are focused on seafood, but the exploration of fish and the ways you can prepare it drives a larger theme in this chapter: that even when you think you know what to expect in Toscana, there's always room for discovery. —MA

BAKED RICOTTA *with* Cherry Tomatoes, Saba, *and* Pignoli Granola

In Toscana, it's common to bake ricotta in a casserole and serve it at the table. This is a stylized take on the traditional baked ricotta in which I portion the baked ricotta into rectangles and serve it with cherry tomatoes and a crunchy pine nut granola. *Saba*, a dark syrup made by cooking down juices from wine grapes with sugar, offers a sweet complement to the tomatoes. I cook cherry tomatoes by frying them very quickly in oil to loosen the skins, then peel the skins upward so the tomatoes resemble ground cherries with papery skins pulled up to expose the fruit. You may peel the skins and remove them completely if you like.

SERVES 6 TO 8

Baked Ricotta

567 grams • 3 cups drained ricotta (see page 281)

30 grams • 1/4 cup grated pecorino

100 grams • 2 eggs

33 grams • 1/8 cup heavy cream

10 grams • 1 scant tablespoon extra virgin olive oil

3 grams • 2/3 teaspoon kosher salt

a nutmeg for grating

Granola

28 grams • 2 tablespoons pine nuts

20 grams • 1 1/2 tablespoons simple syrup (page 256)

8 grams • 1/2 teaspoon honey

2 grams • 1/2 teaspoon extra virgin olive oil

4 grams • 1 scant tablespoon quick-cooking oats

a pinch of kosher salt

Tomatoes

160 grams • 1 cup cherry tomatoes

extra virgin olive oil

a pinch of coarse sea salt

5 to 10 basil leaves, torn

about 1/2 cup purslane or sunflower shoots

extra virgin olive oil

saba for finishing

kosher salt

To make the ricotta: Preheat the oven to 350°F. Coat a 9 by 13-inch baking dish with nonstick spray. Cut a piece of parchment to fit the bottom of the dish, and line it.

In a large bowl, whisk together the ricotta, pecorino, eggs, cream, olive oil, salt, and 10 gratings of nutmeg until smooth. Spoon the batter into the prepared baking dish, smoothing the surface with an offset spatula. Cover with aluminum foil and bake in a water bath for 45 minutes or until the ricotta has set firmly in the center. Uncover and cool to room temperature, about 1 hour. The top may rise in the center as it cooks, but it will fall back down as it cools.

With the tip of an offset spatula, loosen the edges of the ricotta. Turn a baking tray or platter upside down and press on top of the baked ricotta dish. In one smooth motion, pick up the dish and the tray, and invert on the counter. Unmold the ricotta. Cover with plastic wrap and refrigerate until completely firm and cold, about 6 hours or overnight.

Line a baking sheet with foil and coat with nonstick cooking spray. Cut the ricotta into 1 1/2-inch-wide strips. Cut the strips into 5- to 6-inch rectangles. Using a spatula, transfer the rectangles to the foil-lined baking sheet. You will have 8 to 10 rectangles.

To make the granola: Preheat the oven to 325°F. In a small sauté pan over medium heat, toast the pine nuts until fragrant. Pour the pine nuts on a cutting board. Using the tip of a paring knife, cut the pine nuts in half. In a small bowl, mix together the simple syrup, olive oil, and honey. Add the pine nuts and oats and season with a pinch of salt.

Line a baking sheet with parchment paper or use a nonstick silicone sheet. Scatter the granola onto the sheet and bake stirring once, 15 minutes. Cool completely.

{continued}

To make the tomatoes: Score the bottom of each cherry tomato gently (just through the skin) with an X, taking the cuts more than halfway up the side. Heat about 1 inch of olive oil in a straight-sided sauté pan over medium-high heat. Line a platter with paper towels. When the oil reaches 375°F, gently drop a few cherry tomatoes in at a time and fry until the skins loosen, 10 to 15 seconds. Using a slotted spoon, lift the tomatoes out of the oil and drain on the paper towels. Season with coarse sea salt. Repeat until all the tomatoes have been fried. Let cool and peel the skins upward to expose the flesh. Scatter the basil leaves over the tomatoes and drizzle fresh olive oil lightly on top.

Preheat the oven to broil. Put the foil-lined baking sheet with the ricotta in the oven and broil until the tops begin to caramelize, about 5 minutes. Remove and cool slightly.

In a small bowl, season the purslane or sunflower shoots with a few drops of olive oil and *saba*. Season with a pinch of salt and toss.

Using a spatula, divide the ricotta onto plates. Spoon the cherry tomatoes on the top and on the sides and scatter the greens over the top. Crumble the granola across each plate and finish with a drizzle of *saba*.

SCALLOP CRUDO *with* Sunchokes, Hibiscus Agrodolce, Almonds, *and* Cherries

Raw scallops have an inherent sweetness, which I draw out by pairing them with cherries in this whimsical *crudo*. Lightly pickled sunchokes and smoked almonds counter the sweetness, while hibiscus *agrodolce* links the sweet and savory flavors together. While the scallops are raw, I torch them first to firm their texture slightly. For this step, use the same torch you would use to brown a crème brûlée. Powdered hibiscus can be found at spice shops. The glucose in the *agrodolce* sweetens it while thickening it to the consistency resembling maple syrup. To smoke almonds, I use the same stove-top technique that I use for smoking flour (see page 275).

SERVES 6

Scallops

    4 grams • 1 teaspoon coarse sea salt

    2 grams • 1 teaspoon powdered hibiscus

    454 grams • 10 to 16 scallops (10/20 count per pound)

    extra virgin olive oil

    smoked salt

Sunchokes

    113 grams • 1/2 cup white pickling liquid (page 281)

    160 grams • 1 cup thinly sliced sunchokes, peeled

Agrodolce

    50 grams • 1/4 cup sugar

    50 grams • scant 1/4 cup water

    50 grams • scant 1/4 cup white wine vinegar

    10 grams • 1 teaspoon glucose

    2 grams • 1 teaspoon powdered hibiscus

    a pinch of kosher salt

    140 grams • 1 cup almonds

    19 grams • 1 1/2 tablespoons simple syrup (page 281)

8 to 12 cherries, halved and pitted

extra virgin olive oil

a handful of wild wood sorrel and flowers

1 or 2 lemon wedges

To make the scallops: In a small bowl, mix together the salt and hibiscus. Lay a large piece of plastic wrap on a work surface. Place the scallops on the plastic wrap and sprinkle with the cure until lightly coated on all sides. Let the scallops cure for 10 minutes, then pat dry. Rub the scallops with a light coat of olive oil and transfer to a heatproof tray. Using a kitchen torch, brûlée the tops of each scallop briefly (about 30 seconds), just long enough to firm up the edges. Refrigerate the scallops until needed.

To make the sunchokes: Bring the pickling liquid to a boil. Place the sliced sunchokes in a heatproof bowl and pour the pickling liquid over them. Let the sunchokes cool to room temperature and refrigerate until needed. (Alternatively, refrigerate the sunchokes overnight in the pickling liquid.)

To make the *agrodolce*: In a saucepan over medium-low heat, bring the sugar, water, and vinegar to a simmer. Continue to cook until the bubbles become large and glossy and the liquid has turned slightly syrupy, 8 to 10 minutes (avoid browning the sugar). Remove from the heat and stir in the glucose. Let it cool to room temperature, then stir in the hibiscus and salt. The *agrodolce* liquid should have the consistency of a thin maple syrup.

Preheat the oven to 350°F. Toss the almonds in simple syrup until just lightly coated. Scatter the almonds on a baking sheet lined with a nonstick silicone mat and toast for 15 to 20 minutes or until dry and shiny. Smoke the almonds using a stove-top smoker for 8 to 10 minutes, according to the instructions on page 275. Remove the pan from the heat, take off the foil, and let cool.

Slice the scallops crosswise into 3 or 4 thin disks. Lay the slices on a tray. Season with smoked salt and drizzle with olive oil. Spread a thin layer of agrodolce syrup on 6 chilled plates. Arrange the scallops in one even layer on each plate, using 6 to 8 slices per plate. Spoon a few dots of *agrodolce* over the top.

Drain the sunchokes. In a small bowl, dress the sunchokes with enough olive oil and divide the slices among the plates. In the same bowl, mix the cherries with a splash of olive oil. Scatter the cherry halves among the plates. In the same bowl, dress the sorrel with olive oil. Scatter the sorrel (reserving some for garnish) among the plates, then sprinkle the almonds over the top. Garnish with sorrel and a few flowers, squeeze a few drops of lemon juice over each plate, and add a few more dots of *agrodolce* as desired.

ALBACORE TUNA CONFITURA

with Panzanella Salad *and* Anchovies

Panzanella is Toscana's classic bread salad made by moistening stale bread in water until it is soft, then pulling the insides apart into small crumbs and seasoning them with tomatoes, basil, vinegar, and olive oil. My rendition is not so literal. I fry small cubes of bread in olive oil and mix it with the juices remaining from tomatoes and lightly pickled vegetables. I cook the tuna *sous vide* (see page 271) so that it is still pink in the center, retaining its texture, then I serve it with a salty, briny vinaigrette that contains two kinds of anchovies. Salt-packed anchovies need to be rinsed well before using. Cured in vinegar, white anchovies are ready to eat straight out of their packaging. In addition to blending them in the vinaigrette, I drape them over the salad as a garnish.

SERVES 4 TO 6

Pickles and Tomatoes

200 grams • 1 red onion

227 grams • 1 cup pickling liquid (page 281)

4 grams • 1 teaspoon kosher salt

335 grams • 1 cucumber

30 grams • 2 tablespoons pickling liquid (page 281)

1 cup cherry tomatoes

extra virgin olive oil

coarse sea salt

Tuna

about 600 grams • 1¼ to 1½ pounds albacore tuna

2 tablespoons kosher salt

1 tablespoon sugar

about 1 tablespoon extra virgin olive oil

about 5 basil leaves

Anchovy Vinaigrette

20 grams • 2 salted anchovies, rinsed well, boned, and minced

8 grams • 1 white anchovy, minced

15 grams • 1 tablespoon Dijon mustard

15 grams • 1 tablespoon capers

2 grams • ½ garlic clove

30 grams • ⅛ cup mayonnaise

10 grams • ⅛ cup grated Parmigiano-Reggiano

45 grams • 3 tablespoons red wine vinegar

30 grams • 2 tablespoons balsamic vinegar

65 grams • ¼ cup extra virgin olive oil

kosher salt and black pepper

extra virgin olive oil

2 cups country bread, crust removed and torn into ½-inch pieces

kosher salt

1 lemon for zesting

2 or 3 splashes red wine vinegar

8 to 12 white anchovies

a handful of small basil leaves

To pickle the red onion: Slice the ends off the red onion, then slice crosswise into thin rings. Punch out the smaller rings from the center and put them in a heatproof bowl or Mason jar (save the outer onion rings for stock or another recipe). Bring the pickling liquid to a boil and pour over the onion rings. Add a teaspoon of salt to the jar, then cool and refrigerate for at least 3 hours but preferably overnight.

If the cucumber skin is thick, peel it. Otherwise, leave the skin intact. Halve the cucumber lengthwise and scrape out the seeds with a spoon. Put the cucumber halves in a vacuum pouch with the pickling liquid and vacuum seal. Set aside for 10 minutes, then cut open the pouch and drain. Slice the cucumbers into half moons.

Score the bottom of each tomato gently (just through the skin) with an X, taking the cuts more than halfway up the sides. Heat about 1 inch of olive oil in a straight-sided sauté pan over medium-high heat. Line a platter with paper towels. When the oil reaches 375°F, gently drop in a few tomatoes at a time and fry until the skins loosen,

10 to 15 seconds. Using a slotted spoon, lift the tomatoes out of the oil and drain on the paper towels. Season with coarse sea salt. Repeat until all the tomatoes have been fried. Strain and save the oil for frying the bread. When cool enough to handle, peel the tomato skins up to expose the flesh.

To make the tuna: Heat a large water bath fitted with an immersion circulator to 140°F (see *Sous Vide*, page 271). Mix the salt and sugar together and sprinkle over the tuna, covering all sides. Refrigerate the tuna for 20 minutes, then rinse with water and pat dry. Place the tuna in a vacuum pouch with 1 tablespoon of olive oil and the basil and vacuum seal. Prepare an ice bath. Cook the pouch in the water bath for 14 to 15 minutes. (At this point, the tuna will be firm and still pink in the center.) Remove the tuna from the water bath and plunge into an ice bath to chill completely.

To make the anchovy vinaigrette: In a blender or food processor, pulse together the anchovies, mustard, capers, and garlic. Pulse in the mayonnaise and Parmigiano, then pour in the vinegars and process to a fine purée. While the machine is running, drizzle in the olive oil. Taste the vinaigrette and season with salt and pepper as needed.

Using the reserved tomato oil and additional olive oil as needed, heat about 1 inch of oil in a straight-sided sauté pan over medium-high heat. Line a platter with paper towels. Gently scatter the bread into the pan and fry until crisp, about 45 seconds. Using a slotted spoon, lift the bread out of the oil and drain on the paper towels. Season with salt.

Cut open the tuna pouch and drain. Slice the tuna crosswise into 1-inch pieces and grate lemon zest over each piece. Spoon the anchovy purée at the base of each plate and top with tuna. Using about 3 pickled onion rings per serving, in a bowl, mix together the pickled onions, cucumber, and tomatoes with a splash of red wine vinegar and olive oil. Season with a pinch of salt, then spoon over the tuna. Put the fried bread into the same mixing bowl (it should still contain some of the tomato and pickle juices) and toss. Distribute the bread among each portion. Garnish with white anchovies and basil leaves.

BEET *and* RICOTTA PANSOTTI *with* Walnuts *and* Ricotta Salata

Italians are adept at using vegetables and fruits to their fullest potential. The entire plant, from the root to the leaf, is examined for its flavor attributes and culinary possibilities. When beets have impeccable greens, it only makes sense that they find their way to the table. This filled pasta shows one example of root-to-leaf cooking. The slight bitterness in the greens is echoed in the sage and walnuts used to finish the pasta, while the mild ricotta, brown butter, and golden raisins bring sweetness and balance. To underline the star ingredient, I add beet powder to the pasta dough, turning it bright purple, and adding another layer of beet flavor.

Although beet powder is sold through specialty food purveyors, if you have a food dehydrator, you can make your own. Simply dehydrate sliced beets until very dry, then grind them in a clean coffee grinder. Before using, sift the powder to remove larger chunks.

SERVES 4

Filling

200 grams • 7 ounces (6 or 7) baby red beets with attached greens
extra virgin olive oil
15 grams • 1 tablespoon red wine vinegar
kosher salt
8 grams • 2 teaspoons unsalted butter
20 grams • 2 tablespoons minced yellow onion
4 grams • 1 small garlic clove, minced
160 grams • 2/3 cup drained ricotta (see page 281)
18 grams • 1/3 cup grated Parmigiano-Reggiano
a nutmeg for grating

Pasta

240 grams • 1 3/4 cups 00 flour
12 grams • 1 tablespoon beet powder
2 grams • 1/2 teaspoon kosher salt
100 grams • 2 eggs

57 grams • 4 tablespoons unsalted butter
6 to 10 sage leaves
kosher salt
70 grams • 1/4 cup toasted walnuts
2 grams • 1 teaspoon poppy seeds
85 grams • 1/4 cup golden raisins, soaked in warm water to soften
a block of ricotta salata for grating

For the filling: Preheat the oven to 400°F. Trim away the beet greens and reserve. Cut off a long strip of aluminum foil. Place the beets on one side of the foil and coat with a splash of olive oil, the red wine vinegar, and a few generous pinches of salt. Fold the other side of the foil over and crimp the edges closed. Place the packet on a baking sheet and roast until the beets yield to pressure slightly when pressed with your fingertips, about 45 minutes. Once the beets are cool enough to handle, rub the skins off while wearing gloves, and dice into pieces small enough to fit through the large tip of a pastry bag.

Heat the butter in a pot over medium heat. Sweat the onion with a pinch of salt until tender, about 4 minutes. Stir in the garlic and cook just to soften, 1 to 2 minutes. Add the beet greens and cook until wilted, about 3 minutes. Remove the greens from the pot and chop finely. In a bowl, mix the cooked onion and garlic with the ricotta and Parmigiano-Reggiano. Fold in the beets and beet greens, drizzle in 1 tablespoon of olive oil, and season with salt and a few gratings of nutmeg. Taste, seasoning with more salt if needed. Cool completely. You will have about 2 cups of filling. Once cold, transfer to a pastry bag fitted with a large tip and refrigerate until needed.

To make the pasta: In a stand mixer fitted with the paddle attachment, mix together the flour, beet powder, and salt. In a bowl, whisk together the eggs. With the mixer running on medium speed, drizzle in the eggs. Mix the dough for 2 to 3 minutes, then turn it onto the counter and knead several times by hand; it will feel dry and firm. With your hands, flatten the dough into a rectangle. Wrap in plastic wrap and leave on the counter for 30 minutes to soften and hydrate.

Roll out the dough according to the instructions for laminated pasta on page 273. Cut the sheets into 3-inch squares. Lay the squares on the work surface so one corner points up, like a diamond. Pipe about 1 teaspoon of filling slightly off center, closer to the corner facing you. Lightly mist water over the diamonds or dab the edges with a damp but not wet pastry brush. For each piece, fold the bottom of the diamond up to the top to form a triangle. Pick up the triangle and press the edges together with your fingertips to seal, pushing out any air between the filling and the pasta. Repeat until all of the dough and filling is used. You will have about 30 pieces. Place the filled pasta on a baking sheet lightly sprinkled with flour.

Bring a large pot of salted water to a boil. Drop in the pasta and cook until al dente, 4 to 5 minutes. Meanwhile, melt the butter in a large sauté pan over medium heat until it begins to brown and smell nutty. Add the sage leaves and remove the pan from the heat. Drain the pasta, setting aside a cup or so of pasta water. Mix the pasta into the brown butter, return the pan to the heat, and cook the pasta in the brown butter with a pinch of salt for 1 minute or until the butter lightly coats the pasta. (If the pan looks too dry, add a tablespoon or two of the reserved water.) Swirl in the walnuts, poppy seeds, and raisins and toss gently to combine.

To serve, divide the pasta among 4 to 6 warmed plates, and finish with a few gratings of ricotta salata.

TOMATO-BRAISED ABALONE *with* Farinata

Working with abalone is definitely one of my favorite perks of living on the West Coast. While the mollusk was overfished years ago, entrepreneurs have managed to farm red abalone successfully. Not only are abalone visually captivating in their large, decorative shells, but they also are deliciously briny. They are not hard to prepare. Like octopus or squid, you either cook them briefly or for a long time—anything in between will be tough and chewy. In this preparation, I cook the abalone slowly until tender with tomatoes, capers, and garlic, then serve it with crisp disks of *farinata*, a traditional Ligurian chickpea cake. Sold in Ligurian bakeshops, *farinata* is cooked in shallow cast-iron pans inside wood-burning ovens. I've adapted the recipe for a modern kitchen, cooking it in a pot, pouring it into a pan to set before punching out disks and crisping them in a pan. Instead of abalone, you can use squid or octopus in this recipe. Because the weight provided for the abalone in this recipe includes the shell, use half the weight for squid or octopus.

SERVES 4 TO 6

Farinata

225 grams • 2 cups chickpea flour

1000 grams • 4 1/3 cups water

4 grams • 1 garlic clove, minced

15 grams • 1 tablespoon extra virgin olive oil, plus more for frying

7 grams • 2 teaspoons kosher salt

5 turns of black pepper

1 gram • 1/2 teaspoon chopped rosemary

Tomato-Braised Abalone

907 grams • 2 pounds (about 10) red abalone in the shell

extra virgin olive oil

kosher salt

280 grams • 1 yellow onion, thinly sliced

12 grams • 3 garlic cloves

a pinch of dried red pepper flakes

226 grams • 1 cup white wine

454 grams • 2 cups white stock (page 282)

397 grams • 1 (14-ounce) can canned cherry tomatoes

3 tablespoons capers, rinsed well

2 white anchovies, minced

10 to 12 pitted black olives, sliced

extra virgin olive oil

Wondra flour for dusting

a handful of chervil sprigs

1 lemon

2 tablespoons dried black Gaeta olives (see page 278), crumbled

To make the *farinata:* Lightly coat two 9 by 13-inch baking pans or rimmed baking sheets with nonstick spray. In a blender, purée the chickpea flour and water. Pour the batter into a large, heavy-bottomed pot and place over medium heat. Whisk in the garlic, olive oil, salt, and pepper and continue to cook, whisking constantly, until thickened to a paste, about 15 minutes. Stir in the rosemary, then pour the batter evenly into the prepared pans. Tap the pan lightly against the counter to level, then refrigerate, uncovered, until set, at least 2 hours.

Prepare the abalone: Preheat the oven to 325°F. Using a large palette knife or kitchen spoon, pry underneath the foot of the abalone muscle to dislodge it from the shell. Trim away the innards and rinse clean.

Heat a film of olive oil in a heavy-bottomed pot over medium heat. Season the abalone with salt and sear until lightly browned on both sides, then transfer to a plate.

Wipe the pot clean, heat a thin film of olive oil over medium-low heat, and stir in the onions and a pinch of salt. Sweat for 2 minutes, then add the garlic and sweat until the garlic has softened, about 1 minute. Sprinkle the red pepper flakes into the pot, deglaze with the wine, and bring the pot to a simmer. Pour in the stock and tomatoes, return to a simmer, and stir in the abalone.

Cover the pot, transfer to the oven, and braise for 45 minutes to 1 1/2 hours or until the abalone slide off a skewer when pierced. Uncover the pot and let cool for 20 minutes. Fish out the abalone pieces and slice crosswise into thin strips. Return the slices to the braise, then bring the

{continued}

pot to a low simmer and stir in the capers, anchovies, and sliced olives. Turn off the heat and keep warm.

Now finish the *farinata*. With a 3-inch cutter, punch the chilled *farinata* into rounds, cutting as close as possible to limit the amount of trimmings remaining; you will need 12 rounds. Blot the rounds dry between paper towels.

In a large sauté pan with straight sides or a cast-iron skillet, heat ¹/₂ inch of olive oil over medium-high heat. Dust the *farinata* rounds in Wondra flour, shaking off any excess. In batches to avoid crowding the pan, sear the rounds until golden brown on both sides, then drain on paper towels.

To serve, place the *farinata* disks in bowls. Divide the abalone pieces evenly among the bowls and spoon some braising liquid over the top. Grate lemon zest over each bowl. Slice the lemon in half, then squeeze a few drops of lemon juice into each bowl. Garnish with a drizzle of olive oil, a few sprigs of chervil, and a sprinkling of dehydrated olives. Serve with the remaining *farinata*.

SMOKED LINGUINE
with Clams, Cherry Tomatoes, *and* Basil Pesto

The combination of pesto and pasta may be one of the most popular Italian pairings in the world. I make it more savory by adding clams and an accent of smoke. In Puglia, where my family is from, pasta is sometimes made with *di grano arso*, flour milled from charred grains. Smoking the durum flour in this recipe gives the linguine a similar savory, ashy flavor. When smoking flour, I always make more than I need so I have it on hand for next time. For the pesto, I use almonds, which have a lighter, buttery flavor that goes well with the smoky pasta and the clams. In the restaurant, I add oil-blanched cherry tomatoes to this pasta (see pages 253–254); here I peel them after blanching in water.

SERVES 4

Linguine

50 grams • ¹/₃ cup plus 1 tablespoon smoked durum flour (see page 275)

200 grams • 1¹/₂ cups 00 flour

2 grams • ¹/₂ teaspoon kosher salt

100 grams • 2 eggs

9 grams • 2 teaspoons water

Pesto

50 grams • ¹/₂ cup slivered almonds

120 grams • 4 packed cups basil leaves

10 grams • ¹/₄ cup parsley leaves

8 grams • 2 garlic cloves, sliced

100 grams • ¹/₂ cup extra virgin olive oil

kosher salt and black pepper

Clams

20 grams • 2 tablespoons kosher salt, plus extra

2 tablespoons coarse semolina

680 grams • 1½ pounds Manila clams

260 grams • 1½ cups cherry tomatoes

extra virgin olive oil

8 grams • 2 garlic cloves, sliced

¼ teaspoon dried red pepper flakes

75 grams • ⅓ cup white wine

5 to 10 small basil leaves

To make the linguine: In a stand mixer fitted with the paddle attachment, mix together the smoked durum flour with the 00 flour and salt. In a bowl, whisk together the eggs and water. With the mixer running on low speed, drizzle in the egg mixture. Mix the dough for 2 to 3 minutes, then turn onto the counter and knead by hand for several minutes; it will feel dry and firm. Flatten the dough into a flat rectangle, wrap in plastic wrap, and leave on the counter for 30 minutes to soften and hydrate.

Roll out the dough according to the instructions for laminated pasta on page 273. Cut the pasta into 12-inch sheets and dust with flour. Remove the pasta machine rollers and replace with the linguine cutters. (If you don't have linguine cutters, use the narrowest noodle cutter.) One at a time, with one hand, feed the sheets through the cutter. As the noodles emerge from the cutter, catch them with your other hand. Shake the noodles loose, then place on a lightly floured baking sheet and keep on the counter.

To make the pesto: Preheat the oven to 350°F. In a sauté pan over medium-high heat, warm the almonds until they begin to toast. Put the pan in the oven and bake for 5 to 8 minutes or until light brown (starting on the stove will lower the time it takes to toast them).

Bring a large pot of salted water to a boil. Blanch the basil and parsley until soft, about 1 minute. Prepare a salted ice bath. Remove the herbs and plunge into an ice bath lined with a mesh strainer. When the herbs are cold, remove them from the ice bath and squeeze out water with your hands until they are no longer dripping but still damp. Coarsely chop the herbs and transfer to a blender with the almonds, garlic, and olive oil. Add a couple of pinches of salt and pepper and purée the blanched herbs until smooth. Taste, adjusting with more salt and pepper if needed. You should have about 1 cup of pesto.

To make the clams: In a large bowl, mix the 2 tablespoons of salt and the semolina in a gallon of cold water. Submerge the clams in the water and let soak for about 1 hour to purge any grit. Lift the clams out of the water into a clean bowl and cover with a damp towel.

Bring a large pot of salted water to a boil. (You will use this pot to blanch the tomatoes and cook the pasta.) Prepare an ice bath. Blanch the cherry tomatoes briefly, about 30 seconds, then shock in the ice bath. Peel the cherry tomatoes (the skins should slide right off).

In a large sauté pan that has a fitted lid, heat a film of olive oil over medium heat. Add most of the garlic slices and sweat until softened, about 1 minute. Sprinkle in the red pepper flakes, add the clams, and season with salt. Toss the pan once or twice, then pour in the wine and cover immediately. Cook for 2 to 4 minutes or until the clams have opened. Uncover, remove from the heat, and keep warm. Keep the clam liquid for finishing the pasta.

Heat a thin film of oil in a separate pan over medium heat. Sweat the remaining garlic slices briefly, then add the peeled tomatoes. Season with salt and cook until warmed through, about 1 minute.

Bring the pot back to a boil and stir in the pasta. Cook until al dente, 3 to 4 minutes. Drain and return the pasta to the same pot. Pour in the clams and some of the clam liquid and bring to a simmer. Stir in enough pesto to lightly coat the pasta. Simmer another minute, then taste, adding more salt if needed. To serve, divide the pasta among the plates. Spoon the cherry tomatoes over the top and garnish with basil leaves.

RAMP SPAGHETTI *with* Crab *and* Sea Urchin Butter

Pairing ramps with sea urchin takes me back to spring in New Jersey, where I grew up. In early spring, when dark-green ramp leaves began to sprout up from the forest floor, foragers would gather them up and deliver them by the bag to many of the Manhattan kitchens where I worked. My sea urchin experience was a bit different: out to sushi for the first time with my friend and her well-traveled family, I was offered the exotic roe. The taste was a revelation: while rich and buttery, it carried a saline iodine flavor unlike anything I had tasted before. Those two very different flavor memories inspired this pasta.

While the bulb of ramp is often more prized than the leaves, I tend to feel the opposite. I make use of the whole plant in this pasta, puréeing the leaves and then folding them into pasta dough, saving the bulbs to sauté later. The ramp purée makes more than you need for a single recipe of pasta, but it freezes well and can easily be added to risotto or soup.

SERVES 6

Ramp Purée

114 grams • 2 cups firmly packed ramp leaves

57 grams • 1 cup firmly packed spinach leaves

2 grams • 1/2 teaspoon kosher salt

Spaghetti

227 grams • 11/2 cups semolina flour

113 grams • 1 cup durum flour

2 grams • 1/2 teaspoon kosher salt

100 grams • 2 eggs

20 grams • 11/2 tablespoons warm water

70 grams • 21/2 ounces (1/3 cup) sea urchin roe

75 grams • 21/2 ounces unsalted butter, softened but not melted

zest of 1 lemon

extra virgin olive oil

57 grams • 1/2 cup ramp bulbs, sliced thinly

kosher salt

225 grams • 8 ounces crab

28 grams • 1/2 cup thinly sliced, firmly packed ramp leaves

black pepper

about 1/4 cup dried breadcrumbs

To make the ramp purée: Prepare an ice bath. Bring a large pot of salted water to a boil. Blanch the ramps and spinach until soft, about 2 minutes. Using a skimmer, remove the greens and plunge into an ice bath lined with a mesh strainer. When the greens are cold, remove them from the ice bath and squeeze out the water. In a blender or food processor, purée the blanched greens until smooth. (Be patient—this can take a few minutes.) Season with salt. You should have about 1/2 cup of purée. Set aside 1/4 cup for the spaghetti and freeze the rest.

To make the spaghetti: In a stand mixer fitted with the paddle attachment, mix together the flours and salt. In a bowl, whisk together the eggs. With the mixer running on low speed, drizzle in the eggs, water, and ramp purée. Mix the dough for 2 to 3 minutes, then turn onto the counter and knead for several minutes by hand; it will feel dry and firm. Flatten the dough into a rectangle, wrap in plastic wrap, and leave on the counter for 30 minutes to soften and hydrate. Extrude the dough according to the instructions for extruded pasta on page 274.

In a small bowl, mix two-thirds of the sea urchin roe into the butter, then mix in the zest. Heat a thin film of olive oil in a large sauté pan over medium heat. Scatter the sliced ramp bulbs into the pan and season with salt. Sweat until softened, about 1 minute. Remove from the heat and keep warm.

Bring a large pot of salted water to a boil. Stir in the spaghetti and cook until al dente, 3 to 4 minutes. Drain, reserving about 1 cup of pasta cooking water, and return the spaghetti to the pot. Stir in the sautéed ramps and a few tablespoons of the cooking water. Stir in the sea urchin butter, remaining sea urchin roe, crab, and sliced ramp leaves. Season to taste with salt and pepper. Serve the pasta on warmed plates and sprinkle breadcrumbs over the top.

SAFFRON TROFIE *with* Veal Ragù

Hand-shaped pasta comes with built-in advantages. You don't need any extra kitchen equipment to make it, and it's forgiving, since no two pieces can be made exactly alike. Short and spiral-shaped, *trofie* is a fun hand-formed pasta. It's traditionally dressed in pesto in Liguria; here I add saffron to the dough and serve it with braised veal breast to mimic the classic flavors of *osso buco*.

When buying saffron, look for whole strands. While it is more expensive, its quality is often better than pre-ground saffron, which often isn't 100 percent saffron. To extract the saffron flavor and color for the pasta, I toast it lightly until barely fragrant, pulse it in a spice grinder, and mix it with water to form a concentrated paste. This recipe uses saffron paste in two places: the *trofie* and the ragù, but you will still have leftover paste. I suggest freezing it to use later in another pasta dough or in risotto. To blanch and peel cherry tomatoes for this recipe, I use the oil-blanching technique given on pages 235–254.

SERVES 4 TO 6

680 grams • 1 1/2 pounds veal breast

kosher salt and black pepper

extra virgin olive oil

150 grams • 1 carrot, diced

150 grams • 1/2 yellow onion, diced

50 grams • 1 stalk celery, diced

8 grams • 2 garlic cloves, sliced

1 1/3 cups white wine

454 grams • 2 cups brown stock (page 283)

227 grams • 1 cup water

a sachet with 2 sprigs thyme, 1 sprig rosemary, 1 or 2 bay leaves, 5 black peppercorns, 1/4 teaspoon fennel seeds, and 2 cloves (see page 282)

75 grams • 1/4 yellow onion, sliced

1 pinch of dried red pepper flakes

10 grams • 1 1/2 teaspoons tomato paste

30 grams • 1 tablespoon plus 1 teaspoon soffritto (page 282)

Trofie

3 grams • 3 tablespoons saffron

7 grams • 1 tablespoon turmeric

18 grams • 1 tablespoon warm water

250 grams • scant 2 cups 00 flour

a pinch of kosher salt

100 grams • 2 eggs

9 grams • 2 teaspoons room-temperature water

57 grams • 4 tablespoons unsalted butter

100 grams • 1/2 cup cherry tomatoes, blanched and peeled

15 grams • 1/4 cup Italian parsley leaves

75 grams • 1/2 cup crumbled goat cheese

a block of grana cheese for grating

2 sprigs thyme, stemmed

To make the ragù: Preheat the oven to 325°F. Season the veal with salt and pepper. Heat a thin film of olive oil in a large Dutch oven or heavy-bottomed pot over medium-high heat. Sear the veal until golden brown on all sides, about 3 minutes. Transfer the veal to a plate. Add a splash of olive oil to the pot and stir in the carrot, onion, celery, and garlic. Sweat until soft, 2 to 3 minutes. Nestle the veal into the center of the vegetables, pour in 1 cup of the wine, and bring to a simmer. Add the stock, water, and sachet and return to a simmer. Cover the pot and transfer to the oven. Cook the veal for 3 to 3 1/2 hours or until tender enough to pull apart easily when pierced with a fork. Let the veal cool in the braising liquid for 2 hours.

Lift the veal out of the braising liquid and place on a cutting board. Pull off and discard any bones or connective tissue, then cut the veal into 1-inch-long pieces following the grain of the muscle. Strain the braising liquid through a fine-mesh strainer into a clean pot and discard the vegetables. Reserve the sachet for the ragù, squeezing out any extra liquid into the pot. Skim the fat off the top of the liquid with a ladle. You should have about 2 cups of braising liquid for the ragù.

Heat a thin film of olive oil in a Dutch oven or heavy-bottomed pot over medium-low heat. Sweat the sliced onion with a pinch of salt until soft, about 2 minutes.

{continued}

Sprinkle the red pepper flakes into the pot, then stir in the tomato paste and soffritto. Continue to cook over medium-low heat for a few minutes, then add the remaining 1/3 cup of wine and cook until the pot is nearly dry. Pour in the reserved 2 cups of braising liquid and simmer until the sauce coats the back of a spoon, about 5 minutes. Season with salt and pepper. Stir in the veal breast meat and simmer for a few minutes to meld the flavors. Taste, and season with salt and pepper if necessary. Steep the reserved sachet in the ragù as it cools. (At this point, the ragù can be refrigerated overnight or up to four days.) Remove the sachet before reheating the ragù, squeezing out any extra liquid back into the ragù.

To make the *trofie:* In a small, dry sauté pan over medium heat, lightly toast the saffron until fragrant, about 30 seconds. Pulse it in a spice grinder with the turmeric, then mix with the warm water to form a paste. Take half of the paste and freeze it for a future use.

In a stand mixer fitted with the paddle attachment, mix together the flour and salt. In a bowl, whisk together the eggs, half of the remaining saffron paste, and the water. With the mixer running on low speed, drizzle in the wet ingredients and mix for 2 to 3 minutes, then turn onto the counter and knead several times by hand; it will feel dry and firm. Flatten the dough into a rectangle, wrap in plastic wrap, and leave on the counter for 30 minutes to soften and hydrate.

With a rolling pin, roll the dough out to a 1/2-inch-thick disk. Cut the disk into 1/4-inch-thick strips. Roll the strips into thin ropes and dust lightly with semolina flour. Line up all the ropes and cut into 1/4-inch pieces. Roll each piece firmly between your index finger and your thumb to stretch it out and make it take on a spiral shape. The *trofie* will be small, about 1 1/2 inches long and 1/8 inch thick. Place the *trofie* on a baking sheet lightly coated with semolina and keep on the counter.

Bring a large pot of water to a boil and season with salt. Cook the *trofie* until al dente, 5 to 7 minutes. Meanwhile, in a large, straight-sided sauté pan over medium heat, bring the ragù to a simmer with the remaining saffron paste. Add the pasta to the ragù and swirl in the butter. Finish with the cherry tomatoes and heat until warmed through. Scatter the parsley on top and toss to combine. Taste, adjusting seasoning with salt and pepper if needed. Divide the pasta among warmed plates and dot the tops with goat cheese. Finish with a grating of cheese and a sprinkling of thyme leaves.

PASSION FRUIT PANNA COTTA *with* Coconut Spuma

It goes against the hyper-local ethos, but nearly every fine dining restaurant I've visited in Italy appears to be in love with jet-fresh fruit. Da Vittorio, a three-star Michelin restaurant in Lombardia, offers a tropical fruit plate laden with mangosteens, rambutans, and dragon fruit for dessert. Composed of cream, sugar, and gelatin, panna cotta is one of Italy's most flexible desserts. I love the tropical sweetness of passion fruit, which, lucky for me, does grow in California, and find it refreshing at the end of a meal. This dessert combines three of my favorite sweet flavors: Caramel, passion fruit, and coconut. For a bit of crunch, I serve the panna cottas with small coconut macaroons. The coconut *spuma*, or foam, is aerated with a whipper or isi gun, a canister often used for whipped cream. Its lightness balances the richness of the panna cotta, but it is optional.

SERVES 6

Coconut Macaroons

200 grams • 2 1/2 cups sweetened shredded coconut

200 grams • 3/4 cup condensed milk

1 gram • 1/2 teaspoon vanilla extract

20 grams • 1 egg white, at room temperature

1 gram • 1/4 teaspoon kosher salt

Panna Cotta

9 grams • 3 sheets gelatin

175 grams • 3/4 cup plus 1 tablespoon sugar

240 grams • 1 cup whole milk

230 grams • 1 cup heavy cream

250 grams • 1 cup passion fruit purée

1 gram • 1/4 teaspoon kosher salt

Coconut Spuma

70 grams • scant 1/3 cup heavy cream

25 grams • 1/8 cup sugar

1 to 2 grams • 1/2 sheet gelatin

200 grams • 3/4 cup unsweetened coconut milk

To make the macaroons: Preheat the oven to 325°F. Line a couple of baking sheets with parchment paper or non-stick silicone baking liners.

In a large bowl, mix the coconut, condensed milk, and vanilla together. In a separate bowl, whisk the egg white until it holds medium peaks when the whisk is lifted from the bowl. Fold the egg white into the coconut mixture. Form 1 tablespoon balls of batter and place them on a baking sheet. Flatten the balls to 1/8-inch thick disks and bake for 25 minutes or until the tops are light golden brown.

To make the panna cotta: Soak the gelatin sheets in ice water for about 2 minutes. In a small pot over medium heat, bring the sugar and the milk to a simmer to dissolve the sugar, then remove from the heat. Squeeze excess water from the gelatin sheets and dissolve it in the milk. Once the gelatin has dissolved, stir in the cream. Stir in the purée and salt, then strain through a fine-mesh strainer to remove any remaining bits of gelatin. Pour the panna cotta into six 1-cup glasses. Cover with plastic wrap and refrigerate until set, about 4 to 6 hours.

To make the *spuma*: In a small pot over medium heat, bring the cream and the sugar to a simmer to dissolve the sugar. Remove from the heat and add the gelatin. Once the gelatin has dissolved, pour in the coconut milk and mix well. You will have just over 1 cup. Strain through a fine-mesh strainer to remove any remaining bits of gelatin, then pour into the container of a whipper. Charge the whipper with its nitrous-oxide charger, then shake well. Place in the refrigerator until needed.

To serve: Unwrap each glass. Place the tip of the whipper into each glass and top with the coconut spuma. Serve with a few macaroons.

RESOURCES

Kitchen Road Map: Fundamental Techniques, Basic Recipes, and Ingredients

Sous Vide

At its most basic, cooking comes down to controlling two factors: temperature and time. *Sous vide*, a method in which food is gently cooked in vacuum-sealed plastic bags or in tight cylinders of plastic wrap, allows for precise control over both factors. With no smoke and little heat, it is a very clean process, and an immersion circulator set inside a water bath—the setup for *sous vide* cooking—can be put almost anywhere. I nearly always have an immersion circulator going in the kitchen.

I've found several culinary advantages to using *sous vide* over conventional methods like braising or roasting. If I make duck confit, I can cut back the amount of duck fat needed to coat the duck legs if I vacuum-seal the legs and fat in plastic bags. For short ribs*, sous vide* uses less braising liquid to achieve a more tender and consistent result. Sealing carrots in a bag with a splash of carrot juice and some seasoning and then cooking them provides a more intense carrot flavor. Vacuum-sealing ingredients together actually can be a technique in itself: I seal tart green rhubarb with simple syrup, which infuses sweetness into the rhubarb, a reverse of using pickling brine to infuse a vegetable with acid.

To cook *sous vide*, you will need an immersion circulator and a large water bath. An immersion circulator is a box with a wide wand that stays submerged inside the container, circulating the water through a heating coil to hold its temperature constant. If the water bath is too full of ingredients, the water can't circulate efficiently, so a good rule of thumb is to not exceed 50 percent food to 50 percent water in the water bath.

The price of immersion circulators comes down every year; as of this writing they sell for less than $800. For the recipes in this book, I recommend using a rectangular 27-quart professional-grade food storage container or other similar-sized container. You also will need a vacuum sealer and a supply of plastic storage bags that work with the sealer. I use a chamber vacuum sealer, which removes air under pressure, but for most recipes in this book, a home model vacuum sealer will do the job. When vacuum-sealing, always ensure that the edge of the bag is free of oil, food, or anything that could compromise the seal.

THE PROCESS

Before you start, preheat the water bath. Start with hot water that is as close to the needed cooking temperature needed as possible. Meanwhile, bring the ingredients that you will cook *sous vide* to room temperature, to keep the temperature of the water from dropping significantly at the beginning of the cooking process. I cook some ingredients quickly, but typical times run longer than 12 hours. Check the water level periodically, topping it up with hot water if needed. At the end of the cooking time, remove the bag. For meat, put the bag on a baking sheet to cool for about an hour but no more than two hours to allow the proteins to rest (like a roast). Then, unless I am serving it right away, I plunge it in an ice bath to thoroughly chill it and then I refrigerate it.

COOKING IN PLASTIC WRAP

To cook *sous vide* in plastic wrap, wrap the food snugly to prevent water from seeping in. You will need a roll of commercial-size plastic wrap (18 inches wide), available at most kitchen supply stores. Unless the portions you are wrapping are small, smaller rolls of plastic wrap do not provide enough surface area to wrap effectively.

Position the portion of meat so that the long side is parallel with the plastic wrap dispenser. Using a single sheet, wrap the meat tightly at least ten and as many as twelve times around. As you wrap, smooth each layer of plastic over the meat to ensure you're keeping the plastic free of air pockets. Pick up both ends of the plastic wrap and twist the sides in opposite directions simultaneously to expel as much air as possible; the meat should be snugly encased in plastic, like sausage. Tie one end tightly with butcher's twine; then, holding the untied end, start spinning the cylinder in the air like a propeller. While the cylinder is spinning, loop several rounds of butcher's twine around the untied end. (This increases the torque on the plastic wrap, ensuring that the meat is encased tightly.) Cut the butcher's twine and tie snugly. The cylinder should be very firm; if it isn't, repeat the propeller step with the other end. Finally, tie two loops of butcher's twine about two inches apart around the center of the cylinder. This ensures the meat holds the cylinder shape while it cooks.

Once the food has cooked according to the instructions in the recipe, carefully pull it out of the water bath and place it on a tray to rest. When cooled, cut off the plastic ends and, leaving the rest of the plastic in place, drain out the juices that have accumulated, then wrap a

few fresh layers of plastic over the roll, twisting the ends using the same process as before. Look for air pockets, and use a cake tester or other small skewer to poke the plastic and release the air from them. This is especially important with meat: the bag should be taut enough that the gelatin in the meat will bond, holding it together when cut into rounds later. (This whole process can be messy until you get the hang of it.) Finally, plunge the roll in an ice bath and chill thoroughly.

Pasta Primer

This section provides the blueprints for making all of the pastas in this book, whether laminated (pasta rolled out into sheets) or extruded (forced through a die of a pasta extruder to form noodles).

MAKING DOUGH

Flour. The choice of flour for pasta making is never an arbitrary decision in Italy. Some pasta recipes call for finely milled "00" (*doppio zero*) flour. Durum and semolina flours yield pasta with more bite than either all-purpose or 00. The terms durum and semolina can be confusing. In my kitchen we use *semola di grano duro* (coarse) and *grano duro rimacinata* (fine) for dried pasta production. In the United States, the term semolina flour usually corresponds to a coarse semolina flour. Durum is the same flour of a finer consistency. You can use a finely ground semolina flour for any pasta recipe that calls for durum. I also often mix whole wheat with 00 or all-purpose flour, or farro, buckwheat, or chestnut flour. Grain and nut flours have been used for centuries in Italy, as wheat flour was often too expensive. I use "00" flour for rolling laminated dough, and semolina for stacking pasta, for hand-cutting, or filling. For filled pasta, I rest them on a bed of coarse semolina.

Eggs. While egg yolks give a rich sheen and smooth quality to the dough, whites toughen the dough with protein. When I make pasta, I always weigh eggs: on average, one large egg weighs about 50 grams, but size varies widely, particularly if you buy eggs from a small farm. Weigh your eggs, especially when making pasta.

Mixing. I use a paddle attachment and mixer to make dough instead of a dough hook. For small batches, the paddle is most efficient.

Hydration. Pasta dough is hydrated with either egg or water or both. A wet dough is easier to send through pasta rollers, but keeping it from sticking requires several dustings of flour, which toughens it. Too-wet pasta dough also doesn't hold its shape after boiling as well as firmer pasta does. My pasta dough might be drier than you are used to, but I prefer the firm, al dente texture a dry dough gives me once it's cooked.

Rest. Pasta dough needs to relax after kneading; this allows the gluten strands to relax and soften and the dough to hydrate. Dough that may have felt dry and crumbly right after mixing will feel noticeably softer a half-hour later.

MAKING PASTA

Laminated pasta. I recommend an electric pasta roller or a hand-crank model that attaches to a kitchen table; either will give you long, uniform sheets just under 6 inches wide.

Clear a large workspace. Whether you are using a hand-cranked pasta machine or a stand mixer attachment, set the rollers on the widest setting. Unwrap the dough (it should be at room temperature) and divide it into 3 or 4 pieces. If it's too thick to fit through the rollers, flatten it with your hands or a rolling pin. While cranking the pasta machine or with the mixer on, guide the dough through the rollers. Fold the dough in overlapping thirds (like a letter) and pass through again. Repeat a couple of times. Switch to the next thinnest setting and guide the dough through twice. Repeat until you have passed the dough through about the second-thinnest setting, depending on your machine (the dough should be quite thin). If the dough sticks at any point, dust it lightly with flour. If making filled pasta, proceed to filling and shaping or cutting; for fettuccine or the like, you can now replace the dough rollers with a cutter attachment. For wider or thinner strands than your machine's cutters afford, cut the pasta by hand with a knife or a scalloped pasta cutter (see the farro flour pasta on page 130). Before cutting the sheets into noodles, stretch them out

on a table and let them dry for 5 to 10 minutes. This way, you won't have to add as much flour to the noodles to prevent them from sticking together when you cut them.

Extruded pasta. I am fortunate to have a powerful pasta extruder; the machine's power lets me make the pasta dough very dry. Home extruders lack the same horsepower, so if your dough isn't yielding to your extruder, add a splash of water to the dough when mixing it. Clear an ample workspace for making the pasta and set up your extruder near it. Fit the extruder with the disk specified in the recipe, such as bucatini or spaghetti.

Break off pieces of dough no larger than golf balls and feed them through the machine. If you're using a manual extruder, this takes some elbow grease. The noodles will start to emerge from the end fitted with the disk. Once the strands are about 10 inches long for noodles or the desired length for other shapes, cut them with a knife. Lay the noodles out on a lightly floured baking sheet and cover with plastic wrap to prevent the noodles from drying out and becoming brittle. Keep the pasta on the counter if you are cooking it that day; otherwise cover and refrigerate it.

I boil fresh pasta for about 4 minutes in salted water. This is enough time to ensure that the noodles are completely cooked but not too soft. I then drain the noodles, reserving a cup or so of the pasta cooking water to add in increments if the sauce or *condimento* seems dry. In general, I like to simmer the pasta with its sauce for about a minute before serving it.

Stove-Top Smoking

Smoking is a simple technique that provides another means to season food. The easiest way to smoke ingredients at home is to use a stove-top smoker or a large aluminum foil container. Pile soaked wood chips (like cherry or apple wood, which are available at hardware stores and some grocery stores) on one end of the pan. For the recipes in this book, about $1/2$ cup of wood chips will do. Cover with a fitted perforated pan or a wire rack on which to place the ingredients to be smoked.

To smoke liquids: Pour a liquid—like broth or syrup—into a heatproof bowl or a small, disposable aluminum loaf pan and put it on the perforated pan or rack

on the end opposite the wood chips. Cover the bowl or pan tightly with foil or the smoker lid. Put the pan over a pair of front and back burners, with the wood chips in the front. Turn the ventilation fan on and turn the front burner to medium. Allow the chips to smolder for a few minutes, then turn the burner off and let the liquid sit for 15 minutes.

To smoke flour, polenta, or nuts: Cover the perforated pan or rack with foil. Pour the flour or polenta on the side of the pan opposite the wood chips and cover the pan with foil or the smoker lid. Put the pan over a pair of front and back burners, with the wood chips in the front. Turn the ventilation fan on and turn the front burner to medium. Allow the chips to smolder for a few minutes, then turn the burner to low and smoke for 20 minutes. Remove from heat and cool. The flour will be chalky and will have darkened. If it's lumpy, sift it.

To smoke fish: To ensure the fish does not cook while it smokes, I position a foil-wrapped ice pack between the fish and the heat source. For the setup, I use three restaurant-style pans known as hotel pans: a 6-inch deep pan for the bottom layer that holds the wood chips, a 4-inch deep perforated pan above that to hold the ice packet, and a 2-inch deep perforated pan at the top to

hold the fish. You can skip the foil packet layer if you're using a stove-top smoker (there won't be enough room), but the fish may start to cook, so carefully monitor the heat. To smoke, place the fish on the perforated pan or rack as far away from the end with the wood chips as possible. Cover the pan tightly with foil or a lid and put the pan over a pair of front and back burners, with the wood chips in the front. Smoke for 10 to 12 minutes per pound of fish. Take off the foil and remove the fish from the pan.

Basic Recipes and Ingredients

Activa RM

Activa RM is a powdery, vegetarian substance called transglutaminase enzyme, which fuses protein together. It is useful for adhering pancetta to the outside of a roast or for fusing together a boned leg of lamb (page 36). To apply Activa RM, dust it over meat with a fine-mesh strainer as you would confectioner's sugar over a dessert. The enzyme takes about six hours to fully activate; cooking right away will nullify its effect.

Agar-Agar

Agar-agar is a flavorless gelling agent made from seaweed—an alternative to gelatin for stricter vegetarians. I use powdered agar-agar to gel together horseradish water for a garnish with smoked trout. I also use it to clarify fruit or vegetable waters by bringing 1 percent concentration of agar-agar with the liquid, mixing it to a boil and freezing it. As the liquid melts, the agar-agar traps the solids and a clear liquid drips through a strainer.

Basic Cure

For seasoning pig ears or duck legs or for seasoning fish to serve raw, I keep a mix of salt and sugar on hand. For fish, I use $1\frac{1}{2}$ parts salt to 1 part sugar. For meat, I use 3 parts salt to 1 part sugar. For most meat cures, I leave it plain or mix in bay leaf, thyme, black pepper, garlic, fennel, and coriander. For fish, I sometimes add citrus zest.

FISH BASIC CURE

MAKES ¾ CUP

1/2 cup kosher salt

1/4 cup sugar

Citrus zest (optional)

Combine salt and sugar and store in a sealed container. Add 1 to 2 tablespoons of citrus zest before using.

MEAT BASIC CURE

MAKES 1 CUP

3/4 cup kosher salt

1/4 cup sugar

Bay leaf

1/2 teaspoon fresh thyme

1 tablespoon whole spices, such as fennel and coriander (optional)

Combine salt, sugar, bay leaf, and thyme. Toast and crush the spices and mix into the cure. Store in a sealed container.

Dried Fruit

Before using raisins or other sweet dried fruit, I soak them in water to soften the fruit and reduce sweetness.

Burro Fuso

Burro fuso is a silky emulsion made by quickly whisking cold cubes of butter into a small amount of hot water until it reaches the consistency of cream. It is more neutral than *beurre blanc*, though the concept is the same. I use it to finish pastas with a rich gloss of butter that won't break as easily in the pan as butter. To make it, cube 1/2 cup of cold butter. Put a small pot over medium heat and add a couple of tablespoons of water. Gradually whisk in the butter cubes, waiting until the butter looks nearly all melted before adding the next cube. Adjust the heat to ensure the sauce doesn't get too hot or too cold. Make *burro fuso* shortly before using; keep it warm until ready to use.

Cooking Shelling Beans

I use a wide pot so the beans lie in one layer to ensure even cooking. I also avoid old beans, which can cook unevenly. Soak dried beans overnight before cooking in plenty of water. Season the beans toward the end of cooking and as they cool—any earlier and it seems to slow down their cooking. For this recipe, make a parchment paper lid (see above). You can use the same recipe for cooking fresh shelling beans, just skip the soaking step.

MAKES ABOUT 8 CUPS

> 454 grams • 1 pound dried beans
>
> extra virgin olive oil
>
> 1 carrot, cut into large chunks
>
> 1 yellow onion, cut into large chunks
>
> 1 leek, dark green part only, washed well and cut into large chunks
>
> 4 cups white stock (page 282)
>
> 4 cups water
>
> a sachet with 2 thyme sprigs, 1 bay leaf, and 5 to 10 peppercorns
>
> about 2 teaspoons kosher salt

Pick any pebbles out of the beans and rinse them thoroughly but gently. Put them in a bowl and cover with at least 2 inches of water. Soak overnight. Discard any broken beans that float to the surface, then drain and rinse the beans. Heat a film of olive oil in a large Dutch oven or heavy-bottomed pot over medium heat. Stir in the carrot, onion, and leek and sweat for about 1 minute. Stir in the beans and pour in the stock and water—the liquid should cover the beans by 1 to 2 inches; if it doesn't, add more water. Bring the beans to a very gentle simmer, then add the sachet and cover with a parchment paper lid (see opposite). Simmer for about $1^{1}/_{2}$ hours or until the beans are nearly tender (the time will vary depending on the beans' age and variety). Stir in the salt and continue to cook for 15 to 30 more minutes or until the beans are tender. Let them cool in the cooking liquid, seasoning with salt again if necessary. Store beans in their cooking liquid until ready to use, then drain.

Parchment Paper Lids

Covering a pot with a round of parchment paper instead of a lid allows some liquid to evaporate while protecting food that's cooking gently. Fold a square of parchment into quarters, then into eighths. Trim so you make a circle whose radius is about the same as the pot's. For dishes like braised cabbage when you need more evaporation, cut the tip of the folded circle off so the lid will have a small hole in the center. Then place the parchment paper lid directly on top of and touching the liquid in the pot.

Blended Oil

For frying or searing meat, I use a mixture of 80 percent vegetable oil and 20 percent olive oil. Vegetable oil has a higher smoke point; olive oil has more flavor. Do not use your most prized bottle of extra virgin for this blend; a pleasant if bland olive oil works fine.

Calabrian Chile Oil

I keep chile oil on hand to accent everything from fried appetizers to roasted meat. To make it, stem Calabrian chiles and pulse briefly in a food processor. Transfer to a small pot and cover with about ¼ inch of olive oil. Place over the lowest flame possible (a pilot light is optimal) until the chile oil is flavorful and very spicy, anywhere from 15 minutes at a low simmer to an hour over a pilot light. The oil will keep at room temperature for a few days. For longer storage, refrigerate it. You can use this technique with as little as ¼ cup of chiles or as much as a quart.

Canned Tomatoes

Passing canned tomatoes through a food mill is the most consistent way to mix the tomato solids with the juices; puréeing them in a blender introduces too much air.

Dried Black Gaeta Olives

Dark violet, mild Gaeta olives are cured in salt and packed in brine. Before using, I dehydrate them to concentrate their earthy flavors. To dry the olives, place them in a food dehydrator set on medium for twenty-four hours or until the olives are dry enough to easily crumble in your hands. You also can dry them in a 200°F oven for 2 to 3 hours. Make at least a cup of dried olives, then store them in a sealed container at room temperature. I

particularly like using them to accent spring lamb (see page 36) or braised seafood.

Egg Wash

To make egg wash or an egg dip for breaded items, I put an egg in a blender with a splash of water and purée it. This gives me a homogenous egg wash, without the pieces of unblended egg whites you get when you break eggs up with a fork.

Fennel Pollen

You can harvest your own fennel pollen. In the summertime, I forage for wild fennel and when I see it, I harvest a large bunch. To extract the pollen, I let it dry, then shake the dried flowers over a piece of parchment paper. The mild, sweet flavor is excellent with suckling pig and ricotta fritters.

Garlic Confitura

Cooking garlic slowly in olive oil brings out its sweetness and mutes its pungency. Very low heat ensures that the oil doesn't get so hot that it burns the garlic and renders it bitter. Garlic confitura can be mixed with cheese to accent vegetables, folded into poultry stuffing, or just eaten mashed on a piece of bread. Stored in the refrigerator under a cap of olive oil, the confitura keeps for two weeks. When making a new batch of confitura, I use the oil from the prior batch.

MAKES ABOUT 1½ CUPS

20 garlic cloves, peeled, stem ends trimmed off

1½ cups extra virgin olive oil

a pinch of kosher salt

1 thyme sprig

Preheat the oven to 250°F. In a small pot over low heat, gently heat the garlic, olive oil, salt, and thyme until the oil reaches 250°F. Transfer the pot to the oven and cook until soft and caramel-colored but not mushy, about

40 minutes. Remove the pot from the oven and let cool. Remove the thyme sprig. Refrigerate the cloves in the cooking oil, ensuring the oil covers the garlic. If not, top off the container with more oil.

Gelatin Sheets

Clear, brittle gelatin sheets are a higher quality gelatin than powdered gelatin. For desserts like panna cotta, I generally use 1 gelatin sheet for every cup of liquid. To use, soak gelatin sheets in ice water for 3 minutes. Before adding to liquid, squeeze out the excess water.

Lemon Confitura

Poached in sugar water to soften the rind and tame its acidity, lemon confitura is extremely versatile. I mix slices into salads for citrus accents or mince it and stir it into a rich sauce to brighten flavors. Lemon confitura is easy to make and comes together quickly. It will keep, refrigerated, for up to ten days. For longer storage, freeze the slices in a single layer.

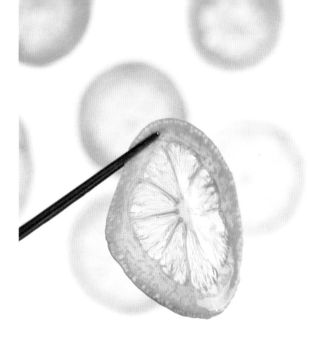

MAKES ABOUT ½ CUP

2 lemons

⅔ cup water

⅔ cup sugar

a pinch of kosher salt

Preheat the oven to 250°F. Starting at one end, slice each lemon into even, paper-thin rounds using a mandoline or very sharp knife. Pick out the seeds. Lay the slices in a single layer on parchment paper and repeat with another layer of parchment paper and lemons until all the slices are used. Stack the layers of parchment and place on a rimmed baking sheet. In a small pot, bring the water and sugar to a boil. Add the salt and pour the liquid over the lemons. Bake for 7 to 10 minutes, until the lemons or translucent but not mushy. Remove from the oven and let the slices cool in the poaching liquid. When cool, drain slices and stack in a storage container and refrigerate. Discard poaching liquid.

Liquid Glucose

Available in specialty grocery stores and pastry supply stores, liquid glucose is a clear, corn-based syrup. I use it for the texture that it imparts to pastry components like ganache. Ganache made with liquid glucose stays pliable and more stable than traditional ganache, which can break when reheated. Glucose also adds body to a liquid without as much sweetness as granulated sugar. It's handy for thickening *agrodolce* (page 254).

Onions

When you slice an onion the classic way—splitting it in half through the root end, then cutting it lengthwise with the root end at the base, you end up with uneven slices. This doesn't matter for stocks, but if the onion slices will be a visible part of the finished dish, there is an easy fix. After you peel the onion, quarter it. Take each quarter and make one clean cut along the inside of the onion to remove the core. Now the quarter should lie flat against the board, making it easier to make even slices with a knife or a mandoline. Save the onion cores for making stock.

Pickles

Pickles accent rich dishes beautifully. I make quick pickles often, which is easy to do when I already have a supply of pickling liquid ready. Below are flexible recipes for pickling liquid and pickled vegetables.

PICKLING LIQUID

If you prefer mildly spiced pickles, drain the pickling liquid after heating it and discard the spices. If you like more spice, leave the spices in the liquid.

MAKES 3 CUPS

200 grams • 1 cup sugar

240 grams • 1 cup water

240 grams • 1 cup white wine or red wine

240 grams • 1 cup white wine vinegar or red wine vinegar

10 grams • 1 tablespoon kosher salt

a sachet of 5 peppercorns, 3 cloves, 2 cardamom pods, 1 allspice berry, and 1 star anise (see page 282)

In a medium pot over medium-high heat, bring the sugar, with the water, wine, vinegar, salt, and spices to a simmer for 5 minutes. Cool and refrigerate until needed. Pickling liquid keeps indefinitely.

PICKLED VEGETABLES

This is a versatile combination of pickled vegetables that works well as an accompaniment with fried foods or braises. It comes together quickly when you have the pickling liquid already made and keeps for several weeks in the refrigerator.

MAKES ABOUT 2 1/2 CUPS

40 grams • 2 baby sweet peppers or 1/4 cup bell pepper diced into 1/4-inch pieces

105 grams • 8 pearl onions

100 grams • 1 cup small cauliflower florets

45 grams • 2 baby carrots, sliced into 1/8-inch rounds

11 grams • 2 cornichons

365 to 400 grams • 1 1/2 to 2 cups white wine pickling liquid

kosher salt

Slice the sweet peppers crosswise into 1/4-inch rounds and remove the seeds. In a large pot of boiling, salted water, briefly blanch the onions. Skim them out, shock them in ice water, then peel and halve or quarter them, depending on their size. In the same pot, blanch the cauliflower until slightly softened, about 1 minute. Repeat with the carrots, blanching for about 1 minute. Drain the vegetables well and place in a glass or ceramic container. Mix in the peppers and cornichons. In a small pot, bring the pickling liquid to a simmer. Pour over the vegetables and add a pinch of salt. Cool completely, cover, and refrigerate. Let the vegetables marinate in the pickling liquid for at least 3 hours but preferably overnight.

Ricotta

I always drain ricotta before cooking with it. This is especially important when making pasta fillings, where any extra water can cause the dough to turn soft and sticky. Fill a large strainer lined with cheesecloth with ricotta and let it drain in the refrigerator overnight. In all recipes using ricotta, the measurements (both weight and volume) are based on drained ricotta.

Simple Syrup

Simple syrup can be made in any quantity by bringing equal parts sugar and water to a boil until the sugar is dissolved. It keeps in the refrigerator for a few weeks.

Spice Sachets and Herb Bundles

A sachet—*sachet d'epices*, or "bag of spices" in French—enables you to steep herbs in a braise or stock and remove them easily before serving. To make a sachet, cut out a 4- to 5-inch square of cheesecloth. Place herbs and spices in the center, then secure the bundle with butcher's twine. An herb bundle is the same idea without the cloth: using butcher's twine, tightly tie sprigs of herbs together, leaving one end of the twine long enough to tie to the handle of the pot for easy removal.

Soffritto

Soffritto offers a way to add concentrated flavor to a dish—I add it to everything from soups to braises or roasts. Making soffritto is straightforward—just grind vegetables fine and slowly cook them in olive oil—but it tastes complex because of the slow, gentle cooking process. Soffritto keeps for at least a week in the refrigerator.

MAKES ABOUT 1¹/₂ CUPS

100 grams • 1 carrot, chopped

100 grams • ¹/₂ onion, chopped

100 grams • 1¹/₂ celery stalks, sliced

100 grams • ¹/₂ cup extra virgin olive oil

5 grams • 1¹/₂ teaspoons kosher salt

In a meat grinder or a food processor, grind the carrot, onion, and celery until the vegetables are chopped finely. Heat the olive oil in a large, wide Dutch oven or heavy-bottomed pot over low heat. Stir in the ground vegetables and salt and gently cook, stirring occasionally, until the vegetables are very soft and the bottom of the pot is dry, about 45 minutes.

Stock

I make stocks with nearly every animal I prepare. In general, I make white stock with chicken bones and brown stock with richer meat, like squab, pork, veal, and beef. But not always: brown chicken stock is quite versatile. Some of the recipes in this book call for reduced stock: simply simmer the stock until it has reduced by nearly half, then strain.

WHITE STOCK

This recipe makes a classic chicken stock, but other poultry bones or even veal or beef bones work as well. Instead of scraping the fat off the surface of the stock once it has cooled, I strain the cold stock through a fine, lint-free kitchen towel, which removes the fat.

MAKES ABOUT 4 QUARTS

3600 grams • 8 pounds bones, cut into 2- to 3-inch pieces

kosher salt and black pepper

vegetable oil

300 grams • 1¹/₂ yellow onions, chopped

150 grams • 2 carrots, chopped

150 grams • 2 or 3 celery stalks, chopped

100 grams • 3 or 4 leek tops

6 thyme sprigs

6 parsley stems

2 bay leaves

10 black peppercorns

Put the bones in a large stockpot and cover with 3 to 4 inches of water. Bring to a brisk simmer, drain, and then rinse the bones, discarding the water. Wash the pot and return the bones to the pot. Cover again with 3 inches of water and bring to a brisk simmer. Lower to a gentle simmer, and cook, skimming the surface occasionally, for 2 hours. Add the vegetables and aromatics and cook for another 2 hours. After four to five hours of total cooking, strain the stock, and cool rapidly over an ice bath, and refrigerate overnight. The following morning strain the stock through a kitchen towel to remove any solidified fat or impurities. The stock keeps, refrigerated, for several days. For longer storage, freeze it.

BROWN STOCK

Brown stock is "brown" because of the addition of tomato paste. To deepen the flavor, I also roast the bones. This recipe makes classic veal stock, but squab, lamb, duck, venison, and chicken bones also make terrific brown stocks.

MAKES ABOUT 4 QUARTS

4500 grams • 10 pounds bones, cut into 2- to 3-inch pieces

kosher salt and black pepper

vegetable oil

113 grams • $^1/_3$ cup tomato paste

300 grams • 1$^1/_2$ yellow onions, chopped

150 grams • 2 carrots, chopped

150 grams • 2 or 3 celery stalks, chopped

100 grams • 3 or 4 leek tops

6 thyme sprigs

6 parsley stems

2 bay leaves

10 black peppercorns

Preheat the oven to 375°F and line a baking sheet with parchment paper. In a large bowl, season the bones with salt and pepper and lightly coat with oil. Spread the bones on a the prepared baking sheet and roast, rotating the bones once or twice, until evenly browned, 35 to 45 minutes. Transfer the bones to a large stock pot and cover with about 3 inches of water (about 8 quarts). Bring to a brisk simmer, lower to a gently simmer, and cook, skimming the surface occasionally, for 1 hour.

Mix the tomato paste with $^1/_2$ cup of water, stir into the stock, and simmer for 2 hours. Add the vegetables and aromatics and cook for another 2 hours. After 5 hours of total cooking, strain the stock through a fine sieve and transfer to a clean pot to reduce by one-third. Strain again and cool. Before using, scrape off any fat that has congealed on the surface. The stock keeps, refrigerated, for 1 week. For longer storage, freeze it.

Tapioca Maltodextrin

When mixed with fats like olive oil or rendered pork fat, or even nut butters, this modified food starch turns the ingredient into a tacky powder. Since it slows down the release of flavor on the tongue, it adds visual and textural interest to certain dishes. It can be purchased at specialty food stores, and online. Powdered dextrose has the same effect on liquids.

Verjus

Made from the juice pressed from underripe grapes, verjus can be white or red. It is an excellent alternative to vinegar or lemon juice when you need to add acidity to a dish. Verjus needs to be refrigerated after opening or it will start to ferment.

Wondra Flour

I use this low-protein instant flour extensively for breading or pan-searing everything from beef cheeks to abalone. Because Wondra dissolves quickly and has anti-caking agents, you need less of it for breading.

Xanthan Gum

For making emulsified vinaigrettes, I find that xanthan gum provides an ideal creamy texture, allowing me to do without adding raw egg yolk. Available online, xanthan gum is a food thickening agent that has recently gained interest for its ability to add texture to gluten-free breads.

ACKNOWLEDGMENTS

Creating this book took all of us on a journey, both literally and figuratively. Along the way, many people opened their doors and shared their expertise, their ideas, and their time. We are grateful to all of you.

To Aaron Wehner at Ten Speed Press, for signing up our Italian adventure. To our editor, Jenny Wapner, who patiently poured over our manuscript countless times and made plenty of smart changes in the process. To Clancy Drake for fearless copyediting and for corralling errant ideas. To Toni Tajima, for designing the book in a way that let our stories truly shine. And to Greg Lindgren, for designing maps that illustrated our path.

Our time in Italy wouldn't have been the same without the generous time and hospitality we experienced from Italian food and wine producers. We would especially like to thank (in alphabetical order) Lucia Barzanò, Giampiero Bea, the Bellavista estate, the Bisol estate, the Bisci family, Chiara Boschis, Ampelio and Vanda Bucci, Roberto Camotto, Giordano Emo Capodilista, Marco Caprai, the Collacciani family and Casale Cento Corvi, the D'Osvaldo family, Giovanella Fugazza and Castello di Luzzano, Angelo Gaja, Ivan Giuliani, Piero Incisa, Luigi Mancini, Sergio Mottura, the Panizzi estate, the Rizzo family, the Sartarelli family, the Taddei family, Giorgio Rivetti and Anja Cramer, Sebastiano Rosa, Walter Scarbolo, Olga Urbani, the Venica family, and the Zoff family. We would also like to thank everyone who has been generous with information, samples, and personal time, including Chiara Di Geronimo, Martin Foradori, Elena Pantaleoni, Portovino, Vittorio Navacchia, Soyoung Scanlan, and Rand Yazzolino.

To Sara Remington, for joining us on our journey, and for capturing unforgettable moments in Italy and California through her camera lens. To Ethel Brennan for lending style to photo shots.

To Amanda Haas for being an enthusiastic recipe tester no matter what we threw her way. And to Inken Chrisman, who helped in these testing efforts.

To Vijay Toke, for getting the paperwork in line from the start. And to Susan McEvers, for keeping us in line once we got going.

We couldn't have undertaken this project without the support of our family, friends, and coworkers.

From Shelley Lindgren:

To Matthew Accarrino for sharing your impeccable precision in your cooking and altruistic approach to food. Your skill and dedication to creating the recipes in this book was admirable through and through.

To Kate Leahy: you're the reason we were able to consider tackling this project. Your amazing ability to bring all of our words together in one book took enormous courage and talent and you also made it a really fun project. I am eternally grateful for your commitment to this book.

To Victoria Libin, my wonderful business partner, for your unending support of research, knowledge, and vision, and for sharing your brilliance in business, food, and wine, it allows me to believe anything is possible.

To our management and wine teams for their ongoing dedication to wine education and customer service. You keep the stories of wines and winemakers front and center every night: Nicholas Sciackitano, Emily Schoonover, Penelope Grill, Nathan Johnson, Rachele Shafai, Tim Baumann, Emily Pacsi, Brian Bittner, Kristen Malotke, Jeremiah Moorehose, Janis Bell, Natasha Dunn, Michael Meier, Aidan Hansen, Jonathan Patch, and so many more who offered their insight and support to help me focus on the book.

And, finally, to my friends, mentors, and family. To Jennifer De Marco, Suzanne Robinson, Marie and Rick Lindgren: you made this book possible because of your unconditional love. A special thank you to my incredibly supportive husband, Greg, and our two sons, Asher and Phineas. Many an hour was needed that didn't exist in the day, and I am in awe of your understanding and patience. Thank you!

....

From Matthew Accarrino:

A moment of thanks . . .

To the many people whose contributions helped make this book come to life and the many culinary and life mentors I've had along the way.

To all the suppliers who cultivate and harvest the bounty of nature that I get to work with each day.

To my staff, past and present, who make this life with food possible. Their focus and dedication, hospitality, and grace inspires and motivates me every day.

To the communities and customers whose faith and participation allows me the freedom to do what I love.

To my Accarrino famiglia, for exposing me to the treasures of their country and the source of my heritage. To my grandparents who have left their legacies and recipes distilled in my memory.

To all of my family and friends here in America, especially Catherine Schimenti and Anthony Amoroso.

Shelley Lindgren, for sourcing her wine like I source my ingredients, honest and delicious, and for always complementing my food with the right wine.

Victoria Libin, for her dedication and input. Your creativity and outlook has always inspired me.

Kate Leahy for her help in telling my story and Amanda Haas for recipe testing.

Sheree Cheng, for the execution and consistency and a tireless passion for the positive.

....

From Kate Leahy:

To Shelley and Matthew for inviting me along this journey. You were always generous when sharing your perspectives on food and wine with me.

To my family, especially to Barbara Sutton for offering her expert eye, keen perspective, and words of support whenever it was needed the most. And to Tom and Kathy Leahy for always believing in me.

INDEX

Garlic, *continued*
    Whole Wheat Fettuccine with
      Funghi Trifolati and Spring
      Garlic, 26–27
Gelatina
    Horseradish Gelatina, 75–77
    Wine Gelatina, 78–80
Gelatin sheets, 279
Gelato, Milk Chocolate, 231
Germano, Sergio, 201
Gewürztraminer, 142
Giacchè, 15
Giacosa, Bruno, 199, 204, 206
Giminiani, Christina, 163
Glera, 106, 110
Gnocchi
    Lamb Ragù with Semolina Gnocchi
      and Pecorino Pepato, 34–35
    Rye Gnocchi with Savoy Cabbage,
      Potatoes, and Crispy Speck,
      149–50
Goat cheese
    Asparagus with Lardo-Wrapped Rye
      Dumplings, Goat Cheese, and
      Sprouting Greens, 124–25
    Goat Cheese and Ricotta Crespelle
      with Orange-Caramel Sauce,
      31–32
    Saffron Trofie with Veal Ragù,
      265–66
    Spring Vegetable Vignarola Salad,
      22–23
Gonzaga family, 141
Goretti, Sara, 70
Graetz, Bibi, 249
Grai, Giorgio, 45
Granaccia, 240
Granita, Sweet Wine, 64–65
Grape varieties
    Albana, 162–63
    Albarola, 237
    Aleatico, 15
    Ancellotta, 164
    Ansonica, 249
    Arneis, 204
    Barbera, 205
    Bellone, 14
    Bianchello, 47
    Bianchetta, 237
    Bonarda, 205
    Bosco, 237, 240
    Brachetto, 205
    Buzzetto, 240
    Canaiolo, 71
    Cesanese, 15
    Ciliegiolo, 250

Colorino, 250
Cornalin, 211
Coronata, 240
Cortese, 204
Corvina, 110
Corvinone, 111
Croatina, 167
Dindarella, 111
Dolcetto, 205
Durello, 111
Erbaluce, 204
Favorita, 204
Freisa, 205
Friulano, 116
Fumin, 211
Garganega, 106, 110
Gewürztraminer, 142
Giacchè, 15
Glera, 106, 110
Granaccia, 240
Grechetto, 70–71
Grignolino, 208
Gropello, 167
Kerner, 142
Lacrima di Morro d'Alba, 50
Lagrein, 139, 144
Lambrusco, 162, 164
Malvasia, 14, 161
Marzemino, 141, 144
Mayolet, 211
Molinara, 111
Montepulciano, 46, 50
Moscato, 201
Müller-Thurgau, 143
Nebbiolo, 197, 198–99, 206
Negrara, 111
Nosiola, 143
Nus Malvoisie, 211
Ormeasco, 240, 242
Ortrugo, 164
Oseleta, 111
Pagadebit, 163, 164
Passerina, 47
Pecorino, 47
Pelaverga, 208
Petite Arvine, 210
Petite Rouge, 211
Picolit, 116–17
Pigato, 236, 240
Pignoletto, 164
Pignolo, 115, 118
Pinot Bianco, 143
Pinot Grigio, 117, 211
Pinot Nero, 144
Premetta, 208, 211
Prié Blanc, 209, 210

Raboso, 111
Refosco, 116, 118
Ribolla Gialla, 117
Riesling, 143
Riesling Italico, 110
Romanesco, 14
Rondinella, 112
Rossesse, 242
Ruché, 206
Sagrantino, 69, 71
Sangiovese, 163, 243, 246–47, 248
Sauvignon, 117
Schiava, 144
Schioppettino, 115, 118
Sylvaner, 143
Tazzelenghe, 118
Teroldego, 141, 144
Timorasso, 201, 204
Trebbiano, 70, 71, 163
Veltviner, 143
Verdicchio, 45, 46, 50
Verduzzo, 117
Vermentino, 236, 240, 243
Vernaccia di San Gimignano, 249–50
Vernaccia Nera, 50
Vernaccia Rosso di Pergola, 51
Vespaiola, 110
Vespolina, 208
Vitovska, 112, 117–18
Gravner, Josko, 112, 142, 236
Grechetto, 70–71
Greens
    Erbazzone Torta with Braised
      Greens, Prosciutto Cotto, and
      Eggs, 187–88
    Farro-and-Bread-Stuffed Quail with
      Chestnuts, Persimmons, and
      Dandelion Greens, 86–87
    Ricotta and Quail Egg Ravioli with
      Wild Greens and Fontina, 179–81
    See also individual greens
Grignolino, 208
Gropello, 167
Grosjean, Vincent, 208, 211
Gruppo Vini Veri, 70
Guanciale, Chestnut-Filled Pasta with
    Broccoli di Cicco, Burnt-Orange
    Sauce, and, 172–75
Guiliani, Ivan, 240

H
Herb bundles, 282
Hofstätter, Josef, 141
Horseradish Gelatina, 75–77
Huckleberry Vinaigrette, 153–55
Hydrosols, 65

Published in the United States by
Ten Speed Press, an imprint of
the Crown Publishing Group,
a division of Random House, Inc., New York.
www.crownpublishing.com
www.tenspeed.com

Ten Speed Press and the Ten Speed Press
colophon are registered trademarks of
Random House, Inc.

Library of Congress Cataloging-in-
Publication Data

Lindgren, Shelley.
SPQR : modern Italian food and wine / by
Shelley Lindgren and Matthew Accarrino
with Kate Leahy.
  p. cm.
1. Cooking, Italian. I. Accarrino, Matthew.
II. Leahy, Kate. III. Title.
TX723.L548 2012
641.5945—dc23
                          2012014120

Printed in China

ISBN: 978-1-60774-052-0

Cover and text design by Toni Tajima
Food styling for pages 18, 21, 53, 76, 79,
99, 126, 131, 173, 177, 180, 185, 252 by
Robyn Valarik
Prop styling by Ethel Brennan

Printed in China

10 9 8 7 6 5 4 3 2 1